ORDERS OF THE DAY

ORDERS
OF THE DAY

The Rt. Hon.
EARL WINTERTON
P. C.

With half-tone frontispiece

CASSELL AND COMPANY LTD
LONDON

CASSELL & CO. LTD
37/38 St. Andrews Hill, Queen Victoria Street
London, E.C.4

and at
210 Queen Street, Melbourne
26/30 Clarence Street, Sydney
Haddon Hall, City Road, Auckland, N.Z.
1068 Broadview Avenue, Toronto 6
122 East 55th Street, New York 22
Avenida 9 de Julho 1138, São Paulo
Galeria Güemes, Escritorio 518/520 Florida 165, Buenos Aires
Haroon Chambers, South Napier Road, Karachi
15 Graham Road, Ballard Estate, Bombay 1
17 Central Avenue P.O., Dharamtala, Calcutta
P.O. Box 275, Cape Town
P.O. Box 1386, Salisbury, S. Rhodesia
P.O. Box 959, Accra, Gold Coast
Calcada Do Carma 55–2°, Lisbon
25 rue Henri Barbusse, Paris 5E
Islands Brygge 5, Copenhagen

FIRST PUBLISHED 1953

SET IN 12PT BEMBO TYPE AND
PRINTED AND BOUND IN ENGLAND BY
HAZELL WATSON AND VINEY LTD
AYLESBURY AND LONDON
F.553

ACKNOWLEDGEMENTS

WHILE making it clear that I alone am responsible for all the statements and opinions contained in this book, I should like to express my great indebtedness to Dr. Orlo Williams, C.B., M.C., D.C.L., for carefully reading through my manuscript and making many useful suggestions as to the form of presentation.

I am also very grateful to my Private Secretary, Miss Vivian Cox, for her assiduous work in typing and checking the manuscript, as well as to her Assistant, Mrs. Sipek.

L'ENVOI

IT was October 4, 1951, the last day of the 1950 Parliament—the day of Prorogation. Normally there is only formal business, and no speeches, when the House prorogues. But on this occasion there were expressions of congratulation to King George VI on his recovery from his illness—a recovery which unhappily proved only temporary. They came from Leaders of Parties and lastly from myself as "Father of the House". It thus came about that I made the closing speech of the 1950 Parliament and of my career as an M.P. at one and the same time—nearly forty-seven years after I had been first elected. I was received as I rose with a long low murmur of sympathetic cheers from all parts of the House, in which both the Prime Minister and Mr. Churchill joined; it is the tribute which the House pays to those who have been for a long time familiar figures in it and who are about to retire from it. Afterwards I sat down on the corner-seat on the front Opposition bench which I customarily occupied to await my turn to walk past the Speaker and shake hands with him, as is the custom on the day of Prorogation.

As I sat there, feeling somewhat emotional, alike because of the occasion and the kindness which the House had just shown to one who had been in the past one of its most turbulent members, a flashback was suddenly projected on to the screen of my memory.

I was in the 1900 Parliament again. Mr. Speaker Gully was back in the Chair in place of Mr. Speaker Clifton Brown; Sir Courtenay Ilbert had taken the Clerk of the House's seat at the Table instead of Sir Frederick Metcalfe. The new, rebuilt Chamber had disappeared, and I was in the old one with its dark varnished oak and its dark green benches instead of the pale grey oak and the pale green benches in the modern House. There was a grille in front of the Ladies' Gallery for the very proper purpose of preventing members from being distracted by female beauty when making their speeches. All the present members of the House had vanished except Mr. Churchill and myself, for we

two alone had then been members. In their place were a number
of men whose features seemed so familiar to me that I forgot
they were ghosts and that most of them had died a quarter of a
century ago or even earlier. The vast majority of them were in
morning or frock coats with high stiff collars and wore top-hats
on their heads; but there were some deviations from the normal;
two or three of the Irish Nationalists were in lounge suits and
without hats, and Mr. Keir Hardie was in his well-known tweeds.
Mr. Arthur Balfour had a turn-down white collar like that worn
by Eton boys; Mr. Joseph Chamberlain was more orthodox—
he had a wing collar and, of course, an orchid in his button-hole
and a monocle in his eye. There they were, the men of fame and
distinction who then sat on the two front benches—Asquith,
Haldane, Austen Chamberlain, Grey, Brodrick, Birrell, Morley,
Long, Campbell-Bannerman, Lyttelton. And behind and below
the gangway were many others whose names were very familiar
to every newspaper reader of the day—Mr. Wyndham, Mr. John
Redmond, Mr. Healy, Sir Wilfred Lawson, Mr. Gibson Bowles,
Sir Charles Dilke, Mr. Labouchere and Colonel Mark Lockwood,
for example.

I reflected sadly that most of them had long been forgotten,
and that mention of them would mean nothing to my colleagues
of the 1950 Parliament. But I noticed with pleasure that Mr.
Churchill was sitting below the gangway; he was a younger
and slimmer Mr. Churchill than the one on the bench beside me
a few seconds earlier, but had not altered in many respects very
much. He was pugnaciously cheering a young Welsh member,
Mr. Lloyd George, who was angrily asking Mr. Balfour, the
Prime Minister, if he did not think the answer which he had
just given was an insult to the House. Mr. Balfour remained
seated with the look of amused indifference which he habitu-
ally wore on such an occasion. There were shouts of "Answer"
from the Liberal and Opposition side of the House and "Sit
down" from the Conservatives; and that noise of the past
brought me back to the present and to reality: so my daydream
ended.

I rose to pass the Chair and shake hands with Mr. Speaker
whose last day it also was in the House of which he had been so long
a popular member. And my chief feeling, as I left the Chamber,

was pride in having been a member of this great assembly for nearly half a century and in having seen it survive, with its essence and spirit unimpaired, when freedom of action and discussion had vanished from half the Parliaments of Europe.

PREFACE

THIS book is not primarily an autobiography. It is an attempt to give a brief and accurate account of events in the House of Commons from 1905 to 1951, and to paint a true picture of the individuals concerned in them, whether or no their political views agreed with mine. My qualifications for the task do not depend upon any merits that I may possess as a statesman, historian or writer, but upon certain advantages, in some respects unusual if not unique, which I have had of close acquaintance with, and observation of, the principal personages, important events and trends in public life during that period.

I was first elected a Member of Parliament in November, 1904, and when I took my seat in February, 1905, I was the "Baby of the House". When I retired at the Dissolution in 1951 I vacated the position of "Father of the House" which I had held for some years. During this unbroken period of parliamentary service, lasting nearly forty-seven years, I was, save from August 4, 1914, to October, 1918, when I was in the Army, a very active Member of Parliament both in the House and the country. I have spent, at various periods, nearly nine years in office, either as an Under-Secretary or a Cabinet Minister in four Governments and under three different Prime Ministers. I have been a member or chairman of innumerable official committees in the House of Commons, and have represented the British Government at international conferences. I was an inmate of a Ministry, as Parliamentary Private Secretary to the Financial Secretary to the Admiralty in 1905, before even those veterans of statesmanship, Mr. Churchill and Lord Samuel, had held office. I was Mr. Joseph Chamberlain's Parliamentary Private Secretary in 1906, and towards the end of my public career I was in Mr. Churchill's "Shadow Cabinet" from 1945 to 1950.

These facts in themselves add up to a long span both of time and experience during an era of flux, world-shattering events and continuous disruption of ideas and ideals—an era to which, even in our turbulent history, no other period of similar length

affords a parallel. But long experience of political life is not my
only advantage as a chronicler. I have another, which I attribute
less to any personal qualities than to the opportunities which
my environment, both social and political, so richly afforded.
I have known, often as an intimate friend, every great figure
in our public life during the last forty-seven years and many
notable men outside it. Apart from politics, for instance, I served
under T. E. Lawrence in the memorable days of the Arab Revolt.
Also, I have a valuable aid to memory in the shape of day-to-day
diaries which I have kept throughout my long public life, during
the whole of which, save when in office, I have been a frequent
contributor to the Press. Before the First World War I was
editor of a weekly paper—The World—for eighteen months,
and after the Second World War I was for some time a political
columnist. Thus I have another storehouse of experience upon
which to draw.

The task of assembling, sifting and endeavouring to present
the mass of data and information at my disposal in a readable form
has been a formidable one. In parts of my book the presentation
may appear repetitive and discursive; in others it may seem that
I have spoilt the narrative by interpolating references to trivial
matters when describing great events and important debates.
But all these things are characteristic of the House itself; it changes
very quickly from gravity to gaiety; it often appears to prefer
the unimportant to the important until recalled to seriousness
by a speech on the part of someone who commands its respect.
It discusses the same point again and again. A record of the House
which did not convey the frailties as well as the virtues of that
great institution would not be a true one.

In my selection of members for mention in each period of the
book, I have chosen those who attracted attention for various
reasons—for example, skill in debate or pertinacity on a particular issue—and not necessarily the men or women who held high
office. This reflects the attitude of the House of Commons itself,
which will often be empty during a Minister's speech and full
when a back-bencher is speaking. The House has its own particular methods for determining who are worth listening to and who
are not.

But there is one thing, above all, that I hope will emerge from my recollections of men and women who have been prominent in politics, and will serve in the reader's mind to strengthen a belief which I hold very strongly. It is that, although events in the field of national and international politics have sometimes baffled and frustrated even the greatest and wisest of British statesmen, their place in history and their claim to honourable memory depends, not upon events but upon character. It is the display in high office of such qualities as courage, conviction, fidelity to truth, chivalry, sympathy and personal uprightness that alone enables them to benefit their country during their lives, and to exercise a lasting influence upon the minds, as well as the fortunes, of posterity. That is the answer to the perennial sneers of persons with little minds at the profession of politics.

CHAPTER I

I WAS elected M.P. for Horsham on November 11, 1904, at a by-election.

The contest attracted some attention for the following reasons. I was only just over twenty-one, in my third year at Oxford, and I was the first candidate to support in principle Mr. Chamberlain's Tariff Reform policy. All the weight of national political organisations and Press support was thrown into the contest. Thanks more to the help which I got and other factors, such as my father's popularity, than to my merits as a candidate, I had a majority of 722, and then became the "Baby of the House".

That they had actually managed to avoid losing a safe seat at a by-election was so unique a happening for the dying Balfour Government that it inspired them with a flicker of hope, and possibly caused the Prime Minister to postpone the General Election. The Conservative and Unionist Party was in a very unhealthy state in 1904. First and foremost of its difficulties was the fissure over Tariff Reform. Not only had Mr. Chamberlain, the most powerful political personality in the Unionist Party, resigned in order to press for Imperial economic consolidation and moderate protection for home industries, but Lord George Hamilton and Mr. Ritchie had also left Mr. Balfour's Government because they were dissatisfied with his attempt to find a *via media* between Mr. Chamberlain's proposals and the official fiscal policy of the Party. They believed, correctly as events showed, that Mr. Chamberlain's suggestion of a small duty on imported flour would supply the Opposition with a powerful and deadly battle-cry of "Dear Food", and they were not satisfied with Mr. Balfour's repudiation of this part of the Chamberlain policy; they believed that any form of protective or retaliatory duty on foreign goods would reopen the bitter controversy supposed to have been ended by the repeal of the Corn Laws half a century earlier. As Free Traders they had the influential support of the powerful Cecil and Stanley families, though members of both families participated in the Government, the former very prominently. This produced another cause of internal friction. Lord Salisbury, though a great and wise statesman in most respects, had neither sought nor obtained personal popularity, and was always a remote figure, even to his own supporters. When he was succeeded as Prime Minister by his relative, Mr. Balfour, whose Ministry included Lord Cranbourne (afterwards the Marquess of Salisbury) as Under-Secretary for Foreign Affairs, and Mr. Gerald Balfour, Mr. Balfour's brother, as President of the Board of Trade, the opportunity for sarcastic comment by the Opposition and by disgruntled Tories on the undue influence of the Cecil family was obvious. Advantage was taken of it by Mr. Gibson Bowles, a brilliant but erratic Conservative M.P., who had quarrelled with his leaders.

He nicknamed the Government "The Hotel Cecil". The jibe did us a great deal of harm at the time.

For all their brilliance, integrity and public spirit, the Cecil family and their collaterals, the Balfours, had little popular appeal severally or collectively. Their opposition and that of the Stanleys to Mr. Chamberlain's policy was considered by some at the time (myself among them, though I subsequently changed my view) to be antipathy to the man himself, to one of a different social class, an iconoclast with prodigious energy and reforming zeal, and a man who was both intensely loved and hated by different sections of the public. The series of brilliant attacks upon Mr. Chamberlain in and out of Parliament made by Lord Hugh Cecil, M.P. (now Lord Quickswood), were deeply resented by the former's supporters, such as myself.

The question of Cecil family influence or predominance in the Government also involved Mr. Balfour's own position. To attempt to discuss and dissect fully the personal and political character of this fascinatingly enigmatic man would take a volume in itself. It is, incidentally, a task which I do not think has ever been satisfactorily performed, and which offers a promising opportunity for some enterprising young historian.

But some facets of that character, at least as they appeared to the public, must be set out here, since they so vitally affected the existing political situation.

Intellectually, he towered over his colleagues, and, as I once wrote elsewhere, I do not believe that any of his successors at No. 10, Downing Street have surpassed him in intellectual capacity and breadth of mental perception. Perhaps because of his gifts, especially those of clear and impartial analysis, he was often slow in coming to a decision where political necessity demanded it. His friends said he was too honest not to admit that every question had two sides to it. His enemies asserted that he was too lazy to make up his mind. The Tory Party is generally suspicious of unusual intellectual gifts, as is shown by its attitude, for many years of their lives, to Disraeli and Churchill. When I first entered the House I heard more than one Tory M.P. say privately: "The trouble with A. J. B. is that he is too clever; far above the head of the man in the street who dislikes cleverness". Supremely dexterous in the ordinary thrust and parry of debate, thereby earning the concealed admiration of the Irish National-ists, who were themselves masters in that art, he often failed to satisfy the House in a big debate when he had to make a set speech; and he had little appeal on the platform. Also there were three or four matters involving either his attitude of mind or his conduct at this period which did him and the Party harm, and which I feel bound to set out despite my admiration for him—a feeling which developed when I was privileged to enjoy his friendship in later years.

Firstly, his book on *Philosophic Doubt* made many in and out of our Party (especially those who hadn't read it) believe that he had no fixed beliefs or principles about this world or the next. Secondly, he was accused, I think unjustly in each case, of having treated Mr. George Wyndham with cruelty and cynicism in the matter of the latter's resignation of the Irish Chief Secretaryship and of nepotism in making his brother, Mr. Gerald Balfour, President of the Board of Trade. Finally, he incurred some unpopularity with his followers by the social environment in which he moved. No man that I have known had greater charm in private life than Mr. Balfour. Not unnaturally, with his gifts, he frequented a small circle of gifted men and women who were the successors or original members of the "Souls". They included a few prominent Liberals, though most of them took no active interest in politics. The inclusion of Liberals in this milieu to which the Prime Minister belonged was a cause of offence to older Tory M.P.s, who remembered that Disraeli and Gladstone never met socially when they were Party leaders.

Though no one could object to the Prime Minister's friends on moral grounds, they were remote from the life and viewpoint of the squires or industrialists who formed the Tory Parliamentary Party of the day, and most of them were separated in their intellectual stratosphere from practical issues of the day, especially the growing political consciousness of the wage-earner. How often one heard it said of Mr. Chamberlain and Mr. Balfour respectively: "Joe understands the working-man; A. J. B. never will and doesn't want to; why, he boasts he never reads the newspapers!" For Mr. Balfour professed, like one of his successors, contempt for Press criticism and indifference to personal criticism alike. I have devoted considerable space to these largely personal and intangible reasons for the Government's unpopularity because, in this instance and in others as this book will show later, they played a greater part than contemporary written evidence showed in the electoral fortunes of the Party.

But there were other more apparent reasons for the Government's decline in authority and popularity which culminated in our crushing defeat in January, 1906. The Tory Party had secured a triumph over its divided Liberal opponents in the Khaki Election of 1900. Any popularity which the Government might have gained from the close of the war in 1902 soon evaporated. The country was tired and disillusioned. We had had, for those days, heavy losses and had gained little credit. The Entente was in its infancy, and generally every foreign country appeared alike to condemn and despise our handling of events.

Again, however justified on economic grounds, the introduction of Chinese indentured labour into the South African mines was a heavy electoral disadvantage at home. The Tory slogan at the 1900 election had been "Every vote for a Liberal is a vote for the Boers". In doubtfulness of veracity, the Liberal battle-cry over Chinese labour far exceeded ours at the 1900 election. The term "Chinese Slavery" was used; by-election candidates such as I were accused of wishing to introduce "Chinese slavery" into Britain; posters depicting a chain-gang of Chinese labourers entering this country appeared on the hoardings.

Another measure of fierce controversy was the Aliens Bill

designed to impose very mild restrictions upon the unregulated entry of aliens, mostly Jews from Central Europe fleeing from Russian persecution. The Liberals believed that, in addition to the "Dear Food" cry, they had winning cards in both Chinese Labour and the Aliens Bill. Their *esprit de corps*, very low at the time of the 1900 election, steadily improved. Their internal divisions and the obvious weakness of Campbell-Bannerman's leadership were forgotten. But about the Aliens Bill they were wrong. It was, on the whole, popular; even among the mild British there is a good deal of hidden xenophobia, and the fact that many of the immigrants were Jews, then one of the principal butts of music-hall derision, did not make the Aliens Bill less palatable. My mother, canvassing on my behalf, was surprised to be told by the wife of an agricultural labourer that, apart from respect for my father, her husband would vote for me against "Them Foreigners". When my mother, perhaps too honest to be a good canvasser, said she was surprised, as there were few foreigners in rural Sussex, she got the reply, "That's where you are wrong, my Lady. Why, there's foreigners from Surrey coming into this parish every day. We've 'ad pretty near enough of them". So much for popular understanding of electoral issues in those days!!

The Liberals also had, quite unfairly and unreasonably, a winning card in Mr. Balfour's Education Act of 1902. The perfectly proper provision contained in the Bill, that support from the rates should be given to Church of England as well as to National schools, was considered an affront to Nonconformists. Their leaders rose in revolt. Some refused to pay rates and were prosecuted, thus providing a precedent for Conscientious Objectors a decade later. Liberals and their allies the Nonconformists protested also against the Licensing Act because of its compensation for publicans and brewers whose licensed houses were classified as redundant by Licensing Justices. We were sneeringly accused of a policy of "Beer and the Bible".

Apologists sought at the time, and have sought since, to assess the relative degree of blame attributable to Mr. Chamberlain or Mr. Balfour respectively, owing to their divergence on fiscal policy, for the catastrophe of the 1906 election: but whatever the assessment, one thing is surely true—namely that, if it is to do its duty, every Government must offend some of the electors all of the time and most of the electors some of the time; but no Government can fail to meet crushing defeat at the next election if it persistently offends one section of voters after the other, and simultaneously fails to evoke among its followers in or out of Parliament any enthusiasm for its leader or its policy. That is the gravamen of the charge against Mr. Balfour's Government and against him personally. It explains and, I maintain, justifies the action which a number of us, especially the younger Tory M.P.s, took from 1906 onwards to secure his resignation—an object finally attained in 1911.

CHAPTER II

THE 1905—and last—session of the 1900 Parliament began on February 14, on which day I took my seat; on March 3 I made my maiden speech, receiving the honour of congratulations from Sir Edward Carson, the Attorney-General, and Sir Edward Grey. Shortly afterwards I became Parliamentary Private Secretary to Mr. Ernest Pretyman, Financial Secretary to the Admiralty. Admiral (afterwards Lord) Fisher, the famous "Jacky" Fisher, was First Sea Lord. The Navy traditionally produces in its higher ranks men of striking personality who temporarily divide that great Service into those who are for and against them. As a controversialist, and as a man determined to get what he believed to be right for the Navy whatever the obstacles, Lord Fisher surpassed them all. He dominated meetings of the Board of Admiralty; the First Lord, Lord Cawdor, a man of small stature and mild disposition, was no match for his powers of persuasion and irony.

The 1905 session requires small space in this chronicle. It was barren of any legislation of importance except the Aliens Act. It added little lustre to either the Government, the Opposition or to parliamentary institutions. Young and inexperienced as I was, I was convinced, from my recent experience as a by-election candidate, that the Government and the 1900 Parliament alike were dying and would not live to see another session.

I found little support for my views among fellow Tory M.P.s. Despite their doubts about Mr. Balfour's leadership and Party differences over fiscal reform, they could not believe that the electors would vote to make a man of Campbell-Bannerman's calibre Prime Minister. There was the same insensitiveness to impending doom among supporters of the Coalition Government in 1922, the Conservative Government in 1929 and the Caretaker Government in 1945.

The debate on the Address was largely devoted to a discussion on fiscal policy. Not very convincingly, Mr. Balfour and Mr. Chamberlain assured the House that there was little or no difference between them. Lord Hugh Cecil, for the Conservative Free Traders, poured scorn on this contention. Mr. George Wyndham, on an amendment to the Address relating to Irish Affairs, defended his conduct over the Macdonell correspondence[1] in a speech of characteristic grace, generosity and eloquence.

Only a few men increased their reputation in this session. Among senior members of the Government, Mr. Austen Chamberlain, Chancellor of the Exchequer, was in this category. One of the youngest ever to hold that office, his modesty, courtesy, knowledge of the House and of the task of his great Department earned him respect and admiration. Of the junior members of the Government, a quiet, self-effacing young Scotsman, Mr. Bonar Law, impressed the House with his efficiency and grasp of figures. But no one at the time prophesied his remarkable future. The senior members of the Opposition on front and back benches took little advantage of the chances offered them in debates by an obviously disintegrating Government. Not so the younger back-benchers. Messrs. Runciman, McKenna, Lloyd George and Winston Churchill in particular were prominent in effective aggressiveness. The Irish Nationalists were, of course, in their element. They could hurl their banderillas with impunity at a goaded Tory bull who had lost the power or energy any longer to use its horns.

The extracts from my diary which I quote give some idea of the muddle, malaise and bad temper which usually characterise the last session of a moribund Parliament.

WEDNESDAY, MARCH 8TH, 1905

Winston's motion on Colonial Preference badly defeated though in a possibly somewhat cowardly fashion by moving the previous question.

[1] While Mr. Wyndham, then Chief Secretary to the Lord Lieutenant of Ireland, was absent on holiday in the summer of 1904, Sir Anthony Macdonell, his Permanent Under-Secretary, had accepted an invitation from Lord Dunraven, the Irish reformer, to assist in preparing a programme of devolution of Irish Government, which was subsequently published in *The Times*.

Sir Anthony was under the impression that he had the Chief Secretary's concurrence to his action; Mr. Wyndham, however, was obliged to repudiate the programme as failing to represent Government policy, and Sir Anthony was formally censured by the Cabinet for his action. Mr. Wyndham offered his resignation to the Prime Minister, Mr. Balfour, and it was accepted.

What I wrote at the time was an understatement; the decision of the Leader and the Whips to avoid a direct vote on this motion was badly received by Government supporters.

Even greater cowardice was shown in the case of another debate on fiscal policy on a private member's motion where the whole of the Government stayed away, with the consequence that no statement of our case was made at all.

WEDNESDAY, MAY 10TH, 1905

Debate in Committee on the Agricultural Rates Act

A curious state of affairs arose when Lambert[1] moved an amendment which Gerald Balfour said we were free to vote on, as we pleased, and which was subsequently discovered to make absolute nonsense if included in the Bill.

Several Opposition speakers, including Fowler,[2] waxed very indignant over this "aberration of intellect" on the part of the Government.

This was not the only instance of Mr. Gerald Balfour's mismanagement of Government business in the House. Later in the session he produced a resolution relating to a modified redistribution of seats to deal with certain anomalies which had arisen; it was subsequently ruled by the Speaker that the resolution would require to be divided into eight or nine parts and committed to a Committee of the whole House; the parliamentary time available rendered such a course impossible, so that the whole project had to be dropped. It is extraordinary that Mr. Balfour should not have ascertained in advance the proper procedure.

MONDAY, JULY 3RD, 1905

Aliens Bill in Committee

Rather a heated debate. Crooks and Burns made two excessively abusive speeches referring to "rich Jews on the other side of the House", "titled aliens", etc.

There are two interesting features of this debate. One is that it exemplified the fact that Mr. John Burns and Mr. Will Crooks, who a few years later in their mellow old age were regarded with affection by the whole House—a "lovable figure" was, I think, the term applied to Mr. Crooks in one of his obituaries—were

---

[1] Now Lord Lambert.　　　　[2] The late Sir Henry Fowler.

in those days very offensive to their opponents; the same could be said, almost without exception, of all the founders of the Parliamentary Labour Party, or "Liberal-Labour", as it was then called. Mr. Bevan in his famous "Vermin" speech was following the traditional line of the father-founders of his party. The other is the insulting reference to "rich Jews". One absolute taboo in the modern House of Commons, since Hitler's persecution of the Jews, is any statement derogatory to the Jewish race. The description to-day by a member of members on the other side of the House as "rich Jews" would, very properly, produce an immediate order of withdrawal by the Chair.

THURSDAY, JULY 13TH, 1905

Volunteer Estimates Debate in the House

Another ticklish debate. Government majority at 7.15 division only 26. A few more Irish there and we should have ended our trouble.

We were, in fact, defeated soon after this (on Friday, July 21) on the Irish Estimates.

The sequel was interesting, as the following extract shows.

MONDAY, JULY 24TH, 1905

The House was packed from top to bottom with people eager to hear the Prime Minister's declaration with regard to the crisis.

Questions were soon over, for the Irishmen, in whose name the majority stood, called out "postpone till next session" or "I will ask that of the Right Honourable gentleman's successor". At 2.25 the Prime Minister got up to make his statement. It was a closely-reasoned speech as to the pro's and con's for resigning and was wonderfully well received. After he had spoken there was some wrangling as to the course to be adopted in order to obtain discussion on the Government's decision not to resign. Finally, Sir A. Acland-Hood moved the adjournment and discussion then began; Winston and Lloyd George were well rebuked by the Prime Minister for their personal attack on him. The debate ended at 7.20 without a division amid loud Ministerial cheers at the cowardice of the Opposition in not taking a vote.

I think the probable reason for the Opposition not wishing to *brusquer* the situation was that they realised, as did most of the

House, though not the Prime Minister, that the longer the Government remained in power the heavier would be its defeat. The discussion on the Irish Estimates was resumed the next day, Tuesday, July 25.

TUESDAY, JULY 25TH, 1905

Irish Estimates in House

A very stormy sitting, the Irish being the most unruly of the Opposition. After ruthlessly opposing the formal stage of every Private Bill, they made a continual uproar until midnight and distinguished themselves by a particularly abusive attack on the Solicitor-General for Ireland,[1] who was described by Devlin as "one of a hungry band of lawyers who had fattened and battened upon Ireland for hundreds of years". After midnight we were kept up until 3.0 a.m. by the Naval Works Bill in an atmosphere which for tropical heat and humidity it would be hard to equal.

M.P.s and others often ask me in these days, when there has been a "scene" in the House, if manners and the relationship between the two sides have not greatly deteriorated in recent years. I always reply that the opposite is the truth. The Irish Nationalists, unlike any other party within my long recollection of the House of Commons, with the exception of the members representing the Clyde for a short period after the 1922 election (they soon adopted a more reasonable attitude), have been the only party or group who deliberately attempted to injure the House as an institution by uproar, insults and obstructions; they atoned for this, to some extent, by their wit and the remarkable standard of parliamentary eloquence among them. But the House has been an infinitely more reasonable place, even in the days of the most acute feeling between the Tories and Socialists—as, for example, after the 1931 election—since the departure of the Irish Nationalists.

The incident in the extract above exemplified this Irish Nationalist attitude. Mr. Campbell was personally a most popular member of the House as well as a very efficient one. His speech was reasonable and conciliatory; yet, without the slightest provocation, Mr. Devlin rose and made the remarks quoted above. His object, in which he succeeded, was to cause a scene and thus,

[1] Mr. J. H. M. Campbell, K.C., M.P., later Lord Glenavy.

by inducing ill-temper all round, make it as difficult as possible for the Government to get their business through.

During the session Speaker Gully resigned and was succeeded by the Chairman of Committees, Mr. Lowther, who had been Under-Secretary for Foreign Affairs in the '90s. A man of fine intellect, magnificent presence and balanced judgment, with a keen sense of humour, he became one of the greatest Speakers of all time. He lived to be ninety-three. Long after his retirement, on his ninetieth birthday, the then Speaker—Colonel Clifton Brown—and I, in my capacity as "Father of the House", sent him a telegram of congratulations. He replied in his own clear and beautiful handwriting, which was wholly unaffected by age.

Two events occurred during this session which, like King Edward's successful visit to Paris the previous year, were intended to help repair the rents in our foreign relationships caused by the South African War.

One was the visit of young King Alfonso of Spain, who shortly afterwards became engaged to Princess Ena of Battenberg, daughter of Princess Beatrice. He was a man of great charm and vivacity, with a keen sense of humour. At a dinner at Lord Lansdowne's (the Foreign Secretary) at which I was present, he said to Mr. Austen Chamberlain: "All my Finance Ministers have been old and sad and they have reason to be sad. But you are young and look happy".

The other event was the official visit of the French Atlantic Fleet, the officers of which were entertained by both Houses to lunch in Westminster Hall. I spent a night on board one of the battleships of the Fleet as the guest of the Captain and sailed back to Brest in her. Naturally the political relationship between our two countries was not discussed between the officers and myself, but there was no concealment of their belief in the value of the nascent Entente Cordiale as a shield for both countries against Germany. Even two years earlier such an attitude would have been impossible for any patriotic Frenchman, since England was then still the hereditary enemy. Though myself biased, perhaps, by affection for and relationship with Lord Lansdowne, I think he has never received his due share of the credit for creating the Entente Cordiale with France which developed into an Alliance in 1914. It is commonly believed that its inception was mainly

due to King Edward VII, and in particular to his famous speech
in Paris in 1903. But he could only have made it, under our
Constitution, with the approval of his Foreign Minister, Lord
Lansdowne. As I have reason to know, the latter shared to the full
his Sovereign's desire for an understanding with France. The
French blood in his veins and his intimate knowledge of France
and the French language helped him greatly in his task.

SATURDAY, JUNE 3RD, 1905

Oxford Polo Match

Oxford University	*A House of Commons team*
Hon. W. H. Pearson 1	Self 1
Mr. R. A. Brassey 2	Sir R. Green, M.P. 2
Lord Balgonie 3	Sir F. Mildmay, M.P. 3
Hon. Neil Primrose (back)	Mr. Winston Churchill, M.P. (back)

The Commons had the best of it all through and won by 9 goals
to 3. A fast game. Drove with Winston in a hansom from Oxford
Station to the Polo Ground, beguiled on the way with political
gossip.

Two of the Oxford team—Harold Pearson and Neil Primrose
—afterwards became Liberal M.P.s. The latter was Under-
Secretary for Foreign Affairs during the First World War, but
resigned in order to join his regiment in Palestine, where he was
killed in action.

This was not my only participation in mounted sport with
Mr. Churchill in the summer of 1905. As the guest of the
Buckinghamshire Hussars, in camp at Blenheim in June, I was
one of the "hounds" in a Hare and Hounds race on horseback.
Mr. Churchill was another member of the pack. A Press photo-
grapher, anxious to get a snap of him—for his fame was considerable even in those days—dashed in front of the pack just as a
View Holloa gave us the signal to start. I was riding a pulling
horse, and, despite all my efforts to avoid him, knocked him
over; fortunately he was not badly hurt, but his camera was damaged and the plates in them ruined!!

CHAPTER III

THE election of January, 1906, brought one of the heaviest defeats in its history to the Conservative Party.[1] Among the rejected were a number of Cabinet Ministers and Under-Secretaries. Mr. Balfour lost his seat.[2] The figures caused consternation to his supporters, and his sister, Miss Balfour, was in tears after the count. He himself, with the philosophic equanimity which never failed him in a crisis, merely observed, "These things *will* happen".

I was fortunate enough to hold Horsham with a slightly reduced majority, though two adjoining seats to mine regarded as safe—one held by a Cabinet Minister, Mr. Brodrick, afterwards Lord Midleton—fell to the Liberals.

The 1906 election had a greater significance even than that involved in a huge transfer of votes from the Conservatives to the Liberals. It marked the end of an era which had lasted since the passage of the first Reform Act. During that period no controversy between political parties nor events abroad had threatened either the stability of Parliament as an institution or the life of the nation. I do not even except the temporary injury done to the House of Commons by the original Irish Home Rule controversy of the 1880s as a result of the obstruction of the Irish Nationalists. But from 1909 until the outbreak of war in 1914 events occurred which shook the Constitution, produced dangerous physical violence in and out of Parliament and involved the menace of civil war. They were, as this book will show, the rejection of the 1909 Budget by the Lords; the passing of the Parliament Act, 1911; the Suffragette campaign; and the bitter controversy aroused by the Home Rule Bill, with the determination of Ulster to resist it by force. Far too many books dealing with this period, in attempting to contrast its alleged serenity

---

[1] The figures were: Liberals 379, Labour 51, Irish Nationalists 83, Conservatives and Unionists 157.

[2] A member resigned and he was elected for the City of London in February, 1906.

with what has happened since, fail to mention that Britain was dangerously divided and distracted over matters of grave constitutional import when war came and, at least temporarily, healed those internal differences.

The new Parliament met in February, 1906. At its first sitting it was obvious that the huge Liberal majority on the back benches was very truculent and overbearing. Many of its members were new to political life; others had won seats which even the Liberal Party management before the election had regarded as hopeless, and for which, consequently, there had been no very careful selection of candidates. A considerable proportion of these had little respect for the House and its conventions, and a sadistic dislike of the Tories. As our front bench came in to take their places for the debate on the Address, they were greeted with ironical cheers from the Government and Nationalist benches and shouts of "Where's Balfour? Where is his brother? Where's Brodrick?"

Mr. Joseph and Mr. Austen Chamberlain retained their seats—as did all the Birmingham Tories—with huge majorities. Mr. Balfour requested the former, who was not in the least dispirited by the result of the election, to lead the Opposition in his absence. Asked by me the rather foolish question (I became his Parliamentary Private Secretary after Parliament reassembled) what he thought of our defeat, Mr. Chamberlain replied: "My motto is never complain, never explain, always attack ; and I propose to put it into practice in this Parliament".

He gave early evidence of this. The motion for the Address was moved in a moderate but commonplace speech. The seconder was Mr. Horridge. He wholly departed from the usual practice on such occasions of being non-controversial, and made a fierce attack, in platform style, on the Opposition, with more than one wounding reference to the absent Mr. Balfour. The excited Liberals cheered loudly, the Tories sat in angry silence. Then Mr. Chamberlain rose, to be received with ironical cheering from Liberal back-benchers and some interruptions. Mr. Chamberlain ignored them completely, and they soon ceased. To the surprise of us behind him, he proceeded to give lengthy and extravagant praise, as it seemed, to the pedestrian speech of the mover, and added that he had created a standard and precedent for such occasions which it would be hard to follow. He made only this reference to the seconder: "The Honourable Member who seconded the motion also created a precedent which I hope for the sake of this House will never be followed". We cheered him at the top of our voices, and it was the Liberals' turn to sit glum and silent. From then until his lamentable breakdown in health a few months later, Mr. Chamberlain continued to have the same hold over the Commons that he had possessed since the '80s. As for Mr. Horridge, he never recovered from the "knock-out" blow given him by Mr. Chamberlain—a rarer event to-day than it was then. His subsequent speeches failed to hold or interest the House, and a few years later, on being given a judicial appointment, he resigned his seat.

During the debate on the Address, a new Liberal M.P.—Mr. Herbert Paul, the historian—in a maiden speech made a ferocious, though somewhat confused, attack upon the Conservative Party. Mr. Bridgeman (afterwards Lord Bridgeman), who held high office after the First World War, followed with his maiden speech. He made one of the neatest retorts I have heard in the Commons. "The Honourable Member's speech", he said, "reminded me very forcibly of a passage in the Bible, 'Paul, Paul, thou art beside thyself; much learning hath made thee mad'".

Members like myself, who belonged to the Tariff Reform League and supported Mr. Chamberlain's policy, were more dissatisfied after the election with Mr. Balfour's attitude towards the question than we had been in the previous Parliament, and were, consequently, anxious to bring the issue to a head. At a dinner on February 5, given by Sir Gilbert Parker, M.P., a number of us, after discussion, decided, in the words of my diary "to press A. J. B. [Mr. Balfour] for a Party meeting, and, in order to carry out that object, arranged to canvass all the Tariff Reform members and ask them to join us in petitioning Balfour. We left the question of proposing a strong Tariff Reform resolution at the proposed meeting and of generally taking the bull by the horns to our next discussion at 20 Carlton House Terrace [1]".

At this dinner I met for the first time a newly elected member who was destined for a great career, and who became a very

[1] Sir Gilbert Parker's house.

good and close friend of mine—Mr. F. E. Smith, afterwards the first Lord Birkenhead. My diary records:

SATURDAY, FEBRUARY 10TH, 1906

Lunch at Sir Gilbert Parker's with practically the same party as Monday. We were able to obtain the signatures of some fifty M.P.s to our petition and, although it appeared that Balfour had in any case decided to hold a Party meeting, we sent the list of names in favour of the meeting to strengthen our position. A letter from Mr. Chamberlain was read deprecating a strong General Tariff Resolution on the ground that it would (1) if carried, practically compel Balfour to give up the leadership, (2) if not carried, do the cause harm. We reluctantly agreed to this; but wrote to Chamberlain through Ridley[1] urging the necessity for some action to emphasise our determination not to let things drop.

What we had really in mind was to run Mr. Chamberlain for the leadership of the Party, both on personal grounds and as the only means of getting his policy officially adopted by the Party. He was aware of our intention, but refused, for reasons which were creditable to him, to do anything to oust Mr. Balfour. The Party meeting was duly held and, after some bickering between the two sides in the fiscal controversy, a resolution of confidence in Balfour's leadership was carried without dissent. But naturally the Liberals continued by debates in Parliament and speeches outside to make full use of the divisions in our attenuated parliamentary ranks on this issue.

One of these debates on fiscal policy[2] was an historic one, for it produced two famous speeches which are still remembered.

MONDAY, MARCH 12TH, 1906

The long-deferred Kitson debate. Mr. Balfour took his seat for the City of London amid perfect silence, broken only by Willie

[1] The second Lord Ridley, then an M.P.
[2] On a resolution moved by Sir James Kitson as follows: "That this House, recognising that in the recent General Election the people of the United Kingdom have demonstrated their unqualified fidelity to the principles and practice of Free Trade, deems it right to record its determination to resist any proposal, whether by way of taxation upon foreign corn or of the creation of a general tariff upon foreign goods, to create in this country a system of protection".

Redmond's: "Welcome, little stranger". Kitson, in a very dull speech, opened the debate. Balfour followed with one of his usual speeches which, though skilful enough as it avoided any direct reference to the question and merely challenged the wording of the resolution, rather justified the Prime Minister's later remark.

The remark in question was Mr. Campbell-Bannerman's famous opening: "I welcome the Rt. Hon. gentleman back to the House. Unfortunately, like the Bourbons, he has learned nothing and forgotten nothing; enough of this foolery!!"

Later in the evening Mr. F. E. Smith made his historic maiden speech—the most brilliant maiden speech in living memory and most effective counter-attack by a party in difficulties and under heavy bombardment which I ever heard in my forty-seven years in the House. Unfortunately, our troubles for the day were not over, for Sir Edward Clarke, a distinguished lawyer member of our party and a former Law Officer, chose to make from our front bench a Free Trade speech and repudiate, in effect, what both Mr. Balfour and Mr. Chamberlain, who earlier in the day had denied any serious difference between them, had said. A few days later, Mr. F. E. Smith and I wrote to Mr. Balfour to protest against this speech and to suggest that Sir Edward be asked to move to one of the back benches. Our suggestion was not accepted, but Sir Edward made no more speeches of the kind.

F. E. Smith's speech was much more than a personal triumph. It marked the end of the period of depression and awe of the huge, overbearing Government majority which at first afflicts a Party that has been in power and then suffered a terrible electoral defeat. From then onwards the members of the Conservative Opposition on the back benches attacked the Government with a vigour that has seldom been surpassed. Some of the younger of us, myself especially, probably went too far and were considered by some of the staider members of our Party to use methods of delaying business, as well as terms of expression, more suited to Irish Nationalists than Conservatives. But we did a good deal to re-establish outside the House confidence in the fighting powers of the Party, and our action was approved by our leader.

On Wednesday, March 21, Mr. Byles, a Liberal back-bencher, moved a resolution of censure on Lord Milner, who had recently retired from the High Commissionership of South Africa, in the following terms:

> That this House expresses its disapproval of the conduct of Lord Milner, as High Commissioner of South Africa and Governor of the Transvaal, in authorising the flogging of Chinese labourers in breach of the Law, in violation of treaty obligations and without the knowledge or sanction of His Majesty's Secretary of State for the Colonies.

The Government, through Mr. Churchill, moved an amendment which was carried by 355 to 135 to leave out from "House" to the end of the proposed words and insert "while recording its condemnation of the flogging of Chinese coolies in breach of the Law, desires, in the interests of peace and conciliation in South Africa, to refrain from passing censure upon individuals".

Mr. Chamberlain, in the words of my diary:

> after defending Lord Milner's action, made a scathing attack on the Government for their infinite cowardice and meanness in neither meeting nor negativing the motion; Winston followed in a very laboured and most offensive speech in which, while he really attacked Milner, he clumsily endeavoured to show that he was protecting him. Balfour wound up the debate and referred to Winston's "insulting protection" of Lord Milner.

The particular passage in Mr. Churchill's speech to which the leader of the Opposition referred was an unfortunate statement that, after all, Lord Milner had left South Africa "honourably poor". It was greeted by roars of anger from the Conservatives. There is no doubt that this first ministerial speech of Mr. Churchill's[1] was a complete failure. His many enemies in the Conservative Party exultantly claimed that he was finished. Influenced no doubt by personal friendship, I thought that they were wrong—and they were. His next speech was a success. Within two years he was in the Cabinet, to display thereafter, as Minister in charge of great Departments, the amazing compound of various qualities of supreme genius—so rarely found in one man—which many years later enabled him to lead the country to victory.

---

[1] He was Under-Secretary of State for the Colonies.

Two of the Government's principal measures of the 1906 session did not pass the Lords. One of them, the Plural Voting Bill, was rejected on second reading. The other, the Education Bill, was dropped after the two Houses had failed to agree on amendments inserted by the Lords. When, in 1910, the Parliament Bill was discussed, the fate of these two Bills was cited, among other examples, to justify the contention that the Lords in recent times had passed the legislation of Conservative and rejected that of Liberal Governments, where a Party issue arose, almost as a matter of course, thereby destroying its own value and reputation as a Second Chamber.

Among other Government Bills passed which did not involve any political issue was one prohibiting street betting. Its most active opponents were Mr. Horatio Bottomley, already famous and afterwards to become notorious, and myself. We pointed out the utter illogicality of making it a legal offence for a working-man to hand a shilling to a bookmaker for a bet in the street, whereas if he posted it to an office in the same street he was committing no offence. We also contended that if the Bill became law it would increase the danger of corruption among the police, because it would be so easy to bribe a constable on duty to walk in the opposite direction when a bet was about to be made. After all these years I still believe that we were right.

By 1907 the Government had established itself as competent in administration and far better able than its predecessor to state a case for legislation in or out of the House. This was not surprising in view of its composition. Men of the intellectual calibre of Sir Edward Grey, Mr. Asquith, Mr. Haldane, Mr. John Morley, Mr. Churchill, Mr. Lloyd George, Mr. Herbert Samuel, Mr. Runciman, Mr. McKenna, Sir Henry Fowler, Mr. Birrell, Mr. Bryce, to mention only a few members of the 1905 Government, are not found in every Administration. But the most interesting feature was the success of Sir Henry Campbell-Bannerman during his short Premiership from 1905 until his death in 1908.

He had been, as I have already recorded, an ineffective and despised leader of the Opposition. As Prime Minister, he commanded the respect of the House. He resembled in some respects two of his successors in that office—Mr. Baldwin and Mr. Attlee.[1]

[1] See also Chapter XV, p. 205.

All three illustrated the fact that the following qualities are useful electoral assets in the King's first Minister: to be mild, tolerant and unimpassioned in debate whilst on occasions hitting hard; and to give the impression of intellectual modesty and claim to no higher intelligence than that of the average man and woman. If to these are added ruthlessness in dealing with recalcitrant colleagues and refusal to be hurried into making a decision in the interests of the Party, but not necessarily of the nation—characteristics common to all the three men mentioned—a Prime Minister or Party leader can reasonably look forward to holding his position for a long time.

In complete contrast to Sir Henry Campbell-Bannerman, Mr. Balfour, who in many respects had failed as Prime Minister, was a highly successful leader of the Opposition. He realised, as not all his successors in that position—Conservative, Liberal or Socialist —have done, that it was his duty to be constantly in the Chamber itself and not merely there for big debates and important occasions; for only by continual vigilance and close personal attention to what is going on in the House at all times can an Opposition leader inspire his followers and give them confidence. Mr. Balfour gave most energetic support to the "young bloods" of the Opposition, such as myself. If one of us, as I frequently did in those days, made an ineffective speech in some unimportant debate he would come to our rescue. After rising in his nonchalant fashion and gazing at the Government supporters with a look of pained surprise, he would observe that he saw no reason for the derision with which his Honourable Friend's remarks had been received; the Government adopted a most arrogant attitude to all who exercised their perfect right of contesting its policy; the Minister's reply had been deplorable; it was regrettable that the Prime Minister was not present, for then he would have been able afterwards to administer in private a rebuke to his colleague for the utter inadequacy of his speech. This invariably produced a cry from us of "Where *is* the Prime Minister? Send for the Prime Minister". The Government Chief Whip would hurry into the Chamber and hurry out again to try to get hold of the Prime Minister, for it is the duty of Chief Whips of the Government to try to prevent a row which may impede the progress of Government business. Equally it is the duty of an Opposition to use every legitimate method, by prolonged discussion where necessary, of supporting their own principles and attacking those of their opponents. The process can naturally be carried too far, but critics of the British parliamentary system who regard such tactics as childish, unworthy and unpatriotic should realise that the logical alternative is that which has prevailed in the legislative assemblies of totalitarian countries in the last quarter of a century. Certainly, in the years about which I am writing, we of the Opposition carried out our duty, of which the following extract from my diary furnishes an example, very fully.

THURSDAY, MARCH 21ST, 1907

Army Annual Bill; this year it affords more opportunities for criticism than usual and Bob Cecil, Helmsley, Claude Hay, Rutherford, Wilfred Ashley, Hunt, myself and several others, kept the ball rolling so well that we managed to sit right on until six o'clock in the afternoon. There were the usual all-night sitting scenes. Jerry McVeagh remarked, as Bull and Hunt came up the Floor of the House as tellers, "Here comes the Prodigal Son and the Fatted Calf"[1] The value of the sitting lies in the fact that the Government will have to sit on Saturday.

By far the most important measure, in its permanent effect, passed in the session of 1907 was for the creation of the Territorial Army. This merged the Volunteers and Yeomanry into a composite Force and abolished the Militia as such, though forming it into a Special Reserve. The Conservative benches were full of Volunteer and Yeomanry officers, and there was some objection to the Bill in its preliminary stage, because it was feared that units of both these auxiliary arms of the Service would lose their value and particular characteristics. Events proved that our fears were unjustified.

Mr. Haldane was undoubtedly the best Secretary of State for War since Mr. Cardwell (1868–74). To him belongs the credit of

[1] This was a good example of the particular type of wit which appeals to M.P.s. Mr. Rowland Hunt, who was nicknamed "Boadicea", on account of a remarkable maiden speech mainly devoted to the British Queen in question, had recently had his "whip" restored to him. It had been temporarily taken from him because of an attack in a speech of his upon Mr. Balfour. Sir William Bull, Member for Hammersmith, was a fat, florid man who closely resembled the legendary "John Bull".

the eventual establishment of the Expeditionary Force, the famous "Old Contemptibles" of the 1914 war. The four divisions comprising it, which fought at Mons, represented the best-trained, munitioned and serviced Force we have ever sent overseas in the early stages of a war. The reasons why it was wholly insufficient for the task which it was asked to perform are stated in a later chapter. The Territorial Army was mismanaged, after August, 1914, by being broken up and having some of its weapons taken away to equip the New Army. As Mr. L. S. Amery has stated, Lord Kitchener had a curious confusion of mind about its character and functions; he believed that it resembled the French Territorial Army which was mainly composed of old men. But that does not detract from the genius and statesmanship of Mr. Haldane in founding it. He has never received his due meed of praise for several reasons. He had a somewhat oleaginous manner in public and private, and was not a popular figure. He once used an unfortunate phrase—"Germany is my spiritual home"—which caused his exclusion, owing to an unfair Press attack, from the Governments of the 1914 war. He offended his old friends and colleagues by joining the Labour Party after the 1914 war.

In addition to the Territorial and Reserve Forces Bill, a useful Smallholdings Bill and two valuable measures of penal reform—the Criminal Appeal Bill and Probation of Offenders Bill—were passed as well as a number of smaller Bills. But the principal characteristic of the session was the growing tension between the two Houses, which resulted in more than one Government Bill being rejected in the Lords or withdrawn in the Commons because it had no chance, in the opinion of Ministers, of getting through the Lords. The result was a resolution passed by the House of Commons, after an angry party debate, as follows: "That in order to give effect to the will of the people as expressed by their elected representatives, it is necessary that the power of the other House to alter or reject Bills passed by this House should be so restricted by law as to secure that within the limits of a single Parliament the final decision of the Commons should prevail". Since this resolution was never communicated to the Lords, that Chamber had no opportunity of expressing any opinion upon it.

In the spring of 1908, Sir Henry Campbell-Bannerman died a few weeks after his resignation owing to ill-health. Mr. Asquith succeeded him as Prime Minister and Mr. Lloyd George became Chancellor of the Exchequer. Momentous events resulted from the latter appointment. It gave Mr. Lloyd George the chance for which he was looking to turn Liberalism into a crusading and reformist army, ready to assault the strong-points of privilege with taxation, a weapon which Gladstone would have been horrified to use for this purpose. It enabled him, as he thought, to forestall the growing claim of the Labour Party to represent the wage-earners, especially the "under-dog", by social legislation advocated in terms of fiery resentment, never before heard from the lips of a statesman of high rank, against those alleged to be responsible for their condition.

A description of the implementation of the Lloyd-Georgian strategy belongs to the next chapter dealing with the 1909 session. But two further results, one remote and one more immediate, arising from his appointment deserve mention here. It sowed the seeds of the eventual Asquith–Lloyd-George dissonance, which eventually killed the political influence of both men and contributed largely to the destruction of the Liberal Party itself. It gave full scope to his political glamour, power of oratory and sense of occasion. So great were these gifts that in the following year they were the main factor in arresting the very serious swing against the Government shown by the loss of by-elections in 1908. I remember Mr. F. E. Smith saying, in 1909, to Mr. Lloyd George at a dinner party: "If you had gone to the country in 1908 before you brought in your budget of this year we should have had a majority of 60". Mr. Lloyd George did not answer, but I could see from his smile that he agreed.

The most serious by-election loss, from the point of view of prestige, was Mr. Churchill's defeat at Oldham in the spring of 1908. He had just been made President of the Board of Trade consequent upon the change in the Cabinet resulting from Sir Henry Campbell-Bannerman's death. By an unnecessary and inconsistent provision of electoral law, now abolished, certain Ministers on appointment had to vacate their seats and present themselves for re-election. He stood again at Dundee, the Liberal member vacating the seat in order to enable him to do so, and after a hard fight was returned. I went to Dundee for two or three days to campaign against him. The following extract from my diary shows that two characteristics of Mr. Churchill—his belief in the value of a personal staff and his generous attitude towards political opponents who are also personal friends—have not changed much in forty-five years.

FRIDAY, MAY 8TH, 1908

Dundee—lunched at the Queen's Hotel where I met Winston surrounded by a sort of staff consisting of Jack Churchill,[1] de Forest,[2] Marsh[3] and Masterman.[4] I addressed a very representative businessmen's meeting in the afternoon; had tea with Winston who seemed very weary.

Another reference to Mr. Churchill in my diary of this year is worth quoting:

THURSDAY, OCTOBER 29TH, 1908

Dined with Fred Smith [Mr. F. E. Smith] in Eccleston Square. Winston and Mrs. Winston and Castlereagh [afterwards the 7th Lord Londonderry] there; a most interesting dinner; had a very instructive discussion with him afterwards about the Pacific question[5] and also Home Rule; this talk more than ever convinced me that in Winston we lost a man who might have rendered signal service to the Imperial cause.

By this I meant that it was a great pity that, partly owing to what he regarded as insufficient recognition of his talents, he had not remained a member of the Conservative Party. However, I need not have worried, since thirty-two years later (in 1940) he rendered the greatest service of any statesman of any time to the British Empire and Commonwealth.

In June, 1908, King Edward VII paid a visit to the Tsar of Russia; there can be no reasonable doubt that the visit was

---

[1] The late Mr. Jack Churchill—Mr. Winston Churchill's brother.
[2] The late Baron de Forest.
[3] The late Sir Edward Marsh, K.C.V.O., C.B., C.M.G.
[4] The late Mr. Charles Masterman, M.P.
[5] I had recently been in the United States, where I learnt of the distrust there, even in those days, of Japanese intentions.

encouraged by Sir Edward Grey, who wished to strengthen the Anglo-French-Russian Entente in view of the potential menace of the growing power of the German Navy. But it caused furious indignation to many Liberal and Labour M.P.s, and was much criticised by what would now be called Leftist newspapers, who regarded the Tsar as an arch-tyrant. I was in Kiel Harbour soon after King Edward had passed through on his way to Russia, and had an interesting experience which is recounted in a book of mine.[1] The Government were themselves to blame for some of the indignation, since a year or two earlier Sir Henry Campbell-Bannerman had made an extremely unfortunate reference to Russian internal affairs. The Tsar had just arbitrarily dissolved the Russian Parliament—the Duma. Sir Henry, in a speech, said, "Le Duma est mort; vive le Duma".

Soon afterwards I managed, in the jargon of the House of Commons, to "get past the Table" a satirical question on the matter—"to ask the Prime Minister if His Majesty's Government propose to use their good offices with the Russian Government to secure the re-election of the Duma". When the Prime Minister rose to reply he said, flushed with indignation, "Does the Noble Lord intend this question to be taken seriously?" I naturally replied that of course I did otherwise I would not have put it down. He then snapped out, "The answer is, No, sir". I was proceeding to ask, in a supplementary question, why then he had used the phrase which he did, when the Speaker very properly stopped me!!

A debate on the King's visit took place on June 4.

JUNE 4TH, 1908

Foreign affairs debate; reduction being moved by O'Grady[2] to protest against the King's visit to Russia; did not hear opening speech but arrived in time to hear Grey who made an admirable speech worthy of "the great days of old"—moderate, dignified and yet pregnant. A. J. B. also spoke. Keir Hardie, to whom I did not listen, made a speech of his usual kind and was nearly "named" for speaking of "atrocities committed by the Czar's Government", but eventually climbed down. He tried to finish amid continual

[1] *Pre-War*, p. 98.   [2] Mr. James O'Grady, M.P. for Leeds (East).

cries of "'Vide", and then Grayson[1] rose when Henderson, for some reason best known to himself, moved the closure. There was at once a —— of a row. Grayson shouting, "I will not be shouted down". The Chairman on his feet calling "Order" and a Labour member chiming in with "Shame, shame". Mr. Emmott[2] at last put the question regardless of Grayson, who continued to yell like a Dervish and kept gibbering at me for calling "Order" to him. At last he subsided, having failed to get suspended, which he hoped to be and having been properly snubbed.

One cannot conceive a debate of such a character on a Royal visit taking place to-day.

It is, however, only fair to the 1906 House of Commons to remember that the occupant of the Throne in those days had, or was supposed to have, more direct influence on public affairs than his successors. I came across a curious instance of this during the same year. I had given notice that I would raise, on the adjournment, the question of the official recognition of Empire Day; the late Lord Meath and others had founded the Empire Day Movement to emphasise, by the hoisting of flags and ceremonies in town and country, on a particular date each year, the meaning and value of the British Empire. The Government refused to recognise this movement officially, and its anti-Imperialist Members of Parliament jeered at our efforts to induce them to do so. Prior to my raising the subject, the Prime Minister, Mr. Asquith, sent for me and told me in his room that he believed that the King objected to flags being flown officially (that is, on Government buildings) on such a day; but when I asked him, he would not say if he had been so instructed in his official position as His Majesty's principal adviser, so I made my speech and received a civil reply to the effect that he would look into the matter again. It is unlikely to-day that any influence from the Crown would be mentioned even in private in a matter of this kind; indeed, if it were, the question of privilege might arise since the House of Commons in recent years has been so jealous about its privileges—real or alleged.

[1] Mr. Victor Grayson, a Labour member of extremist views and considerable talent who mysteriously disappeared (after losing his seat) some years later and was never heard of again.

[2] Mr. Emmott was Deputy-Speaker and Chairman of Committees.

The principal measure of the 1908 session was a Licensing Bill designed further to reduce the number of licensed premises (already limited by an Act passed in the previous Parliament), to impose new conditions, some of them onerous and unnecessary, upon clubs, and to institute a form of local option in respect of new licences. The Bill was clearly brought forward to please the strong teetotal element in the Liberal Party and other opponents of the licensed trade, rather than for any reasonable social or administrative purpose. The Opposition in general, and a small band of young members in particular—Mr. F. E. Smith, Lord Helmsley, Mr. George Faber, Mr. A. Salter[1] and myself—fought the Bill line by line, and it did not reach its third reading until November 20. On this occasion Mr. Salter moved and I seconded the rejection of the Bill. Mr. Asquith, with the kindness and friendliness which he always showed towards young members of whatever Party, praised our persistence and said we were "veterans of the fight whose hair had gone visibly grey under the strain". The debate was one of the stormiest of the session, and ended with the Opposition shouting "Robbery, robbery!!" and supporters of the Government "Snobbery, snobbery!!", as the Speaker put the question. The Bill was rejected in the Lords.

During November the annual conference of the Conservative Party was held at Birmingham. The breach between the "Balfourites" and "Chamberlainites" was virtually healed at this conference. Mr. Henry Chaplin[2] moved a resolution embracing all the cardinal points of Tariff Reform. This resolution was carried unanimously, as it also was when moved by Mr. Bonar Law and seconded by myself three months later at the annual meeting of the Tariff Reform League, the body supporting Mr. Joseph Chamberlain's views. At the mass meeting of the conference Mr. Balfour made a speech to which none of us "Chamberlainites" could take exception in its reference to the fiscal problem.

Earlier in the year Mr. Joseph Chamberlain himself had been laid low by a stroke and was never fully to recover. To his followers and admirers, especially to me, his Parliamentary

[1] Afterwards Mr. Justice Salter; not to be confused with Sir Arthur Salter.
[2] The first Lord Chaplin, affectionately known to political friends and opponents alike as "The Squire".

Private Secretary, this was a calamitous blow, though he himself bore his affliction with great courage and patience, and was much cheered by the circumstances already recorded—the Birmingham Conference and its sequel.

WEDNESDAY, DECEMBER 22ND, 1908

Went to see Mr. Joseph Chamberlain in response to an invitation from Mrs. Chamberlain. It was the first time that I had seen him since his illness and I confess that I dreaded the interview; it was not, however, as bad as I thought it would be. His voice was somewhat thick and halting and the right arm and leg disabled, but his face was unchanged and his perception and conversation as keen as ever; he was, as usual, wonderfully kind and the forty minutes slipped away all too soon; oh, for one year of the old year of the old Joe as leader!! Then we should have an Empire in reality!!

The poignancy of this memory of my Chief—the last time I saw him, save when he was assisted by his son, Mr. Austen Chamberlain, and another member to the Table in the House of Commons to take his seat in the 1910 Parliament, for his constituents refused to allow him to resign, though they knew his condition—is mitigated by the fact that everything he advocated in Imperial relationships and fiscal policy is now permanently established on a basis of all-party support. What a proud memorial to a great statesman!!

CHAPTER IV

THE 1909 session is memorable for the famous "1909" or "Lloyd George" Budget. It was introduced on April 29 in a speech of four hours' duration. In the most recent biography of Lloyd George, by Mr. Tom Jones, C.H., the Chancellor's speech is described as a "parliamentary failure". I do not agree with this judgment. It is true that in the middle of it Mr. Lloyd George showed signs of physical exhaustion and that there was, in consequence, a short adjournment to enable him to recover. But, in the main, it was a good speech. He explained that he had two objects in view in advocating new taxation—financial provision for the Navy and for social reform; the latter category included compulsory and contributory health insurance, and the creation of the Development Fund for the increase and consolidation of grants for afforestation, agriculture, railways and harbours. The principal taxation proposals were: a small increase in Income Tax, a heavy one on Death Duties, a Super-Tax of 6*d.* in the £ on large incomes and higher taxation of the liquor trade. In addition, he proposed a complicated system of land taxes on the future unearned increment of land values and on undeveloped land, realisation of leases and mineral rights.

In his biography, Mr. Jones truly observes that the Opposition might have accepted the Budget but for the Land Taxes. He adds, "this complicated legislation accentuated the decline in house-building which had already begun, by discouraging the small speculative builder who worked on narrow margins of profit."[1] I made the same point in my book *Pre-War*, published in 1932. Contrary to general belief, the gap between the number of new houses built and the number required each year to meet the needs of a growing population did not begin in the First World War; in the later years of the nineteenth and early years of the twentieth century there were more small houses available for wage-earners and others of modest income at reasonable

[1] *Lloyd George*, Thomas Jones, C.H., p. 37.

rents or purchase price than there were applicants for them. With the exception of Mr. Jones, Mr. Lloyd George's admirers have been very reluctant to admit the damage his Budget did to the provision of houses, or the fact that the Land Duties were withdrawn some ten years later with their author's consent because they were impracticable.

The Finance Bill required seventy-two days for its passage through the Commons and a number of all-night sittings; it was the greatest and most sustained parliamentary fight in my forty-seven years' experience as an M.P. Mr. Lloyd George, who *more suo* was often not well versed on the details of the Finance Bill, had the invaluable help of his principal assistant, the late Mr. Charles Masterman,[1] and we on our side had the advantage of the skilled debating power and grasp of detail of men such as the late Sir Laming Worthington-Evans, the late Mr. Ernest Pretyman and the late Lord (then Mr.) Cave. The Finance Bill passed its final stage in the House of Commons on November 4, 1909, by 379 votes to 149 and on November 30 was rejected in the Lords by 350 to 75.

Mr. Lloyd George's treatment of the great national controversy over the Budget in the House was in striking contrast to his methods outside it. In the House he displayed, in words of mine written elsewhere,[2] "a resource, an imperturbability, a vitality and a sense of humour that the longest sittings could not exhaust". During most of the summer of 1909 we spent on an average three days a week on the committee stage of the Finance Bill, never rising before 1 a.m., usually sitting until 3 or 4 a.m., and often much later. I was there most of the time and I never saw the Chancellor lose his temper; it was very seldom that he used unduly aggressive terms about the Opposition or applied the closure; he early gained the admiration of his younger opponents such as myself. On the platform he was very different. There, in Mr. F. E. Smith's words, he raised the "naked issue of class hatred". In his well-known Limehouse Speech and on other occasions he used language about Tories and landlords and members of the House of Lords that has never been exceeded in violence by anything that his conscious or unconscious imitators, such as the late Mr. A. J. Cook or Mr. Aneurin Bevan,

[1] Financial Secretary to the Treasury.   [2] *Pre-War*, p. 148.

have said about Tories and Capitalists. When I was an Under-Secretary in his Government in 1922 I used to wonder if he remembered some of the things he had said before 1914 about the Conservative members of that same Government. It has been a fortunate attribute of many famous men—Mr. Gladstone, Mr. Joseph Chamberlain, Mr. Lloyd George and Mr. Churchill among them—to be able to treat with an indulgent smile and no trace of resentment any reference in debate in the Commons to the antithesis between their views on political parties in the past and the present. No doubt Mr. Lloyd George had two main motives for his attacks. He persuaded himself, quite falsely according to the available evidence, that his early years had been blasted by landlordism. In the same way, Mr. Aneurin Bevan and Mr. Harold Wilson genuinely, though without adducing any evidence to support them, contend that the evils of Capitalism overshadowed them in their youth. His other motive was a belief that his attack on Lords and landlords would be popular in itself and provoke replies that would harm the Conservative Party. Events proved him wrong.

While it is the fact, as I have previously written, that the 1909 Budget arrested the decline, as evidenced by by-elections, in the voting strength of the Liberal Party, this was due in the main to its provisions as a whole in relation to social reform. The Government had a heavy loss of seats at the 1910 election, and gained what support it had, not from any whipped-up indignation against Lords and landlords as such, but because of the unprecedented action of the House of Lords in rejecting a Budget and its obstructive attitude since 1906 to Government Bills passed by a large majority in the Commons. Nor, in the main, were the Peers, who opposed the Budget on platforms in the country, indifferent or inadequate controversialists; some, such as the late Lord Willoughby de Broke, unquestionably gained votes for us by an exposition of the defects in the Chancellor's arguments, especially in his advocacy of the Land Duties; only a few injured their own and the Conservative Party's case. One Noble Lord, whose knowledge of fox-hunting was as extensive as his acquaintance with political questions was meagre, publicly stated that he would like to throw the Chancellor of the Exchequer to his hounds. This observation was frequently quoted in the Liberal

Press and in debate at the time as illustrative of the brutal blood-lust of that debased institution, the British Peerage!

Even in tolerant Britain the first casualty in any furious political quarrel is a sense of humour.

A feature of the 1909 session was the determination of the Conservative Party to arouse public interest in the threat to the nation's safety of the formidable and growing increase in the German Navy and German armaments in general. A year earlier the National Service League had been founded by Lord Roberts to advocate a short term of conscription in the Army. A handful of Conservative M.P.s, of whom I was one, joined it, but its proposals were ridiculed and attacked by the whole Liberal Party and Press. Yet National Service, if adopted, as I wrote, "would not have hastened the Great War; coupled with a declaration that in certain circumstances we should stand by France, it might have averted it; it would certainly have reduced its length".[1]

In 1909 there was a movement inaugurated in the Conservative Party, and led by Mr. F. E. Smith, to press for the building of more Dreadnoughts. We used the slogan, "We want eight and we won't wait". Our agitation had an effect, for the building of an increased number of Dreadnoughts, whose armament completely outclassed the pre-Dreadnought battleships, was accelerated. The contrast between the Conservative and Liberal attitudes towards national defence in 1909 is illustrated by the following incidents. In March, 1909, amid loud cheers from the Liberal Party, a Labour member said, "No one wants more Dreadnoughts except the Noble Lord the member for Horsham [myself] and the *Daily Express*". Mr. Lloyd George in his Budget speech, whilst admitting the need to maintain the country's naval supremacy, said he was not going to squander money "on building gigantic flotillas to encounter mythical armadas". During the critical year of 1917 no one was in a better position than Mr. Lloyd George to realise how false a description "mythical" was to apply to the German Navy.

The terms of the motion rejecting the Budget in the Lords were as follows, "That this House is not justified in giving its consent to this Bill until it has been subjected to the judgment of

[1] *Pre-War*, p. 139.

the country". This was carried by 350 votes to 75. Next day the Government in the Commons moved the following resolution, "That the action of the House of Lords, in refusing to pass into Law the financial provisions made by this House for the service of the year is a breach of the Constitution and a usurpation of the rights of the Commons". After a ferocious debate the resolution was carried by a very large majority. Even his opponents, like myself, could not help admiring the rhetorical and oratorical content of Mr. Asquith's speech in moving it. His main thesis was based upon these words, "The House of Commons would, in the judgment of His Majesty's Government, be unworthy of its past, and of the traditions of which it is the custodian and trustee, if it allowed another day to pass without making it clear that it does not mean to brook the greatest indignity, and I will add, the most arrogant usurpation, to which, for more than two centuries it has been asked to submit".

The Government went to the country in January, 1910, lost over 100 seats, and found themselves dependent upon the votes of the Nationalist and Labour Parties for an effective majority. Nearly all the Conservative M.P.s who had been in the 1906 Parliament increased their majorities. My own went up from just over 600 in 1906 to 2,790 in January, 1910. The result of the election, as often happens, was a surprise alike to the Government and the Opposition. The former expected to get a clear majority over all parties to deal with the "usurpation" of which Mr. Asquith spoke. We thought that we should only slightly improve our position for, as I shall show later, many of us, especially among the younger M.P.s, privately doubted the wisdom of the Lords in rejecting the Budget.

No Conservative contributed more to our success than Mr. F. E. Smith. Indeed, no young "back-bencher" in any party at any time has attracted the huge audiences or made more magnificent platform speeches than he did at the two general elections of 1910. He was putting an enormous strain upon himself at the time for, in addition to all his parliamentary and political work, he was in the first flight as a barrister, dealing, with unsurpassed brilliance, with one leading case after another. I have always believed that this over-burden of work in two spheres was a contributory cause of his lamentably early death at the age of fifty-nine. Mr. F. E. Smith's "opposite number" was Mr. (now Lord) Simon, who had been his contemporary at Oxford. Though equalling him in intellectual attainment and forensic ability, he was less successful than his rival in debate. High as were the style and standard of his speeches, when contrasted with F. E. Smith's full-blooded attack, they gave the impression of an impersonal frigidity. The contrast was all the more noticeable as Mr. Simon was frequently asked by his party to follow Mr. Smith in debate. Usually there was a perceptible lessening of tension, emotion and interest in the Chamber after he had been speaking for a few minutes, though he was treated with the respect which is always shown to brilliant young men who are also good parliamentarians.

No fame or repute, good or bad, is more fleeting and evanescent than that gained in the world of politics. A man or woman may become well known or famous as an M.P., whether a back-bencher or a Minister, in a particular Parliament, enjoying, even in these days of truncated parliamentary press reports, a respectable amount of space for his or her speeches as well as the compliment of members hurrying into the Chamber when their name appears on the indicator as having "risen". Their appearance may become familiar to the public from press cartoons, and their names because of reference to them by music hall and radio comedians. Then he or she retires or is defeated at an election. Save in rare instances, you do not again hear their names mentioned in public or private in the Commons or its lobbies and smoking-room; the Press ignores them completely. Even if one of them, who has suffered electoral defeat, returns at a subsequent general election to the Commons, it is usually necessary for the individual concerned to start afresh to rebuild his reputation. Each new House of Commons differs, to some degree, in its method of evaluating talent and its personal likes and dislikes. A member who is successful and respected in debate in one Parliament may not "go down" at all in the next, nor does this popularity or unpopularity wholly depend upon a different party political majority in each case. The House of Commons is a fickle and changeable institution reflecting, consciously or unconsciously, the mood of the nation at the time; thus it makes and discards favourites—or they make and destroy themselves, whichever way one likes to put it—very quickly.

This is an appropriate place to mention some of the other stars and their attributes as well as lesser members of the cast in the great parliamentary drama that was played at Westminster in the fateful years 1909 to 1914. Mr. John Redmond, leader of the Irish Nationalist Party, was a dignified, handsome man with the nose of a Roman senator. He was much respected by the House as a whole and was a good speaker, though far less exuberant and eloquent than some of his principal followers. He exercised an iron discipline on them, which was not difficult as many of them were dependent for their living upon Irish Nationalist Party funds, and all were liable to ejection from that Party for the slightest deviation from its tenets and policy; the Party had learnt its lesson at the time of the fissure produced by the Parnell case.[1] It is true that there was a small "splinter" party of Irish Nationalists, led by Mr. William O'Brien, M.P., and known as the "O'Brienites". But it had little influence and only two or three M.P.s. It professed the same aims as the Irish Nationalist Party, but very frequently quarrelled publicly with the main Party, from which its members had been expelled.

Irish Nationalist M.P.s were not allowed, by the rules of their Party, to accept hospitality from, or have any social contact with, M.P.s of any other party. They were forbidden to use the House of Commons smoking-room, and none were seen there, except the "O'Brienites". Hence the Strangers' Smoking-Room on the Terrace, which they used, was more full of company than it has ever been since their departure from Westminster. Nevertheless, many of us in the other parties were on pleasant personal terms with the Nationalists in the lobbies. I cherish affectionate recollections of the many friends whom I had among them, despite frequent scenes in the Chamber itself in which we were engaged—on opposite sides.

Mr. Redmond had a younger brother, Mr. William Redmond, M.P.—a charming and talented man—who, despite his previous views which included dislike of and contempt for everything English, joined the Army in the 1914 war and was killed in action

[1] In 1889 Captain O'Shea, a member of the Irish Party, filed a petition for divorce from his wife, citing Parnell as co-respondent. The suit was not defended. As a result of this case, Parnell was deposed in the following year from his leadership of the Party. He died soon afterwards.

in France. Another brilliant and handsome young Irish National-ist M.P., Mr. Kettle, also joined the British Army on the out-break of the 1914 war and was killed in action. Skill in debate, wit and eloquence were more widespread in the Irish Nationalist Party than in any other party that has ever sat in the Commons. The most gifted of them all in this respect was Mr. Timothy Healy, M.P., later to become the first Governor-General of Southern Ireland after partition. Usually intensely bitter in his speeches, with a venomously effective invective, he was a man of great charm, culture and kindness in private life. For this reason the House, perhaps the best judge of character of any institution in the world, forgave him even his most brutally unjust observa-tions. It did not so easily forgive Mr. Dillon, another first-class speaker on the Nationalist benches, because he was a much less attractive figure. I can still visualise the bearded face, and the sinister gleam in Mr. Tim Healy's glasses as he rose to speak, giving me all the pleasure of anticipation, seldom disappointed, of hearing natural, unspoilt and unforced eloquence, spiced with the best type of spontaneous Irish wit, usually directed, with the devastating emphasis conveyed by Irish diction, at some Con-servative or Liberal member who had either preceded him in debate or had been foolish enough to interrupt him. Another formidable speaker among the Irish Nationalists was Mr. Joe Devlin—a Belfast publican. Though inferior to Mr. Healy as a speaker, he shared his advantage of personal popularity in the House despite the brutal bitterness of his speeches.

In the much smaller Ulster Party, only one man could match the best of the Irish Nationalists in effective oratory and hold over the House. This was its leader, the late Sir Edward (afterwards Lord) Carson. Some of his critics after his death (they would not have dared to do it in his life-time) have, in their writings, repre-sented him as a highly successful barrister but in public life a man of lower status than he claimed to be, who attained temporary importance as a party "boss" on the American model, by the threat of civil war if his views were ignored. These critics refer with relish to his apparent failure as a Minister in the Coalition Government of the First World War. I was on service at the time and am therefore not well qualified to judge the truth of the second charge. But the first allegation is a plain distortion of the facts. Sir Edward was one of the finest, most sincere and most effective advocates of a great cause among British parliamentarians, in or out of the House.

Put succinctly, the cause, and the policy based upon it, was this. Ulster was predominantly Protestant and in favour of the Union. Despite the smallness of the land area of Ireland, there was (and is) a deep cleavage between North and South which was (and is) racial, religious and political all in one. To give Home Rule, that is self-government, to Ireland as a whole, Sir Edward and his followers contended, would inevitably lead to civil war and the disruption of the Empire; he further contended that it would be in the highest degree amoral to force Ulster, which has a passionate allegiance to the British Crown and connection, out of both and to leave her to the mercies of a majority in the South, bitterly opposed to everything in which she believes. Thus his conclusion was, in the historic words of Lord Randolph Churchill spoken a generation earlier, "Ulster will fight and Ulster will be right". I was among many young Conservative M.P.s who were ready to support Ulster in a physical sense and took effective means to that end. The number of us was greater, and the extent to which we were committed larger, than was known at the time or has been disclosed since. For instance, I formed what would now be described as a Commando which was ready to give physical assistance to Northern Ireland and the Ulster Volunteers if the need arose.

The question whether Sir Edward and his followers and those of us who supported him in England were justified can be fairly answered as follows. It is probable that the possibility of civil war in Ireland was one of the factors which caused the Kaiser to believe that this country dare not enter a European war, and therefore made him the readier to sanction the invasion of Belgium. It is obvious that to threaten armed resistance to a possible law is a very grave step to take in any country. But it is equally true, though evidence on the matter was not as clear at the time as it is to-day, that to put Ulster under the alien rule of Dublin and the South would in any event have resulted in civil war, which would perhaps have spread to other parts of the Empire where Ulstermen and Southern Irish lived in the same country but despised and detested each other's qualities with intensity. Further, the moral principle that a small community, mainly homogeneous in race and religion, is entitled to opt for the form of governance which it wants and not be forced under the domination of a majority hostile to it is accepted both nationally and internationally to-day, at least in front of the Iron Curtain. One other factor should be mentioned. The conversion of the Liberal Government in 1910 to the full-blooded and comprehensive scheme of Home Rule demanded by Mr. Redmond and his Party was a forced one, necessitated by their dependence upon the Nationalist votes in Parliament. We were entitled to say to that Government as we did again and again in debate: "You are risking civil war and trying to drive loyal Ulster out of her direct allegiance to the British Crown, not because you believe in the Home Rule Bill, but because you are dependent for your retention of office upon Irish Nationalist votes".

Sir Edward's most effective colleague was Mr. J. H. M. Campbell, who was a good debater. The others were inferior in this respect to the Nationalists, though one of them, Captain James Craig (afterwards the first Lord Craigavon), was a man of strong and sterling character who was later the successful and deeply-respected Prime Minister of Northern Ireland. Both the Nationalist and the Ulster Party contained men who, though not first-class debaters, were "characters" very well known at the time. They included several conscious and unconscious humorists. One of the best known was the journalist Mr. T. P. O'Connor. He looked and spoke like a stage Irishman, but, in fact, was seldom in that country and represented the Scotland Division of Liverpool. He was a genial man, though his enemies said his geniality was synthetic. In the '20s he became the respected "Father of the House". He had a namesake in the Party, Mr. John O'Connor—known as "Long John". Nicknames of universal application were more widespread in the pre-1914 Parliament than they are to-day. He was a solemn man who looked like a character in Dickens's novels as portrayed by Phiz. He once administered a pompous rebuke to me which *Punch* afterwards depicted by showing me across his knee being smacked. Then there was a powerfully built ferocious-looking man (he was, in fact, most kindly in private life) named Mr. Flavin who had once been a member of the Royal Irish Constabulary. On one occasion I saw him being carried out of the House by attendants after he had refused to withdraw following his suspension. The attendants' task was not an easy one.

A very well-known Irish Nationalist and a most agreeable man was Mr. Swift McNeill. Of marked simian appearance, his nickname was "Pongo", after a celebrated performing ape of the day. At its best the House of Commons is the most impressive and dignified legislative assembly in the world, but it also has a strong, if somewhat schoolboyish, sense of humour which occasionally causes it corporately to diminish that dignity to vanishing point. Whenever Mr. McNeill got himself into a scene, which he frequently did, and started, as was his wont, to shout and wave his arms about, a low murmur and refrain would come forth from the Conservative back benches: "Order, Pongo; give him a nut; careful, Pongo; Chain! Chain! Pongo". Poor Mr. McNeill, however angry he was, always had to yield to the shouts of laughter which followed.

The most successful conscious humorist among the Irish Nationalists of the time was Mr. "Jerry" McVeagh, a small man with carroty hair and an extremely witty speaker. Among "characters" on the Ulster side was a very good and worthy man, Mr. Corbet, who was known as "Protestant" Corbet. He was a rabid teetotaller whose hatred of strong liquor and the liquor trade equalled his hatred of Home Rule. Once he was speaking when Mr. McVeagh came into the House with a tumbler containing a rich brown liquid which was clearly whisky or brandy. It is not uncommon for glasses of water to be brought into the Chamber for members who feel faint, and Chancellors of the Exchequer in their Budget speeches have a traditional right to something stronger. But the appearance of an obvious glass of spirits on the back benches is so rare an occurrence that everyone was astonished to see it in Mr. McVeagh's hands; he gave it to an elderly Conservative who was very deaf—Sir Francis Powell, known as "The Buzzer" owing to his successful promotion of a Private Member's Bill to prevent factory hooters sounding between certain hours of the night—and asked him to pass it to Mr. Corbet. Sir Francis tried to hand it to Mr. "Protestant" Corbet. With horror and indignation on his face, the latter waved it away. Sir Francis, in the very loud voice which the deaf so often use, called out, "But they said you wanted it". To this Mr. Corbet shouted passionately in a strong Belfast accent, "Take it away, take it away", and then subsided into his seat, for the laughter was so loud and long he felt unable to continue his speech.

These comic interludes, and others like them, were gleams of light in the thunderous lowering sky of bitter partisanship in the Commons from 1909 to 1914. Only once before, in the last hundred and fifty years, at the time of the Reform Bill controversy of the 1830s, and only once since, just after the General Strike of 1926, has there been such dangerous tension. This extended outside Parliament; young ladies of Liberal families were not invited to balls given at houses of Conservatives, and young ladies of Conservative families were excluded from balls given by Liberals. I was, during this period, late for a dinner given by a well-known hostess; she remarked to a Peer, a prominent member of the Conservative Party, "I shan't wait for Winterton, we'll go in to dinner". The Peer, who was rather hard of hearing, replied angrily, "If Winston is coming to this dinner, my wife and I will leave; I refuse to meet any member of this Traitor Government".

In 1911, Mr. F. E. Smith and I gave a fancy dress dance at Claridges at which the Speaker, the Prime Minister, Mr. Churchill, Mr. Balfour and other M.P.s were our guests. Two days later a letter signed "a Peer" was given prominence on the leader page of *The Times*, strongly condemning the presence of the Prime Minister and leader of the Opposition at such a gathering when the country was faced with a constitutional crisis as grave as any in its history. It was suggested at the time that "a Peer" was Lord Northcliffe, the owner of *The Times*, but this seems improbable, as he was a guest at the ball.

One of the ugliest incidents in this era of mutual party hatred in the Commons occurred just after the Marconi case, details of which I shall describe later. Sir Rufus Isaacs, the Attorney-General (afterwards the first Lord Reading), rose to answer a question; he was assailed with cries from the Conservative back benches of "Sticky fingers". Usually calm, collected and complete master of himself, he was so taken aback by this affront that he turned a deadly white and, for a moment or so, was

unable to read out his answer. Mr. Lloyd George glared at our
benches with a look of furious anger on his face which I never
saw on it before or since; Mr. Churchill, the most generous of
friends, ever ready to come to the help of a colleague, shouted
out something at the top of his voice which, perhaps fortunately,
could not be heard amid the tumult, whilst a colleague next to him
put a restraining hand upon his shoulder; Mr. Asquith sat calm
and impassive with his eyes fixed upon the ceiling. The Speaker
managed to restore order just before both sides were apparently
going to start a fist-fight.

When Mr. Speaker Clifton Brown (now Lord Ruffside)
retired at the end of the 1950 Parliament, some commentators
in the Press suggested that he had had a more difficult task than
any of his predecessors, as for six years he had presided over a
turbulent House of Commons with a Labour Government in
power. Such inversions of the truth explain why history is so
frequently falsified. The 1945 and 1950 Parliaments were like a
Sunday School in comparison with the 1906 and two 1910
Parliaments. To say that Mr. Speaker Clifton Brown's task was
more difficult than Mr. Speaker Lowther's is like saying that to
be the Captain of a pleasure steamer taking trippers for a two
hours' run in the Channel on a day of light breeze in June is
harder than to be on the bridge of a small freighter, pounded by
heavy seas, in a winter gale in mid-Atlantic. Indeed, to continue
the maritime metaphor, only the superb seamanship of Mr.
Speaker Lowther and his seconds-in-command, in the shape of
the Chairman and Deputy Chairman of Ways and Means, saved
the good ship *Commons* from sinking between 1909 and 1914.
Lord Ullswater was a thorough master of the craft of Speakership, as not all the Speakers under whom I have sat have been.
He realised when to be mild and tolerant, when to be conveniently
deaf and when to temper rebuke with humour; but he also
appreciated the value of presence and dignity and the careful use
of words, and knew how to command respect for his rulings
in the noisiest and most disorderly House.

The rough-and-tumble of debate in the troublous era which
I am describing was a valuable training-ground for young and
new members; and many in the ranks of the Opposition, who
subsequently attained office, such as the late Sir Arthur Steel-

Maitland, the late Sir William Mitchell-Thomson (afterwards Lord Selsdon), the late Mr. Walter Guinness (afterwards Lord Moyne), the late Mr. George Lloyd (afterwards Lord Lloyd), Mr. Ormsby-Gore (now Lord Harlech), Lord Wolmer (now Lord Selborne), Mr. Samuel Hoare (now Lord Templewood), Mr. Wood (now Lord Halifax) and Mr. Amery, took advantage of it. In the ranks of the Opposition there were also two brilliant and charming young men in the persons of the late Sir Mark Sykes and the late Mr. Auberon Herbert. Both had extensive knowledge of, and sympathy with, the Near East, and both were "characters" in the best sense of the term. Mr. Herbert— "Aubrey" to his friends—in particular had certain delightful and typically British eccentricities. During the Gallipoli Campaign he is said to have risked a court martial by strolling across to the Turkish lines during a lull in the fighting and engaging in a friendly conversation, unconcerned with the military situation, in fluent Turkish with the enemy! Both men died prematurely soon after the armistice of 1918. Others, on the contrary, who afterwards occupied great positions, such as Mr. Max Aitken (now Lord Beaverbrook) and Mr. Baldwin, took little part in debate; indeed, though I had sat for years with him in the House, I did not know the latter by sight until after the 1914 war. No future Prime Minister has ever had, in his early parliamentary life, such an astonishing record of complete unobtrusiveness as the late Lord Baldwin. But his great hold over the House of Commons in the '20s and early '30s, and his supreme success in interpreting its moods were perhaps the result of patient and silent watching and waiting which he practised in the first decade of his membership.

On the Liberal side too, though it is harder to make a reputation when your party is in power than when it is in opposition, many young members who entered the House during or after the 1906 election came steadily to the front. Among them, in addition to those of whose work I have already written, were two Ministers—Mr. (now Lord) Samuel and the late Mr. Montagu. Among young Liberal back-benchers, who had the ear of the House, were three men of great promise: Mr. Gladstone (a nephew of the "Grand Old Man"), Mr. Neil Primrose (second son of the later Lord Rosebery) and Mr. Agar-Robartes.

They were all killed in action in the 1914 war, as were two of their friends and contemporaries on the other side of the House, Lord Helmsley and Mr. Charles Mills. Lord Helmsley and Mr. Mills sat with Lord Castlereagh (the late Lord Londonderry) at the end of the first bench below the gangway. They were affectionately known from their Christian names as "The three Charlies". They were great and dear friends of mine, and often in my mind's eye in the years after the First World War I could, when the House was empty, seem to see them sitting there and, two benches behind, the grim-visaged Mr. John Redmond, with arms folded, keeping an eye on his turbulent followers. Once, when they all three entered the House together in dress clothes during a late sitting, they were greeted by the late Mr. Will Thorne, M.P., with the sally, "Here comes the night-shift".

Members of the Labour Party who afterwards came to high office, such as Mr. Ramsay MacDonald, Mr. Snowden and Mr. Lansbury, made little impact upon the House in those days. The latter was chiefly renowned for the frequency of the scenes in which he was the principal figure. It was hard to believe at the time that the passionate fury into which he worked himself sometimes over the most trivial matters was genuine, but those who knew him well assert that he was a man of deep conviction. His position in the Labour Party was killed many years later by the late Mr. Ernest Bevin in one of the most devastating attacks ever made upon a colleague at a party meeting.[1] By 1910 Mr. Keir Hardie had lost the glamour of the novelty caused by his entrance several years before to Parliament in workmen's clothes, and he failed to hold the House when he spoke.

In every House of Commons there are members who enter the House with a reputation already made in another sphere outside. The House is inclined to be at first slightly suspicious— not to say jealous—of them, especially if they are barristers or writers. It is best for them not to give the impression that their success elsewhere is, by itself, a passport to the affection and respect of the Commons, but that, on the contrary, they are "new boys", with everything to learn, like all the other "new boys". Perhaps because of failure to observe this rule, two famous novelists who were elected to the 1906 Parliament—the late Mr. A. E. W.

[1] See Chapter X, p. 136.

Mason and Mr. Hilaire Belloc—scored no great parliamentary success. Mr. Belloc was the better speaker of the two, as he ought to have been since he was a prominent and brilliant participant in Union debates in his Oxford days. He made one or two good speeches and then committed a fatal error. The late Mr. Harry Lawson, M.P. (afterwards Lord Burnham), a popular and much respected man, had just concluded a mild and unprovocative speech from our benches when Mr. Belloc rose and, in his rather high-pitched voice, began, "In extended observation of the Anglo-Judaic plutocracy I . . .". He got no further. This obvious reference to Mr. Lawson was received by angry cries from the Conservative benches of "Order, withdraw, cad!!", whilst his Liberal colleagues sat in that silent disapproval which is always a sure sign that a member has made a grievous mistake. Neither in the rest of that speech nor in others which he subsequently made did he ever recover from this mistake. The House of Commons did not approve of him for all his talents and many fine qualities which I, as a friend of his, appreciate. Nor, to judge from subsequent reference to politicians in his writings, did he approve of the House of Commons.

CHAPTER V

AFTER the election of January, 1910, the new House met on February 15—the re-election of the Speaker being very appropriately moved by the "Father of the House", Mr. Burt, a Labour M.P. of universal popularity who had begun life as a pit-boy.

Among the new Liberal members was Mr. Trebitsch Lincoln, a Hungarian by birth. He was a man with an aggressive and unpleasant personality. In the course of an argument with him in the House I told him to "Go back to Hungary". He took my advice shortly before the 1914 war and spent the war years in that country and Germany. It was then discovered that he had been a spy for both countries in Britain. Perhaps fortunately for the Liberal Party, he was never brought to trial for high treason; he ended his life as a Buddhist monk in Asia. Another new and aggressive Liberal member was Mr. Handel Booth. In a clash with him I told him to "Go back to your company promoting". He subsequently insisted on making a personal explanation in the House—a course open to any member who considers that something has been said reflecting upon his honour. After remarking that he had not been born with a silver spoon in his mouth as I had been, he contended that his business pursuits were perfectly honourable. They may have been at the time, but after war broke out he was convicted of a serious offence in connection with his business activities. His trial is described in the late Sir Patrick Hastings' fascinating book of reminiscences. At the time there was also on the Liberal back benches a Mr. Joseph King, impolitely known in the lobbies, owing to his appearance, as "The Mad Hatter". Of unimpeachable reputation in private life and a man of some charm, he was notorious for his violent attacks on the British Empire and British policy abroad; he was an extreme exponent of what used to be called the "Exeter Hall" doctrine which meant that, in any international dispute, one was "the friend of every country but one's own". Another Liberal M.P. with the same views on external affairs as Mr. King was Mr.

Byles, one of the members for Bradford. The Conservative Press nicknamed him "Bilious Byles of Bradford".

All parties, especially when in power, suffer damage from the presence on their back benches of a few eccentric, dissident or disreputable M.P.s. The Liberal Party was especially unfortunate from 1906 to 1914 in the proportionate number of such men which it contained. The memory of their records and speeches continued after the 1914 war and was a contributory factor, even if a minor one, in the electoral decline of the Liberal Party. It is worth remembering also that the "Anti-Imperialism" directed against Britain's position in Asian and African territories, which has done this nation and the world such untold harm in recent years, had powerful encouragement from a considerable and influential section of the back-benchers of the Liberal Party when it was in strength and power. It is only fair to the Socialists to state this fact, for they have merely followed the evil path trodden by Liberals in the past.

The situation confronting the Government, the Opposition and the country as a result of the first 1910 election was an extraordinary and unprecedented one. The Budget had not been passed, and therefore new taxes or increase in existing taxes could not be legally collected. The Government were dependent upon the Irish Nationalist vote for their existence. Mr. Redmond and his followers not only disliked many provisions of the Budget which he had described as bad and oppressive, but tried to insist, as a condition of Irish Nationalist support, that a Bill should be introduced to abolish the Lords' veto in order to pass an Irish Home Rule Bill. He wanted a far more extensive measure of Irish self-government in this Bill than Mr. Asquith and the Cabinet were willing to concede. The Conservative Opposition, on the other hand, were not anxious to force another crisis since Mr. Balfour and his Shadow Cabinet believed—and rightly, as the second election of 1910 showed—that a further appeal to the country would not give us a majority and, indeed, show little change.

There was a good deal of unreality and "make-believe" in consequence during the debate on the Address, since everyone knew that there were informal discussions going on between the Government and the Irish Nationalists to try to reach a compromise. These negotiations having been concluded, the Government took the following action. It adopted a novel and special procedure to collect revenue until the previous year's Budget was passed, as it was, with slight amendments, in both Houses by April. In March, amid scenes of violence and fury, the Government got through the House of Commons a number of resolutions on which to found their Veto Bill—in other words, legislative enactment to limit the constitutional powers of the Lords in delaying or destroying legislation passed by the Commons. So angry were the passions roused by these resolutions, and so grave the issue between the two Houses, that more than one Ambassador or Minister in London informed his Government, and continued to do so until the outbreak of the 1914 war, that Britain could not avoid a revolution. Foreign diplomats here have an unfortunate record of inaccurate prophecy in this regard. The French Ambassador at the time of the Gordon Riots said that nothing could save England from civil war. He was quite wrong, and he would have been of more service to his country if he had warned his own Government of the dangers they themselves were running; for thirteen years later Louis XVI was executed.

During this period of parliamentary history—the late winter and spring of 1910—was devised a phrase, made famous and familiar to all by constant repetition, which eventually did its originator great harm. The doubts and confusion regarding the Government's ultimate intention in regard to the Lords and Home Rule naturally prompted a number of parliamentary questions from the Opposition. The Prime Minister, Mr. Asquith, very properly anxious to avoid any disclosure of the course of the negotiations to which I have already referred, answered a supplementary on one of them with the remark, "The Honourable Member should wait and see". Pleased with the cheers and laughter with which his own supporters received his answer, he repeated it on many other occasions. In the circumstances he was justified in the repetitive use of a semi-humorous formula; but, when he was under fire for his alleged lack of decision as a wartime Prime Minister from 1914 to 1916, it was remembered against him. People were wont to say, "Of course the Government has done nothing; what can you expect with 'Old Wait and See' at the head of it".

In May, 1910, King Edward died, to the great grief of his subjects. He was, very rightly, as much beloved and respected during his reign as he had been criticised and condemned by some for his supposed frivolity in youth and middle-age. In the course of my forty-seven years in the Commons, I heard many fine tributes paid to dead monarchs and other famous men, notably by Mr. Churchill in recent years. I never heard a better one than Mr. Asquith's to King Edward VII after his death. Asquith was completely fitted to represent the House of Commons and its best spirit on such an occasion. A handsome and dignified man, with a very fine head and face, he had a voice and enunciation which brought out the highest qualities of the English language. He had also an unforced and natural eloquence that needed no support of a written brief. He summed up King Edward's achievement on this occasion in a sentence, "He was an enfranchised citizen of the world".

Following King Edward's death, there was what the late Mr. J. L. Garvin described at the time in the *Observer* as "The truce of death". A conference on the constitutional issue was formed on the initiative of King George V. The Prime Minister, Mr. Lloyd George, Mr. Birrell and Lord Crewe represented the Government, and Mr. Arthur Balfour, Mr. Austen Chamberlain, Lord Lansdowne and Lord Cawdor were the Opposition members. This conference met throughout the summer. Parliament meanwhile more or less marked time. No conclusion was announced at the time of the August recess. Later in the autumn the country was informed that the conference had failed to reach agreement. It is worth remembering that Mr. Lloyd George, as Mr. Jones records in his biography,[1] favoured a Coalition to avoid a head-on crash which could destroy parliamentary government. There were other men of talent and position on both sides of the House who supported the same view. Though I did not think so at the time, I now consider they were right. Mr. Lloyd George, that astonishing mixture of utter irresponsibility combined with courage, patriotism and statesmanship of the highest order, here most emphatically displayed the best side of his character.

Almost immediately after the end of the conference a dissolu-

[1] *Lloyd George*, Thomas Jones, C.H., p. 39.

tion was announced. I was returned unopposed; so I travelled about the country speaking in various constituencies. In the course of this tour an incident occurred which is worth recounting as it is illustrative of the political temperature of the time. I was sent to a huge mass meeting in Birkenhead, in Mr. F. E. Smith's constituency, to address the audience for ten minutes until he arrived. During the chairman's opening speech a note was handed to him saying that the great man was detained at another mass meeting in Liverpool and would not arrive for half an hour. Instead of concealing this unfortunate news, the chairman conveyed it to the meeting with the comment that he was terribly sorry and upset. He then, amid loud murmurs of disappointment and frustration, immediately called on me to speak. I began with the words, "From all sedition, privy conspiracy and rebellion Good Lord deliver us". A candid critic might have observed that this opening was both lacking in reverence and sense of appropriateness, since I was encouraging Ulster's resistance to Home Rule by violent action if necessary. But the meeting, wholly Unionist in composition with a large proportion of local Orangemen, was delighted with this obvious reference to the Irish Nationalist Party. There were roars of approval and shouts of "Good boy; that's the stuff to give them" and, for the next half hour, I ranted happily and held my audience satisfactorily until Mr. Smith arrived. His characteristic comment afterwards as we enjoyed a champagne supper was, "You're quite a good speaker; I never realised it before!!"

The second election of 1910 produced little difference in the balance of parties; but it weakened Mr. Balfour's position as Conservative Leader. His prestige in the Party and the country had, indeed, improved considerably since the 1906 debacle; the internecine struggle among Conservatives over tariff policy had practically ended, since "Chamberlainites" and "Balfourites" were in agreement as to what should be done if we were returned to power; and Mr. Balfour, as I have already stated, was an assiduous and hard-working Leader of the Opposition in the Commons. But it is a serious thing for the head of any party to fail at three successive elections to lead his followers to victory. After the second election of 1910, Conservatives said, at least in private, "We shall never win under A. J. B."

Before the new Parliament met, an event occurred that had some mild repercussions afterwards in the Commons. A gang of foreign desperadoes and criminals for whom warrants had been issued barricaded themselves in a house in Sidney Street in East London. They fired on the police, with the result that a company of Guards was ordered to attack their stronghold. The criminals returned the fire of the Guardsmen. So, to avoid loss of life, it was decided to summon a battery of artillery from St. John's Wood; I saw it, the streets having been cleared for its progress, galloping past the Mansion House—a most impressive sight. Fortunately, before it reached Sidney Street, the gang had set fire to the house in which they were, and were subsequently found dead in it. Mr. Churchill, the Home Secretary, clad in a fur coat and top hat—the correct dress in winter for a Cabinet Minister at the time—early arrived upon the scene and took charge of the operations at considerable risk of being killed by the gang's bullets. In the Press and Parliament he was critically questioned afterwards for his part in the proceedings. Why was it necessary for him to be there in person? What was his object? Why had he departed from constitutional practice by conducting an unprecedented semi-military operation against a gang of criminals instead of leaving the matter in the hands of his official subordinates, the police authorities? The Home Secretary was cheerful, affable, good-humoured and wholly unrepentant in his replies; we got no change out of him. For Mr. Churchill always was, always is and always will be Mr. Churchill!!

One of his most engaging gifts as a great parliamentarian has always been his ability to get out of an awkward situation and turn aside the wrath of his opponents with a phrase which makes everyone laugh by its audacity or brilliant irrelevance. I raised in the Commons, soon after the Sidney Street battle, the question of the release, on Mr. Churchill's instructions as Home Secretary, of certain young prisoners serving a sentence. He replied that they had been originally sentenced for offences for which "the Noble Lord in his Oxford days would only have been repri-manded". He then gave a description of these offences and, in the course of his narrative, mentioned that one had been sentenced for using obscene language. Asked by me if he suggested that this was the kind of offence I had committed at Oxford, he beamed upon me with that broad smile, so happily reminiscent of a rather naughty schoolboy, that is known to-day to all the world, and said, "Mr. Speaker, we have travelled far from the Noble Lord's Oxford days with all their pomp and pageantry". The House roared with laughter, and on the spur of the moment I could think of no reply.

Mr. Churchill was a good Home Secretary. He humanised and improved the penal system by legislation which he introduced and by administrative action. He showed both courage and restraint in a serious situation with which he was confronted by a coal strike which produced disorder in South Wales in 1910. Instead of despatching troops, he sent a force of Metropolitan Police. His action was criticised at the time as being unconstitutional because the Metropolitan Police should, in the opinion of some, be confined to the Metropolitan area, and it is said that in Tonypandy even to-day Mr. Churchill's action is remembered with indignation. But in all probability it saved bloodshed. This and other strikes in 1911, which I shall describe later, were yet another manifestation of the poison in the nation's blood causing eruptions of a kind which were as unusual as they were alarming on the normally placid face of British public life.

One of them arose out of the movement for women's suffrage, or, in plain English, the demand for votes for women. Few contemporary institutions—except the patient, long-suffering British police—or individuals deserve any credit for their part in the movement for or against extending the suffrage to women in the decade before the First World War. It should have been obvious by that time, though most of us in public life, myself included, were blind to the fact, that the general advance in education and status of women entitled them to a vote—at first on a limited suffrage and afterwards on terms of full equality with men. Instead of granting it, successive Governments and Parliaments hummed and hawed and havered over the matter and did nothing; when the militant suffrage movement came into being it was right not to yield to unconstitutional pressure by giving votes to women, but it should have been done earlier. On the other hand, even the moderate and constitutional advocates, male and female, of votes for women so exaggerated their case as to make it ridiculous; they claimed that all the trouble of the world arose from man-made laws, and that the grant of votes to women in every country would usher in an era of peace and prosperity such as the world had never seen; few prophecies, even by politicians, have been so completely falsified by events. The militant suffragettes were a mild but sufficiently dangerous British variant of the genus terrorist which has proliferated so greatly in recent years; they believed that by violence they could attain their object; for this reason, they injured or attempted to set fire to public property, assaulted Ministers and broke the windows of their houses. Undoubtedly, but for efficient police protection, some of them would have murdered one or two Ministers who had incurred their special enmity; they attempted to commit suicide by refusing to eat when in prison, and one did kill herself by trying to pull down a horse running in the Derby; they tried constantly to interrupt the proceedings of Parliament. The Government took counter-measures, some of them distasteful to them and to the public, such as forcible feeding of suffragettes in prison and the Cat and Mouse Act which enabled the authorities to release them from prison when weak from refusal to eat, and to re-arrest them when they were well again. As a precautionary measure, women, except those employed there and relatives of members, were forbidden to enter the Palace of Westminster and, after the worst of the raids, all access to any street, except for residents in it, and all public transport within a radius of a mile of the House of Commons was stopped, with resultant grave inconvenience. All police reserves, both foot and mounted, were summoned to carry out this operation, to the joy and advantage of London's underworld. Apologists for these violent agitators claim that votes for women would never have been conceded but for their action. There is no evidence to support this contention; the chances of women obtaining votes in 1914, some five years after the militant movement started, were less than before it commenced, for the public deeply detested the violence. The ultimate grant of the franchise after the war was mainly due to grateful appreciation of the gallant part taken by women in that war. Mrs. Pankhurst, the leader of the movement, has been sanctified by her remnant of followers still alive into sainthood, a statue has been erected to her in a public place and she has been compared to Joan of Arc. Anyone who saw, as

I did, the screaming, demented followers whom she had trained
attempting to storm the Palace of Westminster and striking and
kicking policemen who were carrying out their duty of protecting it, with a long-suffering patience and gentleness which no
other police force in the world would have shown, would agree
that this comparison is scarcely fair to Joan of Arc.

When the new Parliament met in February, 1911,[1] it was
obvious that the controversy over the Lords' veto and the
position of the Second Chamber had reached a climax of hatred
and fury between the two sides. The flame had been fanned into
a roaring furnace by the knowledge that Mr. Asquith, the Prime
Minister, before going to the country, had obtained the King's
consent to create 250 new peers—sufficient in his opinion to secure a Liberal majority in the Lords—if all other methods failed
to secure the passage of the Bill curtailing the power of the Lords.
Whilst few questioned the King's constitutional duty to grant
this request, there was great indignation, by no means confined
to purely Conservative circles, that such a request, placing him in
a cruel dilemma, should have been made to a new and young
King. Many suggestions were made that the Prime Minister
should be impeached. Lord Hugh Cecil said in Parliament that
he was a traitor.

The period between the assembly of the new House of
Commons and the passage of the Parliament Bill on August 11
of that year, was one of the most extraordinary in the political
history of Britain. The Government duly produced their Bill.
Meanwhile, the Lords made an attempt, which was, and in the
circumstances was bound to be, abortive, to amend their constitution. The Bill was passed, amended by the Lords, returned to
the Commons, and sent back to the Lords in its original form.
There were, of course, innumerable scenes and periods of disorder
in the Commons over the Bill and on a vote of censure condemning the Government's conduct. In the debate on the Lords
amendments on July 5, Mr. Asquith was shouted down and the
House had to be adjourned "without the question being put".
Before this happened, Mr. Lloyd George was accused of using in
a platform speech an unmentionable phrase, which no newspaper
could print, about his opponents.

[1] It had been summoned for formal business only on January 31st.

The "great surrender", as it was called when the Lords finally accepted the Bill, is described as follows in my book *Pre-War*, p. 216:

A few days later occurred the great surrender. To the astonishment of most people, and to the great indignation of many members of the Unionist Party (including some of the youngest and most energetic), in both Houses, Lord Lansdowne, Lord Curzon and other Unionist leaders in the Lords, gave way when the Bill returned to their House. Lord Halsbury and a number of peers, henceforth to be known as the "Diehards", voted to retain the amendments, so that the Unionist Party was split. The amendments were, of course, lost.

I have not the space to enlarge upon the results of the action taken by the Unionist leaders in both Houses. The immediate effect was to arouse such overwhelming indignation against Arthur Balfour in influential and important sections of the Party that it brought to a head the dissatisfaction against his leadership which had existed since 1906, and, indeed, before it. The result was to be seen in his resignation in the autumn, decently camouflaged (as in all such cases) on the grounds of ill-health and of age. The ultimate effect was to destroy two-chamber Government in this country, because the Lords ceased to have any control over Finance—the one matter of supreme importance in every modern state. It is no answer to say that before the Parliament Act the power of the Lords over Finance was limited—the point is that it was there.

Another effect was undoubtedly greatly to shake the self-confidence of the Upper House in itself. The Lords were like an army whose leader has told it that it must hold its ground at all costs, even to the point of annihilation, and then suddenly says, "I have changed my mind; we must retreat, whatever the cost". Students of military history know that such an army takes months, and even years, to recover its morale. The Peers, though they have done useful work since 1911, have never recovered their morale.

This was written over twenty years ago, but I believe that it accurately represents the situation, and I would to-day only make one emendation. Unquestionably the prestige of the House of Lords has improved in the last ten years by reason of the high level of its debates: and this has been due to the quality of those taking part in them—mainly, though not entirely, new creations for eminent public service—and to the experience gained and position held by peers who were formerly members of the House of Commons. But a fundamental weakness remains. The composition of that House and its powers alike are utterly inadequate for an effective Second Chamber.[1] Yet no country needs a Second Chamber more than Britain. It is not sufficient for the House of Lords to be a high-level debating chamber, though the Press and public opinion alike are becoming increasingly interested in, and affected by, its debates. Every effort that has been made publicly and behind the scenes between and within parties to find an acceptable non-party scheme for making the legal and constitutional power of the Lords correspond with the needs of a Second Chamber for a modern democratic state has failed. I have, as it happens, taken a small part in some of these explorations in the last forty years, and once or twice they seemed near success. They should be continued; so should attempts to find a way to avoid the unanswerable question, "Why should the Lords have greater powers when a man, without any merit of any kind, can sit and vote there because he has a hereditary right to do so?". One obvious method would be a process of selection, by election among themselves, of hereditary peers who alone would enjoy the full privilege of membership of the Lords.

There is little doubt that the astonishing *volte-face* shown by the leaders of the Conservatives in the Lords over the Parliament Bill was mainly due to a wish to avoid the embarrassment that would be caused to the Crown by the creation of 250 peers. But the indignation which such a creation would have caused would have been directed against not the King but the Government. For months previously the plan and the threat had been subjected to merciless ridicule by Mr. F. E. Smith and other speakers in the Commons, in cartoons in the Press and on the music-hall stage; it was always directed against Mr. Asquith and his colleagues, never against the King. But it was too late to keep the Throne out of the controversy by August, 1911; Mr. Asquith had chained the one to the other by his advice to the King before the second election of 1910. Mr. F. E. Smith, whose cool, calm views in counsel on any crisis were invaluable (as was proved again and again—for instance in the General Strike

[1] See also Chapter XXIV, p. 342.

of 1926), begged his colleagues on the front Opposition bench, to which he had recently been promoted, to urge Lord Lansdowne and the Unionist peers in the Lords not to reject the Budget, or, if they did so, not to run away from the consequences of their own action by passing the Parliament Bill. He thought this to be the height of political pusillanimity.

1911 was one of the hottest summers[1] on record in all Western Europe—one of the few when even men and women accustomed to the tropics felt oppressed and irritable because of the prolonged heat-wave. Perhaps these circumstances made people jumpy at home and abroad. At any rate, in August an event occurred which shook Europe and had important other immediate and ultimate results. The German Government ordered a gunboat to go to a small port in Morocco called Agadir, ostensibly to protect Germany's economic interests, though there was no evidence that they were in jeopardy. After considerable negotiations, during which peace hung by a thread, Germany withdrew her gunboat as a result of joint British and French protests, delivered amid a chorus of abuse from the German Press. One immediate result was that an all-England railway strike, over various grievances of the National Union of Railwaymen and other unions, was averted. The leaders of the unions, being informed privately but directly by the Government that war was possible, called it off. Another result was that Mr. Lloyd George, the arch-pacifist of the Boer War, became an ardent advocate of the rights of Britain and France against the pretensions of Germany, even at the cost of a war. He announced his conversion in a famous speech at the Mansion House in the autumn.

Many historians and students of the period believe that, justi-fied as was joint British and French action over the Agadir incident, it made the First World War inevitable, since the injury to German prestige abroad was so great that such moder-ates as there were around the Kaiser and in his Government were unable to stem the indignant demand of the nation for revenge in some form some day. If this view be correct, it surely shows the Munich settlement (with which I deal in a later chapter) in a different light from that in which it was usually regarded. Oppon-ents of Mr. Neville Chamberlain, and of all of us who were

[1] In August the temperature reached 100 degrees in the shade at Greenwich.

associated with him, continue to assert with vigour and venom that appeasement made war inevitable, on the ground that if Hitler had been threatened with war he would have desisted from his action, and real peace would have ensued despite the blow to his own and his country's pride and prestige.[1] The Kaiser and his government, with all Germany behind them, took exactly the opposite view as a result of the check which German plans received at Agadir. It made them more eager than ever for war. Personally, in this summer of 1911, I was astonished that two men who were as courteous and kindly in private life—at least when I met them—as the Kaiser and his eldest son could condone and indeed instigate the ferocious nonsense printed about England in German newspapers after Agadir. Earlier in the year they had both paid what seemed to be a highly successful visit of goodwill to Britain as the guests of the King.

Mr. Balfour resigned in November, 1911, and was succeeded by Mr. Bonar Law. At the time, many of us would have preferred Mr. (afterwards Sir) Austen Chamberlain, who had enhanced the fame and added to the name of Chamberlain in the country; for while never enjoying the status of his famous father, Mr. Joseph Chamberlain, he had been a successful Chancellor of the Exchequer at a very early age, was a man of fine intellect, impeccable character, and great charm in private life, with plenty of friends. Most important of all, he was a good and popular speaker in and out of Parliament. He would undoubtedly have been elected leader but for the fact that the late Sir William Bull, M.P., put forward the name of the late Mr. Walter Long (afterwards Lord Long) and got some—though minority— support among Conservative peers and M.P.s. Mr. Long was the best type of English country squire, had been a success in minor Cabinet offices, and was well liked in Parliament and outside. But in attainments, intellect and position in the country he was manifestly inferior to Mr. Austen Chamberlain. To avoid a contest, both men withdrew their candidature, though some of us, who resented Sir William Bull's action and were certain that Mr. Chamberlain would be elected, wanted him to refuse to withdraw. But, being a most scrupulously fair and honourable man, he resisted our entreaties. Mr. Bonar Law was elected unani-

[1] See Chapter XVII, p. 242.

mously. It seemed at first a leap in the dark to choose Mr. Bonar Law as Conservative leader. It is true, as I have written in an earlier chapter, that he was a very efficient Junior Minister in the 1900 Government; he was also a highly successful debater in opposition, carrying an amazing store of indisputable figures and facts in his mind; he made little use of notes and had a neatly balanced armoury of hard-hitting phrases, coupled with acid politeness, to direct against his opponents. But he was not at the time, nor did he ever become, a great orator able to hold enthralled a full House in the Commons or a great meeting outside. He was very shy and aloof, with a few great friends but no wide circle of acquaintances. This aloofness increased after his wife's death, which had occurred a few years prior to the time of which I am writing; he told a friend of mine occupying a high position in our party just after his wife's funeral that the shock had been so great that he doubted his ability to remain in public life, and it took my friend some time to restore his confidence in his power to do so. He had few pursuits and interests outside public life and both disliked and avoided any social function unconnected with politics. He had little knowledge of country life. In this connection, a front-bench colleague of his told me the following story just after his selection as leader. "I am concerned", said the colleague, "at dear Bonar's apparent ignorance of country life now that he is leader of the country gentleman's party. Last week when he stayed with me at . . . I took him out for a walk. When we saw a pheasant, he said in his strong Scottish accent, 'What might that bird be?'. I hope the Liberals don't get to hear of this question of his; it would deprive us of our best joke against Lloyd George".[1] But Mr. Bonar Law soon proved his worth as leader, and also the truth of Mr. Lloyd George's alleged statement, "The fools have chosen the right man by accident". He was a man of courage and complete integrity of character, with a very shrewd judgment. He was, too, as I realised when I got to know him well as a Junior Minister in his Government

[1] Mr. Lloyd George made an astonishing statement on one occasion in attacking landlords to the effect that their pheasants destroyed their tenants' mangel-wurzels. It became a nation-wide joke, and to the day of his death, one celebrated cartoonist always showed him accompanied by a pheasant and a mangel-wurzel.

just before his death, a most lovable man in whom one could place complete trust. Like so many other statesmen who once stood in the centre of the political stage, he is almost forgotten to-day by the nation which he served so faithfully, but not by his friends.

In addition to the Parliament Bill, the big measure of the 1911 session was Mr. Lloyd George's National Insurance Bill. It was fiercely opposed by the Northcliffe Press and in parts of it by the Conservative Party. I think that the opposition among some sections of the Conservative Party in both Houses would have been greater but for the fact that a private committee of the Party called the Social Reform Committee, consisting mostly of young M.P.s, like myself, was in existence, under Mr. F. E. Smith's chairmanship, to give reasonable support to measures of social reform promoted by the Government and also to counter the efforts of the reactionary and old-fashioned elements in the Party who wanted to fight such measures. The Bill was divided into two parts. Part One provided a contributory system of health insurance based upon payments by the State, employers and employed for all earning less than £160 a year; Part Two provided unemployment insurance for two and a quarter million persons. To bring such a huge and novel scheme into operation was a tremendous task which few Ministers would have attempted. But Mr. Lloyd George was in the full enjoyment of his gifts of energy and vitality, which were unimpaired by the fight over his Budget. The organisation necessary for the implementation of the Bill when it became an Act of Parliament began without an office, staff, address or telephone number; but, with the aid of the late Mr. Masterman, M.P. as his Parliamentary Secretary, and the late Sir Robert Morant as his Civil Servant principal assistant, plus a picked team of other Civil Servants, it was soon functioning.

There were a number of other Acts reforming and improving the social structure of the country brought forward by the 1906 Liberal Government and passed through Parliament before this, such as those dealing with the provision of meals in schools, the medical inspection of school-children, non-contributory old age pensions and Labour Exchanges. It is well that these Acts and also earlier ones promoted and passed through Parliament by the Conservative Party, such as the Workmen's Compensation Act, should be remembered to-day, since the Labour Party has made the audacious and utterly baseless claim that they devised and created the Welfare State. Its foundations were laid long ago by Conservative and Liberal Governments. Mr. Lloyd George's great Insurance Act was the first floor of it; ever since, Governments of different complexions have been increasing its size.

In the minds of all reasonable and instructed men and women, two great monuments to Mr. Lloyd George's humanity, sagacity and statesmanship endure—his National Insurance Act and his War Premiership from 1916 to 1918. They dwarf and should cause to be forgotten and forgiven the uglier memories which he left behind him—his ignorance of, and unreliability in, external affairs after the 1914 war and his disregard of accepted principles in certain personal matters such as the Robinson Peerage, to which I refer in a later chapter.[1] For after all, few men in the front rank of politics have been given a heavier sentence by the electors for their defects of character than Mr. Lloyd George. After he ceased to be Prime Minister in 1922, whilst still at the height of his mental and physical powers, they never allowed him back in Downing Street.

[1] See Chapter IX, p. 114.

CHAPTER VI

THE 1912 session opened quietly in the House, but outside there were few signs of peace or stability, with both the international situation and the Irish crisis growing in intensity. In addition, there was a coal strike affecting every colliery in Britain, which was only settled after it had caused great dislocation of trade and unemployment in other industries (with all the hardship that unemployment meant in those days). It was noteworthy for being the first strike in which the Government directly intervened by bringing the two sides into conference and by the passage of the Coal Mines (Minimum Wage) Act.

Mr. Churchill was, as usual, in the news in the spring of 1912. During the recess he had addressed a meeting in Belfast on the Home Rule issue. Of all the prominent Liberal statesmen none was more detested at the time by Ulster Unionists than he, and threats of physical action against him were uttered before the meeting; consequently there were not only police in numbers at the meeting, but troops to help maintain the peace outside. This procedure was the subject of acid comments and questions in the House, What, we asked, was the cost to the rates and taxes of these elaborate precautions? Did Ministers feel that they and their cause were so unpopular that in future they would only address public meetings hedged around by bayonets? Nevertheless, in his new post of First Lord of the Admiralty, Mr. Churchill received the enthusiastic support of the Opposition for his speech on the introduction of the Navy Estimates. He used a memorable phrase which rang round the world: "We must always be ready to meet at our average moment anything that any possible enemy might hurl against us at his selected moment". Here spoke the real Churchill, showing, as he was to do again and again in the next forty years, his astonishingly versatile gifts of statesmanship; he saw the inner essence of the problem of naval defence, and he put it in a vivid statement that was at the same time simple and clear enough for the least instructed person to understand. However, since this book is intended to be an impartial chronicle,

I have put the controversial Belfast meeting in juxtaposition to this speech since the former illustrated the love of drama—sometimes both irrelevant and unnecessary, as shown by his interposition in the Sidney Street battle and his visit to Antwerp in the early stages of the 1914 war—which is a more disputable feature of Mr. Churchill's character. There is no doubt that he went to Belfast to establish the right of free speech and, being a man of great physical as well as moral courage, he would willingly have faced the mob without a guard. Nevertheless, it was obvious that the precautions, including the use of troops, which the Irish Office very properly took to protect him, could but exacerbate an already critical situation, as in fact it did. "You call out the troops to overawe us", argued the majority of Ulstermen; "very well then, we'll increase our efforts to arm ourselves to prevent our being delivered into the hands of our Southern enemies." In fact, Mr. Churchill, a decade later, had to admit in the Irish Treaty, what he and his colleagues should have realised at the time—that Ulster must be left out of any system of self-government that gave the Southern majority effective rule over that province.

The comparative calm on the Commons front was broken by the introduction of the Welsh Church Disestablishment Bill in April. This produced angry opposition from the Church of England in general and Welsh Churchmen in particular. It was fiercely fought through all its stages by the Conservative Party, and in particular by two brothers, Lord Robert and Lord Hugh Cecil. *Punch's* "Essence of Parliament", a very fair and full parliamentary record, none the less so for being tinged with the charming humour of *Punch's* Commons' correspondent of the time—the late Sir Henry Lucy—truly stated that both of them were nearly "named" by the Speaker on the second reading. To-day these two brothers sit in the House of Lords as Lord Cecil of Chelwood and Lord Quickswood. Lord Cecil, the elder of the two, has a name still familiar to the middle-aged as one of the principal protagonists of the League of Nations. I recount in a later chapter some of the effects of his advocacy. Lord Quickswood's name is now hardly known to the general public, though in academic circles he is remembered as Provost of Eton in the '30s. In the period with which this chapter deals they were two of the best-known figures in political life. No two brothers who have sat simultaneously in the Commons—not even Sir Austen and Mr. Neville Chamberlain in the '20s and '30s—have had a greater hold over that assembly. Both are men of the highest intellectual distinction and personal integrity. Lord Robert, buttressed by his training as a successful lawyer, was the more skilful debater: but Lord Hugh, at his best, could be compared as an orator with giants of the past such as Disraeli, Gladstone, F. E. Smith, Asquith and Lloyd George, or with Mr. Churchill and Mr. Bevan of to-day. Like most men in that class, he could say the most bitter things about an opponent without forfeiting his private friendship with him. He has always been a friend of Mr. Churchill's and was best man at his wedding; but that did not prevent his referring on one occasion, when Mr. Churchill unexpectedly led the House in Mr. Asquith's absence, to the latter's "vicarious insolence", or from describing him as "a cheap actor, playing to a cheap gallery". Lord Hugh deliberately eschewed office, which would have undoubtedly been offered to a man of his gifts in the 1900 Parliament, and showed his sincere opposition to the Government's fiscal policy. He would have, also unquestionably, been given office during the 1914 war, but instead, though no longer in his first youth and of slender physique and sedentary habits, he gallantly joined the Air Force.

Both brothers were in their element during the debate on the Welsh Church Disestablishment Bill, for both are devout Churchmen. Lord Robert, tall, fairly broad, with a permanent stoop caused by an injury when young, gave one the impression, when he was denouncing the Bill, of a benevolent hawk, if there be such a bird, anxious to swoop upon the Liberal Party to remove it from its evil environment of Radicalism and Nonconformity and secure its body and its soul for Church and State. Lord Hugh, on the other hand, tall, pale and very thin, behaved and looked like an English Savonarola, whose mission it was to scarify the impiety of the Government and frighten them into repentance. I shared their antipathy to the Bill at the time, but I must frankly admit to-day that no permanent harm was done to either religion or the Church of England in Wales by disestablishment. Nor, though that is a lesser point, did our opposition help the cause of the Conservative Party in Wales. The only electoral hold the Liberal Party to-day has is in Wales, because the still predominant Nonconformist vote regards Conservatives as the main enemy.

The domestic frictions and difficulties of the Opposition were not, at first, solved by the substitution of Mr. Bonar Law for Mr. Balfour as leader. Everyone liked "Bonar", as he was affectionately named, including strong supporters of Mr. Balfour who resented what they regarded as his forced resignation; but, during the earlier years of his leadership, Bonar Law had an unfortunate habit of making unpremeditated statements in debate which he had subsequently to amend or explain away. One of these indiscretions—during the second reading of the Coal Mines (Minimum Wage) Bill, on March 19, 1912—is described as follows in my diary:—

> B. Law followed the P.M. and, though good on the subject of the danger involved, was foolishly betrayed by an interruption into suggesting alternative courses, none of which he really supported; he is still not firmly in the saddle. A. J. B. was there, but gave no sign of acquiescence or the reverse.

Throughout this period of adjustment to the new leadership, Mr. Balfour behaved like the great gentleman he was, giving loyal support to his successor and never showing in public or private the slightest resentment at his own supercession.

There were, in the Conservative Party at the time, other aspects of internal disagreement, but, like similar aspects in later years, they did the Party no permanent, and little temporary, injury; there is a resilience, respect for minority opinion and ultimate sense of loyalty inherent in the Party's practice and tradition that prevents it from splitting asunder when an incipient rebellion is in progress, as did the Liberal Party, and also the Socialist Party— at least temporarily—in the '30s. There was a body known as the "Confederacy" with an executive committee called the "Allies". The Confederacy was an influential group of Conservative peers and M.P.s, journalists, lawyers and business men, whose rules and list of members were never published, and whose object was to promote the cause of Imperialism and active opposition to the Government by criticising, where necessary, or "gingering-up" the official organisation and leadership of the Party. The more orthodox members of the Party and a section of the Conservative

Press at first ridiculed this body and then, when its power was apparent, threatened it with official action by the Whips. This, in fact, never occurred and could not have occurred without splitting the Party in two. I am convinced, as a member of this organisation which ceased to exist after the outbreak of the 1914 war, that it did good. We were no more rebellious or critical in general of the official hierarchy than the '22 or Conservative Committee has been on occasion in recent years; unlike the Conservative Committee, ours was not representative of the whole Party, but, like it, it provided a useful, vigorous and entirely confidential method of discussing and, if necessary, differing from official policy. After the acceptance of the Parliament Bill following the *volte-face* by the majority of Peers described in the last chapter, an association named the "Halsbury Club" was formed, composed of peers and M.P.s, under Lord Halsbury's[1] chairmanship, who were opposed to the decision. To its members the term "Diehards" was first applied in a parliamentary sense. The Club, to which I belonged, like the "Confederacy", ended at the outbreak of war, but had some useful conferences and discussions of which the decisions were conveyed to the Leader; one took place at Hatfield, under the presidency of Lord Salisbury,[2] whose guests we were, and lasted for three days.

In the autumn there was a parliamentary *cause célèbre* in the shape of the Marconi case. The question at issue was whether Mr. Lloyd George and the Master of Elibank, in purchasing some shares in the American Marconi Company from Sir Rufus Isaacs[3] (who had himself purchased 10,000 from his brother Godfrey, its managing director), and Sir Rufus Isaacs himself were or were not guilty of improper conduct which should have led, as the least possible penalty, to dismissal from office. The position was that, prior to the purchase, Mr. Samuel,[4] the Postmaster-General, had signed an agreement with the English Marconi Company; both companies were concerned with the newly-discovered medium of wireless; the two companies were separate, but there was more than a connection in name, for the

---

[1] Lord Halsbury (1823–1921) was Lord Chancellor from 1885 to 1892, and from 1895 to 1905.
[2] The 4th Marquis (1861–1947).   [3] Afterwards the 1st Lord Reading.
[4] Now Lord Samuel.

English company owned a majority of shares in the American company. Clearly, when the agreement with the English company became known publicly, as it was not at the time of these purchases, the shares of both companies would be likely to rise, as, in fact, they did. The method of handling the issue was unsatisfactory to all concerned. Sir Rufus Isaacs denied in the House that he or the other Ministers concerned had bought any shares in the English company, but neglected to mention their purchase of shares in the American; he also denied the charge made in one quarter—for which there never was any evidence— that he or Mr. Samuel had acted corruptly in their negotiations with the English company. A Select Committee of the Commons, after much squalid wrangling, issued a report, solely supported by the Liberal members on it, completely exonerating the Ministers concerned. Lord Robert Cecil and the Conservatives on the Committee severely condemned the Ministers, two of whom won a libel action against *Le Matin*; an apology was afterwards tendered through one of their number in a statement to the Commons, admitting the unwisdom of their conduct but denying corrupt motives. Much unpleasantness and temporary damage to the three Ministers' reputation was caused, justly or unjustly, by this episode. I have referred earlier to a scene in the House about it: when, at a later date, Sir Rufus was made Lord Chief Justice, Mr. Rudyard Kipling, then at the height of his fame and position, published a poem entitled "Gehazi", containing a scathing and thinly veiled attack upon the new Lord Chief Justice for his conduct in the Marconi case, in the manner and style of similar ferocious assaults upon the integrity of public men of a hundred years earlier. No legal action followed.

I do not know the answer to the question propounded at the beginning of the recital of this case. In private life all three men were friends of mine, though Lord Reading did not become so until a later date when, as will be recounted, I had a particular opportunity of appreciating his great qualities of brain, heart and sense of duty. But so was the late Mr. J. H. Thomas, and I cannot help wondering whether, if the three Ministers concerned in the Marconi case were innocent of any offence in their capacity as Ministers, Mr. Thomas was not too harshly treated for his indiscretion, which I describe in a later chapter. Subsequently, a vote of censure upon the conduct of the three Ministers, officially moved in the House by the Conservative Party, was rejected, the voting being purely on Party lines, by 346 to 268 votes. Here, as in other important divisions, the Liberal Government was saved by the Irish Nationalists.

During the autumn of 1912 and the early months of 1913 the Home Rule Bill was discussed and passed in the Commons but rejected in the Lords. Incessant scenes and frequent prolonged uproar characterised its passage through the Commons. On one occasion, the House was adjourned because of "grave disorder".[1] As members were crowding to the doors amid the angry hum of agitated conversation which always follows such an adjournment, Mr. Ronald McNeill, an Ulster M.P., who after the war became a Junior Minister and eventually went to the Lords as Lord Cushendun, hurled a book at Mr. Churchill which hit him on the chest. Next day Mr. McNeill made a full and complete apology, and Mr. Churchill, made a generous acknowledgement of the form and grace of the apology. Each side of the House loudly cheered both members impartially and gave the impression of great pleasure at the satisfactory solution reached as adding to the credit of all concerned. This characteristic attitude of the House of Commons in such circumstances justifies Mr. Harold Macmillan's witty remark on one occasion in the 1950 Parliament; it was to the effect that if, during an all-night sitting, a member, driven distracted by the snores of another member in the library, proceeded to throttle him and subsequently apologised to the House for his action in appropriate terms, his apology would be accepted and no further action would result!!

Notwithstanding the roaring furnace of controversy caused by the Bills to grant Home Rule to Ireland and enact the Disestablishment of the Welsh Church respectively, the Government produced another most contentious measure in the 1913 session. This was to abolish plural voting, and it was rejected by the Lords.

It should be recorded in their favour that in both Houses in this session the Conservative Opposition made strenuous efforts to induce the Government to increase the strength of the nation's Defence Forces. For whilst Parliament, the Press, and that portion of the public that takes interest in the nation's affairs

[1] Under Standing Order No. 21 (now No. 24).

were mainly preoccupied with the growing danger of the Irish situation, Germany was every month becoming more bellicose in the utterances of her leaders and more formidable in armaments. Some of us pressed for a modest form of National Service in the Territorials. Colonel Sandys, M.P.,[1] brought in a Bill to that end which was "talked out" by the Liberals. A speech I made on the subject was interrupted by a Labour member observing, "Working men ain't going to fight each other, mate". He was loudly cheered, not only by his own Party but by every Liberal in the House. Here, they argued in their own minds, was a working man putting the true and common-sense point of view in his own homely language to the nonsensical militarism of a foolish young Tory Lord. Unhappily, both for the world in general and the accuracy of the Labour M.P.'s statement, eighteen months later, on August 4, 1914, "working men" as well as others started killing each other, and have been doing so at intervals ever since, to a greater extent than in any previous epoch in history.

In both Houses we pressed for more aeroplanes—a plea to become very familiar, indeed customary, in later years—and the acceleration of the naval building programme. In the Lords there was one debate on defence in which acrimony of a kind seldom heard in their Lordships' House arose. Lord Curzon described Lord Chancellor Haldane as "the greatest master of copious irrelevance this House has ever seen" and Lord Denbigh said "all the slackers, funkers, wasters and loafers are on the Liberal side". Those—and this includes some historians who should know better—who inaccurately state that the terrific impact of the 1914 war, with its shattering effect upon our national life from which we are still suffering, burst upon us without warning, should read the debates to which I have referred in the Hansards of 1913 and earlier on the same subject. The Government and the nation had plenty of warnings, but wouldn't listen to them.

Following the rejection of the Home Rule Bill by the Lords, to which reference is made earlier in this chapter, the preparations in Ulster for armed resistance to it increased, and a Commander was appointed in the shape of General Richardson. Further, a

[1] Father of the Rt. Hon. Duncan Sandys, M.P.

provisional Government was formed with Sir Edward Carson at its head. Some Liberals in and out of Parliament urged that he should be tried for high treason. But other and more influential Liberals began, for the first time, to see the need for compromise. Lord Loreburn, an ex-Lord Chancellor, stated that an enforced settlement on Home Rule would lead to disaster, and he advocated a conference. Mr. Churchill in his speeches in the summer gave unmistakable hints that Ulster might have to be excluded from the Bill. At the same time Mr. F. E. Smith, in the words of his biographer, the present Lord Birkenhead,[1] "had talked with various dispassionate men in high position in England who were anxious about the situation and he communicated their views to Carson, and the outcome of these conversations is shown in this memorandum which he wrote at the time". The memorandum is too long to quote here. Mr. Smith's advocacy was in favour of the exclusion of Ulster, in return for which Sir Edward Carson would, if necessary, use his influence to "make Home Rule, so limited, a success in the rest of Ireland". Sir Edward, apparently, was unwilling to commit himself for or against such proposals. But Mr. Bonar Law and Mr. Churchill, who was clearly personally in favour of a compromise, discussed the matter when they met at Balmoral in September, and Mr. Lloyd George, as a letter to Mr. F. E. Smith printed in Lord Birkenhead's life of his father shows, was of the same opinion. It is interesting to note that these three men—Mr. Churchill, Mr. Lloyd George and Lord Birkenhead as he then was—were the negotiators for the British Government and the real architects of the Irish Settlement and Treaty in 1921.

The fruits of this new spirit of conciliation were seen in a debate in the House of Commons on March 9, 1914, which is described in my diary as follows:

> The P.M. made his speech, containing so-called "offers to Ulster"[2]; the gist of them was that Ulster can "contract out" of the Bill (voting by Counties) for six years, but, at the end of that time, she will have to come in, unless Parliament otherwise orders.
> The offers are not in themselves very helpful; but the fact remains

[1] *Frederick Edwin, Earl of Birkenhead.*
[2] A White Paper was issued on the subject on the same day.

that the Government do, at last, realise what a fix they are in and are making an effort to get out—a very different atmosphere we are in now in the H. of C. than that in which we used to be when any reference to Ulster's preparations were greeted with sneers and jeers. B. L.[1] made a good speech in reply; Carson was not conciliatory but promised that, after the exclusion was made permanent, "unless Parliament otherwise orders", he would submit it to the Ulster Convention.

Unfortunately this new spirit soon evaporated, as a further extract from my diary shows:

The debate was resumed on the so-called "Irish Offer" of the Government. B. L. remarked that little progress had been made. Carson made a splendid fighting speech, fiercely attacking the Government, and ended by saying that it was no use parleying any longer; he was off to Belfast. Devlin made a vitriolic rejoinder in the course of which Carson said that he had told a deliberate lie. The Speaker objected, whereupon Carson substituted "wilful falsehood" which the Speaker accepted.

It is difficult for anyone not fully acquainted with the nuances of parliamentary life and procedure to understand why "wilful falsehood" is in order, as a parliamentary phrase, and "deliberate lie" is not. But it is only fair to Mr. Speaker Lowther to mention that, owing to the bitterness between the two sides of the House, he had been undergoing a strain such as no other occupant of the Chair had experienced since the Irish rows of the '80s and '90s. This was shown in a scene between him and Mr. Bonar Law on May 21, when disorder had arisen over an attempt by Lord Robert Cecil to move the adjournment. The Opposition, led by a number of the younger members such as myself, had been chanting "Adjourn" when the Speaker rose and said, "As Honourable Gentlemen seem determined not to hear their own leader, may I ask the Leader of the Opposition if it is with his sanction that this disorder is taking place?" The Leader of the Opposition rose and said, "I do not presume to criticise what you consider your duty, Sir, but I know mine, and that is not to answer any such question". To quote from my diary:

[1] Mr. Bonar Law, the Leader of the Opposition.

Half the Tory Party rose and cheered and waved papers (including some of the oldest and staidest Members) and the Speaker then adjourned the House.

At the next sitting of the House the usual apologies followed from the two participants in the episode. When, on one or two occasions during the 1945 and 1950 Parliaments, Mr. Speaker Clifton Brown and Mr. Winston Churchill came into mild conflict, there were expressions of surprise and regret in many quarters; no doubt the occurrences were regrettable, but nothing like as regrettable as the angry scene between Mr. Speaker Lowther and Mr. Bonar Law. Such incidents, however, are soon forgotten, and this particular one in no way affected their position or popularity in the House of Commons.

All chances of an Irish Settlement were destroyed by the Curragh incident or, as some Liberals called it, "the Curragh Mutiny". This occurrence, which has fortunately been almost forgotten, can briefly be described as follows. The Government, in view of the existence of the Ulster Volunteer Army, decided to move troops from the military camp of the Curragh to Northern Ireland. General Paget, the General Officer Commanding the British Army in Ireland, after seing Colonel Seeley,[1] Secretary of State for War, and having apparently received from him the idea that the troops might refuse to shoot Ulstermen, had a confidential talk with the senior officers of the Third Cavalry Brigade at which he gave a strong hint to any officer unwilling to serve against the Ulster Volunteers to send in his papers. The sequel to this talk was immediate and electrifying. Brigadier-General Sir Hubert Gough and fifty-seven of the officers of his Brigade stated that they would "prefer to accept dismissal if ordered North". There resulted a situation which was painfully like that which has frequently arisen before and since in the smaller South American Republics. Colonel Seeley sent for the senior officers of the Brigade and assured them that they would not be used to coerce Ulster. There was a furious debate in the House of Commons in which the Government was accused of trying to start a civil war, while the Opposition was accused of treason. I forgot, at the time, to notice whether the representatives

[1] Afterwards Lord Mottistone.

of Guatemala, Haiti and San Domingo were in the Diplomatic Gallery; if they were, they must have fancied themselves back in their homelands, especially when Mr. Asquith repudiated Colonel Seeley's pledge. The upshot was that Sir John French,[1] the C.I.G.S., Sir John Ewart, the Adjutant-General and Colonel Seeley himself, resigned. Six months later the temporary harm done to the Army was completely eradicated by the magnificent conduct of the "Old Contemptibles". The incident or mutiny, call it what you will, would probably never have arisen if not only Colonel Seeley but the Chief Secretary to the Lord Lieutenant of Ireland, Mr. Augustine Birrell, had been more suitable occupants of their respective posts. Mr. Birrell was a scholar and a well-known writer of literary essays; he had a talent for witty and epigrammatic remarks which were known as "Birrellisms". Unhappily for him, they seldom appealed to the House of Commons, and by the use of them he acquired a not wholly deserved reputation for frivolity when seriousness was necessary. Further, he gave the impression that he had some intellectual contempt for the House as an institution and for its members; there is no surer road to unpopularity and failure in the Commons than this, which has been followed by several men (and women, too, in recent years), especially lawyers and University representatives. Colonel Seeley was a gallant and lovable man with hosts of personal friends in every part of the House and outside; but few people took him seriously, partly owing to a gasconading habit of reciting exploits, some of them partly apocryphal, in which he was the principal figure.

In the early summer of 1914, while the *jeunesse dorée* danced the fashionable rag-time all through the night with a feverish intensity that came subconsciously, perhaps, from a feeling that the boys would never see another English May or June and the girls because of that would never feel the same again, Government and Opposition in the Commons roared and snarled at each other across the floor about Ireland like angry lions and tigers. But privately, in the lobbies and smoking-room, people said, "Which is coming first—war or civil war?" So much for the astonishing fantasy—one of many attacked in this book—manufactured by modern writers and journalists to the effect that

[1] Afterwards Lord Ypres.

everything was peaceful and serene in Britain until the Kaiser's troops invaded Belgium in early August, 1914. That event settled which came first—war or civil war. On the surface Ireland was peaceful and almost united after war broke out, with Irish Nationalists and Ulstermen alike joining the Forces. In fact, the civil war was only postponed.

I was not there to witness the historic and emotional scene in the House of Commons on August 3, when Sir Edward Grey made his famous speech, and Mr. Will Crooks led the singing of "God Save the King", for I joined my Yeomanry Regiment that day on mobilisation. Had I been in my place in the Commons, I do not think I should have been as impressed as some were by the occasion. Mr. Crooks was a most likeable and upright man who, according to his lights, faithfully represented the wage-earners as a Labour Member. But I could not forget that he and his colleagues had opposed the provision of the armaments necessary to fight a major war and had sneered at us for advocating them. These last-minute conversions to patriotism, which were very common among "leftist" M.P.s at the beginning of both world wars, do not atone for the evil done by pacifist opposition to adequate defence urged by the same men before war starts.

There was a conflict of opinion at the time as to whether the late Lord Morley and the late Mr. John Burns were or were not justified in resigning from the Cabinet on the outbreak of war; were they or were they not committed, by previous acquiescence in Cabinet decisions, to support their colleagues in the situation which arose on August 4, 1914? They sincerely believed that they were not. There was an obvious connection between their resignation and the circumstances of the Anglo-French conversations. Sir Edward Grey made clear in his autobiography that there was no agreement, secret or otherwise, with France to go to war in the event of a German attack upon her; but there was a contingent liability furnished by the military conversations,[1] for

[1] Lord Grey, in his book *Twenty-Five Years* (I, pp. 96, 97), makes this reference: "The Agadir affair had thus brought the military conversations into prominence. They must have been familiar to several members of the Cabinet in discussion at the Committee of Imperial Defence, and in 1912 the fact of their taking place became known to other members of the Cabinet. Those Ministers

otherwise they would have been purposeless. Moreover, it was obvious, in view of the bad state of Anglo-German relationship, that, apart from any other reason, we could not afford to see France overrun and would have to come to her aid. A public announcement of this intention might have averted the war. The secrecy surrounding the mutual defence conversations did great harm during the First World War to Anglo-French relationship, for a section of French opinion wrongly believed—and believes to this day—that we promised more than we performed. It is impossible to avoid the opinion that the conversations were concealed, not because of fear of alarming Germany, but because the Liberal leaders thought their disclosure would lose them votes. This must detract from the place in history of Sir Edward Grey as a statesman, though not from his charm, uprightness and fine gifts as a man.

There is another grievous aspect of this question of prepared-

who had not been directly informed of them were entitled to know exactly how we stood with the French. There was no reluctance to have the whole matter discussed at the Cabinet. The only difficulty arose from the thing having gone on so long without the Cabinet generally being informed. Ministers who now heard of these military conversations for the first time suspected that there was something to conceal. If the conversations really did not commit the country, as I stated, why should the knowledge of them have been with-held? There was a demand that the fact of the military conversations being non-committal should be put into writing. I had the impression that some Ministers, who had not been members of the Committee of Defence, expected some demur to this, and were suspiciously surprised at the immediate assent to the proposal given by myself and Asquith. I had made it so plain to Cambon that the Government must remain absolutely free and uncommitted, that I anticipated no difficulty whatever in getting a satisfactory exchange of notes with him on behalf of ourselves and the French Government. I knew he understood and accepted the position and would make no difficulty; and, if there had been any doubt raised, I was prepared to contend that the military conversations must stop and not be resumed till the condition of them was made clear. I therefore agreed, readily and at once, to the proposal that this condition should be put in writing." There follows in Lord Grey's book a reproduction of the letters exchanged in November 1912 between him and M. Cambon, the French Ambassador in London. Lord Grey makes this ad-mission on page 99 of his book: "I have always regretted, however, that the military conversations were not brought before the Cabinet at once; this would have avoided unnecessary suspicion. But it has also been a great satis-faction to me that they did come before the Cabinet some two years before we were called upon to face the outbreak of war."

ness. As I have shown in an earlier portion of this chapter, the Conservatives advocated a modest but efficient scheme of conscription which was angrily opposed by the entire Liberal and Labour Parties; worse still, the Asquith Government which fell in 1916 refused to impose National Service during the first two years of the war. For this the Conservative members of that Government and the Party in the House must share the blame. Perhaps, had a large number of young M.P.s, who were, like me, on service with their units, come home and formed a group to urge conscription on a reluctant Parliament, we should have succeeded in our efforts; but, rightly or wrongly, we felt that our duty lay elsewhere. The results of this Governmental and parliamentary reluctance to face an obvious duty were grievous. The least of them was internal dissent and bitterness which took the form of the "white feather" campaign.[1] Far more serious were the appalling losses among the first "Hundred Thousand" and the cream of the Regular Army. Though few people dare say so openly, one moral and practical advantage of National Service in war-time is to distribute the casualties evenly—and not to confine them merely to the best and bravest men in the nation who have volunteered to serve their country.

Our lack of adequate man-power in the Army had a bearing on the appalling losses of the French. In the first four months of the 1914 war the French had over 850,000 casualties, which was more than eight times the strength of the original British Expeditionary Force. In four and a half years they had on the Western Front alone nearly one and a half million men killed, which was more than double the losses of the British. It is an indisputable fact that the memory of this frightful holocaust had an effect alike upon the morale and fighting qualities of the French Army in the Second World War, and no one can blame the French nation for it; the memory still lingers, and British statesmen must, and no doubt do, make allowance for it in discussing Western Defence. The sins of political forefathers are visited upon their successors. No Frenchman of my generation, among whom I include many friends—some alive, some dead—will accept as an

[1] A number of excitable women gave white feathers to men in mufti—many of whom were complete strangers to them and some of whom were medically unfit to join the Forces.

answer to the disproportionate losses of the two countries the facile point, "You forget the contribution which the British Navy made to our common victory; where would you have been without it?" He would reply, "No Frenchman who is not an ignorant fool lacks in gratitude to the British Navy; but that does not atone for your fantastic folly in refusing to impose conscription for two whole years when, at any rate by the middle of 1915, you knew how desperately short your armies were of man-power, and when you were able to arm at least a large portion of that missing man-power".

Though the fact was carefully concealed by the Press when National Service was at last introduced, the "old sweats"— Regular Army, New Army and Territorials of 1914—were very averse at first to their new comrades, though this feeling soon evaporated when it was seen how well they fought. One day, in 1916, I was returning at the head of my company of the Imperial Camel Corps from a five days' desert operation against Bedouin sympathisers with the Turks, in the hills on the Asiatic side of the Suez Canal. We were desperately tired, dusty, dirty and unshaven, for the small quantity of water we carried in containers on our saddles was not sufficient for shaving; no doubt, too, even in those days, though the Camel Corps had a useful military function, its outward appearance was somewhat old-fashioned. Near El Kubri on the Canal, which is much in the news at the time of writing, we passed a hutted camp full of newly arrived conscripted men. As we rode by, one of them said, "Gorblimey! Look at the blooming circus! What have you done with the elephants, mate?" The company was marching at ease, and one of my men shouted out, "You dirty —— white-livered cur! You and your like have been staying at home for two years stealing our jobs—and our girls, too, when you could—while we've been sweating and fighting from Gallipoli to here and seeing our best pals killed; you dare to jeer at real soldiers, do you!! Well, I'd like ——". He got no further, as I ordered the company to march at attention and the sergeant-major to take the name of the man who had insulted us in order that it might be reported to his Commanding Officer, and of my man for his remark, though I didn't subsequently punish him. As I rode angrily on, after watching with interest the look of bewilderment and alarm on the face of the conscript when the sergeant-major sternly asked him for his name and number, I almost decided at once to ask for parliamentary leave, which was granted to M.P.s on service, in order to report this story to the House of Commons and base upon it a furious denunciation of members of all parties who had remained at home, for shirking their duty in not insisting upon Conscription in 1914. Fortunately I rejected my impulse, having recovered my equanimity after a bath, shave and good dinner in camp.

CHAPTER VII

There is perforce a gap of nearly four years in this parliamentary chronicle, since I was absent on military service for the whole of the time between August, 1914, and the Armistice, save from October to November 1918, and when on leave I only went to the House of Commons on five or six occasions. Since this book is a personal record of parliamentary events written by one who can claim, whatever his demerits in other directions, to have attended very regularly for nearly forty-seven years to his duties as an M.P., save during this period, it would detract from its value to describe happenings of which he learnt only at second hand. Moreover, the actions and reactions of Parliament during the 1914 war seemed very remote, and I fear also unimportant, to regimental officers like myself. The Army was not interested in politics or in the views of politicians whose names, except for one or two of them, such as Mr. Lloyd George and Mr. Winston Churchill, were almost unknown to the average soldier. I took a certain malicious pleasure, when I returned from active service in Palestine just before the armistice, in acquainting with this fact some of my parliamentary colleagues who had stayed at home and become, as they believed, public figures of consequence.

Very rightly, the Prime Minister, Mr. Lloyd George, appealed to the country soon after the armistice in 1918; for the war had been won, universal adult male suffrage (by reason of an Act of Parliament passed earlier in the year) and votes for women over thirty had fundamentally altered the previous electoral roll, and the nation had the right to be consulted as to how it was to be governed now that it was again at peace. What was in dispute, from an ethical point of view, at the time of the election and for years afterwards, was the method adopted by the Prime Minister for ensuring an adequate majority, and his policy and tactics during the election.

With the support of the Northcliffe Press, and most newspapers, the Conservative and Liberal leaders in the war-time

Coalition had decided during the summer of 1918 to continue it after the war was over. The Labour leaders in the Government differed from this view, and three days after the Armistice most of them resigned. Some of them, like the late Mr. Barnes, who remained in the Government, had given most valuable public service in high office during the war. On November 12 the Conservatives at a Party meeting, not without some misgivings, decided to maintain support of the Coalition, thus destroying an incipient revolt which started with certain Conservative M.P.s possessing more sincerity and enthusiasm than brains, who tried in the summer of 1918 to form an independent party or group which would disassociate itself from the Coalition. At a meeting the same day, the Liberals supporting the Government decided to continue that support during and after a General Election.

With the tremendous prestige attaching to him on account of his position as Prime Minister of a victorious country, with his personal popularity then at its zenith and backed by overwhelming political support, Mr. Lloyd George, with his colleagues' approval, then took a drastic step. Only those candidates who supported the full election programme of the Government and who, if they were M.P.s, had voted with the Government in the Maurice Debate[1] would receive a certificate, or coupon[2] as it came to be called, of worthiness. All others were to be opposed, and opposed they were, with overwhelming success for the Government. This was the second big blow to the integrity—and indeed existence—of the Liberal Party, the first being the overthrow of the Asquith Government and subsequent division in the Liberal ranks in 1916. Angry recriminations followed this decision, which was condemned by *The Times* and other papers. I thought then, and still think, that Mr. Lloyd George was justified in the action he took; he had a right to request a mandate and to

[1] On May 8, 1918, Mr. Asquith moved that a Select Committee be appointed to enquire into charges which had been made by Major-General Sir Frederick Maurice, in a letter to the Press, alleging that Mr. Lloyd George and Mr. Bonar Law had made inaccurate statements in Parliament about the strength of the army in France. The Government let it be known that Mr. Asquith's motion would be regarded as a vote of censure, and it was defeated by 293 votes to 106.

[2] Hence the term "Coupon Election" for the 1918 contest.

ask the electors to reject those who were only prepared to give him conditional support or had opposed the war-time Government on a big issue of policy.

In addition to promising social reform in all spheres and rehabilitation of those broken in the war, which pledges were redeemed in the subsequent four years' tenure of office of the Coalition, Mr. Lloyd George gave an undertaking to prosecute the Kaiser and all responsible for atrocities, and to make the Enemy Powers pay indemnities to the limit of their capacity. From the middle '20s to the early '30s critics from both right and left ridiculed these pledges, and accused both Mr. Lloyd George and us who supported him of dishonestly advocating aims which we knew could never be attained in order to "cash in" on the national bellicosity against Germany and Austria immediately after the Armistice. Some of the most distinguished of these critics, including Lord Keynes, are dead, but I wonder if they would be so confident that they were right if they were alive to-day?

Britain, in conjunction with her Allies, not only tried, but executed or sentenced to long terms of imprisonment, scores of Germans after the Second World War, and demanded and obtained, as she is still doing, heavy reparations in the form of occupation costs and in other ways from the Germans. If the nation had given continued support to the Coalition policy *vis-à-vis* Germany at the time of the Peace Conference and afterwards, and demanded that the Government should range itself on the side of France in her demands for strong action, whatever President Wilson might say, the pledges could have been redeemed. A threat of force or a raid across the border would probably have produced the Kaiser from his refuge in Holland. Whether such a policy would have prevented or accelerated the rise to power of Hitler is a moot point. It is easy to argue both ways. One can assert that the impossible and tragic economic condition of Germany in the late '20s and early '30s was the result of Allied action, and in turn produced Hitler; contrariwise one can contend that, if the Allies had occupied all Germany for ten or fifteen years, arrested and tried the Kaiser and his principal Ministers, and squeezed every penny from the country, the rise of Hitler would have been impossible, because he would have been arrested or shot directly he started his agitation. What is certain is that the

shrill chorus of University professors, economists, zealots of the
League of Nations, and pacifists who, anticipating Mr. Noel
Coward's famous song in the Second World War, kept up a
chant during the '20s of "Don't let's be beastly to the Germans",
had a powerful influence on a war-weary public, and made it
impossible for any British Government to take, with popular
support, strong action against Germany. The chorus appeared
to have a plausible basis at the time. Victorious nations, said the
professors and their friends, can't hold down conquered countries
for long after the war has ceased. Yet some of them have lived
to see Soviet Russia perform this allegedly impossible task ever
since 1945.

The Government obtained an immense majority in the election, and, as has often happened before and since, the absence of
an effective Opposition eventually did them considerable harm,
for it encouraged, as it always does encourage, fissiparous tendencies in the ranks of their supporters. The non-Coalition
Liberals made a poor show. Their leader, Mr. Asquith, who lost
his seat at the 1918 election but was returned as member for
Paisley in 1920, was an ageing and disappointed man, though
occasionally he recaptured the ear of the House with his command
of the English language, his clear and beautiful enunciation, and
his handsome and striking profile. The Irish Nationalists had been
nearly obliterated by the Sinn Fein Party, most of whom refused
to take their seats; those of us who had sat in previous Parliaments
missed the presence of Mr. John Redmond, whom even his
opponents greatly respected. Most of the leading men who were
on the Government side in the 1900 Parliament when I entered
it had disappeared. Mr. Joseph Chamberlain, Mr. Arnold
Forster, Mr. Alfred Lyttelton, Mr. George Wyndham and many
others were dead. I had had before the war a boyish hero-worship
for Mr. Wyndham and Mr. Lyttelton; no two members of the
House, in my long experience, were more talented, more charming, or more helpful to young M.P.s. Mr. St. John Brodrick[1]
and others were in the Lords. Several men well known to the
public ten or fifteen years earlier were no longer M.P.s, and had
been forgotten. Among them was Sir Charles Dilke—a tragic
figure possessed of great gifts, with a rare perception in foreign

[1] Afterwards Lord Midleton.

affairs, who had ruined his career by becoming involved in a divorce case in which his conduct was such that no Government, even in the laxer atmosphere of to-day, could have afforded to number him among its members. In the 1906 Parliament he was invariably called in debates on foreign affairs and spoke well, but he had entirely lost his grip on the House. He usually emptied it. Another famous M.P. died before the 1914 war. That was Mr. Henry Labouchere—"Labby", the redoubtable, talented and irrepressible editor of *Truth*, a scourge alike to Governments, especially those whom he nominally supported, "confidence men" and criminals of all sorts, whom he attacked with savage relish in the columns of his paper. Once, soon after I took my seat in 1905, I was walking home from the House to St. Anne's Mansions where I lived. I overtook in the courtyard a bowed, wizened little man who said to me, "You live here too do you? Do you know who I am?" I replied quite honestly that I didn't. He replied, "I am Labouchere", and went on to mutter, half to himself, that no one took any notice of "Labby" to-day.

Many new figures had come into political prominence during the war and were returned at the 1918 election, among them the "war-time recruits", by which term I mean men of reputation and authority in various walks of life, such as the brothers Geddes and Sir Robert Horne, who were elected to the House of Commons or created peers in order that important offices might be given to them. With one or two exceptions they were not a parliamentary success when the war was over. They compared unfavourably with the similar "new entry" in the Second World War; Mr. Churchill's choice of successful and talented men from outside either House of Parliament to hold high office in war-time was happier than that of Mr. Lloyd George.[1]

Among the M.P.s who had blazed into a temporary effulgence during the war was that extraordinary man Mr. Horatio Bottomley. Before 1914 he had created something of a parliamentary record. Whatever the quality of their speeches, the House of Commons, to its credit, usually pays scant attention to those of its members who are known to be crooks in private life—however great their following may be outside. The case of Mr. Bottomley is an exception to that rule. From the time he entered the House

---

[1] See Chapter XVIII, p. 255.

in 1906 onwards, though his dishonest methods in business were well known, he could always count on a well-filled House to listen fascinated to his remarkable powers of oratory. During the war, both as editor of *John Bull* and as one of the most popular platform speakers, he attracted a huge public and unquestionably aided the war effort. Lord Birkenhead once told me that, in his opinion, had Mr. Bottomley become a barrister and refrained from dishonest financial dealings in the City, his forensic ability would have enabled him to become Lord Chancellor or Lord Chief Justice. Certainly no other layman has conducted his own suit in court with such ability as he did. For all his crookedness he had one saving grace—the golden gift of a sense of humour in the direst calamity. With characteristic kindness of heart, Lord Birkenhead wrote him a friendly personal letter just after his heavy prison sentence for fraud in the early '20s. In the course of his reply Mr. Bottomley said, "We had a very inaccurate statement in a sermon from a visiting parson in the prison chapel last Sunday. After assuring us that we were all his brethren, he urged us not to despair; our trouble in life had been that we lacked conviction. I longed to rise in my place and point out to him that he was wrong; the one thing we all shared in common was a conviction"!

Few Governments and their supporters have started with higher hopes and brighter prospects than did the 1918 Coalition Government; but no Government within living memory, not even those of 1945, 1950 and 1951, has been faced with more intractable problems at home and abroad from the beginning to the end of its term of office. It is true, as I shall show later, that its own ineptitude and its particular constitution added to the difficulties of finding a solution to a few of these problems, but the most perfect Government would still have had to deal with factors that were beyond its power to control. Behind the many immediate symptoms of a sick world, such as mutinies in the Army soon after the Armistice (for by no other name can certain incidents in France and Egypt be called), strikes, including a serious police strike, and labour trouble of every kind, civil war in Ireland, threatened insurrection in India, murderous attacks upon British soldiers and civilians in Egypt, abortive expeditions against Soviet Russia, serious unemployment and trade depression from

1920 onwards, with continuous and angry recriminations at top level between the Allied Delegates at Versailles—behind all this lay an ominous background—the state of British public opinion in general. It would be outside the scope of this book to attempt a close analysis of this state of mind, but in order to explain the course of parliamentary events a summary description of it is necessary.

The year 1919 inaugurated an era of disillusion and denigration with, at the opposite pole, a most dangerous self-delusion regarding the new instrument devised to make future wars impossible —the League of Nations. The appalling casualties in France suffered by the young manhood of the nation scarred and seared the public mind as the much heavier material damage and civilian losses in the Second World War never did. "Why this awful waste of life?" people asked in private. Was it due to the incompetence of the generals, those remote "Red Tabs" whom so many fighting soldiers disliked? Or was it the result of the vanity and folly of the politicians? There was, with the exception of Lord Allenby (to those of us who served under him in Palestine), no popular figure among the Commanders-in-Chief on the various fronts such as Lord Roberts and Kitchener had been in the South African war, and Lord Montgomery and Lord Alexander were in the Second World War. "No more fighting for us", said the ex-Service man and (in secret) some who were still in the Services. "We are not going to be such fools as to fight", said the young men after the war who during it had been below military age; "we've seen how our fathers and brothers were massacred, we've no use for national honour and patriotism; that's all out of date. The League of Nations which prohibits that sort of thing is the show for us. Meanwhile let us dance and be merry and have a good time. We couldn't care less about your political problems." Many of the girls of the period eagerly embraced this philosophy and rejoiced in the new freedom of their sex.

The idealists of the League of Nations quite legitimately made full use of the "no more fighting" side of youthful opinion at the time. They urged that support of the League would ensure peace, and that armaments for national purposes would soon be abolished. Many went further and identified its ideals with those of

Christianity. The Episcopal and other Protestant Churches at home and abroad (outside the United States) eagerly embraced this conception; but the Roman Catholic Church stood somewhat aloof and apart. I still remember with amusement how a Church of England clergyman of distinction made a statement to the effect that he failed to follow this reasoning, since many of the Member States were heathen—supporters of Islam, or Buddhism or Hinduism. He was fiercely assailed for his attitude by bishops and clergy of all denominations. No humane or reasonable person can deny that the League of Nations was a fine conception which in certain fields, that of international health for example, did work of great and permanent value. Nor should the possibility be ignored that it may have laid the foundations for an organisation which at some distant date will really unite the world. But its mistakes were grievous. Its worst mistake was to lay down the general principle that war for national purposes and national self-defence was morally wrong and that, in consequence, disarmament to the point of endangering national security was necessary, whilst at the same time emphatically asserting that "sanctions" which could in many cases lead to war must be employed against an aggressor. In other words, the people of each nation were told that they must not fight on behalf of their own country but must be prepared to fight for other countries and risk heavy casualties, with inadequate forces as a result of disarmament, in somebody else's quarrel in which their national interests were not concerned. Such a doctrine is antagonistic to human nature; nor does the Korean war of the United Nations disprove this fact, for it is to the interests of all the anti-Communist powers to repel Communist aggression wherever it occurs and where it is militarily possible to check it.[1] Further, by following the precepts of its originator, President Wilson, in favour of "self-determination", a laudable aim in itself, supporters of the League of Nations encouraged the framers of the Peace Treaty to create a number of new States, some of which were united and happy, while others, such as Czechoslovakia, were full of racial rivalries or permeated by a fierce xenophobia that helped to prepare the way for a second world war.

Two men of great distinction and probity, the first of whom

[1] On this subject see Chapter XXIII, p. 327.

is a lifelong friend of mine, Lord Cecil of Chelwood and Prof. Gilbert Murray, O.M., bear a heavy responsibility for the manner in which they used the British Branch of the League of Nations Union as an instrument of policy, through the Peace Ballot and in other ways, to hinder British rearmament in the '30s. The trouble with both men was that they had had little experience of the darker side of international politics. They had not seen with their own eyes, as I had done, the foul and horrible nature of the system of government prevailing in certain countries in both hemispheres. They did not realise that the members of those governments lived in luxury on tolls or blackmail extracted from the white slave trade, drug traffic, and every form of human vice and corruption both moral and financial. They apparently supposed that the representatives of these countries at Geneva or at League of Nations' Conferences elsewhere were gentlemen and statesmen like themselves; whereas, in fact, these men had never said or done an honest thing in all their lives. At least the United Nations Organisation to-day is free of some of these illusions; for the most ingenuous person does not believe that unity exists except in name, or that through U.N.O. alone Western Europe can avoid being destroyed by Soviet Russia and her satellites. Few can harbour the delusion that many of its Member States are actuated by anything but the mixed motives of fear, self-interest and the principle of "I'll scratch your back if you scratch mine".

But in the '20s, to hold such views about the League of Nations was a political heresy punished by the voters. Those of us who held office in more than one Government during the '20s, including myself and Mr. Churchill, whose tenure of the Air Ministry was marked by the reduction of an overwhelming air strength to a few squadrons, cannot escape responsibility for the ultimate results. Nevertheless, we can urge in our defence that the nation was resolutely opposed to what it termed "militarism" and the defence of national interests. Researches, both in and out of office at the time, convinced me that in the early '20s the country was determined to avoid a major war at any cost, and was seething below the surface with a dangerous unrest which reached its climax in the General Strike of 1926. There was, indeed, a revolutionary mood abroad, partly instigated and inspired by the Russian Revolution. A well-known Trade Union leader at the time said in a speech that, while he wished no personal harm to Their Majesties, he hoped to live to see the day when "six-inch 'Hows' will be dropping their shells on Buckingham Palace".

As evil in their effect upon public opinion as the disillusionists and illusionists of the League of Nations Union were the denigrators. Whether Lord Keynes was or was not right in the contentions of his book *The Economic Consequences of the Peace* is mainly a question for economists. That its publication did great harm to international relationship, strengthened American isolationism and handicapped the British Government in its foreign policy, I can assert from official experience. More remote in their effect upon political policies, but nevertheless a deterrent to legitimate national pride and moral purpose—the foundation-stones of any country which wishes to retain its greatness—were the efforts of the new school of biographers and novelists. Lytton Strachey, despite his genius and many gifts as a writer, did harm by his *Eminent Victorians* in smashing the belief of many simple people in their national heroes, and thereby helping to undermine national self-confidence. Much can be urged against parts of Mr. Kipling's philosophy, though, perhaps biased by personal friendship, I regard him as a great poet and a supreme man of letters; but at least he succeeded, in his heyday, in making us proud of ourselves. Mr. Strachey's apparent object was exactly the opposite. The new school of novelists, which had started before the 1914 war and had many additional pupils after it, introduced characters who had no moral or Christian purpose in life; many of them gloried in marital infidelity; most of them, openly or by inference, sneered at patriotism and the country's institutions, including parliamentary government. These novels shocked and offended many ex-Servicemen who believed that the first two objects were worth fighting and being prepared to die for; but they obtained, nevertheless, a huge number of readers and greatly pleased and helped those whom are now known as extreme "leftists".

Many of these men and women really believed that in Soviet Russia you could do and speak as you liked, and that all old-fashioned conventions had been abolished. They were particularly attracted by the fact that one of the conventions thus destroyed was marital fidelity. Those of them who are still alive must be pained to learn that the present Supreme Council of the Soviet has completely reversed this policy. To-day sexual immorality is severely punished in Russia. The "new school" of novelists went happily hand-in-hand with the "leftists" and the numerous admirers of Bolshevism to be found in all ranks of society at the time. They were all iconoclasts together. They made the task of Government harder than it need have been, because the impression was given at home and abroad that Britain had lost faith in herself and her historic past.

I have devoted considerable space to the recital of these diverse factors, which largely conditioned the public mind at the time, because they had an influence upon the policy and legislation of all Governments in the first decade after the 1914 war, and also an effect on the attitude of the House of Commons.

CHAPTER VIII

THE first session of the Coalition or "Coupon" Parliament opened very appropriately, in view of the prevalent labour unrest, in the midst of a Tube strike, on February 4, 1919. As a result of the war few M.P.s had cars, and taxis were almost unobtainable because of the demand upon them. Indeed, the late Sir Henry Norman, M.P., a man of great talent and ingenuity, astonished his fellow-members and the police on duty in Palace Yard by arriving there on a motor-scooter. Mr. Lowther was re-elected Speaker. Later in the same year he was offered, but declined, the post of British Ambassador to Washington. One day when I was dining with him he said that his refusal was due to the fact that he was "too old to begin all over again". I think he underrated his great vitality and intellectual power.[1]

It was presumably on the occasion of the opening of the session that Mr. Baldwin noticed that the new Parliament comprised among Government supporters a number of "hard-faced men who looked as if they had done well out of the war". I was unaware of this opinion of my future leader until years afterwards, but I arrived at much the same conclusion during the session. For instance, I recorded in my diary on March 17 that during the debate on the Transport Bill there was

> rather reactionary opposition among some of the fat, prosperous-looking Coalition supporters.

On the same day Lord Birkenhead took his seat on the Woolsack for the first time as Lord Chancellor. *Punch* stated that "a trifling error in the setting of his three-cornered hat, whose rakish look was for the moment reminiscent of the 'Galloper',[2] was quickly corrected by one of the Lords Commis-

---

[1] See Chapter II, p. 12.

[2] A reference to a nickname bestowed on Mr. F. E. Smith (before he became Lord Birkenhead) by his political opponents because he had acted as an amateur Aide-de-Camp or Galloper at a review of the Ulster Volunteers before the 1914 war.

sioners at his side". *Punch* went on to pay tribute to his dignity and poise at this, the beginning of a notable Lord-Chancellorship.

Soon after the session started a small number of young Conservative M.P.s, of whom I was one, formed a "group". The original members were Mr. Edward Wood (now Lord Halifax), Viscount Wolmer (now Lord Selborne), the late Mr. Walter Guinness (afterwards Lord Moyne), the late Sir John Hills, Sir Samuel Hoare (now Lord Templewood), Mr. Ormsby-Gore (now Lord Harlech) and Mr. Philip Lloyd-Graeme (now Lord Swinton); Mr. Walter Elliot, Sir John Davidson and one or two others afterwards joined us. Our critics suggested, though not to our faces, that we were a mutual admiration society designed to force attention upon ourselves in order to obtain office. If that had been our intention we were signally successful, for every one of the original members eventually became a Cabinet Minister with the exception of Sir John Hills who, however, from 1922 to 1923 held the most important ministerial post outside the Cabinet as Financial Secretary to the Treasury.

Office, however, was not our aim. Indeed, when I was first offered an Under-Secretaryship in 1922, I declined it because of dissatisfaction with certain aspects of the Coalition Government, including Mr. Lloyd George's leadership; I only finally accepted under strong pressure from the late Sir Austen Chamberlain, who advanced certain reasons, not of a personal character, in favour of my acceptance. The object of this group was, in essence, the same as that of two somewhat similar unofficial organisations within the Conservative Party in Parliament, to both of which I have belonged. These were the Conservative Social Reform Committee, under Mr. F. E. Smith's chairmanship before the 1914 war, and the Tory Reform Committee, which came into existence in the later years of the National Government.

There is a tendency in every political party, especially in parties of the Right, to cling to political thoughts and policy that are outmoded. Equally, Prime Ministers and Leaders of the Opposition are naturally prone to listen to those sections of their Party who will give them no trouble. To oppose this tendency, groups or committees of young and ambitious men and women M.P.s who believe in their own and the Party's future can do valuable work by sweeping aside the cobwebs, countering the purely

"Yes-Man" and giving to their side a sense of youthful vitality and enterprise. Conversely, if they are merely self-seekers and wreckers, they can do great harm. But this was emphatically not true of the three organisations to which I have referred, nor of another group in the '30s under Mr. Churchill's leadership to advocate re-armament, to which I also belonged. "The Group", as we called ourselves, worked cohesively during the 1919 session to support the Government when it needed support against reactionary elements on the Coalition back benches, and received in private the thanks of the Chief Whip. Less palatable to the authorities, but not really resented, was the independent line we took on some matters.

Compared with its pre-1914 predecessors, the House of Commons in 1919 was a very quiet and placid institution, since no great issue divided the parties, and both the Labour and Liberal Oppositions were small and ineffective. The latter, facetiously known as the "Wee Frees", not content with their already exiguous numbers, split into two halves led by Sir Donald Maclean and Mr. George Lambert[1] respectively. The most remarkable feature of Liberalism in the last thirty years has been its masochism. Its members delight in inflicting the maximum of harm upon their Party, its principles and their own electoral prospects, by splitting into mutually hostile fragments whenever possible.

In this tranquil atmosphere—so far as domestic politics were concerned—Parliament passed a number of measures, such as the Government of India Bill, of which I shall have a good deal to say in a later chapter, a Bill to continue conscription and one to create the new Ministry of Health. It also foreshadowed events to come by passing the first of innumerable Transport Acts and also of equally innumerable Housing Acts. The latter was the well-known Addison Housing Bill, called after the late Dr. Addison[2]. Lord Addison was a man of both character and talent, but the housing scheme contained in his Bill was a calamitous failure, and was used for the next thirty years as the classic example of what to avoid in schemes of housing with the aid of grants from public funds.

Outside the House, storms raged at home and abroad. Labour

[1] Now Lord Lambert.   [2] Created Viscount Addison in 1945.

unrest of every kind was prevalent, and there was a railway strike in the late summer. At Versailles, after weeks of bitter wrangling between the Allies, and angry recriminations between them and the Germans, the German Peace Treaty was finally signed on June 28. Mr. Lloyd George seemed to be higher than ever in the esteem of the House of Commons and of his fellow countrymen. When he rose to announce the signature of the treaty in the Commons, the cheers that greeted him were as long, loud and pervasive as any Mr. Churchill received during or after the last war. Once again Members sang "God Save the King", in which only Mr. Neil Maclean, M.P., refused to join; but the Ladies' Gallery made up for this defection by adding, contrary to the rules of the House, their voices to the anthem. However, this mood of exaltation and hero-worship for the Prime Minister soon passed, and before the end of the year there were complaints that he was seen too seldom in the House. He suffered a significant setback in the debate on the adjournment before the recess on August 18, less than two months after his triumphal return from Paris. The incident is described as follows in my diary:

AUGUST 18TH, 1919

L. G.'s speech on the adjournment. He started by a long and rather platitudinous discourse that was a mixture of Philip Kerr[1] and Callisthenes[2] on our national outlook and the need for increased production. . . . The interesting thing about the speech was that while it contained some good matter it utterly failed to thrill or even hold the House, and for the first time in my recollection L. G. didn't produce his own special H. of C. atmosphere; and he knew it! Was it because we are all tired? Or is it because L. G.'s stock is really down with the clay feet of the Idol peeping out?

On December 1, 1919, Lady Astor made her historic entry into Parliament as the first woman M.P., having retained at a by-election the seat held by her husband, who went to the Lords on the death of his father. She remained a member for the same

[1] The late Lord Lothian, who was one of Mr. Lloyd George's principal private secretaries at the time.
[2] The pseudonym of a gentleman who wrote the advertisements of Selfridge Stores in the newspapers.

seat for over a quarter of a century, and earned the affection and respect of the whole House despite frequent participations in "scenes" and a style of speech which, though witty, was usually both irrelevant and too discursive. The admittance of women M.P.s during the last thirty-three years has confounded alike both the pessimists and the optimists among the prophets of the early days of the Women's Suffrage Movement. It has not, as some feared, lowered the tone of the House or produced a "Women's vote for Women". Most women electors vote, like men, according to their political views and not on sex grounds. The presence of women M.P.s has not notably advanced the cause of women as such, though the feminine vote in the constituencies has undoubtedly done so—on the whole to the advantage of the whole nation. There has been no great woman orator among M.P.s who could hold a "full house" in the Commons and sway opinion there and outside. There have been, on the other hand, many successful woman Ministers, notably the late Miss Margaret Bondfield, the late Miss Ellen Wilkinson, Dr. Edith Summerskill and Miss Florence Horsbrugh.

Women in the Commons suffer from a disadvantage I have never seen discussed in print, though it is perfectly obvious to every close observer of its proceedings. The House of Commons has what may be termed a Restoration Comedy relish for a phrase or statement made in all innocence which can be turned into a bawdy joke. It greets such remarks with so much loud laughter that the Press, for obvious reasons, has often to ignore the incident altogether. Most of the victims in the last thirty years have been women M.P.s, and I have often felt, however much I may have been amused, sorry alike for the individual concerned and the other women M.P.s sitting there silent and embarrassed at their colleague's predicament, often made worse by the fact that in some instances she had not the slightest idea at what the House was laughing. An extract from my diary on February 23, 1919, illustrates what I mean, though the debate occurred before there were any woman M.P.s:

Particularly amusing debate on the Dogs Bill fathered by "Peckham".[1] This was the Report Stage, and in passionate terms he talked

[1] The nickname (because of his Constituency) of the late Sir Frederick Banbury, M.P., afterwards Lord Banbury.

of "The Dog; the friend of man". To this an irreverent interrupter said, "What about the monkey the ancestor of man?"

Then the fun began. One Elliot,[1] a Scotch doctor, the Scots Greys M.O. with a very fine war record, accused John Butcher[2] who supported the Bill of being concerned with a German Princess —Princess Löwenstein-Wertheim—on the Dogs' Protection League. Butcher was furious, the House hilarious. After several humorous (conscious and unconscious) speeches, Butcher rose and said quite seriously amid shouts of laughter, "I have not had intimate relations with this lady".

The comment of keen feminists would, I suppose, be that only when the majority of M.P.s are women will the House of Commons cleanse its mind and cease to be amused at ribald jokes; but that day looks like being a long way off.

The session of 1920 opened quietly and somewhat dully, which was not surprising, as there was no big issue of principle between the huge Government majority and the small, factious, and divided opposition of "Wee Frees", Labour members and the remnants of the Irish Nationalist Party; but this did not prevent squalls on occasions, as the following extract from my diary shows:

FEBRUARY 4TH, 1920

Little Benn[3] made an impassioned attack on the extension of D.O.R.A.[4] to Ireland. He quoted Fox. I produced an anti-climax (vide *The Times*) by asking him to quote Pitt's reply; he wouldn't. Old T. P.[5] made a very dishonest and foolish speech about Ireland and Poland. I replied and I believe that I trounced him well. Anyway the Speaker congratulated me next day.

The holder of the great office of Speaker has to repress his feelings, at least in public, but every Speaker, in my experience, has his own method of expressing approval or disapproval of the content of speeches. Mr. Speaker Lowther's took the pleasant form of telling young or new members, in private, if and when

[1] Now the Rt. Hon. Walter Elliot, C.H., M.P.
[2] The late Sir John Butcher, M.P. [3] Now Lord Stansgate.
[4] The Defence of the Realm Act.
[5] Mr. T. P. O'Connor, known as "Tay Pay", one of my predecessors as "Father of the House".

they went to talk to him, whether he thought they had spoken well or badly, and how the debate in which they had spoken had gone. Both Mr. Speaker Fitzroy and Mr. Speaker Clifton Brown had their particular methods of showing disapproval of bad, tedious and too lengthy speeches. Mr. Speaker Fitzroy would remark to himself in a voice audible at least to the two front benches "What a speech", or "When is this boring fellow going to sit down?" Returning to the Chair after his dinner he once said to the Deputy-Speaker of the time, "You might have called this dreary woman as I asked you as soon as I left the Chair to have my dinner. Now I suppose I shall have to listen to fifteen minutes of the invariable nonsense which she talks!" Mr. Speaker Clifton Brown drummed angrily and repetitively with his fingers on the sides of his chair when he thought a speech had lasted too long—a frequently effective method of unofficial closuring. It is a tribute to the fairness of Speakers of the House of Commons that they give the male and female bores, of which that assembly contains, as is natural, a proportion, their reasonable share of speaking. Sometimes I have suspected them of deliberately "calling" a bore after a stormy scene in order that he or she may empty the House and give members a chance of cooling down.

The mention of Mr. Wedgwood Benn in the extract from my diary affords an opportunity of describing his work and that of others in the 1918 Parliament who followed the tactics of mosquito attacks upon the Coalition Government. Lord Stansgate, as he now is, has always loved opposition, at which he is an adept; he has been less successful in Office. His occasional undue aggressiveness, to use a mild term, is forgiven him because of his lovable personal character and fine record in the 1914 war. He will go down to history as the subject of one of Mr. Churchill's most famous phrases. Lord Stansgate is a small man who works himself into a paroxysm of indignation over some alleged grievance. "The Honourable Member", Mr. Churchill once said, "should not engender more heat than he can contain".

Lt.-Commander Kenworthy, M.P. (now Lord Strabolgi) was a persistent, and at times effective, critic of the Lloyd George Government. *Punch* of the day described him as a "hullaballoonist". It is an apt description of Lord Strabolgi to-day. During his long political life, first as a Liberal and then as a Socialist, he has always seen in the action of any Government to which he is opposed a dark and sinister plot against the forces of light. He has one piece of powerful and personal political armament. He is utterly impervious to ridicule, of which he has been a constant target.

A very different and most complex character who attacked the Government with vigour was Colonel Wedgwood.[1] It is hard in the space available to describe him adequately. A man of great integrity, with a most kind, affectionate and generous nature, known to his myriad of friends as "Josh", he belied in public his real character; for in the intense espousal of causes in which he believed, such as self-government for India, and Zionism, he was often grossly unfair and offensive. He was also at times unbalanced. I once saw him as he was leaving the Chamber after a debate, kick a Conservative member, Mr. Mitchell Banks,[2] on the shin with the remark "Take that, you swine!" The latter said nothing, the Chairman of Committees discreetly averted his eyes, no one raised a point of order so the incident passed unreported. Mr. Banks's sole offence had been to attack Zionism in debate. With a fine record in the First World War, Colonel Wedgwood yet consistently maintained on Foreign Affairs the attitude of a pacifist and Little Englander. He was a poor speaker and a failure when in office, but for all his faults was beloved in the House of Commons. He was the founder of the History of Parliament Trust, which is now an officially recognised institution.

Two persistent "Wee Free" critics of the Government were Messrs. Hogge and Pringle. The Liberal Press, eager to seize upon any evidence of youthful vigour in the Parliamentary Party during the early years of its decline, "wrote them up" as successful parliamentarians with a great future, and even suggested that Mr. Pringle had invented a new form of activity by his skill in asking supplementary questions known as "pringling". Neither man had a really successful parliamentary position, and both are completely forgotten to-day. A far more formidable adversary of the Government was one of its nominal supporters—Lord Robert Cecil.[3] He could find little good to say of it, notwithstand-

[1] Afterwards Lord Wedgwood.   [2] Later Sir Reginald Mitchell Banks.
[3] Now Lord Cecil of Chelwood.

ing that he had been a member of the war-time Coalition Government. Though his parliamentary gifts were great, as I have written earlier, he gave an impression of personal disappointment and bitterness, and did not improve his position in the House. An opponent of a different kind was Mr. (now Sir) Oswald Mosley, who crossed the floor to join the Socialist Party soon after his election as a Conservative M.P. Despite his grave faults, for which he has paid dearly, he was a first-class debater, able to make an angry House, however bitterly opposed to him on both public and personal grounds, listen to his views.

Among Ministerial successes at this stage of the 1919 Parliament was Sir Alfred Mond.[1] With a very acute brain, an excellent taste in art, and a humorous and charming manner and method in debate and in answering questions, he held the esteem of the House and made an excellent First Commissioner of Works. He also had great moral courage. An eccentric Scottish peer who, *inter alia*, believed that fairies inhabited his castle and appeared on the staircase to welcome him from time to time, had a dispute with the Ministry, and in a personal letter to Sir Alfred stated that his ancestors had forcibly extracted the teeth of the race to which he (Sir Alfred) belonged, and that he would stand no nonsense from such a man. Very properly, Sir Alfred, so rumour said at the time, sent the letter to the King, who ordered his strong displeasure to be conveyed to the peer for writing so offensively to one of his Ministers.

During the session of 1920 there was the usual trouble in the coal mines, the usual new legislation to try to appease the miners and the usual declaration (in this case in a speech on the Address made by a respected miners' M.P., Mr. William Brace) that only nationalisation of the mines would satisfy the miners and produce peace in the coalfields. There was also, an event that was to become the normal rule in the next twenty years, a tremendous row between the Prime Minister and a "Press Lord"—in this instance Lord Northcliffe. The personal attacks of the Northcliffe Press on the Prime Minister died down after Mr. Lloyd George had made a furious counter-attack in the Commons on Lord Northcliffe. Pausing dramatically in the course of his speech he said, "There is reason to believe that the noble Lord is . . ." and

[1] Afterwards the first Lord Melchett.

he tapped his forehead. It is a tribute to the reticence of the British Press that not a word of this was stated in print at the time; in the United States such an unprecedented form of attack by a leading statesman on a famous newspaper proprietor would have been front-page news.

A Bill establishing the Ministry of Health had been passed after considerable opposition from some Government supporters. Friction developed between individual right-wing members of the Conservative party and left-wing members such as Lady Astor and Lord Henry Bentinck. The former's particular *bêtes noires* were Sir Frederick Banbury,[1] who might be described as a legendary "back-woodsman", and Mr. Macquisten, a talented and witty Scottish K.C., who believed (though not in a personal sense) in the virtues of alcoholic liquor, whereas Lady Astor believes it is the main source of all the evil in the world. Many angry scenes, both in Committee upstairs and in the House, occurred between these protagonists, usually to the great amusement of the onlookers. But the main troubles the Government experienced in this session were outside Britain or, at any rate, England. The Government's foreign policy and Lord Curzon's handling of it as Foreign Secretary were attacked at intervals alike by political foes and friends. There was particularly heavy criticism of His Majesty's Government's direct or indirect support of Kolchak and Denikin's military attempts, with the aid of White Russians, to overthrow the Bolshevist régime.

Mr. Churchill, who was Secretary of State for War, got into trouble with Socialists and "Wee Frees" alike for a speech in which he said that peace with Soviet Russia was only another form of war and apparently (to quote from *Punch*) invited the co-operation of German militarists to fight the Bolshevists. To-day such a statement would excite little comment; indeed, it would seem very up-to-date, except that we are tactful enough to refrain from calling the future members of the new German Army militarists. But the War Secretary's speech raised a furious clamour in the House, and Mr. Lloyd George had considerable difficulty in defending him. History, as has been so often and so boringly pointed out, is full of irony; it is, therefore, not surprising that Mr. Churchill's political career, which is an essential

[1] Afterwards Lord Banbury.

part of British history in the last half-century, also contains ironical contrasts. His speech in July, 1920, was distant in time from Yalta and his speech at Fulton; but the streams of his fertile ideas flowed parallel, if not in exact confluence, in his 1920 and Fulton speeches. The Yalta decisions went in an opposite direction.[1] In justice to him, however, it must be recorded that at Yalta he was in a terrible dilemma. He could not fundamentally alter President Roosevelt's terrible misinterpretation of the Soviet's ultimate aim, unless he was prepared to risk smashing the whole Alliance.

The Government had a heavy loss of votes from their own side and a defeat in the Lords in a debate on the Dyer incident.[2] Mr. Edwin Montagu, Secretary of State for India, defended his own action skilfully, and I think he was right, though many of my constituents with Indian experience disagreed with me. Though General Dyer stopped the rioting and the danger to the life of British and Indian officials, I believe less drastic methods might have succeeded equally well.

In this year 1920 and later, some of the members of the "Group" to which I have referred earlier, who had served in the Middle East in the war, such as Mr. Ormsby-Gore, the late Mr. Walter Guinness and I, were seriously concerned at the turn events were taking. With the advice of Colonel T. E. Lawrence (under whom I had served) and the powerful help of Mr. R. D. Blumenfeld and the *Daily Express*, of which he was editor, we launched a modest campaign in and out of Parliament to call attention to the confusion caused by the difference between the Balfour Declaration in regard to Palestine and the Sykes-Picot Agreement.[3] The Government at the time denied that there was any such difference, and many good friends of mine, who have held high office—some of whom are still alive—have often engaged in furious private controversy with me over this issue, by denying that there is any discrepancy between the two agreements. But I had the melancholy satisfaction of hearing the late Mr. Ernest

[1] See also Chapter XVII, p. 243.

[2] General Dyer was compulsorily retired from the Indian Army for giving orders to fire on a riotous mob of Sikhs at Amritsar. The firing caused heavy casualties.

[3] The agreement between the late Sir Mark Sykes for Britain and the late M. Picot for France defining British, French and Arab spheres of influence in the Middle East.

Bevin, in one of his speeches on Palestine in the 1945 Parliament, frankly admit, without contradiction from anyone, that the two sets of promises conflicted. The *Daily Express* headed one of its leading articles supporting our case with the caption "The Muddled East". The caption was a happy one and still applicable to-day. Few British Foreign Secretaries, Colonial Secretaries or their official advisers in the last thirty years can escape some blame for the setbacks, and in some case disasters, that have overtaken British policy in that area. The treatment of devoted British servants on the spot has been calamitous. For instance, Sir Reginald Wingate, the late Lord Allenby and the late Sir Henry MacMahon were successively compulsorily removed by the Foreign Secretary of the day from the official position of chief British representative in Egypt, and a similar procedure was adopted in the case of the late Lord Lloyd. In July, the French expelled from Damascus the Emir Feisal (afterwards King Feisal I of Iraq). Mr. Ormsby-Gore, supported by me, objected to this course in a speech on the adjournment. I was, incidentally, very accurately pictured in *Punch* over the caption "An Arabian Knight at home" in an Arab head-dress exactly similar to the one I actually wore in the Arab revolt! In reply, Mr. Bonar Law denied that His Majesty's Government had any right of interference in the matter. There was an interesting sequel to this debate. About ten months later, the late Lord Lothian (Mr. Lloyd George's principal private secretary at the time) said to me one day, "The Prime Minister has authorised me to tell you in the strictest secrecy that he is prepared to offer the crown of Iraq to your friend Feisal if he will accept it. He will not offer it unless he is sure of the Emir's acceptance. Can you unofficially get a promise from him?" This I did, with the invaluable aid of Colonel Lawrence, Lord Harlech and the late Lord Moyne, at 3 a.m. in my house in the country after five hours' continuous discussion. King Feisal was a brave, most talented and charming man, and one of the greatest gentlemen I have ever met, but like most geniuses he was temperamental. For hours, to all our collective persuasion he made the same answer. He was sick of politics, especially European politics, and indeed of all Europeans except personal friends such as ourselves. He had been abominably treated in Damascus; was there any reason to believe we should treat him any better in Baghdad? At last he assented to our request and said he believed Iraq and Britain could and should work together, which would be his great aim in his new position.

The Government's greatest and most dramatic difficulties were over Ireland. In March, 1919, the Government had brought in a Bill which established Parliaments for both Southern and Northern Ireland, with a joint council as a link and the reservation of certain powers to the Imperial Parliament at Westminster. It created intense controversy and did not receive Royal Assent until December 23, 1920. Meanwhile there had been an appalling deterioration in the situation. The memories of the Easter Rising[1] were still a suppurating sore. Sinn Fein mourned its casualties and made them into national heroes; even the tolerant English, so quick to forgive those who fight against them, were furious at this attempted "stab in the back" in one of the most critical periods of the war. During 1920 what was, in effect, an alternative Government was set up by Sinn Fein. The Government applied a form of martial law and to aid the Royal Irish Constabulary, that magnificent body of men who had hitherto never failed to deal with any situation, established a special armed force of picked men derisively known as the "Black and Tans". They met violence with violence, being as "quick on the draw" as any sheriff's posse in a Western film. But in creating the force the Government made the psychological mistake of forgetting that the humane English will never allow the forces of law and order to use the same methods of unrestrained ferocity against actual or potential revolutionaries that are required to stop a rising. If it were not so, we should still be in India and Palestine. It was legitimate, so runs the peculiar English reasoning, to kill in Hamburg in a week 60,000 German civilians by bombing and by the fire caused by bombing, because we were at war with their country; but when Indians or Palestinian Jews, or Southern Irish, assassinate or torture Englishmen trying to do their duty by restoring law and order, you must not allow the police or troops under their command to show equal craft and cruelty, even if it

[1] During Easter 1916 there was an attempted rising by Sinn Fein—the Irish Revolutionary body. There were casualties on the sides of both the insurgents and the police and military. Sir Roger Casement and others were executed for their part in it.

does end the rebellion; that would put us wrong with the world and our own consciences. So the Black and Tans were the constant target of angry questions in Parliament, where it was alleged that outrages had been committed by them. It was a bit·hard on them, since they were in constant danger of being shot in the back, as many were, in Ireland.

A number of members of our "group" visited Dublin as the guests of Mr. Ernest Guinness in the spring of 1921. We were appalled by what we saw. The Lord Lieutenant and his devoted and most able Civil Servant assistants, Sir John Cope and Sir John Anderson,[1] were virtually prisoners in the Castle. The Dublin division of the Black and Tans, housed in most uncomfortable barracks, could not go out save in a lorry with rifles at the ready, whilst the double sentries at the gate stood back to back to avoid being shot from behind. We communicated our views to Mr. Lloyd George in a private interview and told him that the new Act could never be implemented. At that time he did not share our views, and the Chief Secretary[2] to the Lord Lieutenant showed a wholly unjustified optimism in the Commons, constantly repeating a phrase which became a grim House of Commons' joke: "We've got them on the run". At last, in the summer of 1921, when the campaign of murder, arson, hunger-strike by Irish political prisoners, and terrorism with savage reprisals by the Black and Tans and the British Army, were at their height, Mr. Lloyd George opened negotiations with Sir James Craig[3] for Northern Ireland and with Mr. De Valera for Sinn Fein and the South. The eventual result was the Irish Treaty, which recognised the separate entities of Northern Ireland (inside the British Commonwealth and a part of the United Kingdom) and Southern Ireland—at first not nominally, but actually, and in later years, as to-day, both actually and nominally—outside the British Empire and Commonwealth. After the treaty was signed Mr. Lloyd George both literally (by clasping in turn the hands of the Irish delegates) and figuratively "shook hands with murder", which he had asserted in Parliament he would never do. In this *volte face* he is not an isolated historical

[1] Now Lord Waverley.
[2] The late Lord Greenwood, then the Rt. Hon. Hamar Greenwood, M.P.
[3] Afterwards the first Lord Craigavon.

figure. Many a British statesman and many a distinguished soldier, sailor and airman has in recent years shaken hands with former leaders of enemies or revolutionaries after having previously described them as more evil than the devil. The only thing quite certain about this cruel and fantastic world ever since 1914 is that present enemies, whether their enmity takes the form of war or rebellion, may become future allies and present allies future enemies. I remember, as a soldier in the 1914 war, how we were deluged with propaganda about our allies "The gallant little Japs", and the "Brave Italians who like Garibaldi, their national hero, would face any odds". Twenty-five years later the Japanese were officially described as a race of foul and brutal monsters, and the Italians as cowards to the core. I have no doubt that the advantages of the Irish Treaty outweighed the disadvantages. For reasons also mentioned in a previous chapter, British public opinion would have prevented any Government from fighting a real war to re-conquer Ireland. Anti-militarism, too, was at its height in Britain in 1921–2. The intake of regular Army recruits from 1918 onwards was of poor quality; some British Army units, bearing honoured names with a splendid record of service in the 1914 and 1939 wars, made as poor a showing in operation against the Irish rebels as their predecessors had done against the American rebels in 1774. Their hearts were not in the fight. We could not afford then, any more than we can to-day, to earn the permanent hostility of the majority of Southern Irish in Ireland, or of the big Southern Irish population in the United States and Australia. Of course the loyalists in the South suffered. I am afraid that those who stand by Britain just before she evacuates a country always do suffer. Some Indian and Pakistani friends of mine, who were on our side all through the years of trouble and terrorism in India from the 1920's to the evacuation, have caustic comments to make in private on this subject. At least the Southern Irish loyalists suffered less than the American loyalists after the War of Independence. Though both British and American histories are unduly reticent on the subject, neither the young United States in 1778 nor the British Government of 1920 showed up to advantage. After the War of Independence was over, the supporters of King George, whose only crime was that of allegiance to him whom they regarded as their rightful King, were physically molested, their property confiscated and in some cases their houses burnt. They fled destitute in tens of thousands—men, women and children—to Canada, where they proudly termed themselves, as do their descendants (many in positions of great power and responsibility) to-day, United Empire Loyalists. The British Government did nothing whatever to help them before or after their departure.

Naturally, the Irish Treaty caused heart-burnings in the Conservative Party. M.P.s like myself who voted for it lost a number of supporters. The "Diehards" of the day, under the influential leadership of the late Col. Gretton[1] and Mr. Rupert Gwynne, put up a fight in the Commons, but in the Division lobby were defeated by 343 votes. The voting was closer in the Lords: 166 For, 47 Against. The scene in the Lords is thus described in my diary:

Carson delivered a most biting, embittered attack on the Treaty and on Curzon, whom he accused of betrayal. From an oratorical point of view he was splendid, from a national point of view deplorable. It was a dramatic scene. Carson with all the old incomparable fighting force. The crowded red benches with so many of one's friends on them—Salisbury, Midleton, Alan Northumberland, etc.; F. E.[2] aloof and inscrutable on the Woolsack; the press of eldest sons and Privy Councillors on the steps of the throne; the crowded Peeresses' gallery full partly of young and beautiful women, partly of old and sad ones listening with anguish to Carson's tale of woe; the eager M.P. listeners at the bar; a great occasion.

Lord Carson (he had been made a Peer only a few months earlier) lost some influence in Ulster by that speech; henceforth the Ulstermen looked more to the wise, firm, unemotional leadership of Sir James Craig.[3] Gradually Lord Carson faded into the background as a leading political figure.

No assembly changes so quickly from grave to gay or vice versa as the House of Commons. On a day during this period when things in Ireland were at their worst, there was, during question time, a whole series of scenes, with the Speaker constantly on his feet. Questions and answers which mainly dealt with the activi-

[1] Afterwards Lord Gretton. [2] Lord Birkenhead.
[3] Afterwards Lord Craigavon—their first Prime Minister.

ties of the Black and Tans were greeted with shouts of "Tyrants!" and "Murderers!" from the Irish Nationalists and the Labour Party directed against the Government and Dublin Castle, and cries of "Rebels!" and "Cowardly Assassins!" came from us about Sinn Fein. Once the two sides were on the verge of fisti-cuffs. Then the ordeal of the Chief Secretary ended, and the next question—to another Minister—was reached. It was to ask what was the condition of affairs in Austria then, as now, under Allied occupation. The reply was that there had been a great change for the better in recent weeks: there had been no political murders, no attacks upon the occupying troops, no attempt to derail trains, and no cases of arson, whilst the relationship between the occupation authorities and the local inhabitants showed a pro-gressive and gratifying improvement. Mr. "Jerry" McVeagh, M.P., then rose and in his strong Irish brogue, which his enemies said was that of a stage Irishman, solemnly said: "Can the Right Honourable Gentleman give an assurance that all this is a long, long way from Tipperary?" There were shouts of laughter from members in all parts of the House, and for the rest of question time all was gaiety and good humour.

The remainder of the 1921 session largely followed a pattern that was becoming painfully familiar at the time and has become even more painfully familiar over thirty years later, to-day. There was industrial and economic trouble of every kind. There was a serious and total strike in the mines with the usual stop-gap solution to end it after the usual lachrymose appeals by Ministers to employees and employers alike to remember that the country was being ruined. "The Geddes Axe"[1] was wielded to cut down expenditure in order to avert national bankruptcy, so it was claimed. Among the victims of the axe were the farmers, who lost their guaranteed price for wheat under the Corn Production Acts (Repeal) Bill. Even at this distance of time I regret having voted for this Bill and not having opposed it with all my might. I did not realise at the time, though I should have, how grievous the effect on agriculture would be. The housing situation was desperate. Mr. Addison, having failed to provide houses, became Minister without Portfolio. His leading Government colleagues in

[1] So called because Sir Eric Geddes, Chairman of the National Expenditure Committee, devised the measures for the Cabinet.

both Houses found it hard exactly to define where his duties began and ended, as do the colleagues of the present Ministers of Co-ordination to explain the beginning and end of their duties. There was one of the inevitable Unemployment Insurance Amendment Bills. There was a furious and open quarrel between France and Great Britain over the French occupation of the Ruhr. The unfortunate Lord Curzon, Foreign Secretary, was again the subject of almost universal attack over this matter, though few of his critics agreed among themselves. A moderate Tariff Bill—the Safeguarding of Industries Bill—introduced by a modest and unassuming Minister, Mr. Stanley Baldwin, President of the Board of Trade, produced loud lamentations from the official Liberal Party on the ground that the sacred edifice of Free Trade was again being undermined. At this period the "Wee Frees" were trying desperately to prove how out-of-date were their views and policies alike—an activity their successors are still pursuing. Finally, there were two Government pronouncements which will not sound unfamiliar to members of either House to-day. His Majesty's Government were seriously considering the reform of the Lords; and the railways were in a dangerous financial position and had been losing money even before the 1914 war.

There were many changes in the personnel of the Commons through the disappearance or temporary eclipse of well-known figures and the emergence of others. Mr. Speaker Lowther, after a long and honourable occupancy of the Chair, resigned and became Lord Ullswater. Mr. Speaker Whitley succeeded. I took a modest part behind the scenes in securing his nomination, for which he was good enough to thank me. His potential opponent (though his name was never officially put forward) was the late Sir Frederick Banbury,[1] who, in my opinion, did not possess the requisite qualities for the post. Yet Mr. Speaker Whitley proved a disappointment to many of his backers besides myself. He never had the power over the House possessed by his immediate predecessor, or by his successor, Mr. Fitzroy. Moreover, many Conservatives mistrusted him because of his allegedly partial handling of a difficult situation when he was in the Chair before the 1914 war. He was accused of allowing a debate to continue,

[1] Afterwards Lord Banbury.

having been suddenly apprised by the Chief Liberal Whip (in a whisper from the Front Bench) that the Government were without a majority in the House, after he had "collected the voices"—in other words, put the question. The allegation was that he "called" a Liberal member in order to give time to bring ministerial supporters to Westminster, when the House, by its rules, should have at once proceeded to divide. I do not myself think that he intended to act against the rules, but he certainly appeared to do so.

Mr. Walter Long, a familiar figure for so many years in the Commons, went, like Lord Carson, to the Lords in 1921. Mr. Bonar Law retired from the Government because of ill health, and Mr. Austen Chamberlain succeeded him as leader of the Conservative Party. Mr. Bonar Law recovered sufficiently to make a most useful speech from the back benches in support of the Irish Treaty. Sir Gordon Hewart[1] was a brilliant success as Attorney-General, as were the late Sir Robert Horne as Chancellor of the Exchequer, and Mr. Hylton Young[2] as Financial Secretary to the Treasury.

Mr. Clynes made a dignified and responsible leader of the Labour Party, whilst one of his followers, the late Mr. Jack Jones, M.P., became one of the best conscious humorists in the House, especially when in one of his over-convivial moods. He was sometimes very offensive, and frequently involved in scenes, but he had a real and genuine wit—on the whole not an unkindly one. In contrast to him was one who might be described as an extremist of pre-1914 days—the late Colonel John Ward, M.P. With a fine record as an amateur soldier in the war he shed all his anti-Imperialist prejudices as a result of his experience. A magnificent figure of a man, with all the best attributes of a British wage-earner, much respected in all quarters of the House, in his rough, homely voice he fiercely attacked again and again his former pacifist and Little-Englander colleagues in the Labour Party.

[1] Afterwards Lord Hewart, Chief Justice from 1922 to 1940.
[2] Now Lord Kennet.

CHAPTER IX

THE parliamentary session of 1922, that year of political crisis and excitement, opened quietly so far as the debate on the Address was concerned; but two great and menacing shadows lay over the Government and the country.

The first was Ireland. The signature of the Treaty had not ended the trouble of that blood-stained country. An internecine war broke out between the moderates and the extremists of Sinn Fein, in which Michael Collins, the most able and charming of the rebels (if a man who was responsible for the death of many Irish policemen and British soldiers doing their duty to their King can be called charming), and other moderates were killed. With the British Government powerless to restore law and order, and Sinn Fein torn by dissension, Southern Ireland was in a state of anarchy. In the North, also, there were murderous attacks on police and Protestants, but under Sir James Craig order was eventually restored and, from then onwards, the Northern Irish Government never lost its power to suppress those who sought to destroy its constitution by violence. It treated with contempt then, as it does to-day, those in the British House of Commons and elsewhere who believe that the enemies of Ulster's status as an integral part of the British Empire should be treated with "kisses and kindness", even when they have revolvers in their hands and bombs in their pockets. In the summer, Field-Marshal Sir Henry Wilson, M.P., was assassinated by a couple of Southern Irishmen as he left his house in Eaton Square. He was in uniform and, as he fell, he tried to draw his sword. At imminent risk of being shot, two road-workers pursued the assassins; there are few countries in the world where such cool courage and sense of duty would be shown in peace-time. The conduct of these two men made a profound impression, and was in striking contrast to the attitude of the "man in the street" in Southern Ireland who usually hurried, with eyes averted, from any assassination he had witnessed in order to avoid getting into trouble with either side. The two murderers were eventually arrested and hanged. Sir Henry Wilson was an Ulsterman and a great soldier, but a somewhat controversial one who disliked his political chiefs, whom he described as "frocks". When I once told him, in one of the few conversations I had with him, that regimental officers like myself in the war had the same feeling of contempt for most staff officers in the higher ranks such as himself, he smiled good-naturedly. His death, which shocked the country, caused an angry debate in the Commons. "What", members asked, "were the Government doing to protect us from the murderous attacks of Irish revolutionaries?" As a result, security measures were tightened. Not until December, 1922, under the Bonar Law Government, did the Irish Constitution become promulgated by decree and both parties to it settle down to comparative peace.

The other dark and gloomy shadow was the state of India. In 1909 there had been a very tentative advance towards self-government through the Morley-Minto reforms[1] which abolished the official majority in the Provincial Councils. In 1919 a new Government of India Act, usually known as the Montagu-Chelmsford Act,[2] became law. This Act was based upon Mr. Montagu's announcement of 1917, which was, in fact, embodied in the preamble to the 1919 Act. This included the phrases, "The increasing association of Indians in every branch of the administration", and "The gradual development of self-governing institutions with a view to the progressive realisation of responsible government in British India as an integral part of the Empire". Though in some important respects the 1919 Act departed from the Montagu-Chelmsford Declaration, its main features were based upon it and were as follows:

The greatest possible popular control in local bodies.

A large measure of devolution of powers to provincial Governments and Legislatures, and the institution of 'dyarchy'—the division of subjects between those transferred to Indian Ministers and those reserved to official control by the Governor.

The continuing responsibility to Parliament of the Government

[1] So called because Lord Morley was Secretary of State for India and Lord Minto Viceroy.
[2] Lord Chelmsford being Viceroy and Mr. Edwin Montagu Secretary of State for India.

of India, coupled with the enlargement of the Indian Legislative Council to which greater powers of influencing Government were assigned.

The gradual relaxation of the control of Parliament and the Secretary of State over the Government of India and provincial Governments, in proportion as the foregoing changes took effect.

Unhappily, trouble and disorder marked the inauguration of the new constitution; not only was India cut in two "by a great volcanic rift", as I once said in introducing the Indian estimates, by Hindu-Moslem hatred and rivalry leading to riots, burnings, tortures and murders, but there was something else. "Gandhiism", in the shape of Mr. Gandhi's remarkable personality, creed and influence, was a most disturbing factor in the Indian situation in the early '20s and for years afterwards. Put succinctly, his maxims and creed were as follows:

(a) Simplicity of life, self-abnegation, kindness to all mankind and animals, avoidance of all violence and hate, the universality of God, together with the common purpose and ethics of all religions, were the key to personal happiness and harmonious human relationship;

(b) The British must be got out of India but only by "non-violence". There must be disobedience to unjust laws, hunger-fasts, impediment of traffic by squatting in the road, etc.

Unfortunately, his millions of followers, unable exactly to understand what (b) meant, did their best by methods which were often far from "non-violent" to make the maintenance of law and order impossible, and he and they were frequently sent to jail.

Up to the day of his assassination, Gandhi was the subject of furious controversy in Britain. Some, including many clergy, with over-simple minds, believed him to be the greatest follower of Our Lord since the Apostles. Others regarded him as many regarded Premier Stalin in his day—as a double-dealing, sinister, all-powerful revolutionary. I never met him, but my long years of official experience at the India Office convince me that, notwithstanding his exceptional gifts and many virtues, including his courageous rebukes to his own fellow-countrymen for their faults of character, his attitude under Article (a) was in such contrast to that under Article (*b*), thereby causing unnecessary suffering and harm, that his behaviour can only be explained on one of three suppositions:

(1) that he was a conscious hypocrite;

(2) that he was an unconscious hypocrite;

(3) that he was mentally deranged.

Being charitable, I prefer the second theory.

Mr. Edwin Montagu was a man of great ability, idealism and charm, who had a natural sympathy with the East, based, I think, partly upon his Jewish blood. He believed in appeasement rather than the "strong arm". He was not wholly popular with the Conservative Party in Parliament, and was mistrusted by the "Diehards". So was Lord Reading, the Viceroy. I once heard a "Diehard" say in private that India was being lost because two Jews, one in Whitehall and one in Delhi, were afraid to grapple with the extremists. This was a gross libel, but Mr. Montagu's position in Parliament deteriorated as Gandhiism increased in violence. Sir W. Joynson-Hicks,[1] in a debate on the Address in the 1922 session, said Montagu had "broken the heart of the Indian Civil Service", and, in the same debate, Mr. Rupert Gwynne compared him in turn to a mole and a hippopotamus. On March 9 it was announced that, at the Prime Minister's request, he had resigned for having authorised the Government of India to publish a statement advocating, in the interests of Anglo-Moslem friendship, a revision of the Turkish Treaty of peace. The House, being in one of those, happily, rare moods when it is unfair and ungenerous to an individual, cheered the announcement ecstatically.

Mr. Montagu was succeeded by the late Lord Peel as Secretary of State, with myself as Under-Secretary of State in the Commons. As recorded earlier, I at first refused the post, because of growing concern at the general conduct of events by the Prime Minister and the Government; but eventually, under pressure from Mr. Austen Chamberlain, I accepted it, salving my conscience by the fact that I was not a "Diehard" over India and sympathised with the official policy. The House of Commons, always most kind to me in my long membership, was generous, as was the Press to the "poacher turned gamekeeper" as *Punch*

[1] Afterwards Lord Brentford.

called me; that journal had a cartoon entitled "The new Mahout" showing me guiding an elephant with Lord Peel in the howdah. Helped by this sympathy, I managed to sustain, during the spring and summer of 1922, the onerous task of representing single-handed a great Department of State in the House of Commons, piloting the new Constitution of Burma Bill, getting the Indian Estimates passed, and answering scores of questions each week, mostly hostile ones from Conservative "Diehards", who disliked the new constitution. My principal Conservative opponent was a charming and genial, if not highly intelligent, old gentleman called Colonel Yates, M.P. for Melton Mowbray. He enjoyed a reputation in the House, where he was very popular, as an expert on Indian affairs—a qualification denied him by some of his contemporaries in the Indian Army. Knowing that his constant denigration of Lord Reading and the Government of India was doing harm, I decided to put him in his place and gave a very offensive but effective reply to one of his supplementaries. Almost the whole Conservative Party roared its disapproval, the Press criticised me next day, and Colonel Yates sat red, gasping and at a loss for any retort. From henceforth he tackled me more warily.

I was well served by my Private Secretaries both Civil Service and Parliamentary. The former was Mr. Gilbert Laithwaite,[1] and the latter Lord Ednam (now Lord Dudley), and I could not have found a better or more congenial staff to work with than that in the India Office—a government itself in microcosm. Its members and I had our moments of humour amid the grim preoccupations of the Indian situation. I had a huge mail each day, and among it was once a letter from an Indian resident in Algiers. It ran as follows: "My Lord, Please advise me. Every time I read a speech by Mr. Lloyd George it makes me so angry I want to go out and murder someone; what am I to do?" I sent a "rag" minute to a distinguished Civil Servant in the office, asking if he thought the writer was mad or sane. To this he replied, "Parliamentary Under-Secretary of State—I hope that the writer is sane as, until I ceased reading them, the Prime Minister's speeches had the same effect on me. Signed . . ." (with initials).

[1] Now Sir Gilbert Laithwaite, British High Commissioner to Pakistan.

The growing tension within the Conservative Party was shown by an incident in the early spring of 1922. Sir George Younger, M.P.,[1] was Chairman of the Conservative Party. Small, sturdy, highly efficient, full of humour and completely fearless, he was immensely popular in the Party. He was deeply concerned at the growing disagreement among Conservative members of both Houses as to whether or not to continue to support the Coalition, and was very critical of Mr. Lloyd George's leadership, so much so that the latter threatened in private to resign if Sir George remained in his post. Eventually a temporary truce between them was arranged. But the event which really started the avalanche that eventually overwhelmed the Coalition and once and for all ended Mr. Lloyd George's official career was the incident of the Robinson Peerage. The late Sir John Robinson was a wealthy man who was alleged, rightly or wrongly, to have amassed his South African fortune by dubious means. It is only fair to his memory to say that almost all the Rand magnates of those days had the same charge brought against them—usually by unsuccessful rivals. The announcement of the conferment of a peerage upon him in the Birthday Honours of 1922, and information which leaked out that just prior to the conferment he had subscribed a huge sum to the "Lloyd George Fund"—a party fund for the benefit of the Prime Minister's Liberal followers—caused furious indignation. The Duke of Northumberland, a young man of great promise and courage whose untimely death in 1930 all his friends deplored, raised in the Lords the question of how recommendations to the Crown for honours were made and asked whether money payments were previously extracted by the Government from those whose names were submitted. Similar questions were raised in the Commons. At first the Government spokesmen in both Houses, supported by certain elder statesmen who should have known better, were exceedingly evasive in their replies. Some peers threatened action of a perfectly constitutional kind, which they believed would result in their Lordships refusing to "receive" the new peer so that he could not take his seat. At last the Government yielded. A Royal Commission[2] was appointed to consider the whole matter and,

---

[1] Afterwards Lord Younger.

[2] Called the Dunedin Commission after its Chairman, Lord Dunedin.

as a result, there is to-day a far more proper and decent method of examining the claims and records of those whose names are submitted to the Crown for honours. After a somewhat stormy scene Sir John was induced by one of the Prime Minister's supporters—Captain the Hon. Frederic Guest, M.P.—to petition the Crown to have his name removed from the list of peers to be, and the Crown consented. But the mischief had been done.

One day in the summer of 1922 I said in the lobby to a fellow Under-Secretary, who has since occupied positions of great authority and is an old and dear friend of mine, that I was deeply disturbed at the extraordinary infelicitous selection of names in that part of the Honours List for which the Prime Minister was responsible, culminating in the Robinson peerage. He replied, "So am I, and so is Willie Bridgeman.[1] I'll have another word with him. It might be advisable for us to ask for an interview with Austen".[2] Shortly after this I went to stay with Lord Birkenhead. He said, "What's all this I hear about you and other junior Ministers intriguing against the Prime Minister because you don't like his Honours List? It is both disloyal and foolish. Winston, Austen and I are behind him. We four are the most powerful combination in political life. Who is going to lead you to victory if you smash the Coalition? Someone like Bonar or Baldwin? You would not stand a chance". I replied that we were entitled to state our views to our leader, Mr. Chamberlain. But for the rest of the day I was profoundly disturbed, for Lord Birkenhead was my guide, philosopher and very dear friend in public and private; nevertheless, I was convinced that he was wrong; and wrong he was.

The meeting between the junior Conservative Ministers and Mr. Chamberlain, supported by other senior Conservative Ministers, was duly held. The proceedings were stormy, most of the Under-Secretaries supporting Mr. Bridgeman, myself and others who shared our views, and the majority of the Cabinet Ministers remaining silent, though Lord Birkenhead vigorously rebuked us but smiled good-humouredly when, with equal vigour, I counter-attacked him. Mr. Baldwin sat, *more suo*, silent and aloof, but I detected a gleam of sympathy for us in his face.

[1] The late Mr., afterwards the 1st Lord, Bridgeman, then a junior Minister.
[2] Mr. Austen Chamberlain was leader of the Conservative Party.

Finally, Mr. Chamberlain promised to convey our views to the Prime Minister. Mr. Balfour, when I asked him afterwards what he thought of the meeting, replied, "It was not a very happy occasion, nor one that was very tactfully handled on either side". I was certain that he, with his great discernment and experience, considered that the Coalition was doomed.

In August, 1922, I went to India to discuss certain matters on behalf of Lord Peel, with the Viceroy, Lord Reading. I had a most interesting, though strenuous, tour, staying with various Presidency and Provincial Governors and interviewing scores of people, but I had to cut my tour short as I received a warning from Lord Peel that an immediate election was probable. The Cabinet had barely survived an internal crisis caused by Mr. Lloyd George's misguided determination to aid the Greeks against the Turks in military operations in Asia Minor; he even appealed for military help to the Dominions. Lord Reading told me privately, as he had already told my Chief, Lord Peel, that if we went to war against Turkey, India would be ungovernable, as we should lose the only firm support which we had at the moment—that of the majority of the Moslem population. Fortunately, owing to the tact and discretion of Sir Charles Harington, the British C.-in-C. on the spot, and the statesmanship of Mustapha Kemal, an armistice was signed and the danger averted.

Before I reached home the Government had fallen as a result of the famous Carlton Club meeting at which Conservative M.P.s had decided by 186 votes to 87 that under a Conservative leader there should be an appeal to the country at once, without any agreement or understanding with the Liberals. Lord Balfour,[1] Lord Birkenhead, Mr. Austen Chamberlain, Sir Robert Horne and Sir Laming Worthington-Evans refused to support either the "break-away" or Mr. Bonar Law, who became the new Prime Minister.

I wrote in my diary at the time:

I am sorry we are separated from Austen, Winston and F. E., but it is their own fault that they are where they are. Goodness knows, they had enough warning—F. E. and Winston from me

[1] He was made a peer in 1922.

among others—as to how things were going and how the big guns alone, the three super-guns particularly, could not hold together an Army whose rank-and-file had lost all morale.

The principal cause of the loss of morale in the rank-and-file was that all faith in the Commander-in-Chief had gone; the Conservative Party in particular had in the last few months become completely mistrustful of Mr. Lloyd George.

Despite the handicap of having to fight not only Liberal and Labour opponents but to face some shells (Lord Birkenhead being particularly ironical and scathing about Mr. Bonar Law's team) from the "big guns" of their own Party, the new Government obtained a good working majority over all opponents. The "big guns" learnt a lesson which my old Chief, Mr. Joseph Chamberlain, once said that all politicians should know—"No one is indispensable, especially in politics"—and were ready enough to accept office, a little over a year later, in the wholly Conservative Government of 1924. This result was largely due to two remarkable men, the late Sir George Younger, the chairman of the Party, to whom I have previously referred, and Colonel (now Sir) Leslie Wilson. The latter was the first of the five most able and successful Chief Whips the Conservative Party has ever had—the others being Commander Eyres-Monsell,[1] Captain Margesson,[2] Mr. James Stuart and Mr. Buchan-Hepburn; no one who has not worked under them and with them, in and out of office, as I have done, can realise the immense extent to which they have contributed to what has been an era of very considerable Conservative power and influence in the last thirty years. Bitter reproaches were directed at the time against Sir George and Colonel Wilson for supporting the break-up of the Coalition. They did so because they were rightly convinced that the Conservative Party would be split asunder if it continued to support Mr. Lloyd George when a large proportion of its members in both Houses and some of its most influential supporters in the country would no longer consent to do so. Sir George and Colonel Wilson performed a plain and simple duty by acting as they did.

Mr. Baldwin became Chancellor of the Exchequer in the

[1] Now Lord Monsell.　　　[2] Now Lord Margesson.

Bonar Law Government. Lord Curzon remained at the Foreign Office, and Lord Peel at the India Office with myself as Under-Secretary. There were several interesting promotions and new appointments. For instance, Mr. Bridgeman became Home Secretary, Mr. L. S. Amery First Lord of the Admiralty, Sir Samuel Hoare Secretary of State for Air, whilst Sir Philip Lloyd-Graeme went to the Board of Trade. Sir Arthur Griffith-Boscawen, the Minister of Agriculture, who lost his seat at the general election and at a by-election as well, resigned his post and Sir Robert Sanders was appointed. Mr. Edward Wood (now Lord Halifax) was President of the Board of Education. But the most significant appointment, in view of what was to happen in the next twenty-five years, was that of a new member, Mr. Neville Chamberlain, during March, 1923, to the Ministry of Health. The son of Mr. Joseph Chamberlain and half-brother of Mr. Austen Chamberlain, he early proved his parliamentary ability and grasp of detail by securing, without much difficulty, the passage of important Bills relating to rent restriction and the relief from rates of agricultural land.

The Labour Party at the election increased its representation to 138. Whereas in 1918 pacifists or conscientious objectors during the 1914 war who stood for Parliament could scarcely find a constituency in Britain to elect them and were in considerable physical danger from the enraged populace when they appeared on a platform, by 1922 they were welcomed in many constituencies. I was returned unopposed at the 1922 election, and after my return from India, going to speak for Captain Gee, V.C., M.P., I was astonished and shocked by the following exchanges:

CHAIRMAN: Our candidate fought most gallantly in the war.

INTERRUPTER: More b——y fool he. (*Loud cheers from Socialist supporters.*)

At the 1918 election such an interruption in any constituency would have caused intense indignation and resulted in its author, at the very least, being forcibly ejected from the meeting. No wonder the world finds it hard to understand the amazing changes of the national mood in Britain.

Thus many of the leading Labour pacifists—Mr. Ramsay MacDonald and Mr. Snowden, for example—returned to the

House of Commons, and many more were elected for the first
time. There was a big irruption of what appeared at the time to be
angry and dangerous revolutionaries from Glasgow and the
Clyde; they included Mr. Shinwell, the late Mr. John Wheatley,
the late Mr. Campbell Stephen, the late Mr. Maxton, Mr.
David Kirkwood, and Mr. George Buchanan. Of the whole group
the last three were perhaps the most detested by Liberals and
Conservatives: yet, when in course of time they ceased to be
Members owing to death or resignation of their seats, no three
men stood higher in the estimation of the House. Among other
new Members was a quiet little man called Major Attlee. Every
new House of Commons produces a fresh crop of "eccentrics"
in a parliamentary sense, though they may be sane enough in
ordinary life. The choicest in the 1922 Parliament was a diminu-
tive Parsee called Mr. Saklatvala. Though coming from a
wealthy family, he was a Communist, and sat for North Battersea, a place in which he enjoyed great esteem; when he went
canvassing he was followed by children shouting "Good old
Uncle Sak." He poured out, in questions and speeches, a flood of
insinuations and abuse against the Government of India, but I
rather liked him and we were on friendly terms outside the
Chamber. The House treated him as a great joke—not because
of his race or colour, for there had been much-respected Indians
in the House in the past—but on account of the furious and incoherent rage into which he worked himself when speaking.

A serious Cabinet crisis took place in the early months of 1923
over Mr. Baldwin's settlement, in his capacity of Chancellor of
the Exchequer, of the United States loan to Britain. It was stated
at the time—and it was true—that the Prime Minister, Mr. Bonar
Law, was opposed to the agreement. In fact, the Cabinet only
just averted a split on the subject which would have destroyed
the Government. For years afterwards, Mr. Baldwin's many
Press enemies gloated over his alleged mistake in this matter.
Personally, I have not sufficient knowledge of the facts to pass
judgment.

In general, the first and only session of the 1922 Parliament
was a quiet one, though there were some prolonged sittings and
some scenes, mainly caused by the "Clydebankers". One such

¹ Now Lord Kirkwood.

scene caused the House to be adjourned on account of "grave disorder". One of the Glasgow Labour members, passing the Government Front Bench after the adjournment, called out, "Take that grin off your face!" to one of the Under-Secretaries. He was unaware that the Under-Secretary in question invariably and unconsciously smiled in moments of tension. (Most people have their particular reactions to such moments. In my case the centre vein of my forehead swells—a characteristic I share with Sir Alfred Duff-Cooper.[1]) Not being obeyed, the Labour member aimed a blow at the Under-Secretary, but hit another Minister, the late Lord Moyne (then Lieut.-Colonel Guinness) who, with great self-control, did not hit back, and the Labour member rushed angrily out of the House. Apart from its unpleasantness, there was irony in the incident, for Colonel Guinness had been in the 1914 war as a front-line soldier of great courage which earned him the D.S.O., whereas the Labour member was a conscientious objector.

In the summer of 1922, Mr. Bonar Law resigned from ill-health to die a few months later of a painful disease; I happened to speak to him in the lobby a short time before his resignation and was deeply shocked by his haggard, pain-stricken face. I shared Mr. Baldwin's feelings towards Mr. Bonar Law, expressed in his moving phrase when tributes were being paid to the dead leader in the House: "I loved the man." What a ghastly commentary it is upon the limitations of human thought and endeavour that in the twenty-nine years that have elapsed since Mr. Bonar Law's death, the scientists have perfected means for reducing the whole world to a cemetery and a desert through the invention of the atomic bomb and its even more destructive successor, but still have not discovered either the cause of, or an effective cure for, cancer!

Mr. Bonar Law was succeeded as Prime Minister by Mr. Baldwin, the Chancellor of the Exchequer. The status, attainments and experience in high office of Lord Curzon were considerably greater than those of Mr. Baldwin; many people, including Lord Curzon himself, believed that the King would choose him for his First Minister. The reason given by the Press for Mr. Baldwin's selection was that the time had passed when it was

[1] Now Lord Norwich.

possible, or at least convenient and in the public interest, for a Prime Minister to sit in the Lords. This explanation was never either given or controverted officially, but, since it appeared to emanate from official circles, it is to-day, in general, accepted as true and as establishing a precedent that would preclude any member of the House of Lords from holding the office of Prime Minister. Therefore, at the risk of causing pain and offence to some, I am obliged to state certain facts that were known to me and others moving at the time in the inner circle of the political world.

Lord Curzon was a man of great gifts of intellect, of statesmanship and of artistic perception. He was, as I know from my own experience during a long tenure of the Under-Secretaryship for India, a highly successful Viceroy of India, despite certain discords for which he was partly to blame during his Viceroyalty. Prominent Indians and senior European Civil Servants have often said to me, "With all his faults, he was the greatest Viceroy we ever had". He was less successful as Foreign Secretary, but in the 1918 Government his position was made difficult by Mr. Lloyd George's persistence in trying himself to devise and conduct the foreign policy of the country. Unfortunately, Lord Curzon had two grave defects of manner and personality which earned him scores of bitter enemies. He suffered fools most ungladly; and he presented to equals and inferiors, especially to inferiors, a façade of extreme pomposity and aristocratic class-consciousness that would have been tolerated, and indeed considered natural, in one holding his position in the eighteenth century, but was deeply resented in the twentieth. I believe it was only a façade for, in private life, he was a kind and affectionate man with hosts of friends, including many men and women of genius who were devoted to him; he was an excellent host and a witty and charming companion in company which he liked and which liked him; he could, too, laugh at himself in such company. But the public and the "man in the street" saw the façade and heartily disliked it.

Just as in my time at Oxford in the early 1900's undergraduates invented stories about Canon Spooner,[1] the Warden of New

[1] "Spoonerisms" were originally based on an alleged mistake made by Canon Spooner in a sermon when he referred to the words of a well-known

College, and retailed them as evidence of his inability to talk intelligently, so that "Spoonerisms" became a feature of the University, in the same manner witty and malicious people invented "Curzonisms" to illustrate his foibles. There was, for instance, a wholly apocryphal tale current in London at the time that, on visiting France during the 1914 war and seeing some soldiers bathing, he exclaimed, "I had no idea that the skins of the lower classes were so white". Obviously, this outward aspect of Lord Curzon's character made it unlikely that he would be a successful Prime Minister. Feeling this very strongly, after Mr. Bonar Law's death, elder statesmen of great position in the Conservative Party, on whose support the Cabinet largely relied, privately submitted to the King that Lord Curzon would not be *persona grata* to them as Prime Minister. I have no doubt that George V took these submissions into serious consideration, as he had both a right and a duty to do; I have no doubt also that they affected his ultimate decision to send for Mr. Baldwin to ask him to be Prime Minister.[1] Lord Curzon was deeply disappointed at being passed over, but he showed his generosity and breadth of mind by supporting Mr. Baldwin's elevation to the Premiership in an admirable speech at the customary Party meeting after the King's choice had been notified; he also gave his complete support to Mr. Baldwin in his new office.

hymn, "Conquering Kings their titles take" as "Kinkering Kongs their tatles tike". I was never able to discover when at Oxford if he ever did use these words, but I myself have heard him in private conversation make some transliteration of sentences which made amusing nonsense; but he was, despite this failing, a most popular, successful and lovable Head of a great College.

[1] This passage was written before Mr. Harold Nicolson's *George V, His Life and Reign* was published. It confirms my statement that George V was approached on the subject of Lord Curzon's fitness for the Premiership. It is doubtful if the Crown could refuse to accept as Prime Minister a Peer who was a member of the House of Lords, if the Party with a majority in the Commons wished such a man to be Prime Minister and if its leading members refused to accept or retain office, as the case might be, unless he were appointed; for, in that event, a grave constitutional crisis, in which the Sovereign would be involved, would arise.

CHAPTER X

THERE was an orgy of high wages and profits with little unemployment in the first years after the Armistice; but by 1923 a serious trade depression, with much unemployment, had supervened. Mr. Baldwin decided in the autumn of 1923 that he must appeal to the country for a mandate to introduce protective tariff measures in order to reduce unemployment. According to a statement subsequently made by him, he had other motives as well; he believed that this issue would unite the party, including those whom he called the "Lloyd George malcontents"—in other words, those Conservatives who had refused, when the Coalition broke up, to join or support the new Conservative Government; he also thought that Mr. Lloyd George, whom he always regarded as the most wily old fox in the political covert, was about to become a protectionist and would attract the support of Mr. Chamberlain and Lord Birkenhead. This, in his words, "would have been an end to the Tory Party as we know it".[1] In the same statement he said that he got the Cabinet into line with his views. This is a euphemistic way of stating the case. It was later understood that he announced at a Cabinet meeting, without previous discussion of the matter, that he intended to go to the country. There was some indignation at the method pursued because it has always been considered that Cabinet Ministers in such circumstances had either to resign or support the Prime Minister in his action, as the Cabinet did. It was thought that it would have been more courteous for Mr. Baldwin to have consulted the Cabinet before making his decision, notwithstanding the fact that the last word in such circumstances rests with the Prime Minister. Some say that he was badly advised by Admiral Hall, M.P., who at that time was organiser of the Party. Admiral Hall did immensely valuable service as head of British naval intelligence during the 1914 war, but was not wholly successful as a political organiser.

I think that the Government's defeat was due less to dislike

[1] *Lord Baldwin, A Memoir*, a pamphlet published by *The Times*, 1947.

of a tariff than to resentment at the action of a Government with an adequate majority in plunging the country into a general election within a year of its formation after success at the polls. The Government suffered heavy losses at the election, the figures being, Conservatives 254, Labour 192, Liberals 149. The Liberal Party was united for the election, but the respective hatchets of Mr. Asquith and Mr. Lloyd George, after being temporarily buried, were soon unearthed, as will be seen later. The Labour Party, too, repaired the breach in its unity between the war-time patriots and pacifists. After the election both sections thronged the Albert Hall to cheer Mr. Ramsay MacDonald and to sing at the end "The Red Flag" instead of the National Anthem. I have never understood why the Socialists sing this song in moments of triumph, in view of the harm it does them by suggesting that they are dangerous revolutionaries, since that is the only meaning to be attached to this dreary dirge. They even sang it as late as 1945 in the House of Commons.

The Baldwin Government retained office until Parliament met early in 1924, when they were defeated and resigned. Mr. Ramsay MacDonald then formed a Government that contained many men of ability and integrity such as Lord Haldane (Lord Chancellor), Mr. Philip Snowden (Chancellor of the Exchequer), Mr. Arthur Henderson (Secretary of State for the Home Department), Mr. J. H. Thomas (Secretary of State for the Colonies), Lord Olivier (Secretary of State for India), Lord Chelmsford (First Lord of the Admiralty), and Mr. Thomas Shaw (Minister of Labour); Mr. MacDonald himself was Foreign Secretary as well as Prime Minister. With a few exceptions, however, none of them had been in ministerial office or had official administrative experience elsewhere. Moreover, the characteristic feature of all "leftist" parties—the rift between moderates and extremists —was accentuated in the case of the first Labour Government by its dependence upon the Liberal votes to keep it in office. There was trouble between the front bench and their supporters from the very start. The Government, too, as might be expected from its lack of experience, was a naïve one given to dangerously foolish statements. The most famous of these, which lost the Labour Party thousands of votes in the 1924 election, was Mr. Thomas Shaw's remark, when asked what he was going to do about the million unemployed, that he could not produce a plan "like a rabbit out of a hat" after a few weeks in office.

But internal strains and stresses were not confined to the Labour Party; they afflicted the other two parties as well. So much so that many of us in private took the gloomiest view at the time of the prospect of any Government lasting the full normal term of a Parliament with an adequate and united majority. Events proved us to be wrong, as they will, I hope, falsify similar gloomy prophecies to-day.

"The Liberal Party", said Mr. Austen Chamberlain[1] at the time, "is visibly bursting up. It holds constant Party meetings to decide its course; then forty vote with the Government, twenty with us and the rest (including the leaders) walk out or absent themselves." What Mr. Chamberlain wrote about the Liberals in 1924 remains true to-day. It is strange that they cannot realise that what keeps them out of power and influence is not mainly, as they allege, the unfairness to small parties of the electoral system, nor the country's disregard for Liberal principles, but the fact that they can never agree among themselves how those principles should be applied in particular instances and, consequently, that their members display a ludicrous lack of unity in public.

In the short 1924 Parliament the Conservative Party was not in a happy state of mind, as the following extracts from my diary show:

DECEMBER 9TH, 1923

Wild rumours going about in the Lobbies and elsewhere and disreputable efforts to get rid of Baldwin and re-create some sort of Coalition.

FEBRUARY IITH, 1924

Attended a meeting of former Conservative Junior Ministers addressed by S. B.[2] at Bobby Monsell's[3] house; he outlined in an able and business-like speech what the policy of the Party should be; Ronnie MacNeil[4] and Billy Gore[5] foolishly and reprehensibly attacked the inclusion of Austen and F. E. in the "Shadow Cabinet". Several of us replied, including Walter G.[6] and me. Then S. B.

[1] *Life and Letters.*   [2] Lord Baldwin.   [3] Lord Monsell.
[4] The late Lord Cushenden.   [5] Lord Harlech.   [6] The late Lord Moyne.

made a conciliatory little speech and the incident closed, but I had a word with Billy outside who was full of threatenings and mutterings against F. E. and against the party for recognising him.

It would be improper to record this private conversation but for the fact that an account of the proceedings subsequently appeared in the *Daily Express*. I asked Lord Beaverbrook some days later how his paper got the information. He replied, "I got it, Eddie, from Baldwin's mistress". The point of this joke, delivered in appropriately solemn terms, was that Mr. Baldwin was most happily married and known to have no intimate friendships, platonic or otherwise, with any other woman.

MAY 5TH, 1924

I lunched with Philip Sassoon[1] at a party consisting of Balfour, Bertie Horne,[2] Austen, Philip Lloyd-Graeme,[3] and Walter G. We had a rather important political talk after lunch, especially about Winston and the right-wing Liberals. It was decided that Balfour and Austen should see Winston who goes on Tuesday to speak at Liverpool.

As the following extract shows, the negotiations with Mr. Churchill at the time proved unfruitful.

JUNE 20TH, 1924

There appeared on Sunday in the *People* an interview with S. B. containing some very true but crude and indeed libellous reflections about Max Beaverbrook, Rothermere, F. E. and others, and dealing scathingly with the intrigues to bring in Winston. The *People* is owned by Colonel Grant Morden, M.P.,[4] whose reputation is not of the highest, and is the only really Conservative Sunday paper. Baldwin promptly repudiated the interview through the Central Office and the *People* has promptly issued a communiqué reasserting its truth through the Press Association; most of the newspapers have ignored the matter, but the Beaverbrook Press has "stunted" it (Max being very excited about it when I saw him yesterday) and, to make matters more intriguing, the *Morning Post*

---

[1] The late Sir Philip Sassoon.   [2] The late Sir Robert Horne, M.P.
[3] Now Lord Swinton.
[4] The late Colonel Grant Morden, M.P., a Conservative who was born in Canada.

has written an article to say in effect "it is true even if Stanley Baldwin did not say it".

Lord Northcliffe had died a few years earlier, to the grief of friends such as myself who appreciated the many great qualities of that remarkable man; but the ferociously bitter fight between Prime Ministers and the "Press Lords" was to continue almost without intermission until the Second World War. To-day there is peace, or at least an armistice, possibly because, with the exception of Lord Beaverbrook, the proprietors of great newspapers are a milder lot than their predecessors. At the time of writing, the "Overlords"—Ministers with co-ordinating or overriding authority—have taken the place of the "Press Lords" as targets of political abuse.

With one or two exceptions, such as Mr. John Wheatley's Housing Act which proved a disappointment in operation, the Government introduced no legislation of importance. Its precarious position afforded every opportunity for young backbenchers to make a name for themselves, and among those who took advantage of the situation were the late Mr. Kingsley Wood, M.P.,[1] and Mr. Leslie Hore-Belisha, M.P. The Government crashed and the Parliament came to an end over the Campbell case. Campbell, a crippled ex-Serviceman and Communist editor of the *Workers Weekly*, urged soldiers to disobey orders. The Law Officers advised a prosecution for sedition, but eventually, under pressure from their supporters—according to those supporters—withdrew the prosecution. Campbell and his friends openly rejoiced in their victory. The Liberals demanded an enquiry into the circumstances of the withdrawal of the prosecution, whilst the Conservative Opposition tabled a vote of censure. In the debate, as will be seen from the extract from my diary below, the Conservatives voted for the Liberal motion and the Government fell, and an immediate election followed.

OCTOBER 8TH, 1924

The debate on which so much hangs! I think in 20 years I have never known the issue of a debate so doubtful or where the result was going to be so momentous. Horne was there; had an angry

[1] Afterwards the Rt. Hon. Sir Kingsley Wood.

question time, but the actual debate was quiet and dignified, partly owing to the Speaker's intervention. Horne made a completely effective and virile, though un-impassioned, attack on the Government; Patrick Hastings[1] spoke next and was, I must say, very good —so much so that I was shaken in my own conviction as regards his guilt and that of the Government. Simon followed and was also brilliant but, as usual, coldly chiselled.[2] The Prime Minister followed and was poor; up to dinner the issue was still in doubt. After dinner, however, it was clear that we were going to refuse to fall into the trap which the Government were anxious to set and S. B. put our doubts at rest by announcing that we should vote for the enquiry. Douglas Hogg[3] and Thomas[4] followed for their respective sides in a shouting House and the division was taken. The Government were heavily defeated. There were the usual scenes inside and outside the House.

Some years afterwards I met the late Sir Patrick Hastings for the first and only time at dinner. I found him most agreeable and entertaining. When I happened to mention the House of Commons he said, "Don't talk to me of that place; it treated me as no honourable man should be treated". I tried in vain to persuade him that, though he had made a good speech, the House was entitled to put its own interpretation upon his actions.

Mr. Asquith also took part in the debate; it was his last speech in the House, as shortly afterwards he was made a peer; he died in 1928. By his death, a great figure was removed from the parliamentary scene; whatever mistakes he may have made, he brought a brilliant intellect and complete integrity of purpose to bear upon all the problems with which he was confronted.

The election that immediately followed the Government's defeat was a triumph for the Conservative Party and a personal one for Mr. Baldwin; 415 Conservatives were returned with 151 Labour members and 42 Liberals as against 158 in the previous Parliament—Mr. Asquith lost his seat and, as I have said, was shortly afterwards made a peer. In addition to being weighed

[1] The late Sir Patrick Hastings, K.C.

[2] "Coldly chiselled" is, I admit, a curious phrase and might be regarded as a wounding description of a speech, but at the time it seemed adequately to express the precision, untouched by passion or invective, with which Lord Simon presented the case against the Attorney General.

[3] The late Lord Hailsham.   [4] The late Rt. Hon. J. H. Thomas, M.P.

down during the election by the Campbell case, the Labour Party were shackled by Mr. Ramsay MacDonald's inept handling of the Zinoviev letter. Zinoviev, president of the Third Communist International, wrote a secret letter to his British "comrades" urging them to encourage mutinies in the British Armed Forces. The *Daily Mail* obtained a copy of this letter and published it. Mr. MacDonald at first expressed doubts as to its authenticity, but then had to admit that, as Foreign Secretary, he had initialled a draft letter of protest to the Soviet Government. On platform after platform in the country the Conservative leaders, Lord Birkenhead in particular, castigated him for his cowardice and folly.

The new Government emphasised, on its formation, how completely the breach in the Party caused by the break-up of the Coalition had been healed, for Mr. Austen Chamberlain was Foreign Secretary and Lord Birkenhead Secretary of State for India. Even more significant was the appointment of Mr. Churchill as Chancellor of the Exchequer. Mr. Churchill had gone through many political vicissitudes since 1922. At the election of that year he lost, as he explained ruefully at the time, his office, his seat in Parliament and his appendix almost simultaneously. There followed a period when he was, *more suo*, the centre of bitter controversy during which he made an unsuccessful attempt to re-enter the House; finally he was elected for Epping as a "Constitutionalist". Among the less instructed members of the Conservative Party there was some raising of eyebrows at this famous, but, as they thought, incalculable man being given a key office in a Conservative Government in his new role of a "Constitutionalist". However, except possibly in one or two instances, he proved a successful Chancellor. Inheriting, as he generously admitted, a surplus from his predecessor, Mr. Snowden, he devoted part of it to a contributory Old Age and Widow's Pension scheme. The Bill to effect this important advance in social reform was piloted by Mr. Neville Chamberlain, the Minister of Health. The distinguished sons of two distinguished fathers—Mr. Joseph Chamberlain, the Radical reformer, and Lord Randolph Churchill, the Tory reformer—thus admirably maintained their personal and political heritage.

Other principal appointments were Lord Cave (Lord Chancellor), Sir William Joynson-Hicks[1] (Home Secretary), Mr. L. S. Amery (Secretary of State for the Colonies), Sir Philip Cunliffe-Lister (President of the Board of Trade), Mr. Wood (Minister of Agriculture), Sir Arthur Steel-Maitland (Minister of Labour), Mr. Bridgeman (First Lord of the Admiralty), Lord Eustace Percy (President of the Board of Trade) and Sir Samuel Hoare[2] (Secretary of State for Air)—the last-named becoming responsible for the first civil air line to India, an act of policy which was rightly regarded at the time as showing that the British people were determined to be as active and energetic in air as in sea travel. To the regret of his numerous friends, Sir Robert Horne was not included in the new Government since he declined, as being unsuitable for him, the office he was offered; but he occupied in later years, before his lamentably early death, a position of great authority on the back benches in the House of Commons. His speeches were noteworthy for the charm, good temper, integrity, courage and great ability which were characteristic of the man.

I obtained, with the distinguished aid of Mr. Richard Law[3] as my personal assistant and private secretary, a huge majority in the Horsham and Worthing Division—one of the safest in Britain for the Conservative Party. Asked by me how he had got on at a meeting which he took for me, Mr. Law replied, "The audience had not the slightest idea what I was talking about and I had only a very faint idea myself, but they seemed to be delighted with my speech and unanimously passed a vote of confidence in you".

I returned to the India Office. The following is an extract from my diary:

NOVEMBER 12TH, 1924

I had a telephone call from the Prime Minister's secretary asking me to go to 10, Downing Street. The P.M. asked me if I would "carry on at your old job". I told him that there was nothing that I desired better and that my thoughts were turning more and more eastwards—so much so that I might some day ask for a Presidency Governorship in India, which seemed to surprise S. B. He asked if

[1] Afterwards Lord Brentford. [2] Now Lord Templewood.
[3] Now the Rt. Hon. Richard Law, M.P.

F. E. and I would get on all right, and I replied that I believed that we should. He then said, "I may tell you that no one can answer better for India in the House of Commons than you", which was very nice of him. He then talked very interestingly on general political topics for ten minutes or so. Watching him sitting and talking with the light on him in that historic room, I thought him a better and finer man than I had ever considered him before; success and responsibility have certainly improved him. At his request went to see Mima Gore[1] to ascertain if Billy,[2] who is somewhere in unknown Africa, would take the Under-Secretaryship at the Colonial Office.

In fact, I never asked for a Presidency Governorship, but was offered and refused no less than three. It is only honest to admit that the main reason for these offers was the difficulty at the time of obtaining candidates willing to have their names submitted to the Crown for these great and honourable, but extremely onerous, posts, the emoluments of which did not adequately cover the cost of maintaining them. I refused largely because I decided I would like some day to be, as I subsequently became, "Father of the House".

Despite its defeat, the Labour Party quickly recovered its morale after the election. It deserved to do so because it contained, as it still does, in addition to the "flibberty-gibbets" and careerists with whom it has always been encumbered, many men and women of great integrity and ability who had given a lifetime of devoted service to the Trades Union movement and in most cases risen from humble circumstances to positions of great authority.

The Liberal Party, on the other hand, continued steadily on its downhill course. Furious quarrels broke out in it behind the scenes, mostly centred on the "Lloyd George Fund" which Mr. Lloyd George had collected during his Premiership from—so his enemies alleged—those anxious to obtain honours. The Party wanted to use it, Mr. Lloyd George wanted to keep it for his own purposes. For the rest of his career Mr. Lloyd George produced a number of statements on policy, some of them very wise and some the reverse, and made a series of magnificent

[1] Lady Beatrice Ormsby-Gore, now Lady Harlech.
[2] Mr. Ormsby-Gore, now Lord Harlech.

speeches in the Commons which filled the House. But the electors had completely lost their faith in him and in the Liberal
Party alike, so that all this tremendous effort was in vain. His
lack of judgment, in his latter years, was strikingly shown in
the session of 1924–5 of the new Parliament. The Liberals moved
a resolution of censure on Mr. Speaker Whitley for his alleged
negligence in interpreting the rules of the House. Though he
knew that not only the Conservatives but the Labour Party as
well were going to support the Speaker who was, incidentally,
a respected member of the Liberal Party before he occupied the
Chair, Mr. Lloyd George rushed into the fray in support of the
motion and was highly indignant at being called to order for
irrelevance; he was effectively answered in a dignified and
admirable speech by Mr. Clynes, speaking for the Labour
Front Bench.

A few months later, Sir Alfred Mond[1] joined the Conservative
Party; Mr. Lloyd George promptly compared him to Judas
Iscariot and by this comparison lost the Liberal Party a few more
thousand votes, this time among the Jewish community. Soon
after his political conversion, Sir Alfred attended the eve-of-the-
session reception given by Lord and Lady Londonderry at
Londonderry House. As he ascended the great staircase, the
cynosure of all eyes, the orchestra by accident and not design
played a popular tune of the day, "I want to be happy" to the
delight of the assembled peers and M.P.s!

The Government had an acknowledged mandate to introduce
a protective tariff system, which they did by the passage of the
Safeguarding of Industries Bill. But that did not prevent the
Liberals from tramping through the lobbies to oppose it, bearing
aloft the mummified relic of their patron saint—Free Trade—
thereby offending thousands of voters who were suffering personally from the effects of "dumping".

There was, I need hardly say, in 1924 and 1925 trouble both
in Egypt and India, for very few of the between-war years were
free from such troubles. Sir Lee Stack, the Sirdar, was assassinated
in the streets of Cairo in November, and further attempted outrages against Englishmen occurred in Egypt and the Sudan.
Lord Allenby took very strong and effective measures in Egypt

[1] The first Lord Melchett.

after the murder, which did not, however, prevent his virtual dismissal by the Government a little later. When the new Parliament met, a Socialist M.P., Sir Charles Trevelyan, who during his membership of the House enjoyed the dubious distinction of being the most unpopular member of his Party with his opponents, attacked the Government and Lord Allenby for the latter's action. Mr. Austen Chamberlain, in the opening words of his reply to this speech, said amid thunderous cheers, "I have been to Paris and Rome recently, but it was not until I returned to the House of Commons that I heard a thoroughly anti-British speech."

The Swarajists were very active and mischievous in India and Lord Birkenhead and I, in our respective Houses, had constantly to rebut the charges of the "friends of every country but their own" that the Government of India had dealt harshly with those who had broken the law. Both being blessed with sharp tongues, we hit back with such effect that most of the attackers retreated with their tails between their legs. Lord Reading's term of office as Viceroy, which was marked by infinite patience, great and conscientious industry and his delightful personal qualities of charm, courtesy and brilliant intellect, ended in 1925, and Mr. Edward Wood[1] was appointed in his stead. Recommendations to the Crown for the Viceroyalty were, until the Indian Empire ended, the responsibility not of the Secretary of State, as in the case of other Indian appointments, but of the Prime Minister. Mr. Baldwin, however, as was proper, consulted Lord Birkenhead privately about the matter before approaching anyone, and he, in turn, asked my opinion.[2] Unhesitatingly, I suggested Mr. Wood; meeting him in the lobby a few hours later, I told him

[1] Now Lord Halifax, created Lord Irwin on his appointment.

[2] The King, Mr. Nicolson states in *George V, His Life and Reign* (p. 504) suggested that Mr. Wood should be made Viceroy. I do not know whether this was before or after my conversation with Lord Birkenhead; certainly Lord Birkenhead had no knowledge of the King's views at the time. It was the custom for the Prime Minister, after, of course, previous private discussion with the Sovereign, formally to submit the name of a person to be Viceroy for the Sovereign's approval. But he would naturally consult the Secretary of State for India before doing so. In the case of Presidency and Provincial Governors of Provinces in India, the initiating responsibility for submission rested with the Secretary of State.

what I had done. Looking absolutely astonished, he said, "You must be mad"; then, seeing that I was rather upset, he added, "Nevertheless, I am very grateful to an old and dear friend for his confidence in me". He made an excellent Viceroy.

Two important events in external affairs were the Irish Treaty and the Locarno Pact. The tripartite treaty between the British Government and those of Northern and Southern Ireland is still the main foundation of the relationship between the three parties to it—a foundation which is as stable as the circumstances permit. The Locarno pact was signed by three great statesmen who held in common the belief that the tortures, so many of them self-inflicted, which modern humanity has to bear can only be ended by mutual forbearance, conciliation and willingness to forget the past. They were Austen Chamberlain for Britain, Briand for France, and Stresemann for Germany. I consider that this agreement afforded the best hope of any reached between the wars and might have succeeded but for the hardship and chaos caused by the world economic crisis of a few years later which was a primary cause of Hitler's rise to power in Germany. Mr. Chamberlain was honoured by the King and congratulated by all parties in the Commons for his part in the agreement.

Two famous statesmen died in 1925. One was Lord Curzon. In a true and charming tribute to him,[1] Mr. Harold Nicolson has written, "To the nation he had given Tattershall, to the nation also he would bequeath his lovely Bodiam. What memorial could any man desire more lovely or more durable? The memory of these last few months is not, therefore, a distressing memory. It is a memory, not of a self-pitying egoist, but of a genial philosopher." The other death was that of Lord Milner, whose work of humane and wise statesmanship in Egypt and South Africa should be remembered when to-day foolish and evil men in both countries are attempting to destroy the remaining fruits of it.

As always in a new Parliament, new names began to figure prominently in the parliamentary news. One was Mr. Austin Hopkinson, who spent nearly a quarter of a century in the House as an independent member until he was defeated in the 1945 election. Universally known as "Hoppy", and a man of great

[1] *Curzon, the Last Phase*, p. 380.

courage and integrity, he was independent in more than name.
During the First World War, in which he served most gallantly,
he preferred to be a private soldier. The owner of a business, he
claimed to live on terms of equality with his work people and as
simply as they. He was an effective speaker and infuriated the
Labour Party, whom he constantly attacked, but he also kept some
of his invective for those whom he regarded as the wealthy and
worthless on the Conservative side. The redoubtable Miss Wilkinson was very active in 1925 and 1926. She was in those days one of
the bitterest of the Labour speakers, but greatly modified her tone
when she became a Minister in 1945, and was much respected
by her opponents, who lamented her early death. On the debate
on the Address in 1926 I noted in my diary that Major Cadogan,
the late Sir Frank Meyer, the late Colonel Oliver Stanley and Mr.
Robert Hudson all made good speeches. I added, "There are at
least ten back-benchers capable of filling (i.e. the Under-
Secretaries) places".

There was a very unpleasant scene in the House on March 11
recounted in my diary as follows:

MARCH 11TH, 1926

We had an all-night sitting on the Trade Facilities Bill; in the
evening, Lansbury, on the introduction of Navy Estimates, made a
disgraceful attack on this country's action in the war, saying that it
was fought for capitalistic reasons and that the Navy had been used
for most despicable objects. It made the whole House extremely
angry, causing some of us (including myself) to interrupt even from
the front bench. He was answered by Willie Bridgeman[1] in an
admirable speech, with Slesser[2] and Jack Jones both speaking
against him from the Socialist benches in the debate. It is an outrage
that such a man, as a result of his election to the executive committee
of the Socialist Party, should sit on the front bench, though he is an
embarrassment to his own Party.

The ex-Servicemen of the last war in all parts of the House
in the 1945 and 1950 Parliaments were luckier than we, their
predecessors, who served in the 1914 war; for the few pacifists,
such as Mr. Rhys Davies and Mr. Emrys Hughes, who expressed
their views in debate, as a rule avoided offending those who

[1] The late Lord Bridgeman.   [2] Afterwards Lord Justice Slesser.

differed from them. We, on the other hand, in the '20s and '30s had to listen, as patiently as we could, to foul attacks in the Commons upon our national honour in the first world war with insinuations that we, and our dead comrades, who had taken part in it had done a foolish and ignoble thing. However, we had our revenge, so far as Mr. Lansbury was concerned, when Mr. Ernest Bevin killed him politically at the Socialist Party Conference in October, 1935, with his devastating phrase: "It is placing the Executive and the Movement in an absolutely wrong position to be taking your conscience round from body to body asking to be told what you ought to do with it. . . . I have had to sit in Conference with the Leader and come to decisions, and I am a democrat and I feel we have been betrayed".

The parliamentary year 1926 was dominated by the General Strike. In 1925 there had been the usual trouble in the coalfields, and, to avoid a strike, the Government gave a subsidy in order to enable higher wages to be paid. Some of us, in the junior ranks of the Government, doubted the wisdom of the decision at first, but were reconciled to it when we learnt the true facts. For a general strike by all Trades Unions, in support of the miners, was threatened. The Government needed time to produce the organisation to meet and defeat this threat to the nation's existence. When the General Strike took place in May, 1926, this organisation was completely prepared. Its outward manifestation was a Chief Commissioner, in the person of the Postmaster-General[1] with Civil Commissioners, in the shape of Under-Secretaries such as myself, in charge of groups of counties. We had authority, both supervisory and advisory, over all the public services, whether they were normally in the control of Whitehall or the local authorities. We also had—most important of all—similar powers over transport and local authority utilities. We were given further instructions in the event of a complete breakdown to take drastic action of a comprehensive character. Since there was happily no need to carry out these instructions, it might be a breach of the Official Secrets Act to state their nature, because, though the powers conferred upon the Government by the Proclamation announcing an emergency were debated in both Houses of Parliament amid angry and noisy scenes and suspension

[1] The late Sir W. Mitchell-Thomson, afterwards Lord Selsdon.

of Socialist members in the Commons, the Government rightly refused to state the extent to which they would use them. Certain things about the organisation created can, however, properly be stated. Its completeness and the fact that the Trades Union leaders knew almost nothing of its nature until the strike began show the complete efficiency and discretion of the Civil Service in our country; no other Civil Service in the world could have produced a scheme which worked so smoothly, even in districts with an overwhelming Labour majority in sympathy with the strikers, and which, notwithstanding the power placed in the hands of us who were responsible for working it, involved the minimum of interference with the rights of individuals going about their lawful occasions.

At the end of April the miners came out on strike. The Government, nevertheless, continued negotiations with the Trades Union leaders. But these were abandoned on Sunday, May 2, when the Trades Union Congress ordered a General Strike for next day and the *Daily Mail* chapel refused to print a leading article for the Monday's edition criticising the decision. Next day there were few trains and no newspapers, but a few days later the Government produced a newspaper whose orginator and editor-in-chief was none other than Mr. Winston Churchill. My area, as a Civil Commissioner, comprised the counties of Hampshire, Buckinghamshire, Berkshire and Oxfordshire, and my headquarters were in the abandoned Reading Gaol, made famous by Oscar Wilde's residence in it and poem about it. (At a dinner given me by my staff when the strike ended, I was presented with a copy of this poem. In making the presentation, my chief assistant observed that he thought it appropriate that I should remember that there had been well-known inmates of the gaol before me.) My office staff began with three Civil Servants, including my India Office Private Secretary, Mr. Tomkins, C.B.E., a tower of strength who worked during the ten days of the strike even harder than I did—eighteen hours a day against my sixteen. Within a few days I had over sixty in the office. These voluntary workers—business men, retired generals and Civil Servants—were in most cases far more distinguished than I was, but made a most happy team. Men and women of all classes thronged our headquarters and district offices offering to drive cars, to move food and goods, or do any other work required. On the last day of the strike, I had 10,000 more voluntary workers than I could find work for. One lot of young wage-earners from a certain village asked to be sent as special constables to Glasgow. When I asked why, their spokesman replied, "To have a crack at them dirty bolshies on the Clyde". I had heard the same sentiments in a more violent form put by a sergeant of a Scottish Territorial regiment in Gallipoli, who said he would like to get his bayonet into the stomachs of the leaders of a strike in Glasgow at the time. I have in a previous chapter paid a tribute to the many fine qualities of the group of Socialist M.P.s known as the Clydebankers; I doubt, however, if they realised the intense hatred they aroused in hundreds of thousands of their own class who fought in the war. Even in the hectic and strained ten days of my Civil Commissionership there were lighter moments. At the Headmaster's request, I visited Eton to discuss how food was to be supplied to the boys. I found on arrival in School-Yard that the Headmaster, Provost, Vice-Provost and Housemasters were waiting patiently (I was late for my appointment) with note-books and pencils ready to receive my instructions and advice. I was wholly undistinguished as a boy at Eton, and among the expectant throng I noticed a few elderly "beaks", as masters are called in Eton jargon, who had made wounding remarks about my intellect a quarter of a century earlier. Being desperately tired after a hard day's work I had difficulty in preventing myself from saying to one old gentleman in particular, "Don't stand there shuffling and fidgeting, you always were an old fool though I may have been a young one, as you once told me I was".

At Oxford my car was surrounded with undergraduates begging for a favourable answer to two requests. One was to be given the job of special constable driving a food lorry or doing anything which would excuse their attendance at lectures. The other was that I should arrest or allow them to kidnap the Master of Balliol (the late Lord Lindsay) a prominent Socialist who, they alleged without any solid evidence to support the allegation, was trying to impede the smooth working of our organisation in Oxford.

I found working with the various local authorities in my area pleasant and easy, even at Swindon where there was a strong

Labour element on the Council. I found efficient liaison with the various police authorities more difficult, despite the most valuable assistance of my police adviser—the then Chief Constable of Reading. There were two reasons for this. Chief Constables are often "kittle cattle". They do not always relish advice, let alone instructions, from the Home Office in ordinary times. To a certain extent they are right, for the essence of the British police system is that the provincial police are under democratic control divided between the Watch and Standing Joint Committees and the Chief Constables, and not under Whitehall. Naturally, some Chief Constables in my area were slightly suspicious of the authority vested in me. The other reason is the localised nature of British police organisation. There was then—and I fear that the defect has not been entirely remedied even to-day—a clumsy system of liaison between the different police forces, some of them ridiculously small; one of them, indeed, in my area consisted of sixteen men. When I told Chief Constables that during the emergency ordinary police boundaries must be disregarded and that convoys with regular police and special constables protecting them might have to pass through from other police authority areas and would resist and, if necessary, arrest strikers molesting them, a few of them were clearly somewhat perturbed, but, being disciplined Englishmen, accepted my decision.

The counties within my area obtained their imported food supplies, in normal times, almost entirely from London and not, as one would have supposed, from Southampton. My head office organised convoys of lorries with police and special constables on them to London each day to bring down the supplies without which the people of the area would have starved, or at any rate been very short of food. The Home Office, however, would not allow these provincial police to cross the Metropolitan Police boundary and, consequently, from that boundary the lorries went without any protection. After the first week of the strike the strikers in Fulham Road and in the East End succeeded, by obstruction and threats of violence, in turning back a number of my lorries, with the result that I received warnings to the effect that my area was getting dangerously short of food. I sent an urgent message to my chief, Sir William Mitchell-Thomson, to say that unless the Home Office and the Metropolitan Police afforded my lorries more protection I could not be responsible for the food supply in my area and, in consequence, should have to resign my post, even though it involved the resignation of my Under-Secretaryship. I said I was not going to be a party to the huge law-abiding population in the four counties in my area being short of food because Sir William Joynson-Hicks, the Home Secretary, and the Cabinet, had apparently not got the courage or initiative to use the large forces which they had at their disposal in London to prevent disorder in the streets. I was both tired and angry at the time, and realised afterwards that my message had been couched in unnecessarily strong terms. Immediately he received my message, Sir William Mitchell-Thomson telephoned me to go and see him. He said that I was not alone in my complaints, that he had made the strongest representations to the Prime Minister and Cabinet for a "showdown". Consequently, there would be inaugurated that very day a system of convoys to the docks protected by troops and machine-guns. The convoy reached the docks without incident; forty-eight hours later the T.U.C. called off the General Strike, though the miners remained on strike until the autumn.

Many conflicting versions have been given at various times of the real reason why the T.U.C. capitulated. Some commentators have said that the tremendous response from all classes to the appeal for volunteers to keep essential services going and the astonishing ease with which they carried out unfamiliar work, some of it supposed to require years of training, broke the morale of the strikers; others that the T.U.C. leaders realised the growing resentment against them owing to the inconvenience and economic loss which the strike caused; some ascribe the ending of the strike to a speech by Sir John (now Lord) Simon saying that it was illegal; some, again, to a proposal made by Sir Herbert (now Lord) Samuel, who had been chairman of the Royal Commission on the Mines, in which he recommended that the Government should grant a further subsidy to the coal industry; others to the result of the discussions between members of the Government and leaders of the T.U.C. held in secret. No doubt all these factors and others, including the resentment of many of the wives of the strikers accentuated by the fact that their husbands, owing to the wet and cold weather, remained at home most of the day and had to listen to their reproaches, played a part; but in my opinion, when the first convoy, protected by guardsmen in steel helmets with live ammunition in their pouches, went to the docks, the T.U.C. knew that they were beaten. Unless you have the armed and police forces of the country on your side, you can't carry out a revolution without being prepared to kill and be killed. To their credit, the T.U.C. did not want to kill anyone, nor did the Government.

Undoubtedly, the prestige of Britain abroad was enhanced, despite the calamitous effect in other directions of the General Strike, by the absence of serious violence on both sides. Like all human follies, the motives which produced the General Strike were not entirely bad. There were some evil men among the leaders and their followers who were ready to overthrow the existing order by violence, hoping to find themselves the commissars of the new régime. There were dangerous, though sincere, fanatics, like the late Mr. A. J. Cook, the miners' leader, consumed with a burning hatred for the evils he considered that the private ownership of mines and minerals entailed which he believed he could overthrow. There were more moderate leaders, such as the late Mr. J. H. Thomas and the late Mr. Ernest Bevin, who thought that only by a display of complete Trades Union solidarity could the recognised aim of political labour—public control of production and distribution, and equality of opportunity for all—be obtained. But there were thousands of Trades Unionist strikers in a different category; some struck out of loyalty to the "cause" without being concerned with the consequences or the aim of their leaders. Thousands of others, many of them ex-Servicemen, were deeply discontented at their lot. During the war Mr. Lloyd George had promised them, "A land fit for heroes to live in", instead, they had seen widespread unemployment and a far wider gap between poverty and wealth than exists to-day. It was the Second World War, plus a Socialist Government after it, that destroyed hereditary wealth and most of what had been acquired by industry and hard work as well, with the result that the incentive to make money has largely disappeared, with evil effects upon our national economy. Nevertheless, the virtual disappearance of that which Disraeli called "the two Nations" has been of national psychological benefit. In the early '20s, the Labour Party, in and out of Parliament, laid great stress on this gulf between the rich and the poor. Some illustrated weekly newspapers, concerned with the frivolous doings of a section of rich people who were in many cases neither representative of capitalists generally nor particularly respectable, were distributed free, so it was stated at the time, by Labour Party organisations in industrial areas to support this propaganda. Ascot races were then, and still are, a target of abuse by the Labour Party, anxious to prove their case against wicked extravagance "by the Tory and capitalist classes". One Labour lady in the 1950 Parliament spoke of "rich women wearing furs, dripping with jewels at Ascot". She seemed surprised to learn that, even in a normal British summer, women seldom wear furs at Ascot races, nor do those furs, when worn, drip with jewels. Indeed, the Labour Party has an *idée fixe* about this harmless national spectacle which brings much foreign wealth to Britain and which many of its most prominent members have attended in the past. Only the other day I heard a Labour peer denounce Ascot in the House of Lords. One thing is certain; never again, in any circumstances, will the T.U.C. attempt a General Strike. The painful experience of May, 1926, taught that body that it can never attain its aims by such unconstitutional means. When the strike ended, an abscess burst, which in time healed, and organised Labour has been healthier ever since.

As I shall show later, Mr. Baldwin, as the wiser Labour leaders admitted in private, contributed greatly to this healing process. But first of all it was incumbent upon the Government to produce legislation to enact in peace-time that a General Strike was illegal and to prevent the abuse of Trades Union rights which had arisen. The majority of public opinion both demanded and supported this action which took the form of a Trades Disputes Bill—the most important measure of the session of 1927—whose principal features were that a General Strike was made illegal, as was intimidation to induce Trades Unionists to strike against their will, and any coercion to subscribe to political parties; in addition, Civil Service unions were forbidden to affiliate themselves to political parties.

There were furious denunciations by the Labour Party in and out of Parliament against the Bill. In the Commons, members of

the Party attempted a rather feeble imitation of the Irish Nationalists' opposition to coercion Bills thirty and forty years earlier.
There were constant scenes and conflicts with the Chair, which
had every appearance of being prepared in advance. Labour
M.P.s were suspended and when leaving the House, sometimes
when they had refused to withdraw after a division suspending
them, under the escort of the Sergeant-at-Arms, they screamed
insults alike at the Speaker and the Government. But the
eloquence, the knowledge of procedure and the wit with which
the Irish Nationalists so seasoned their obstruction and breach
of the rules of the House that it became almost palatable to their
opponents, was wholly absent. There was little public response
to Labour and Trades Union indignation.

The Conservative Party organised meetings, usually under the
chairmanship of a Minister, in Hyde Park on Sundays in the
summer of 1927 to explain the need for the Bill; at one of these
meetings I was agreeably surprised at the respect accorded to our
views by an audience largely composed of wage-earners. The
majority of them showed no sympathy towards the minority of
excited Socialist and Communist youths who interrupted the
speakers.

Public opinion was undoubtedly influenced by the courageous
action of Mr. G. A. Spencer, M.P., leader of the Notts Miners'
Union, who, with the full approval of the majority of the members of his union, supported the Trades Disputes Bill. It was also
influenced by the statement made by Mr. Churchill, Chancellor
of the Exchequer, in his Budget speech of 1927, that the miners'
strike of the previous year had cost the country £150 million.

Shortly before this, there had been serious trouble with the
then Government of China, which commenced the process
which has been brought to fruition by its various successors, of
destroying the most valuable trade, from the point of view of
both visible and invisible exports, of Britain in China. When
political leaders to-day assert, as they can do with perfect accuracy,
that the main cause of our dangerous economic position is the
immense loss the Nation sustained in two world wars, they
should add that there are important subsidiary reasons for this
state of affairs. One is the injury done to our export trade by the
troubles in the coal industry in the last thirty years, and the other

the manner in which country after country has deprived us of our legitimate trade interests. The record of the treatment of British financial and commercial interests in China, the Argentine, Persia, Egypt and many other countries since 1918 is a sorry one. When protests are made about this treatment in and out of Parliament, almost invariably the reply of the Government in office, whatever its political complexion, is "that the days of Lord Palmerston are over"; there is much to be said against the late Lord Palmerston as a Foreign Secretary, but there is this to be said in favour of his memory—that he made it clear to all and sundry that a British firm or individual going about their lawful occasions in foreign countries was entitled to the protection of Her Britannic Majesty's Government. To-day, and for the last thirty years, that protection has not been available because British Governments, for reasons which are sound enough, have bound themselves to refer all international disputes to international bodies; but the result has been almost completely unfruitful in securing redress for British interests.

CHAPTER XI

THREE young men, all with a fine record in the 1914 war—Captain Crookshank, Captain Macmillan and Captain Anthony Eden—were among those whose names began to be familiar to the public in the 1927 session, from parliamentary press reports. Even in those days I had been long enough in the House of Commons to be, or to flatter myself that I was, a fairly good judge of those among the young and new members who were likely eventually to attain high office; I was confident that such a position in the future would be reached by the three captains in question. On the Opposition side of the House there was a young member who was very active at the time in the person of Captain Garro-Jones,[1] known by the nickname of "Garrulous" Jones; he was popular with his opponents, even when, as often, he greatly irritated them.

In the period of the second Parliament of 1924, I had an extremely busy time and a very responsible task in my position as Under-Secretary of State for India. The representative of the India Office in the House of Commons, whether he was a Secretary of State, or the Under-Secretary with his Secretary of State in the Lords, which was my position, had to answer for the actions of a whole Government. He thus, in a sense, combined the functions of half a dozen Ministries at home. In addition, during the period in question, India was going through a most difficult time in her history, and was only saved from disaster by the wise governance of two great Viceroys—the late Lord Reading and Lord Halifax—and by a number of Presidency and Provincial Governors of eminence and supreme ability, such as the late Lord Lloyd, the late Lord Willingdon, the late Sir Harcourt Butler, Lord Hailey and Sir John Maffey.[2] I paid a second visit to India, on this occasion accompanied by my wife, and by Sir Victor Warrender[3] and his wife, again to discuss with the Viceroy and with the Governors certain confidential questions on behalf of my chief, Lord Birkenhead. In the course of these

[1] Now Lord Trefgarne.   [2] Now Lord Rugby.   [3] Now Lord Bruntisfield.

two visits I was in every Presidency and Province in India, except
Madras, and had the advantage of enjoying alike the hospitality
and the friendship of the distinguished men to whom I have
referred above, as well as that of a number of the Indian State
rulers. I was responsible for piloting numerous Bills concerned
with Indian Government through Parliament as well as grappling
with various members of the Labour Party and some Liberals
who openly and covertly sympathised with the cause of Swaraj
in India at a time when Mr. Gandhi was causing the maximum of
trouble to all concerned: but my task was made both as easy as
it could be in the circumstances and extremely happy by my
relationship with Lord Birkenhead who, as I have indicated
earlier, was one of the best friends whom I have ever had in
political life.

In 1928 a Commission under the chairmanship of Sir John
(now Lord) Simon was appointed to consider and report upon
the next step to be taken in Indian self-government, for which
purpose it twice visited India. The Swarajists boycotted it and
greeted its arrival with childish slogans such as "Simon; go back".
Lord Olivier had been Secretary of State for India in the Labour
Government of 1924, and was the principal spokesman of the
Party on India after the second 1924 election. He was a talented
man who had had a distinguished career in the Colonial Civil
Service, but he was an indifferent Minister and poor speaker; it
was indeed difficult to follow the trend and purport of his
speeches. I was once sitting on the steps of the Throne in the
House of Lords, listening to an exceptionally confused speech
by him, when the lights failed. With that equanimity which
distinguishes them, their Lordships continued their deliberations
in total darkness as if nothing had happened. A distinguished
Privy Councillor, happily still alive and a colleague of mine in
the Lords, who was sitting next to me, when I asked why on
earth the Leader of the House had not proposed an adjournment,
replied: "Well, as you will have observed, Olivier is no more
obscure in his utterances in the dark than he is in the light. The
Lords as a body are full of common sense; that's why, I've no
doubt, since Olivier is speaking, the Leader of the House has not
suggested an adjournment!!"

An astonishing incident arose out of my Under-Secretaryship

in the summer of 1926. The late Colonel Wedgwood[1] wrote to
me enclosing a letter received from a lady who alleged that her
husband had been murdered by the late Maharaja of Alwar, in
whose service he had been. He asked me for information on the
subject; and I replied in a letter marked "private and personal" to
the effect that the India Office and the Government of India had
no reason to believe that there was any truth in the allegations,
adding that there was unhappily reason to suppose that the
writer's mind had become slightly unhinged as a result of the loss
she had sustained. Colonel Wedgwood, who, as I have previously
recorded, was at times somewhat eccentric, sent the letter to the
lady in question, having failed to notice that it was marked
"private and personal". The sequel was that a week later an agitated India Office messenger came to my room to tell me that a
lady was waiting outside to serve me with a writ for libel! However, with the aid of my private secretary, he succeeded in inducing her to leave the building, and she was informed a few hours
later that the Treasury Solicitor would accept service of the writ.
The case duly came to the Courts with the Attorney General (Sir
Douglas Hogg, afterwards Lord Hailsham) as my leading counsel.
The prosecutrix conducted her own case and, in a speech of some
five hours' duration, proceeded to describe the treatment which
she alleged her husband had received at the hands of the late
Maharaja of Alwar. The Maharaja of Alwar did not bear a very
good reputation either with the Government of India or with his
fellow Princes, and it may well be that some of the allegations
about him which the prosecutrix made were true, but, as the
judge pointed out, they were totally irrelevant to the case. When
she had completed her statement, she announced that she did not
propose to call any witnesses, and the jury shortly afterwards
informed the judge that they had found in my favour and did not
want to hear the Attorney General, who was going to plead
privilege on my behalf. Immediately after the case was over, I
was talking to Sir Douglas when his junior came up to him and
said, "Attorney General, Colonel Wedgwood is in Court and
would like you or me to ask the judge to allow him to make a
statement in which he wishes to express his deep apology to Lord
Winterton for the trouble caused him". Sir Douglas replied, "I am

[1] Afterwards Lord Wedgwood.

not going to make the application; you can if you like, though the judge will very probably snub you. The best thing you can do is to get Josh 'chained up' as soon as possible". At that moment, I looked round and, to my horror, saw Colonel Wedgwood standing behind us, having obviously heard everything Sir Douglas had said. He had a strained and grim look on his face and, for one awful moment, I thought that he was going to show his displeasure at Sir Douglas's remarks in the same physical fashion as he had to a remark of Mr. Mitchell Banks[1], to which reference is made earlier in this book: however, after listening to the judge's ruling that "of course Colonel Wedgwood cannot make a statement", that he was surprised at anyone supposing that he could; "it was a completely improper submission", he hurried from the Court. He then wrote me a most charming letter, which was typical of his kind and affectionate nature, begging me to forgive him for an unpardonable offence and, with the Speaker's permission, next day he also apologised in the House of Commons for the mischief he had caused.

During the years 1927 and 1928 Mr. Baldwin was at the height of his power and authority—an authority derived as much from his personal qualities as from his high position. "Baldwinism" has become in recent years, like "Chamberlainism", a derogatory term to describe the mistakes of British policy in its dealings with German and Italian aggression in the '30s. But just as there was another form of "Chamberlainism"—Mr. Neville Chamberlain's many fine contributions to the advance of social well-being—so there was another aspect of "Baldwinism". After the General Strike a man of lesser calibre would have yielded to the clamour of the right wing of his supporters and similar right-wing opinion in the country and used every opportunity in his speeches to scarify and sneer at the defeated leaders of the trades unions. Some of these extremists said in private: "We have a unique opportunity, with public resentment against the T.U.C. for producing the General Strike still hot and vigorous, to smash the powers of the unions once and for all. It is only Baldwin's weakness and cowardice which prevents it". Mr. Baldwin's attitude was the exact reverse of weak or cowardly; it showed moral courage and high purpose. Though the Government had, perforce, for reasons

[1] Afterwards Sir Reginald Mitchell Banks.

which I have stated, to pass the Trades Disputes Act into law, the
Prime Minister, with the full approval of his colleagues, preached
this doctrine incessantly in and out of Parliament: "Make a fresh
start and forget the past". There was no future, he maintained,
for this densely populated country, with its dependence upon
export trade, unless there was a better understanding between
Capital and Labour, and especially between the active management and the wage-earner in every works. Each side was to blame
for the growing estrangement between them. In his own family
business the owners had known most of the workers by their
christian names, but now relationship was conducted through
cold and formal channels. The existence of what Disraeli had
called "The Two Nations" was a terrible deterrent to British
effort. They must be merged and fully united. The common
sacrifice of the war and the common heritage of the lovely English, Scottish and Welsh countryside, of Shakespeare and all the
other poets, writers and painters of these islands, and the immense
achievements of Britain at home and overseas bound us all
together—rich and poor, whatever our political opinions were.
Mr. Baldwin developed this theme in a series of speeches which,
by reason of their clarity, lucidity and beauty of expression, stand
very high in the illustrious record of British oratory. I have no
doubt that they were an important contributory factor to the
improved relationship, in comparison with a quarter of a century
ago, between employers and employed to-day. Mr. Baldwin
would have desired no better memorial.

There is an extract from my diary early in the year 1928 which
is worth quoting because it shows how completely false is the
contention of Mr. Bevan and others that the '20s and '30s were a
period of unrelieved misery for wage-earners.

FEBRUARY 13TH, 1928

An excellent speech by S. B.[1] on the same King's Speech amendment by the Opposition as that on which Philip[2] spoke on Friday
on trade, industry, the cost of living and real wages. He showed
that over a million more people were employed in industry than
was the case six or seven years ago which is an amazing fact; he also
stated that the prosperity and expansion of the "new" trades—

[1] Lord Baldwin.   [2] Sir Philip Cunliffe-Lister, now Lord Swinton.

motor car manufacturers, artificial silk, gramophones—is going far to absorb the displacement of labour from some of the depressed "heavy industries". Thirty thousand miners, for example, found work in other trades in 1927—he also showed by careful statistical calculation that real wages are higher and hours shorter than before the war and better even than two years ago—this speech of S.B.'s in my opinion pulverised the Opposition; indeed, this is borne out by the results of recent by-elections. The public feels that prosperity is slowly and certainly coming and that we are helping to bring it.

Unquestionably, the facts stated by the Government in the King's speech of 1928 were a remarkable tribute to British recovery from the injury caused by the General Strike, and I have no doubt myself that that recovery would have continued but for the tremendous blows given to British industry by the world trade depression of 1930 and 1931; the extent to which the British Labour Government was responsible for Britain's share of the injury is discussed later in this book.

On December 15, 1927, there was a famous debate in the House of Commons when a measure for a revised Prayer Book for the Church of England was thrown out after most heated controversy between members belonging to the Low Church Party, supported by several Nonconformist M.P.s, and members of the High Church Party, in addition to a number of those with broad Church views who supported the measure. It was, of course, a non-party debate, and members in all parts of the House could vote without the intervention of the Whips. The measure was largely defeated by a remarkable speech from Mr. Rosslyn Mitchell, Labour M.P. for Paisley[1]; he never made before or afterwards any noteworthy addition to debate, but, unquestionably, his speech on this occasion was of the highest order. After the defeat of the measure the Church Assembly endeavoured to meet the points raised by the objectors, but were not successful. A description of the second debate appears in my diary as follows:

JUNE 13TH–14TH, 1928

Jix[2] opened against the measure but was not, I think, as good as last year; Hugh Cecil, in support, made a very good speech, much

[1] He had defeated Mr. Asquith at Paisley in 1924.
[2] The late Sir William Joynson-Hicks, afterwards Lord Brentford.

better, I thought, than last year. Most of the speeches were good, but the issue was seldom in doubt and the measure was defeated by a larger majority than last year. I voted for the measure with much of the same doubt and reluctance as I voted against it last year, but for the reason that since its rejection last year an honest attempt has been made to clarify the meaning of the doubtful passages in it, and an equally honest assurance has been given that the Bishops will do their best to enforce it if it is passed. There was a great deal of feeling on the matter and the protagonists opposed each other rather like a Hindu-Moslem mob.

An important Bill was passed in the session of 1928 extending the franchise to women on the same basis as men; the Bill in question was known at the time as "Votes for Flappers". Sir William Joynson-Hicks, who was in charge of the Bill and who, despite a sharp tongue, was a most amusing and delightful man with a great hold on the affection of the House, described its seven opponents among Conservatives—who were Lord Hugh Cecil[1], the late Sir William Bull, the late Sir Charles Oman, the late Sir Henry Nield, the late Colonel Cuthbert James, the late Colonel Gretton and Colonel Applin—as "prehistoric men".

Another important Bill was passed into law in the shape of the Agricultural Credits Bill designed to allow farmers credit on easier terms than they would have obtained by ordinary borrowing; the late Colonel Guinness[2] was in charge of the Bill as Minister of Agriculture. This Bill, like the Bill to exclude agricultural land from rates, and a number of other measures to benefit farming passed in the '30s, should rebut the charge that nothing was done by Parliament to assist agriculture between the wars.

In the summer of 1928 Mr. Speaker Whitley retired and was succeeded by the Chairman of Committees, Mr. FitzRoy, who proved to be a very great Speaker. Soon after he was elected to the Chair, he stated one day that there were far too many supplementary questions, as this meant that members with oral questions some way down on the list had little chance of getting them answered, which was unfair to them. He announced that he would have to take steps to curtail the number of supplementary questions. His action raises an interesting point as to what should be the attitude of the Speaker towards undue delay over questions,

[1] Now Lord Quickswood.   [2] Afterwards Lord Moyne.

through the insistence of members on asking supplementary questions. On more than one occasion Mr. Speaker Clifton-Brown[1], when his attention was called to the matter, said that the remedy was in the hands of the House, and apparently, the present Speaker takes the same view; but both Mr. Speaker Lowther and Mr. Speaker FitzRoy believed that they had a duty to ensure that a reasonable number of questions were answered each day, and both of them were more strict in preventing lengthy or unnecessary supplementaries than either of their successors have been. It would be improper and impertinent for me to say which school of opinion is right, but that there is a contrast between them is clear from looking at the average number of oral questions answered to-day compared with the number answered when Mr. Speaker Lowther or Mr. Speaker FitzRoy were in the Chair.

In November Lord Birkenhead, whose health had been giving rise to concern, resigned the Secretaryship of State for India. The following is an extract from my diary:

NOVEMBER 15TH, 1928

Saw F. E. and took affectionate leave of him. Willie Peel[2] is to succeed him, of which I am glad. F. E. hopes that I may get the vacant Commissionership of Works.[3]

The 1928 session ended in the late summer of that year and the new session opened on November 6; the following is an extract from my diary:

NOVEMBER 8TH, 1928

Debate on the Address. An excellent speech by Winston reviewing the industrial and national situation. This is not the first time he has made this admirable kind of speech on a broad and lofty basis, thereby confounding alike the critics and comforting the doubters in our own Party.

It was known at the time that the Government was going to the country in the spring or summer of 1929, but the King's

[1] Now Lord Ruffside.   [2] The late Lord Peel.
[3] In fact I did not get it, but was given reason to suppose that I should receive promotion after the General Election if the Government were returned again—a contingency which did not occur.

Speech announced that before the Dissolution one important measure would be passed in the shape of the Local Government Reform Bill. The second reading debate on it is described as follows in my diary:

NOVEMBER 26TH, 1928

Neville C[1] moved the second reading of the Local Government Reform Bill; it was a masterly speech of over $2\frac{1}{2}$ hours. There was almost complete silence and the closest attention I think which I have seen since the war given to a speech of this character. Apart from its lucidity, the speech had more human touches and humour than is customary with Neville's speeches. The P.M. who sat next to me was as much impressed as I was; Neville received a tremendous ovation when he sat down.

In the summer of 1929 the Government went to the country. The Conservative organiser was Mr. John (now Lord) Davidson who had been a Civil Servant but had retired and entered Parliament a few years before. He is an able man, of great charm and integrity, but he had had at the time very little political experience. He was a great friend of Mr. Baldwin. Every Prime Minister and Party Leader has his *fidus Achates* on whose loyalty and discretion he can rely and who is on terms of such close friendship with his Chief that he can tell him things—often unpleasant things—that his colleagues may hesitate to mention. The late Mr. Sanders, for example, who was Mr. Balfour's Private Secretary, both when he was Prime Minister and Opposition Leader, was said to be the only man who knew his Chief's inner thoughts and views about people. Lord Bracken and Lord Cherwell in recent years are commonly supposed to be Mr. Churchill's most intimate friends in public life. A political *fidus Achates* performs a useful and necessary function, but, from the nature of it, is seldom popular. So Mr. Davidson was accused by many Conservatives, at least in private, of being responsible for the defeat of the Government and the invention of the Party's election slogan, "Safety First". Personally, I thought at the time, and still think, that it was a good slogan, for the danger of putting the Socialists back into office was manifest. But the Press and a number of electors thought otherwise. The election result was as

[1] Mr. Neville Chamberlain.

follows: Labour 289, Conservatives 260, Liberals 58, Others 8. Despite a small increase in their number, the Liberals were deeply disappointed at the result, as Mr. Lloyd George, after much beating of drums and sounding of trumpets in the Liberal Press and elsewhere, had produced a manifesto, published in what was called *The Orange Book*, under the title "We Can Conquer Unemployment". This followed three other pronunciamentos described as the *Brown*, *Green* and the *Yellow* books, in which Mr. Lloyd George had thundered denunciations against the Conservative Party and had suggested his own cures for the evils from which the world was suffering. Voters, however, were almost completely unimpressed.

With vague and contingent promises of support from the Liberals, Mr. Ramsay MacDonald formed a Government with Mr. Snowden as Chancellor of the Exchequer and Mr. Arthur Henderson as Foreign Secretary. Other appointments were: Lord Sankey, Lord Chancellor; Lord Parmoor, Lord President of the Council; Mr. J. H. Thomas, Lord Privy Seal; Mr. J. R. Clynes, Home Secretary; Lord Passfield, Colonial Secretary and Secretary of State for Dominion Affairs; Mr. Thomas Shaw, Secretary of State for War; Mr. Wedgwood Benn, Secretary of State for India; Lord Thomson, Secretary of State for Air; Mr. W. Adamson, Secretary of State for Scotland; Mr. A. V. Alexander, First Lord of the Admiralty; Mr. William Graham, President of the Board of Trade; Mr. Arthur Greenwood, Minister of Health; Mr. Noel Buxton, Minister of Agriculture; Sir Charles Trevelyan, President of the Board of Education; Miss Margaret Bondfield, Minister of Labour; Mr. George Lansbury, First Commissioner of Works.

Mr. Snowden (afterwards Lord Snowden) was the biggest individual asset possessed by his party in the '20s, and his courageous action in and after the 1931 crisis is highly commendable. A little man in stature, permanently lame from a cycling accident in his youth and often, I believe, in physical pain, he glared aggressively at all and sundry like a terrier of his native Yorkshire. He had a bitter tongue and often said unfair things, but he was a first-class parliamentarian with a cool, calm brain who earned the unstinted admiration of Civil Servants working under him for his good judgment, integrity and fearlessness. During the

1929 Parliament there was an all-night sitting on the committee stage of the Finance Bill which lasted from 4 p.m. on one day until 11 a.m. or thereabouts on the second. It was mainly a bare-fisted all-out fight between Mr. Snowden and his immediate pre-decessor, Mr. Churchill. In a series of mellifluous and magnificent Churchillian phrases and aphorisms, Mr. Churchill smashed into Socialism in general and Mr. Snowden's budget in particular; the Chancellor was, his theme ran, the narrow, rigid, pedantic and fanatical high priest of this dangerous and fantastic new religion. Mr. Snowden, with icy sarcasm, congratulated Mr. Churchill upon his success in his new part—that of the exponent of orthodox high Toryism; he had been a rebel Conservative in his youth, then an advanced Liberal, then a Constitutionalist, now a Tory again. Of course, he played his new part well; this most magnifi-cent of all political actors would always do well so long as he could command a full house. It was immaterial to him whether he believed in the part or not. In political life to-day no one but Mr. Bevan, and then on occasions only, could stand up to Mr. Churchill as Mr. Snowden did during that long sitting. It would have been difficult for any referee to decide on points who won the fight. Just before the end of the sitting, on the motion "to report progress", Mr. Churchill rose and, in his chivalrous way, con-gratulated the Chancellor on the patience, devotion to duty and skill in debate which he had shown; with a smile of real pleasure and emotion on his grim, tired face, the Chancellor rose and, in equally felicitous terms, thanked Mr. Churchill and paid a tribute to his eloquence and endurance. The two men left the Chamber together in friendly and cheerful conversation. I remember at the time feeling proud of belonging to an assembly where such incidents occur.

As always at the beginning of a Parliament, new names began to appear in *Hansard* and the political newspapers, and fresh faces in the cartoons, whose owners had attracted attention in the House after the 1929 election. A young member, Mr. R. A. Butler, made a successful maiden speech on the Address. There were friendly references in the Press to the speeches of two other new Members—the progeny of famous parents who had been nur-tured and reared in political circles—Lady Megan Lloyd George and Mr. Malcolm MacDonald. The famous quiff of the new

Minister of Transport, Mr. Herbert Morrison, appeared for the
first time in a *Punch* cartoon. Then there were the two redoubtable Browns. Mr. W. J. Brown, Labour M.P. for Leicester, was
a pertinacious critic not only of the Conservative Party but, on
occasion, of his own Party as well. Standing in later years and
being elected as an Independent, he became, until defeated at the
1950 election, one of the most effective speakers in the House.
As it happens, I have worked with him in one or two connections
and learnt to admire his courage, integrity and ability. The voice
of Mr. Ernest Brown, Liberal M.P. for Leith, frequently boomed
across the Chamber of the Commons. It was always a matter of
dispute whether Mr. Brown was the fastest or the loudest speaker
in the House—or was both. What is not in dispute is that in the
next few years he did most useful and honest work in various
ministerial offices and was missed in all sections of the House when
he lost his seat in 1945. A great figure was removed from the
parliamentary scene when Lord Balfour died in the spring of 1930.
His faults as a leader, to which I have referred in earlier chapters,
had long been forgotten. He was mourned as an elder statesman
of immense charm, grace and intellect; for those who were
honoured by his friendship there has been no one to replace him,
for "A. J. B." was unique. Among his qualities was that of making the most stupid and unimportant person whom he might
chance to meet at dinner or a party feel entirely at ease by listening
intently and sympathetically to the most banal or unintelligent
observations. Most great men suffer fools very ungladly. Mr.
Balfour's high standards of conduct and courtesy precluded him
from doing so.

CHAPTER XII

As invariably happens to a Party Leader following a defeat at a general election, Mr. Baldwin was subjected to considerable criticism after the 1929 election, though some of this, as I have stated earlier, was deflected upon Mr. Davidson. Lords Rothermere and Beaverbrook and their respective papers were very hostile—the latter demanding an official affirmation from him in favour of Free Trade within the Empire. Some of us, too, who moved in the inner circles of the Party, were concerned about its present and future, and especially the policy to be advocated. The late Lord Lloyd, who had resigned his position as British representative in Egypt after a dispute with the Foreign Secretary, Mr. Henderson, came to stay with me in the spring of 1930 and, after talking through most of the night, we determined to use what influence we possessed to induce Mr. Baldwin to adopt a more positive and less enigmatic attitude towards policy in general and that regarding the Empire in particular. I went to see two Press friends of mine—the late Mr. Gwynne, redoubtable editor of the *Morning Post*, and Lord Camrose of the *Daily Telegraph*, whose shrewd and balanced judgment in a crisis I have always found invaluable. The effect of the efforts of a number of us, working not as a "group" or in any conspiratorial sense, to induce our leader to produce an Imperial policy and improve his relationships with important sections of the Press are described in my diary as follows:

MARCH 5TH, 1930

The political situation has been completely transformed since S. B.,[1] at a meeting of the Executive of the Party yesterday, stated his willingness to submit any proposals put forward by the Dominions at an Imperial Conference called *ad hoc* to consider inter-Imperial fiscal arrangements and to refer them, even if they included food duties on non-Imperial produce, to the electors by a referendum. This plan has advantages and seems feasible and will be supported by "Max" and his newspapers. What Rothermere will do

[1] Lord Baldwin.

is problematical, but this would seem to be the end of the "United Empire Party"[1] as an organisation hostile to us. S. B. has also declared in favour of a subsidy for wheat and the prohibition of dumped German oats; with food duties intended specifically to help British farmers ruled out and almost universal safe-guarding, this announcement on policy was essential.

No one who is devoted, as I am, to the cause which my old chief, Mr. Joseph Chamberlain, first propounded, of Imperial Unity and integration, should fail to be grateful to Lord Beaverbrook for his powerful support of it in the last forty years. Other politicians and newspaper owners have sometimes enthusiastically, sometimes lukewarmly, supported it whilst at periods ignoring the subject altogether. Lord Beaverbrook has been its constant and persistent supporter, though sometimes his enthusiasm has caused him to minimise the difficulties of its achievement. It is a fine thing to have devoted a lifetime of fervent and loving support to a great conception.

But the doubts and difficulties surrounding Mr. Baldwin's leadership were not resolved by his declaration on Imperial Policy. In the late summer of 1929 and in 1930 a breeze blew in the Conservative Party over Indian affairs which, though it died down temporarily, later developed into a gale which nearly blew that tough old oak out of the leadership. During the summer recess of 1929 Lord Irwin[2], the Viceroy of India, who was home on leave, asked me to meet him in the absence from town of the two senior members of the Conservative Party—the late Lord Peel and the late Lord Birkenhead, who were, as ex-Secretaries of State for India, concerned with Indian affairs. He lunched with me at the Belgravia Hotel. I was surprised and alarmed by the views he expressed. The sequel was as follows:

OCTOBER 25TH, 1929

Lunched with Willie Peel at the Carlton; F. E. was there too; a somewhat serious situation has arisen. Edward Irwin is anxious to make a declaration defining "Dominion Status" as the final goal. Now "Dominion Status" has a very special meaning (especially since

[1] The United Empire Party was one of the many mushroom groups formed as a result of newspaper action in the Conservative Party in the past.
[2] Now Lord Halifax.

the Imperial Conference of 1926), and use of the term would be in advance of any of the definitions hitherto attempted such as "self-government within the Empire" because of that meaning—I knew of Edward's[1] desire some time ago but the disturbing thing is that S. B. seems to have given contingent assent on behalf of the Party—contingent that is on the agreement of all three parties and the Simon Commission. Even so, some of us think it is dangerous to do so without prior consultation with former colleagues.

During the Press controversy on this matter it was alleged that when a distinguished official of the India Office, who at Lord Irwin's request (and with the Secretary of State, Mr. Wedgwood Benn's, permission) was sent to Aix-les-Bains where Mr. Baldwin was having a cure, to discuss the subject with him, Mr. Baldwin showed little interest in it and merely remarked: "If Edward says it is all right, I'll agree". In fact, as the next extract from my diary shows, Mr. Ramsay MacDonald must share the blame for any mistaken impression by Lord Baldwin of what Lord Irwin's views involved.

NOVEMBER 1ST, 1929

Edward[2] has made his statement about a new conference between the Government of India and representatives of British India and the Princes, following the report of the Simon Commission. This matter he discussed (with Benn's permission) with Willie Peel and me in July. It was accepted by the Simon Commission and popular opinion here seemed fairly favourable to it. I do not very much care for the plan, but at least it is an advance to bring the question of the Indian States into the picture; Edward's other announcement defining the demand of 1917 as meaning "Dominion Status" has had an even more deleterious effect than it did when Edward astonished and almost horrified me by telling me of the idea when we lunched at the Belgravia Hotel in September. The Commission was never consulted, Simon himself says he never agreed to it (though Benn says he did). Reading and the "Goat"[3] are against it, and so far as S. B.[4] gave his conditional assent when his opinion was asked in August, that consent was founded on conditions never fulfilled. Ramsay's[5] letter to him on the subject was misleading (I have now seen it) to say the least of it. To-day at question time the fat was in

[1] This refers to what Lord Irwin told me at the Belgravia Hotel.
[2] Lord Irwin (now Lord Halifax). [3] Mr. Lloyd George.
[4] Lord Baldwin. [5] Mr. Ramsay MacDonald, the Prime Minister.

the fire. The *Daily Mail* made a most ferocious attack on S. B., and incidentally on Edward, too, accusing S. B. of committing our Party to "Dominion Status" without consulting it or his former colleagues and then being forced to withdraw; the *Daily Mail* also said that Edward was in fact a Socialist and that S. B. had appointed him well knowing this fact. S. B. at question time to-day emphatically denied that there was the faintest truth in the *Daily Mail's* allegations.

NOVEMBER 4TH, 1929

A great Press controversy has arisen over Edward and S. B.'s statements, respectively. The "Dominion Status" announcement is, as I supposed it would be, commonly criticised—but there is almost universal Conservative support for S. B. against the *Daily Mail*.

NOVEMBER 7TH, 1929

The day of the Indian Debate in the House of Commons, S. B. led off and spoke very vigorously (though too fast in delivery), about the *Daily Mail's* attack on him and, on the whole, gave a completely satisfactory denial to the allegations made. He then went on to speak about the conference and the "Dominion Status" announcement—approving the one and enquiring about the other in a mildly critical way, very different from F. E. in the other House, or L. G. who followed. In a passage of high eloquence he spoke of the "split migration of the Aryan peoples". L. G. was aggressive and provocative; he got a nasty retort from "Wedgy",[1] whom he described as "Moses dancing before the Ark"; the latter immediately sprang to his feet and said "I have never worshipped the golden calf!" The House roared with laughter for several minutes; in any case the "Goat's" speech was a very dangerous one, calculated to do considerable harm in India. I thought the Secretary of State good, but many people did not. At any rate he was careful not to say anything to make the position worse, as were the Prime Minister, Baldwin and most of us—but not so Winston and L. G.; indeed, some credit the latter with having intrigued with Rothermere to bring off a treble event—the defeat of the Government, the downfall of S. B. and a coalition. I can hardly think that Winston is in favour of this course. Simon continued the debate and made a most discreet and statesmanlike speech and there it ended—a day of tense excitement but far less mischief done than in the Lords.

Mr. Churchill, I should explain, did not actually speak in the debate but cheered Mr. Lloyd George, to the concern of some of

[1] Mr. Wedgwood Benn, Secretary of State for India.

us, very loudly—thus presaging the line which he was to take later when the internal conflict in the Conservative Party on Indian affairs reached its height.

The charges and counter-charges in the controversy between Mr. Baldwin and the "Press Lords" continued throughout 1930 to reach a crescendo later on, as will be recorded, in due course, in this book; they were intermixed with reconciliations or truces which seldom, however, lasted long. For instance, I find this entry in my diary for June 18, 1930:

> Had tea with Max Beaverbrook at Stornoway House and heard an interesting exposition from him, with which I was not in agreement, as to the reasons for his new break with S. B.

I have the advantage of a retentive memory, but so complicated, drawn-out and many-sided was the controversy in question, that I have completely forgotten the nature of this particular breach and Lord Beaverbrook's justification for it; which is perhaps as well, for otherwise he might justifiably accuse me of giving away confidences by mentioning it!

The Government announced in the middle of June that a Round Table Conference on the next steps to be taken in the advance towards Indian self-government would be constituted; it would consist of Indian and British representatives. This announcement quenched momentarily the flame of angry recrimination in some right-wing Conservative Party and Press circles about Mr. Baldwin and Lord Irwin's position; for no one could find any reason for objecting to the Conference nor to its composition, except on one score—the Party was unanimous, and had indeed Mr. Lloyd George's support, in favour of Sir John Simon's membership of it, to which the Government refused to agree. As it happened, a bitter, though temporary, internecine controversy in the Parliamentary Labour Party served to divert attention from the disputes over some aspects of Mr. Baldwin's policy as leader among the Conservatives. I was largely instrumental in producing it, but my primary object was to protect the good name of the House of Commons; however, to hurl the apple of discord among one's parliamentary opponents and thereby induce them to fight like tiger cats is a perfectly legitimate political weapon. The question of Sir John Simon's exclusion from the Round Table Conference and how the "row" among the Socialists in Parliament arose are described in my diary as follows:

JULY 28TH, 1930

Another discussion on Indian Affairs in S. B.'s room at the House of Commons. We have now secured "All-Party Representation" in the Indian Round Table Conference in face of Benn's and, apparently, Edward's[1] opposition; but the Government steadily refuses to put on Simon. I raised at question time the matter of a speech (as a question of privilege) made by Sandham, the Labour member for Kirkdale, on Saturday in which he accused Socialists of bribery and drunkenness. Sandham was not present and my motion declaring him to have stated a gross libel was adjourned until tomorrow. The House, especially the Socialists, cheered me loudly, and *The Times* wrote approvingly of my action.

JULY 29TH, 1930

Went to see S. B. in morning; he is consulting me freely about Indian affairs and said affectionately that I was "a man after his own heart". L'affaire Sandham developed this afternoon and has now become a matter of first-class importance. Sandham made a more or less defiant speech (though he was quite polite to the Speaker and to the forms of the House) in reiteration of his charges which, however, he still left completely vague. He quoted long extracts from his speech when the Speaker stopped him, as he did also when he tried to quote my incident with Will Thorne[2] twenty-one years ago.

[1] Lord Irwin, afterwards Lord Halifax.

[2] During an all-night sitting in 1909, in a moment of folly, I made the unfounded allegation, by inference, that the late Mr. Will Thorne, M.P., was under the influence of drink; in a scene which followed he was suspended for his retort to me. Next day his suspension was rescinded on a motion moved by the Prime Minister [Mr. Asquith] and supported by my own leader Mr. Balfour on the ground that he had been greatly provoked. I then apologised for my allegation. By 1930 the incident had long been forgotten and Mr. Will Thorne and I were on excellent personal terms. The House greatly resented Mr. Sandham's reference to the matter, with Mr. Thorne leading the protests, because there is a strong unwritten rule of conduct and etiquette in the Commons that there shall be no mention in debate of a "scene" after the participants in it have made it up and apologised to the House. Had the Speaker not risen Mr. Sandham would undoubtedly have been shouted down, in any case his reference had no relevance to his charge which concerned the conduct of members in the then House of Commons and not in a previous one.

Sandham then sat down and Maxton protested on his behalf that he had been unduly curtailed; the motion to refer the matter to the Committee of Privileges was carried by an enormous majority.

JULY 30TH, 1930

Meeting at S. B.'s house in morning about India. After some discussion it was decided to try to move the adjournment if Austen,[1] who was to raise the question, could get no satisfaction about Simon's exclusion from the conference. In point of fact he did not, as the adjournment cannot be carried on a closure of supply day; so Austen gave notice he would raise the matter again tomorrow, the Speaker having said that the right to ask for permission to raise the question as a matter of urgency would not be prejudiced by the delay.

JULY 31ST, 1930

Report of the Committee of Privileges came out this morning; it was to the effect that Sandham had failed to produce evidence and they recommended that he should be censured. An angry debate ensued on the report; the Attorney-General moved the motion agreeing with the report. Unfortunately, the Speaker put the question directly the Attorney-General had sat down. Several of us thought that it would have been better, had it been possible, to induce the House to consent to the matter going to some sort of judicial committee who would be able to call for evidence on oath. It was probable that most of the members of the Committee of Privileges would not have objected to this. They are in the position of a grand jury and must find for or against on evidence which Sandham couldn't or wouldn't produce, though he and Brown[2] said that they would do so before a proper tribunal. Had this happened the charge would have been proved or disproved. But the Speaker's action prevented this so we had an undignified wrangle on Snowden's motion to censure Sandham, whom Brown, Maxton and others defended. The rest of the House angrily demanded facts and called for Sandham who at length reluctantly spoke but said nothing. Then the motion of censure was carried, only four or five voting against it; the sequel was that the Speaker, in full-bottomed wig, with his hat on, looking as he always does a magnificent figure, in solemn tones amidst dead silence in the House censured Sandham. After all this turmoil Austen raised the question of Simon's exclusion from the conference, L. G. and I spoke in support of him; Benn said nothing in reply—and there the matter ended.

[1] The late Sir Austen Chamberlain.   [2] Mr. W. J. Brown.

The legislative fare on the parliamentary table during the 1929–30 session was neither attractive nor novel, including as it did further amending Acts to deal with such painfully familiar subjects as unemployment and the mining industry. The session ended on August 1, 1930.

During the recess I visited Northern Rhodesia where I owned some property. My visit coincided with one of the periodical crises with the Colonial Office which occur in every colony where there are British European inhabitants who have either been born there or made it their home.

SEPTEMBER 26TH, 1930

Reached Livingstone and stayed at Government House. Maxwell, the Governor, is home for the Colonial Governors' Conference, and when he returns will find a difficult situation confronting him —for the whole country is up in arms about the White Paper, that is the memorandum on native affairs issued by the Colonial Office. Originally applied to Kenya, the contents refer to Arabs and Indians (who are practically non-existent in Northern Rhodesia) and says native rights must be paramount, and where emigrant and native rights are in conflict, the latter must prevail. Whatever the intention of the framers of the document it is both injudicious and offensive, and the people here are as indignant and apprehensive as they are in Kenya. They have written a reply couched in very aggressive terms and asked for the expenses of a deputation home to be paid. Passfield[1] has replied in the negative in terms which are not very courteous so "the fat is in the fire". Northern Rhodesia is being supported openly by Southern Rhodesia and at least one South African Minister—Groller—has expressed his sympathy with them. The unofficial members of the Northern Rhodesian Council are meeting the private members of the Southern Rhodesian legislature at the Falls to-day.

SEPTEMBER 27TH, 1930

Met the Northern Rhodesian unofficial members at the Falls Hotel. They had been during the day at the conference with the Southern Rhodesians. A proposal in favour of amalgamation with Southern Rhodesia had been proposed, but finally withdrawn, because though the majority of the Northern Rhodesians [including

[1] The late Lord Passfield, Colonial Secretary at the time.

Moore[1] who had hitherto been opposed] were in favour, John Brown and Chad Norris were not prepared to vote for it without further considering it. They wanted the resolution to pass unanimously or not at all. The elected members asked me what steps they should now take. I advised them to send a cable to Passfield, couched in courteous terms, which would acknowledge his reply to their memorandum and to go on to ask him, as and when conditions in Northern Rhodesia approximated to those in Southern Rhodesia, at the time that the country was granted self-government, would His Majesty's Government accept a proposal for such amalgamation emanating from the elected representatives of both territories. . . . They gratefully accepted my proposal and drafted a telegram and we despatched it at midnight, Moore sententiously stating that we would make history.

To-day, at the time of writing—twenty-two years later—the form of juncture between Northern and Southern Rhodesia is still under discussion, though its eventual inevitability in some form is certain. The time is past when any British Government or any section of opinion in Britain can prevent two growing European communities, even those set in the midst of much bigger African populations, from deciding between themselves what their future constitutional relationship shall be. Britain is too old, wise and experienced a nation to repeat in Africa the mistakes which she made in North America in the eighteenth century in her treatment of European overseas settlers.

In the train on my way back to the coast I heard of the death of Lord Birkenhead. I put in my diary this epitaph on him which I think merits reading because it seems to me to be a true estimate of his character:

> never was supreme genius and the most vivid and surpassing intellect joined to quicker wit, more *joie de vivre* or such a capacity for loyal and true friendship. The less creditable aspects of his character should be forgotten and submerged in these facts.

[1] The late Mr. Moore, owner and editor of the *Livingstone Mail*. He afterwards became Sir Leopold Moore and was at the time a very prominent man in Northern Rhodesia; he was extremely aggressive in controversy and not always tactful, but with great courage and considerable talent both as a writer and a speaker. He was not popular either with the Colonial Office, the Northern Rhodesian Government or the Chartered Company, who were his three principal bugbears.

I added that I had a most gloomy four-day journey to Cape Town, for I was deeply saddened by an overwhelming sense of loss.

I arrived home to find in full progress a fresh crisis in the Party over the leadership. The following passages from my diary describe the situation and its sequel:

OCTOBER 19TH, 1930

A crisis has arisen in our Party as some forty M.P.s have said that they will not support S. B.[1] at the meeting tomorrow. The report of the private meeting at which this was decided came out by accident but there seems reason to think that the report was accurate.

OCTOBER 20TH, 1930

The Party meeting was held in Caxton Hall on a clear, bright day. S. B. in the Chair—grim, determined, fierce—and, incidentally, very good. Support for his policy was carried by about 500-1 (Max Beaverbrook dissenting), and then he retired from the Chair whilst the question of leadership was discussed, Salisbury taking it in his stead. He had speeches for and against with the usual excitement and ill feeling. Max,[2] among others, spoke and quite well, though greeted with hoots. Hailsham[3] made an eminent speech for the leader and he frankly admitted some weaknesses in his leadership in opposition but strongly stressed the fact that (a) a change would be hailed with triumphant delight by the Press, (b) the difficulty to bring about, as who would be the man to succeed him? When someone shouted "You", he said emphatically, "No". He showed, too, the value of S. B.'s name and prestige in the North of England. Resolution of confidence carried by over 500 to 110 and the minority at once, through their spokesman, announced their acceptance of the verdict.

The House met on October 28, 1930, and in the next session there were a number of good speeches on the Address, including one from Sir Oswald Mosley and the late Colonel Oliver Stanley, respectively. Sir Oswald, even by then, had had a chequered career. Very angry feeling between Conservatives and Socialists was shown in more than one debate during the last weeks of 1930.

[1] Lord Baldwin.   [2] Lord Beaverbrook.   [3] The late Lord Hailsham.

NOVEMBER 4TH, 1930

"Wind-up" of Address debate. I did not hear S. B. but Ramsay was appalling, and because he was interrupted sat down saying "and they call this the gentlemanly party—the swine". This was faithfully reported in *The Times*.

The Times reported this remark probably because it was of a novel character for a Prime Minister to use, though Mr. Lloyd George had said far worse things about us before he became Prime Minister, during the budget controversy. Other members of the Labour Party in the Commons, in moments of stress and emotion, when a Conservative says something of which they disapprove, have at intervals ever since called out, "And they call themselves the gentlemanly party!", despite the fact that no Conservative is on record for having made such an extraordinarily snobbish claim for the composition of his Party. Another scene occurred on November 27, 1930:

> Censure debate on the Government for their failure to accept the offer of the Dominion Premiers. I did not hear S. B. who opened, but I am told he made too academic a speech. Jimmy Thomas who followed was better but made an outrageous reference to Bennett, the Canadian Prime Minister's speech as "humbug"; Amery who made quite a good speech was bitterly interrupted and we retaliated on Snowden and when he made an offensive reference to S. B.'s speech and said that soon there would be a renewed demand for "Baldwin must go" we all yelled at him.

As we were filing out to vote, a Labour member, Mr. Simmons, M.P. for Erdington, struck me with an Order Paper. In those days I did not know Mr. Simmons, who had a fine record in the 1914 war and was an "old Gallipolite" like me, though in recent years we have become friends. So I was naturally somewhat surprised and annoyed, but decided to take no notice of the incident. However, both our Chief Whip and Mr. Baldwin said it must be brought to the Speaker's attention, which it was by Mr. Baldwin himself. The Speaker ruled that Mr. Simmons must apologise, which he did, explaining that he thought that I had called Mr. Snowden "an insulting dog". It is quite likely that he was so

---

[1] Mr. Ramsay MacDonald, the Prime Minister.

described by somebody on our side in the exchange of insults, but it was not I who made the observation.

As I was leaving the House, a Labour M.P. offered to fight me somewhere outside the precincts of the Palace of Westminster. I ignored his offer by making no answer but, perhaps unwisely, I referred in a humorous manner to this challenge at a public meeting; it immediately became front-page news in the popular Press, so I deemed it right to make a personal explanation when the House next met in order to deny that I had ever made the alleged remark which caused the tap with an Order Paper and the challenge to a fight. I had the satisfaction of being assured by both *The Times* and the *Morning Post* that I had behaved with tact and discretion and that no blame attached to me.

CHAPTER XIII

THERE was not much parliamentary excitement in the early months of 1931. The Government produced an Electoral Reform Bill which was a frank and crude attempt to secure Liberal support by providing for the alternative vote. Mr. Clynes, the Home Secretary, who introduced it, was too honest a man to give more than a very tepid proclamation of his belief in it. It was ridiculed by the Conservatives and attacked by the "Clyde"; like the Consumers Council Bill and a Bill to amend the Trades Disputes Act, it failed to pass. Indeed, only a few minor and non-controversial Bills got through all their stages in the last session of the 1929 Parliament. Most Ministers appeared to be unhappy and indecisive, as must be members of any Government with no assured majority, since every Minister, of keenness and capacity, wants to mark his term of office by fresh administrative action or by the production of legislation which his departmental officers convince him is necessary for that particular part of the public interest which his Ministry serves. A Minister in a minority Government is often precluded from taking either action, since controversy is likely to result therefrom, unless he is assured in advance that all the various elements in the two separate parties which sustain the Government in office will support him. An exception to this general impression of ministerial sterility in the 1929 Government was the late Mr. Lansbury's tenure of the Office of Works. He did a good deal to improve the London parks, including the provision of a bathing place in Hyde Park known as "Lansbury Lido". His knowledge of, and love for, London, which resembled that of Mr. John Burns, did something to atone for grave errors of taste and judgment which I have described earlier.

There were two important events in foreign relationships in 1930; the Five-Power Naval Conference took place in London in January, 1930, and, as a result, there was agreement between Great Britain and a number of Powers on the ratio of construction of their respective Navies; following it there was also agreement between some of the Powers on the relative strength of their Navies; at the Hague Conference in the autumn of this year, after an acrimonious discussion between Mr. (afterwards Lord) Snowden and M. Charon, the French Minister of Finance, this country obtained an increase in the amount of reparations from Germany to which she was entitled; unhappily, as happened with the agreements of so many international conferences between the wars, the march of events entirely obliterated any good which was done by either of these conferences.

The domestic affairs of the Conservative Opposition in the first half of 1931 were as strained as those of the Labour Party, whose back-benchers were alarmed and indignant at the growth of unemployment and the Government's failure to arrest it. There were serious differences of opinion in the sub-committee of Conservative M.P.s on India with the gradual emergence of a group of members led by Mr. Churchill in opposition to the official policy of the Party. In particular, the group objected to the negotiations between the Viceroy, Lord Irwin,[1] and Mr. Gandhi, and wanted the Leader of the Party and those like myself responsible for dealing with Indian affairs from the Front Benches in both Houses to protest against these negotiations. How the group in question eventually, when the Government of India Bill was produced, went into open opposition to the official policy is described later. But the biggest "row" in the Party arose over a by-election in Westminster. The official candidate, Mr. Duff Cooper,[2] was opposed by the late Mr. Erskine supported by a number of dissident Conservatives, mainly because of dissatisfaction with Mr. Baldwin's leadership, and by the *Daily Mail*. Mr. Baldwin described the latter organ as the "Harlot of all the Ages", and the candidates and their supporters abused each other with greater vigour, not to say venom, than is customary between candidates and supporters of different parties. The City of Westminster indeed reverted to its electioneering habits of 150 years earlier. Returning one day from Parliament to my house in Eccleston Square I saw a scene more reminiscent of Falls Road in Belfast than peaceful Pimlico. A well-known speaker for the Conservative Party, his arms held by two police constables, was on his way to the police station, and a cordon of police, the

[1] Now Lord Halifax.   [2] Now Lord Norwich.

sergeant-in-charge with a large and blood-stained handkerchief on his head under his helmet, stood across the entrance to the Square. He let me through on my assurance that I was not one of a band of rival Conservatives who had been fighting each other and the police in Gillingham Street a few minutes earlier. He said, pointing to his head, "You can see, sir, what we've got to put up with in this election. I and my men will be glad when it is over". It soon was, with Mr. Duff Cooper an easy winner.

One day in the early summer of 1931 I was on the terrace of the House of Commons and met two prominent Labour M.P.s from the Clyde walking up and down. They invited me to join them. They said their leaders were losing their nerve at the growth of unemployment and the increasingly serious financial position of the country, and that the Prime Minister was carrying on secret negotiations with Mr. Baldwin. I told them that they were talking nonsense and that if there had been such discussions I should have heard of them. One of the "Clydebankers" replied, "You can say what you like, Winterton, but I tell you as a fact that those two wily old birds, your leader and ours, have put their heads together and have decided on a Coalition some time in the autumn". From that day to this I have never been able to find the slightest evidence to support my Labour friends' contention that such discussions were going on in May, 1931; nor would they, in after years, when pressed on the subject, tell me where they got the information which they gave me; but their prophecy about a Coalition proved to be completely accurate. At the time it was made no newspaper or politician had even hinted that there was a possibility of such a happening. Indeed it was not until more than two months later when the May[1] Committee reported that public opinion was seriously alarmed by the country's financial position. The report, which came out just after

[1] So called because the Chairman was Sir George (afterwards Lord) May. The Committee's terms of reference were "to make recommendations to the Chancellor of the Exchequer for effecting forthwith all possible reductions in the National Expenditure on Supply Services, having regard especially to the present and prospective position of the Revenue. In so far as questions of policy are involved in the expenditure under discussion, these will remain for the exclusive consideration of the Cabinet; but it will be open to the Committee to review the expenditure and to indicate the economies which might be effected if particular policies were either adopted, abandoned or modified".

Parliament had adjourned for the summer recess, estimated the deficiency on the budget for 1932 at £120 million, and recommended economies of the most drastic kind. These included a reduction in the amount paid in unemployment insurance, large cuts in the salaries of the police, of teachers, and in the pay of the Army and Navy. It also advocated the abolition of the Road Fund and of the Empire Marketing Board. The next steps on the road that led to the downfall of the Labour Government are described as follows in an extract from my diary of August 14, 1931, when I was staying with my wife in France:

Exciting and disturbing events are occurring in England. It appears that when the German financial crisis caused a general investigation by foreign bankers, Finance Ministers and others, it became apparent that the British financial position was bad. Though still creditors to a large extent on long term account we are debtors to a disturbing degree on short term account. This plus the following facts: (1) The warning of the Chancellor of the Exchequer as to the seriousness of the budgetary position; (2) The continued drop in exports and rise in unemployment; (3) The "rigging" by the Treasury of the Unemployment Fund; (4) The May Report and the Government's failure as yet to say if they are going to accept its conclusions and, less certainly, the desire of sections of foreign financial interests to ensure our credit has produced some serious results. There has been a drain of gold from London, the bank rate has had to be raised, and French and U.S. financial interests have lent £50 million temporarily to the Bank of England.

The Prime Minister has come to London to consult Snowden.

AUGUST 15TH, 1931

The English and French papers are full of the crisis. S. B. who has returned especially to London from Aix-les-Bains and Neville Chamberlain have both seen the Prime Minister. The latter and Snowden have spoken of the need of economy and sacrifice by all classes to meet the situation. No one knows what these sacrifices will be as the Committee of the Cabinet who are considering the May Report have apparently not made up their minds, so the wildest rumours are extant.

AUGUST 16TH, 1931

The newspapers say that next week (when the Cabinet will consider the situation and apparently consult informally both the

T.U.C. and representatives of the Opposition in regard to their proposals for meeting the financial situation) will be the most anxious period since August 4th, 1914. It is suggested that the House of Commons will meet in September to consider a fresh budget.

AUGUST 21ST, 1931

The Government have apparently not yet reached any final decision for meeting the deficit; according to French papers they are consulting with Herbert Samuel and Maclean[1] representing the Liberals, and Neville Chamberlain and Sam Hoare representing us, and have consulted the T.U.C. Apparently, the Opposition leaders were not yet satisfied that the economies went far enough, whilst the T.U.C. were evidently as yet unconvinced and probably hostile. The Cabinet sat all day before they could reach agreement —while the British press is getting impatient and the totally un-justified credit which the Government got for "being busy" and calling the Opposition into conference is fading away.

AUGUST 23RD, 1931

The Times of yesterday reports that there is still no plan produced by the Government, and there is a strong leader demanding one at once. French local papers of to-day contain even more exciting news. The King is to return to London to-day and S. B. has again come back from Aix-les-Bains. The despatch says that Ramsay and the Cabinet nearly resigned on Saturday, but that in the end it was decided to amend the plan produced and see if the Opposition would accept it then. There was to be another Cabinet to-day (Sunday). The communiqué says that the Cabinet adjourned after their Saturday meeting until Sunday in order to afford the opportunity of giving the finishing touches to a plan which had been produced. It is said that if Ramsay resigns there will be no election, but S. B. will be asked to take office. This would be "handing us the baby" with a vengeance, and I hope he will hesitate to accept.

AUGUST 25TH, 1931

The Government has resigned and a new "National Government" is to be formed of Conservatives, Liberals and Labour.

The new Cabinet was a small one. Mr. MacDonald was Prime Minister and Mr. Snowden remained at the Treasury. The other

---

[1] The late Sir Donald Maclean.

members were: Mr. Baldwin, Lord President of the Council; Mr. Philip Snowden, Chancellor of the Exchequer; Sir Herbert Samuel, Home Secretary; Lord Sankey, Lord Chancellor; Lord Reading, Secretary of State for Foreign Affairs; Sir Samuel Hoare, Secretary of State for India; Mr. J. H. Thomas, Secretary of State for Dominion Affairs and for the Colonies; Mr. Neville Chamberlain, Minister of Health and Sir Philip Cunliffe-Lister, President of the Board of Trade.

The principal offices outside the Cabinet were filled as follows: Lord Crewe, Secretary of State for War; Lord Amulree, Secretary of State for Air; Sir Archibald Sinclair, Secretary of State for Scotland; Lord Peel, Lord Privy Seal; Sir Austen Chamberlain, First Lord of the Admiralty; Sir Donald Maclean, President of the Board of Education; Sir John Gilmour, Minister of Agriculture and Fisheries; Sir Henry Betterton, Minister of Labour; Lord Londonderry, First Commissioner of Works; Mr. Pybus, Minister of Transport; Major Tryon, Minister of Pensions; Lord Lothian, Chancellor of the Duchy of Lancaster; Sir William Jowitt, Attorney General; Sir Thomas Inskip, Solicitor-General; Mr. Ormsby-Gore, Postmaster-General.

I have recorded in full the names of the holders of all the important offices in the National Government, because the list is an interesting one on account both of its composition and of its omissions. There is little reason to doubt that both Mr. Churchill and Mr. Lloyd George, had they so wished, could have been included in the Cabinet. In the circumstances of the time, two men of such pre-eminence would have been fully entitled to approach the Prime Minister and offer their services. So far as I am aware, no offer was made to Sir Robert Horne, though he had been Chancellor of the Exchequer and was a first-class parliamentarian. Mr. L. S. Amery, who had held high office with distinction in the 1924 Government, was also not included in the new Government, nor was Sir Arthur Steel-Maitland, though he was an accomplished and well-known member of the Party with considerable and varied ministerial experience. Lord Hailsham was another distinguished Conservative not in the Government. Lord Lothian, afterwards to become one of the best British ambassadors ever sent to Washington, was Mr. Lloyd George's intimate friend and great admirer. He had served him as principal private secretary during the war and been entrusted by him with the most delicate and important tasks at home and abroad. He told me one day soon after the 1922 election that, whether I liked it or not, Mr. Lloyd George would soon be back at No. 10, Downing Street. His inclusion in the Government and Mr. Lloyd George's omission from it was yet another example of the unhappy main feature in Mr. Lloyd George's later years. He failed again and again to agree with, or retain the support of, those who had worked with him in the most intimate political relationship.

The age of the members of the National Government when it was first formed was higher than that of most Governments; this was due to the Prime Minister's wish to include elder statesmen of all parties in order to restore confidence in a grave emergency. The British, unlike the French, are usually kind and respectful to Governments on their first formation; but this principle was not observed when the new administration was nicknamed "The Government of the unburied dead". However, as the subsequent election showed, it could afford to laugh at its critics.

I was not offered office in the 1931 Government. I think that Mr. Ramsay MacDonald neither liked me nor thought much of my ability. I did not reciprocate this feeling; on the contrary, I consider that his life record as a politician and statesman has been besmirched by unfair criticism. There is an interesting parallel between the motives of those who to-day seek to blacken the memories and destroy the reputation as statesmen of Mr. Ramsay MacDonald and Mr. Neville Chamberlain, respectively. It is that they wish to divert attention from their own shortcomings. Socialists fasten upon Mr. MacDonald the charge of disrupting their Party in 1931, whereas it split into two halves because a number of its members, as I have already stated, obstinately refused to recognise that there had occurred one of the gravest world economic crises of all time, that it had hit Britain with tremendous force, and that her destruction could only be averted by measures dissonant from their Party's principles. Members of all parties (with the honourable exception of Mr. Churchill, Lord Norwich[1] and a few others) wish to conceal the fact that they either supported or did not oppose the Munich settlement at the time it was made by representing Mr. Chamberlain as the man

[1] Then Mr. Alfred Duff Cooper.

who, by making that settlement, rendered war inevitable. As I endeavour to show in later pages of this book, there was never a crueller libel uttered against any British Prime Minister.

His critics invariably begin their attack upon Mr. MacDonald by asserting that he was a fantastically vain man. All Prime Ministers and Leaders of Parties have perforce to have a good conceit of themselves or they would never have got where they are or be able to remain there when they have got there. If Mr. MacDonald showed vanity in obstinate insistence upon a wrong course in some matters against the advice of his colleagues because he thought he knew best, he did what every Prime Minister before or since has done in a greater or lesser degree. It is said that one form of his vanity was an appetite for social adulation. Mr. MacDonald was a handsome man, with great charm of manner; this made him an asset to any dinner party and attractive to the women members of it in particular; even if he was, as his enemies assert, fond of moving in "high society" when he was Prime Minister, it is not a particularly serious offence, especially as he was a most abstemious man; nor did he indulge in dangerously emotional female friendships as some Prime Ministers, to the damage of their character and reputation, have done. Indeed, all who knew him intimately assert that he was always faithful to the memory of his dead wife, a lady of great goodness, character and charm. Finally, it is asserted that he was a very weak man with no principles. I consider, on the contrary, that he showed great courage and devotion to principle on two memorable occasions in his life. The first was when he refused to support the 1914 war, thereby, as it seemed certain at the time, destroying the fulfilment of his ambitions one day to lead the Labour Party to electoral victory, since many of its most prominent leaders and the vast majority of its members supported the war. That his views on the war were utterly wrong does not diminish his honesty and courage in adopting them. All Socialists were pacifists prior to 1914 and thereby did a great deal of mischief to national safety, as I have shown earlier in this book; unlike his colleagues, Mr. MacDonald retained his pacifism when it was no longer popular in the Socialist Party or the country. His action in forming the National Government in 1931 showed courage and patriotism of the highest order. Few people thought it would last more than a few months; most people believed that Mr. MacDonald, in taking the steps which he did to prevent national disaster, was filing his own petition in political bankruptcy. The estimate of the Chief Whips of the three sections of the National Government—Conservative, Liberal and Labour—before 1931 was that it would have a majority of only some 30 seats. These good qualities of the late Mr. Ramsay MacDonald's character as a statesman should be set against his defects, of which the most pronounced was his tendency, as his colleagues alleged, to veer suddenly from one opinion on an issue to another; even so, the harm done by this process in a leader is probably less than that of clinging obstinately to a point of view long after events have proved it to be wrong. Few Prime Ministers or Party Leaders are able to maintain the mean between the two extremes.

The reasons for the economic crisis of 1931 which destroyed the second Labour Government were various, and were summarised, I think adequately, in the extracts from my diary which I have reproduced. A large portion of the Labour Party contended at the time, and still contends, that there was no crisis at all, only a "bankers' ramp". Certainly, some foreign financial interests may have benefited from the crisis, but that is not what the Labour Party meant by a "bankers' ramp". Many of its members believed, apparently with conviction, that British banks deliberately provoked a crisis in order to destroy the Government and make money for their shareholders. It is alarming that a considerable portion of one of the great parties in the state should believe in such obvious and fantastic nonsense; the first institutions to have been injured had the national financial system been destroyed would have been the joint stock and other banks. Unquestionably, the world economic crisis was a major factor in producing the British financial crisis. Perhaps Conservative and Liberal critics of the Government at the time made insufficient allowance for this in their speeches at the election; unhappily, pure and undiluted statement of facts is not a common feature of electioneering: but the Cabinet made matters far worse, and indeed endangered the whole fabric of the nation's trade, industry and ability to buy the food which it required to avert starvation, by its pusillanimity over the May Report and its failure to take any other steps to avert bankruptcy. Like all "leftist" bodies, it feared to tell its own supporters the truth, for that would have meant shedding cherished beliefs, such as the supposed desire of employers for widespread unemployment in order to depress wages and the parallel contention that unemployment in Britain was the fault of the capitalist system and was unaffected by world conditions.

There was a strained and unhappy interlude between the formation of the new Government in September and the general election in October. This interlude was necessary to allow the Government to pass a fresh budget and an Economy Bill for the purpose of drastically reducing Government expenditure. The Bill lowered both Service and Civil Service pay and that of the employees of local authorities. Some of these, the teachers in particular, were resentful. But the most serious repercussion to the pay cuts was among certain naval personnel at Invergordon; their action was officially described "naval unrest"[1]; in fact, it was a mutiny. Foreign newspapers, not unnaturally, believed that a British revolution had started. The pound slid further in value and the Chancellor had to abandon the gold standard. On the first day that the new House met, Mr. Winston Churchill expressed grave doubts on the wisdom of the Conservatives in joining the Government, thus heralding, as some thought—quite wrongly as it proved—a fresh "break-away" from that Party. This period of tension and uncertainty was ended by the general election with its overwhelming victory for the Government. The figures were: Government supporters 552, others 63. My majority was over 33,000, a considerable rise from that of just over 700 which I obtained at my first election in 1904. It is true that the boundaries of the division had been altered and the electorate increased six or sevenfold. Nevertheless, the result, like that in other southern constituencies, emphasised the vast change in the fortunes of the Conservative Party since the early 1900s.

Then, if I may interrupt my main narrative for a moment, the agricultural and residential seats were by no means safe for the

---

[1] Some scientist, who is also a good writer, should produce and publish an essay to explain what is the psychological reason for the modern dislike of a nation, as tough as the British have proved themselves to be in the last forty years, for describing unpleasant events or occupations by their right names. Why, if we possess any national sense of humour, do we allow rat-catchers to be officially designated "rodent officers" by the local authorities who employ them?

Party. Both Brighton seats fell to the Liberals in 1906. On the
other hand, even in that most disastrous general election for Conservatives, some industrial areas such as Birmingham remained
predominantly Conservative or Unionist. This was, of course,
largely due to the influence exercised by Mr. Joseph Chamberlain
and other former Liberals, who, when they changed their allegiance, brought a large number of their supporters with them.
To-day, the south and the constituencies surrounding but outside
the County of London are still in the main Conservative, though
the irruption of works and their employees from London has
made serious inroads into their solidarity, as in the case of Eton
and Slough for instance; many of the former safe Liberal seats,
predominantly agricultural in character, in England, Scotland and
Wales are now equally secure for Conservatives. But we have no
safe seats that are purely industrial; those of that nature that return
a Conservative usually do so because of the exceptional personality and popularity of the member.

The problem of the Conservative Party in the next decade is to
persuade millions of wage-earners, both male and female, of
whom a large number are neither Socialist nor enamoured of the
policy of the Labour Party, that it is not, as they think, to be
disloyal to their class and to their trades unions if they vote
against the local Labour candidate.

There were important changes in the composition of the
Government after the election, among which were the substitution of Mr. Neville Chamberlain at the Treasury for Mr. Snowden, who became a peer and was made Lord Privy Seal. Sir John
Simon succeeded Lord Reading as Secretary of State for Foreign
Affairs, Lord Londonderry succeeded Lord Amulree as Secretary
of State for Air, and the Secretaryship of State for Dominion
Affairs was separated from that for the Colonies, with Mr.
Thomas in the former office and Sir Philip Cunliffe-Lister in the
latter. Sir Austen Chamberlain retired from the Government
altogether. In my opinion, the Prime Minister was foolish to lose
his services, as Sir Austen was greatly respected both in Parliament
and in the country and was a very wise counsellor in every sense
of the term.

I noted, soon after the new Parliament met, as follows in my
diary:

NOVEMBER 26TH, 1931

Some ninety M.P.s gave a dinner to Max Beaverbrook in the H. of C. Henry Page Croft[1] and I were responsible for the arrangements. Neville Chamberlain proposed Max's health and did it very well. Max made a good speech in reply.

An interesting feature of the last forty years in British politics has been the number of tearful partings and joyful reconciliations between Lord Beaverbrook and the official hierarchy of the Conservative Party. Unhappily, the reconciliations have seldom lasted long, but I would not presume to say whose fault that is, especially as I don't really know.

As a corollary to the India Round Table Conference to endeavour to reach agreement between British and Indian representatives on the form of self-government for India, with which I deal in a later portion of this book, a Burma Round Table Conference, of which I was a member, was constituted in 1931. The late Lord Peel was the very efficient, tactful chairman, and a valuable report was produced early in 1932. In their sense of humour and in other ways Burmans are, I think, closer to the British than Indians. At any rate, I found the Burmese delegates most congenial and delightful colleagues. But it is easy to make the mistake of supposing, at any international conference, that the meaning of an English colloquialism is fully understood. On one occasion, when there was an angry scene between two of the Burmese delegates, I suggested that they should cease this "cat and dog fight" and let the Conference proceed to the next business. One of the delegates concerned then said in tones of great indignation, "I tell the Noble Lord that I am not a cat and I am not a dog. I have been insulted and shall leave the Conference and not return". He then bowed to the chairman and left the room. Fortunately, a day or two later I was able, with the aid of another Burman, and over a drink, to convince him that I was only speaking metaphorically, and he returned to the Conference.

When Parliament reassembled, a Bill was introduced which buried Free Trade in Britain and with it any hopes of the official Liberal Party ever being returned to power. The grave had been prepared in earlier years—during and immediately after the First World War—but the Import Duties Bill was the real interment.

[1] Afterwards Lord Croft.

Its provisions included imperial preference to as full an extent as the Dominions approved; unilateral exemption from the general tariff for Empire goods pending the assemblage of an Imperial Economic Conference to consider and, if necessary, extend the protection afforded to Empire goods, an all-round ten per cent tariff on foreign goods other than certain raw materials and important food-stuffs, with power to the Government to raise the duty to a hundred per cent for the goods of countries discriminating against us; a tariff commission to examine the protective machinery as it worked and recommend, if necessary, additional duties on luxury imports.

The introduction of the Bill was marked by an astonishing and unprecedented action by a section of the Liberals in the Cabinet led by Sir Herbert (now Lord) Samuel. They announced that they could not support the Bill but, with the Prime Minister's and their other Cabinet colleagues' approval, they had "agreed to differ". One of the characteristics of the Samuelite Liberals, as they were then called, was their lack of any sense of humour or proportion. Unfortunately for that section of the Liberal Party which to-day Mr. Clement Davies leads, those qualities have been inherited from the Samuelite Liberals. This utterly unconstitutional arrangement, made worse by its fantastic nomenclature of "agreement to differ", was attacked and ridiculed in Parliament. I took a part in both processes. This book is not an autobiography and therefore I have hitherto, in writing it, refrained from quoting from any of my own speeches. But since the one in which I opposed the "agreement to differ"—on a censure motion by Mr. Lansbury, Leader of the Opposition—created considerable interest at the time and even produced a denial from Mr. Baldwin's Secretariat [1] that the Press had correctly interpreted his departure from the Chamber in the middle of it as a sign of his disapproval, I feel entitled to incorporate some points from it in this narrative:

> The doctrine of Cabinet responsibility has been thrown overboard, not, as the newspapers say, on a mere item of domestic policy but in a vast fiscal change from the system of free imports

[1] The official statement explained that Mr. Baldwin had left the Chamber for the sole reason that he had to attend an official committee. The loud ironical cheers, from all sides of the House, which greeted his departure, were therefore obviously misplaced.

to the system of protection. . . . How can a change that is going to affect the whole trading relations of the world be only an item of domestic policy? . . . . The doctrine of Cabinet responsibility is not a mere abstract constitutional theory. It has been found to be a practical necessity in order that administrative action and legislation may have a fair chance of success. If a minority of members of the Cabinet are at liberty to criticise the actions of the majority of their colleagues on a matter of prime importance, the policy dealing with it is subjected from the start to an unfair handicap. . . . We all tend to rate our services to the country too highly. Everyone on the Front Opposition Bench in any Parliament or on the back benches on either side who has ever been in any Government thinks that the Government would be carried on better, or the particular office which he has in mind would be better filled, if he were in the Government; and all those in the Government, especially the leaders, believe that they personally are indispensable and that they alone stand between their beloved country and disaster. I believe that to be a complete delusion; I believe that if all those in this House who are in office or have ever held office were suddenly removed, the Government of the country could be carried on by back-bench members or by men outside, such as those who run the great municipalities of the country, almost as well as it can be carried on by experienced Ministers. . . . I believe that, if all those who have held office or are in office, were taken out in a ship and if by some terrible misfortune the ship was lost, what would happen would be that our families would mourn us, there would be a service in Westminster Abbey, and foreign statesmen would shed their crocodile tears, but life would proceed as before and the "man in the street" would probably say, "Well, the old gang has gone west at last. I feel very sorry for the poor blanks, but I wish some of them had been drowned ten years before.

I stated in my diary at the time:

I have leaped into fame by my speech; the *Daily Express* "double leaded" the report of it and Low published a cartoon "If Winterton comes", showing me as Charon bearing Mr. Baldwin, Sir Herbert Samuel and the P.M. across the Styx; nearly seventy of my colleagues in the House wrote or spoke to me in praise of the speech and they included, which was both interesting and surprising, several members of the Government. Mr. Duff Cooper[1] told me that "I was inspired".

[1] Now Lord Norwich.

Real benefit to British trade resulted from the Imports Bill and the complementary provisions in the budget. Unfortunately, the results of the Ottawa Conference on Imperial Trade, held in the summer of 1932, were more meagre than had been hoped. Owing to pressure and objections from various interests, the representatives of the Dominions were only prepared to advance a short distance towards the aim of an integrated Imperial trade system and not at all in the direction of Lord Beaverbrook's more idealistic conception of "Empire Free Trade". Nevertheless, immense progress had been made since I was the first member to be elected to Parliament in 1904 in favour of Imperial preference and tariff reform.

A Bill was passed to give British farmers a guaranteed price for their wheat; another Government Bill, on which, however, the Whips were off, was passed to regularise Sunday entertainments, including Sunday cinemas. The late Colonel Oliver Stanley was in charge of the Bill and produced the wit, charm, tact and oratory which carried him, before his lamentably early death, to the very top rank of parliamentarians. The late Sir Thomas Inskip[1] and the late Mr. Joynson-Hicks,[2] those formidable sabbatarians, opposed the Bill from the Government Bench, while Mr. Lansbury and I, in an alliance which *Punch* regarded as so strange that it depicted us as colleagues in a three-legged race, organised support for the Bill in our respective parties with some success.

Among the younger Ministers, Mr. Hore-Belisha steadily improved his position, and among the older ones, the late Mr. J. H. Thomas delivered some smashing blows, in his own inimitable style, against his former colleagues, the Opposition Socialists. Among them, Mr. Attlee began to attract attention. His quiet manner in debate and his fine war record, which was well known despite his modest concealment of it, commanded respect. Mr. Robert Boothby commenced his series of addresses, whenever opportunity offered in the Commons, on the financial policy of the country. He has been delivering them at intervals ever since; as he is a first-rate parliamentarian, one of the best in recent Parliaments, he is always certain of a good audience; but it never appears to share his strongly-held views on how the finances of the country should be managed.

[1] Afterwards Lord Caldecote.   [2] Afterwards Lord Brentford.

At the Lausanne Conference the question of German reparations was finally disposed of, to the advantage of Germany. Mr. Churchill made some satirical comments on the matter in the subsequent debate. At Geneva, there was a Disarmament Conference. It failed completely of its main purpose. It was not the fault of Lord Simon, the British Foreign Secretary, who, like almost every British statesman of note who held office in the '30s, has been cruelly traduced, mostly by politicians who did their best to make their task impossible. It failed because of the suspicion, resulting from two wars and sixty years of mutual hatred, between France and Germany. The problem of reconciliation has not yet been fully solved. Readers of this book will notice in this parliamentary record of forty-seven years how certain intractable problems were brought again and again to the attention of Parliament in the unrealised hope that a solution for them would be found. One of these was and is Franco-German relationship. Another was and is the mining industry of Great Britain. They will not be surprised to learn that yet another Bill relating to that industry was passed in the session of 1932.

In 1932 Mr. William Graham, M.P., one of the ablest members of the Labour Party in the Commons, died. Like Mr. Lees-Smith, another prominent Labour M.P., who also died at a comparatively early age in the last war, he had a quiet, persuasive manner of speaking which contrasted strongly with the flamboyant, loud-voiced aggressive style of his leader, Mr. Lansbury, and many of the older members of the Party. It was also far more effective, for the House of Commons does not take kindly to the constant re-iteration, shouted out in furious tones, of some Socialist M.P.s that they and their Party alone understand the sufferings and needs of the working classes. It may be true, but the House, like every other institution of any value, dislikes being bullied and bored at the same time. Quite a number of Labour M.P.s in the last twenty years have injured their chances of success in the Commons by forgetting this.

CHAPTER XIV

THE Samuelite Liberals, now known as the official Liberal Party, their departure undoubtedly speeded by the debate on the "agreement to differ" to which I have referred, left the Government at the end of 1932, whilst the Simonite Liberals, now known as the National Liberals, remained in it. Thus a wide chasm, which has never since been bridged, opened in the dwindling ranks of Liberalism. Mr. Lloyd George and his family, in the persons of Miss (now Lady) Megan Lloyd George and Mr. Gwilym Lloyd George, stood magnificently aloof from all this. Perched, amid his offspring, on a political peak of his own, he impartially condemned both Samuelite and Simonite Liberals, Tories and Socialists.

There were, in 1933, interesting increases and decreases in the parliamentary position of those who were famous or prominent members at the time or who were afterwards to become so. In the declining category were Mr. Lansbury, the Leader of the Opposition, and the Prime Minister. Mr. Lansbury became more and more a figure whom no one took seriously, whilst Mr. MacDonald, probably because of the strain which he had undergone in the previous few years, showed signs of premature senile decay; indeed, some of his speeches were completely incoherent. Mr. Churchill's parliamentary position temporarily deteriorated. He was accused, by his enemies within and without the Party, of having tried, by his espousal of "Diehardism" over India, to bring off a *coup d'état* which would unseat Mr. Baldwin from the leadership and eventually put in office himself and his followers in both Houses, who included men of great ability, such as Lord Wolmer, M.P. (now Lord Selborne) and the late Lord Lloyd. The fact that the "Diehards" failed to carry their point was a serious defeat for Mr. Churchill. A "whispering campaign" about him sedulously encouraged by, if not originating from, Ministers, started in the lobbies of the House of Commons and in the country. He was, it was hinted, another but a lesser Lloyd George, with the same brilliant gifts and powers of oratory, but unstable in character: he would never be in any Government again, because he invariably tried to domineer over his colleagues and persist in wrong courses. Some of his most vocal critics in private were—none the less—delighted to receive office and favour from him ten years later.

Many members began to attract attention or improve their parliamentary position. Mr. Eden was proclaimed as the best Under-Secretary of State for Foreign Affairs for years. An ebullient young man, with flaming red hair, named Mr. Brendan Bracken[1], M.P., as ferocious and formidable in debate as he was in appearance, with a gift for witty invective, successfully concealed at first the fact that he had one of the keenest brains and most generous and courageous natures of any man in public life. Other young men who showed promise, which was not fulfilled in all cases, were Mr. Dingle Foot, from the Liberal benches, Mr. Kenneth Lindsay, a National Labour member (who, having been elected to Parliament in November, 1933, made a most successful maiden speech in seconding the Address in November of that year), and two Conservatives, Mr. Crossley and Captain Cunningham Reid. Among older men, on the Labour benches Mr. Attlee, Mr. Thomas Williams, Mr. Greenwood and Mr. Shinwell improved their position. A number of members, both male and female, also established their right to be classified as first-class parliamentary bores. To be a successful House of Commons bore several qualities are needed. You must be prepared to speak as often as you can and get yourself "called" on any subject, whether you know anything about it or not; when you do speak you must pour out a string of platitudes, un-enlivened by any apt or original phrases or a single gleam of humour. You must be impervious to criticism, whether it be direct or indirect. Direct criticism will come, on frequent occasions, from the Chief Whip of your party when you persist in addressing the House at a time when he wants the debate brought to an end. Indirect criticism will come every time you make a speech. Immediately you are "called" the House will empty. But you have your uses and your little niche in the Commons' temple. When the House is very angry, the Speaker or Chairman, as I have stated in a previous chapter, often "calls" you in order to lower the temperature and induce members to leave

[1] Now Lord Bracken.

the Chamber. If your party is in Opposition and it wants to delay business, you are one of its chosen instruments to do so.

Parliament in 1933 was chiefly concerned with external affairs. The sinister shadows of things to come were observed in the following extract from my diary:

FEBRUARY 27TH, 1933

Two events of first-class importance have just occurred—in China and Germany. Japan has successfully invaded the Province of Jehol to protect herself, or rather Manchukuo, as she says, from attack, and Hitler, at the head of the Nazi Nationalists, having won the German election, is allowing his followers to behave with shameful violence to all their opponents—Pacifists, Jews, Socialists and Communists. The French are, not unnaturally, very disturbed at this, especially as Mussolini is known to be sympathetic to Hitler.

The complete failure of the League of Nations to prevent the Sino-Japanese war or counter the threat, already apparent in 1933, of German re-armament in no way abashed its supporters, in the shape of the League of Nations Union, in Britain. They continued for some time afterwards, as I have stated earlier in this book, to press for unilateral disarmament by Britain and to assure a gullible public that national security could safely be entrusted to the League. As regards Hitler's victims, it was not the League, but an organisation with which I was closely connected, the Inter-Governmental Committee for Refugees, which saved many thousands of them before the 1939 war. That organisation, as I shall show later, owed its origin mainly to the initiative of the late President Roosevelt, whose Government was not a member State of the League.

Another grim shadow of future mischief, which dominates the lives though not—happily for our sanity—the thoughts of the nation to-day, namely, the problem of Anglo-Soviet relationship, was cast by the case of certain employees of Metropolitan-Vickers in Russia. Without a shadow of foundation these men were charged with sabotage; some of them, as a result of the brutal treatment they received in prison before the trial, which reduced them to nervous wrecks, "confessed". Great indignation was caused in Britain by this case, even though the employees in question were released and allowed to return home; it did not, however, abate the enthusiasm of the "left" in general for the Soviet and its system.

The Indian controversy continued to boil in the Conservative Party and threatened its unity as nothing had done since the Tariff Reform controversy of thirty years earlier. In the early months of 1933, the Government produced a White Paper containing its proposals for a further advance in Indian self-government: so far as the Provinces were concerned, these were based, in the main, upon the Simon Commission's Report, which recommended complete responsible Government for the Presidency and Provincial Legislative Councils, subject to reserved powers vested in the Governor for certain purposes. A debate took place in March, 1933, on the White Paper; the following is an extract from my diary concerning it:

MARCH 29TH, 1933

Winston's speech, which was to be the *pièce de résistance* of the "Diehards", was a failure, partly I think because he sat on it too long, giving me an easy task in reply (it having been arranged that I should follow), and producing for me favourable notices in the Press as well as a cartoon in *Punch*, with encomiums from a number of people, including S. B.

This was the only occasion in my forty-seven years in Parliament that I was able to compete with Mr. Churchill on equal terms and get the better of the contest; but I had many advantages, since I had a personal knowledge of Indian Government far greater than his and the advantage of being briefed officially.

There had been in the previous year a second Indian Round Table Conference of which I was a member. A fresh means of dealing with the subject was put into operation in 1933. This took the form of a joint Committee of both Houses which contained representatives, not only of all the political parties in the State, but of the varying points of view in the Conservative Party on the subject. I was also a member of this body and was, from the very outset, greatly impressed with the chairmanship of the late Lord Linlithgow. In dignity, fairness, shrewdness, sense of humour and knowledge of procedure of so difficult a body as a joint committee of both Houses, he surpassed any chairman under whom I have ever sat. Prior to his appointment, he could not be described as having been prominent in the world of public life; but he owed to his chairmanship of the Committee his appointment, later, as Indian Viceroy, in which post he was an outstanding success. We had one or two dramatic occasions in the Committee, especially when Mr. Churchill and the late Sir Michael O'Dwyer, former Governor of the Punjab, who was one of the "Diehards'" principal assets, gave evidence. The findings of the Committee formed the basis for the Government of India Bill, the passage of which through the House I describe in a later chapter. I think that the reason which, apart from loyalty to Mr. Baldwin, induced the majority of the Party to support these recommendations and the Bill based upon them, and to reject Mr. Churchill's advice, can be stated briefly as follows:

We had created in the great peninsula during the last fifty years a new type of Indian "after our own image"; these were the Indian members of the Civil Service and of the Provincial Service. In the main, they were men of culture, keen intelligence and probity; most of them, as I know from friendship with many of them, were also gentlemen in the true sense of that misused term. In the All-India Assembly and in the Presidency and Provincial Legislatures there were many members with not only dialectic skill, which is natural to most Indians, but administrative ability as well. Making allowance for the environment in which they lived and the traditions of the continent in which they were born, where political corruption is accepted as natural, their standard of conduct was good; it was certainly higher than that prevalent in British political life before the first Reform Bill. Though only a few of the boldest admitted it, they copied that standard from modern Britain, and were sufficiently aware of the gross nepotism and dishonesty of administration in eighteenth-century Britain to try to avoid it in endeavouring to make a new constitution work in their country. Of course, the number of this class was infinitesimal in comparison to the huge uninstructed Indian masses, but here again there is an historic parallel with British history. Every extension of self-government in Britain— in the eighteenth century this country was in effect an oligarchy— from 1832 onwards has been opposed on the ground that power was being placed in ignorant hands. The plea, which was the real basis of the opposition to the Government of India Bill, that British rule in India should continue because we knew what was best for India was exactly the same as the argument used by opponents of the British Reform Bill of 1832, against extension of the franchise.

To my mind, two most powerful reasons for progressive extensions of Indian self-government were these. Firstly, British rule had, in the last hundred years, brought many advantages to India which she would not have had, at any rate in such profusion, without it. These were a good administrative system, education, roads, railways, ports, irrigation and at least a rudimentary public health service; our administration had also countered the worst effects of the famines which are endemic in most Asian countries; it had abolished suttee and other evils; it had established law and order. But British rule could not, because it had not the power to do so, also abolish other features of the Indian social system—caste, the untouchables, the worship of cows and the refusal to kill old and decrepit ones because they are associated with the Hindu religion. It would be wrong for any member of a Christian Church, like myself, to assert in print that these things are morally wrong, whatever one's private views may be, because it would cause grave offence to orthodox Hindus, including many good friends of mine. That they were and are a preponderating cause of Indian poverty and suffering is indisputable, as thousands of Indian reformers have admitted for decades past. But we could neither abolish them nor some systems of land tenure enmeshed in the Hindu social system, which increased the hardships of the masses, without the certainty of causing an all-Indian Hindu insurrection. Thus we were blamed by our critics throughout the world for tolerating the existence of conditions which we were powerless to remove. Only a self-governing nation can deal effectively with the social and religious factors of this kind. Whether India will do so or not remains to be seen; there are hopeful signs, in some directions, that she will.

The second reason, though it is little mentioned in public discussion of the matter, why the extension of Indian self-government leading eventually to Indian self-determination was advisable from a British standpoint is this. The original British connection with India was for purposes of trade. Only slowly and reluctantly did the East India Company assume the responsibilities of administration. The Indian Mutiny disclosed the weakness of that administration, so that an Indian Government, under the control of the Crown, was established. Gradually and progressively, the directorates of British businesses in India associated Indians of probity and commercial and financial experience with those businesses. There has been, throughout this century, an intermingling of British and Indian capital in great enterprises in India. All the most progressive and intelligent British directors of such enterprises asserted, both in public and private, that support for eventual Indian self-government was necessary for British financial and economic interests in India. To oppose it would be to lose the goodwill of the customers of British trade in India. Further, so the argument ran, the interaction and common interests of Anglo-Indian trade were such that, given goodwill on both sides, it would flourish after India attained her independence; some prominent British business men in India went further, and told me that they thought it would increase, because the objection to buying British goods would disappear. On the whole, these assumptions have proved in the event to be true.

It is not surprising that among the "Diehards" with Indian experience who opposed the advance of Indian self-government there were hardly any British business men of experience. The majority were former Civil Servants and officers in the Indian Army who objected, for reasons with which one can sympathise, to the threatened disappearance, at least in its then form, of two splendid Services. They have, I hope, some consolation to-day in the fact that the traditions of both remain embedded in the Army and Civil Service of both India and Pakistan.

In the summer of 1933, following a short but sharp bout of undulant fever, I went with my wife to Austria, Hungary, Czechoslovakia, Poland and Germany for a recuperative if somewhat strenuous trip. In Budapest I had an interview with Admiral Horthy, and in Berlin with Herr Dieckhoff, then a prominent member of the official staff of the German Foreign Office. Admiral Horthy informed me that it would be necessary to re-create Austria-Hungary as a country and that this would surely be done in the next ten years. Herr Dieckhoff said that, though he himself was not a Nazi, he was impressed by the fact that Hitler had already, in his short term of office, brought internal security and decent administration to Germany and would in time, he was convinced, produce lasting peace and prosperity for Western Europe. Since both autobiographers and biographers like reporting the prescient and prophetic remarks of celebrities whom they have met, I feel it is justifiable to record two instances when such remarks were falsified by events.

The poignant and perennial question of unemployment on a large scale was much to the fore in and out of Parliament in 1934. A series of "hunger-marches" to London occurred during the year; these were organised by Communists and left-wing extremists in general with a view, undoubtedly, to promoting disorder which, in fact, did not occur. Those who took part in them were mostly not extremists but people out of work who believed that their plight would be remedied by their pilgrimages and the effect which they would have upon Parliament. Some Members of Parliament, notably Mr. McGovern, tried to persuade the House that the "hunger-marchers" should be allowed to present a petition at the "Bar", and there were angry scenes when these suggestions were rejected.

A Bill effecting important and most beneficial alterations in Unemployment Insurance was passed during the year; this took the form of the creation of an Unemployment Assistance Board which made provision outside unemployment insurance for assisting and promoting the welfare of able-bodied persons, within the definitions in the Bill, who were unemployed and in need. Its sponsor was the late Sir Henry Betterton.[1] His good work, like that of one or two others who held high office between the wars—for example, Lord Eustace Percy, a former President of the Board of Education—has been almost forgotten to-day, mainly for the reason that these Ministers were not well-known figures when they were in office or in great demand as platform speakers. It is customary for opponents of the Conservative Party and the National Liberal Party to-day to sneer at the alleged incompetence of the men who held office between the wars; this is the reverse of the truth—in fact, the general standard was high and much good work was done by many Ministers. Mr. Walter Elliot, for example, during the year under review—

[1] Afterwards Lord Rushcliffe.

1934—was a very successful Minister of Agriculture who, by the beef subsidies and the wheat quota and in other ways, continued the rehabilitation of British agriculture to which I have previously referred. Mr. Hore-Belisha, too, was a most useful and energetic Minister of Transport.

It is appropriate to say something at this juncture about unemployment generally between the wars. No record of events, policies and tendencies in the House of Commons over a series of years would be complete without a consideration of this grave and poignant problem and of the extent to which political parties and Parliament as a whole were responsible, by action or inaction, for failure to solve it. In my judgment, an impartial review whilst not absolving either parties or Parliament from criticism, would present facts which were half-veiled at the time because they were unpopular and because to state them in debate in the Commons immediately produced a "scene" from the Labour Party. One such fact is that unemployment was increased by the immobility of labour. During the worst periods of unemployment in the industrial districts there was little in large and growing areas of the south and south-east. There was room for more employment in agriculture and the building trade. Some men from Wales and the north took advantage of this, but they were not encouraged to do so by their unions, who loudly demanded that work must be found in the depressed areas for all its working inhabitants. Moreover, the rigidity of trades union regulations, devised with the laudable intention of protecting their members, prevented men from obtaining work in a trade in which there were vacancies, even when the trade in which they normally worked and to whose union they belonged was so depressed that there was no immediate prospect of the re-engagement of more than a fraction of the men out of work. Women workers, also, who had lost their industrial employment, were loth to accept domestic service, which was regarded by many as degrading. Housing difficulties also affected the mobility of labour. Emigration after the world depression of 1930–1 was for obvious reasons difficult, but before it neither Governments nor Trades Unions were willing to advocate organised migration to the Dominions with enthusiasm or to use any powerful advocacy to induce the Dominions to relax their immigration regulations; both were afraid to incur the unpopularity of being charged with trying to drive people out of the country. Neither migration within Britain or emigration from it (save on an impossible scale) would have solved the unemployment problem in the '20s and '30s, but it would have mitigated its effect. Nothing that any British Government could have done would have prevented serious unemployment in the worst years of the world trade depression, nor is it likely that the present or any future British Government will be able to prevent unemployment on a big scale if a similar world-wide trade recession occurs again: but, prior to those years, just before the General Strike, there was, as I have shown earlier in this book, a remarkable and growing improvement in employment which the General Strike arrested owing to the loss of trade which was its aftermath. Bitter memories of the unemployment between the wars still remain in many areas of the country; indeed, they dominate much political thinking to-day. It is a justifiable complaint against Members of Parliament like myself representing residential or agricultural constituencies at the time, that neither we nor the bulk of our constituents realised fully the despair and injury to self-respect and morale caused by mass unemployment in other parts of these islands. Indeed, the same consideration applied to some of the newer industrial districts outside London and elsewhere in which expansion was constant between the wars. As against this must be set the fact that the provision for the maintenance of people unemployed was much more generous than in any European country or, indeed, in any country except possibly Australia and New Zealand, whilst voluntary effort by the Churches and other bodies to mitigate the effect of it was greater than in any Continental country.

The year 1934 was notable for the growth in Britain of the Fascist movement in the shape of the British Union, under the leadership of Sir Oswald Mosley. Sir Oswald had had, prior to this date, an extremely chequered political career. He was elected as a Conservative for the Harrow Division in 1918 and continued to call himself a Conservative until 1923, when he announced that he was an Independent Conservative; in 1924 he stated that he was an Independent and, having been defeated in his previous constituency, unsuccessfully contested a Liverpool Division in

1924 as a Labour candidate. Eventually he was elected Labour Member for Smethwick in 1926, which seat he held until his defeat in 1931. He was made Chancellor of the Duchy of Lancaster by the Labour Government in 1929, but resigned in May, 1930, because of a difference of opinion with the Government on unemployment policy. For the rest of the period he spent in Parliament he was a most bitter opponent of the Socialist Government. The founders of the British Union were men of evil intent in a political sense; they intended, if they obtained power, to overthrow the existing parliamentary form of government and substitute for it a form of dictatorship; they deliberately provoked anti-Semitism and encouraged disorder by their provocative action; they were all the more dangerous because Sir Oswald Mosley, in his prime, was a first-class speaker in the Commons or on a platform. He could hold his own in the most hostile and disorderly House. He also possessed the personal magnetism which is a necessary accomplishment of the successful orator. Many decent young men joined the Union in its early days who were either ignorant of, or disregarded, the sinister side of it; they did so because they believed it would counter the anti-national and unpatriotic attitude of many of their contemporaries as expressed in speeches in and out of Parliament and in various leftist organisations. Because some Jews, especially on the Continent, had enriched themselves at the expense of the community in the years of depression, they regarded all Jews as enemies of humanity and accepted the foul slanders of the anti-Semites.

During 1934 there were frequent clashes between the British Union, whose members had adopted a distinctive uniform, and their opponents—Jews, Communists and others—in the East End and elsewhere. During the session, Mr. Oliver Locker-Lampson, M.P., brought in a Bill under what is known as the "Ten Minute Rule"[1] to prohibit the wearing of distinctive uniforms by any political organisation; I opposed the introduction of the Bill and it was rejected. I did so (with, I may say, the subsequent approval of the Press) because I thought it was an undue interference with

---

[1] "The Ten Minute Rule" is a rule of the House by which a member may ask for leave to introduce a Bill in a short speech; permission is also given for an opponent of the Bill, if there be one, to make a speech opposing it. The question is then put to the vote.

the liberty of the subject; but, having afterwards seen for myself some of the activities of the Fascists, I changed my mind and supported the Bill which was eventually brought in by the Government of the day to achieve the same object. In the course of the year, Sir Oswald addressed an immense meeting at Olympia at which some 15,000 people were present, though a number of them were there as curious spectators and not as supporters of the Union. Most elaborate police arrangements had to be made outside Olympia to prevent the Fascists and their opponents from engaging in serious fighting. Order was kept in a ruthless manner by stewards in Fascist uniform within the building. Sir Oswald's appearance on the platform surrounded by a bodyguard and banners, had a close resemblance to similar proceedings when Hitler or Mussolini addressed public meetings. This, and the disorder outside the meeting, aroused the apprehensions of many people who had not hitherto taken the Union very seriously, and was one of the originating causes of the subsequent decision of the Government to prohibit the wearing of uniforms by political parties.

Earlier in this chapter I referred to the sinister shadow of things to come when Hitler came into power in Germany; these shadows deepened ominously in 1934. In France the Stavisky[1] scandal not only destroyed a French Government, which is not a difficult achievement, but endangered the lives of the members of the Chamber of Deputies when a blood-thirsty mob, shouting "Death to the Traitors!", attempted to storm the Chamber and was only stopped by the fire of troops and police which inflicted casualties upon them. The crowd, in the opinion of a Frenchman who witnessed the proceedings and had been in Paris in the days of the 1871 Commune, was the most ferocious which had assembled in that City since the Commune. Many people believed a new French Revolution had begun. The scandal and its aftermath seriously diminished the weight of France in the counsels of Europe. It increased, too, a right-wing movement in France in favour of some form of dictatorship which was based partly on reluctant admiration of Hitler's success in ending internal disorder in Germany. This influenced opinion in France's hour of

[1] Stavisky was a dishonest financier whose transactions involved many Frenchmen in public life.

defeat and desolation in 1940 and produced support for "Petain-ism".

In the summer, Dollfuss, the Prime Minister of Austria, was assassinated, and thus started the series of events which led to Austria's second Calvary within a generation.

A disarmament conference was held, but was abortive despite Mr. Anthony Eden's strenuous efforts, by visits to various European capitals in turn, to secure its success. "Mr. Punch", that impartial and accurate chronicler of parliamentary events, describes the sequel in words which it is worth while to quote because they illustrate the eternal irony of history and the alternating and sometimes entirely conflicting parts which the statesmen who help to make it perform from time to time.

PUNCH, WEDNESDAY, MARCH 21ST, 1934

Impressions of Parliament
The Dove Still on the Wing

Commons' debate was opened by Mr. Morgan Jones, who alleged that Government had bungled disarmament. He was followed by Mr. Eden, handicapped by absence of official comments from Paris on his mission, but well able to repudiate such a contention. The Lord Privy Seal deplored General Goering's recent swashbuckling utterance, but refused to be pessimistic about chances of reconciling French insistence on security with German irritation at postponement of her equality. Failure would of course necessitate review of armaments, but he felt confident that France and Germany had been brought closer by British Memorandum and his own visits.

This statement brought an ironic Mr. Churchill to his feet, politely incredulous that Mr. Eden's tour, though harmless, could have done any good. It was only a little while back that he had heard Ministers reading diplomatic documents saying that rearmament was unthinkable ; now all our hope was to regulate the unthinkable. Our present policy of continually asking France to weaken herself was full of dangers.

In reply Sir John Simon refuted Opposition's statement that American proposals had exceeded British willingness to disarm, praised skill with which Mr. Eden had prosecuted his mission, and spoke of need for quick action in disarmament.

Two contrasting currents began fighting for mastery in the river of British public opinion this year, and continued their

struggle until the outbreak of the Second World War. The
pacifists and the illusionists continued, even after the failure of
the Disarmament Conference, to press for unilateral disarmament
by Britain. Mr. Churchill and a group of members led by him,
whose activities I describe later in this book (since the group only
came fully into action in 1936), pressed for more rapid rearmament than the Government was prepared to achieve. A start was
made, in this year of 1934, under the late Lord Londonderry as
Secretary of State for Air, in enlarging and re-equipping the
Royal Air Force. Lord Londonderry deserves more credit than
he has received for fighting against formidable odds in the
Cabinet in favour of this policy, for, despite Mr. Baldwin's famous
statement in the Air Estimates' debates of 1934, that "our frontier
was on the Rhine", his colleagues were reluctant to make as firm
a start as was desirable in measures to meet the new situation
arising from Hitler's threats and rearmament in Germany. An
amendment to the Address pressing for an acceleration in re-
equipment and the enlargement of the R.A.F. was tabled at the
beginning of the new session in December, 1934, by Mr. Churchill. It was supported by the late Sir Robert Horne, the late
Captain F. E. Guest, Mr. Leo Amery and myself, who put our
names to it. Seldom, if ever, have five Privy Councillors supporting the Government in power put their names to an amendment
to the Address, and the Government wisely gave a conciliatory
reply to Mr. Churchill's speech in moving it. Mr. Churchill, as is
not unusual with him, was fighting on two fronts this year. He
continued his struggle against the Indian policy of the Government with unabated vigour, being assisted by important members of the Party to whom I have already alluded. With the help
of an entirely different lot of ex-Ministers, he espoused the vital
cause of the advocacy of Britain's rearmament.

Mr. Churchill is always ready, quite legitimately, to forge new
weapons or adapt old ones for the discomfiture of those, whether
political foes or political friends, with whom he is in disagreement
at the moment. During the session of 1934, he launched a missile
at Sir Samuel Hoare and the late Lord Derby, the two most
prominent supporters, within and without the Government, of
the official policy on India. He made what the Speaker ruled was a
prima facie case of breach of privilege against them for alleged

undue influence upon the Manchester Chamber of Commerce to alter the evidence which it was going to offer to the India Joint Committee of both Houses. When the Speaker rules that there is a *prima facie* case of breach of privilege it means, in plain English, that he considers that there is a case to be argued and considered by the House itself or, as is the more usual custom, by the Committee of Privileges, which in due course reports to the House its finding whether a breach of privilege has or has not been committed. The Speaker's ruling does not imply a judgment on the case. The incident caused a political sensation, especially as the late Lord Derby was one of the most respected and popular figures in the whole Conservative Party—being rightly beloved, by political friends and opponents alike, for his charm, geniality and public services in his native Lancashire. I stated in my diary at the time my opinion that Sir Samuel Hoare and the whole Indian policy of the Government would be "busted" if the Committee of Privileges found against Sir Samuel and Lord Derby. Alternatively, if the Committee found there had been no breach of privilege, I wrote that Mr. Churchill would suffer a serious decline in his status and position at least in the present Parliament. The Committee found against Mr. Churchill's contention, and the incident did him some harm, though it is pleasant to record that it did not affect his personal relationship with either Lord Derby or Sir Samuel Hoare.

CHAPTER XV

THE House of Commons reassembled after the Christmas recess on January 28, 1935, to be faced with a heavy programme of legislative business including a housing bill, in the competent hands of Sir Hilton Young[1], and the Government of India Bill. Sir Samuel Hoare (now Lord Templewood) conducted this Bill through all its stages with great lucidity, competence, equanimity and a complete grasp of detail. Like most prominent Ministers between the wars, he had a chequered official career in the '30s. His fall from the office of Foreign Secretary and the reasons for it are described later in this chapter. It ought not, in an assessment of his career, to obscure his great services to his country in other directions, especially as Secretary of State for India. Here, he was most ably seconded by Mr. R. A. Butler as his Under-Secretary. Mr. Butler's appointment, at the direct request of Sir Samuel Hoare, to this Under-Secretaryship at a very early age for a ministerial post and after a comparatively short time in the House was criticised in private by many Conservative M.P.s at the time on the ground that there were many men of greater experience in the Party more suitable for such a post. The event proved them to be completely wrong. Mr. Butler was a first-class Under-Secretary—in the House and in his office.

There is an interesting resemblance between Lord Templewood's official career and that of another great servant of the State—Mr. Leo Amery. Both share two contrasting qualities. Neither is an orator of the first order on a platform or in Parliament. They lack the instinctive quality, which is the fortunate possession of really great speakers, of being able to use, if necessary without preparation and on the spur of the moment, the apt phrase and the emotional appeal which grips the attention of a full Chamber of the Commons or causes a crowded and excited public meeting to cheer and counter-cheer with all its might; though it is true that once in his career Mr. Amery did make a

[1] Afterwards Lord Kennet.

great House of Commons speech—in the debate which led to the defeat of the Chamberlain Government in 1940. But no two men alive to-day have contributed more, by the power alike of their intellect, enthusiasm and conviction, to the remodelling of the British Commonwealth to meet modern conditions. Both men willingly incur unpopularity and abuse for the sake of a cause in which they believe.

The India Bill was carried on second reading by a majority of 267 votes, Mr. Churchill and his followers, and Mr. Lansbury and the official Socialist Opposition having to vote in the same lobby against the Bill. Mr. Baldwin offered both of them his ironical commiseration, but hoped that the objection of two completely different sets of extremists to the Bill would commend it to moderate opinion in India.

Mr. Churchill did not increase his waning popularity at the moment with the majority of the Conservative Party by the support which he and the *Daily Mail* gave to the unofficial candidature of his son, Mr. Randolph Churchill, at a by-election at Wavertree Division of Liverpool. The result of a split vote, in which the number who supported Mr. Churchill was less than that cast for the official candidate, was to lose the seat for the Conservative Party. Mr. (now Sir) Charles Williams, M.P., asked Mr. Hore-Belisha, the Minister of Transport, following a question about "Belisha Crossings" if "there had been any 'double-crossings' at Epping?"—Epping being then Mr. Churchill's constituency. The roar of cheers and laughter which followed from the Conservative benches was indicative of the resentment against Mr. Churchill over the Wavertree election.

But Mr. Churchill, in his other role, that of an advocate of quicker rearmament, could give instance after instance in 1935 to sustain his case and that of Sir Austen Chamberlain, Sir Robert Horne, Sir Edward Grigg and others of us who were supporting him on that issue. In particular, in a defence debate on May 22, the Government admitted that they were in error in their previous comparison between the strength of the German and British Air Forces. On the previous day, I had motored back with Mr. Churchill from T. E. Lawrence's funeral, following his fatal accident, and I remember how, in conversation, we sadly contrasted the present decline in Britain's power and prestige with the proud position which she occupied in 1918. It is interesting also to recall that just prior to Lawrence's death, Mr. Churchill held the view that he should be appointed Minister of Defence. To some people such an idea might have seemed fantastic, but not to me who had served under him and who knew the width and height of his astonishing genius.

The unsatisfactory course of events in Europe prejudicially affected Sir John Simon's position as Foreign Secretary. In the natural course of events Ministers lose weight in their own party when things go wrong with their policy, whether it is their fault or not. At a meeting of the Foreign Affairs Committee of the Conservative Party in June a strong attack on Sir John was made by two influential and respected Conservative M.P.s—the late Sir Terence O'Connor (who later became Solicitor-General) and the late Mr. Sidney Herbert. By inference, though he did not mention Sir John's name, Sir Austen Chamberlain, who at the time occupied, both in his own Party and in Parliament, greater authority than any ex-Minister including Mr. Churchill, attacked him also. I commented at the time in my diary that "the meeting evidently agreed with this condemnation of the Government's foreign policy but also agreed with me that it is wrong and un-constitutional to attack a single Minister". By which I meant that the whole Government must be held blameworthy for the vague-ness and inefficiency of our foreign policy at the time.

The proceedings in this sub-committee of the Conservative Party and similar occurrences when dissatisfaction was expressed about Ministers, undoubtedly influenced the Government changes in the summer of 1935. The principal ones were as follows: Mr, Ramsay MacDonald resigned the Premiership and became Lord President of the Council and Mr. Baldwin followed him as Prime Minister. The Lord Chancellor, Lord Sankey, retired, and Lord Hailsham, who had been one of the most valuable supporters of Conservative policy for the previous twelve or thirteen years, whether in or out of office, became Lord Chancellor. Like his son, the present Lord Hailsham, he could use some very pungent in-vective when he had need for it; also, like his son, he enjoyed great personal popularity among both supporters and opponents in the House of Commons. He had suffered a tragic loss a short time previously by the death, at an early age, of his stepson, the late Mr. Edward Marjoribanks, who seemed to many of us to be the most brilliant young man of his generation in the House of Commons at the time. Lord Halifax took Lord Hailsham's place as Secretary of State for War; Sir Philip Cunliffe-Lister became Secretary of State for Air—the former holder of that post, Lord Londonderry, having been made Lord Privy Seal and Leader of the House of Lords; Sir Samuel Hoare became Foreign Secretary, and Sir John Simon Home Secretary. Sir Kingsley Wood was sent to the Ministry of Health, a Department for which he was obviously well suited and in which he did excellent work; and to the surprise of some, because he was not very well known in the country, or a prominent figure in the House, Mr. Malcolm MacDonald became Secretary of State for the Colonies, and proved his worth there, as he was to do in later years in other posts. Lord Eustace Percy was made Minister without Portfolio, for the purpose, as it was stated at the time, of studying and planning a policy. Critics of our political system might observe with some justice that the habit of appointing a Minister over Ministers, whether they be called "without Portfolio" or, in the slang of the moment, "Overlords", has grown undesirably in recent years and that in some instances such appointments, so far from simplifying administration, have confused it, because no one knows where one Minister's responsibilities begin and another's arise.

Soon after the re-formation of the Government, Sir Samuel Hoare was called on to justify his new position in a debate in the Commons, an account of which is worth quoting from my diary because it created considerable interest at the time at home and abroad and illustrates the fact that in the 1930s there was no substantial measure of agreement among parties on foreign affairs such as has existed, until recently, since the last war.

JULY IITH, 1935

Foreign affairs debate in the House of Commons. Rather a testing time for Sam in his new position, since everyone is worried about the Italo-Abyssinian situation which is surely going to lead to war and will put the League of Nations, already weakened by the defection of Japan and Manchuria, into an impossible position; there is almost bound to be some criticism of Anthony Eden's offer to Italy of a strip of British Somaliland.

Sam made a long carefully prepared statement—on the dull side, but what was wanted for both home and foreign consumption since a detailed statement of British policy and aims was required; we have not had such a statement for some years and it was particularly welcomed abroad. Herbert Samuel followed and was mildly critical and then Attlee made a "forcible-feeble" attack on Sam for his alleged "Imperialism". Then came Winston in a clever speech, half praise and half criticism, then L. G. followed in a tremendous Philippic, which was a histrionic triumph, against our own and every other Government; Austen made a most effective reply to him.

Debates of this character, of which there were many in the '30s, as I shall show later in this book, gave an impression abroad, not unnaturally, that there was no consensus of opinion on foreign affairs between the three parties, and that the leaders and prominent members of those parties disagreed among themselves. This impression, which was by no means unjustified, weakened our prestige abroad. The fault lay, not, as the opponents of the Conservative Party have tried sedulously to prove ever since, wholly with that Party, but with all parties and their leaders and followers.

In June, 1935, King George V celebrated his Silver Jubilee; and, in accordance with precedent, the Lords and Commons presented Addresses to him in Westminster Hall through the Lord Chancellor and Speaker respectively. The formal presentation of these Addresses is, by custom, preceded by short speeches for which the Lord Chancellor and the Speaker respectively, and not the Houses in which they sit, are responsible. Mr. Speaker FitzRoy's speech was so admirably phrased and delivered in such clear tones as to make it far superior, as oratory, to the usual performances on such formal and ceremonial occasions. Its effect was enhanced by the fact that Mr. FitzRoy—tall, commanding, beautifully proportioned in face and figure—was one of the most handsome men who has ever held the office of Speaker. There was a piquancy about the occasion, in that Mr. FitzRoy made his speech within a few feet of the spot where his ancestor King Charles I was tried for his life and found guilty.

Mr. Baldwin went to the country in November and secured a majority of nearly 250.

A most curious thing happened to me in the process of Cabinet-making. For the good reason that I was a critic of the slow pace of the Government's rearmament efforts and known to be associated with Mr. Churchill's movement to accelerate it, I did not think I was likely to be offered office. I was therefore astonished to read, in the *Daily Mail, Daily Express, News Chronicle, Daily Telegraph* and *Daily Herald* of November 22, that I was to be made Secretary of State for War. The statement in two of the papers in question was strongly headlined and accompanied by laudatory references to my services. I went to London from my home in Sussex on business for the day without being unduly elated, as I knew the slips between the cup and the lip which politicians experience when a Cabinet is in process of formation. Later in the day, it was announced that Mr. Duff Cooper had been appointed Secretary of State for War. Next morning I received a very friendly letter from the Prime Minister much regretting that he could not fit me into the Cabinet and asking if I would like to have my name submitted to His Majesty for an English Peerage. I declined this offer, which constitutes the customary solace for the disappointed politician, because I wished to remain active in the political world and because I was not particularly disappointed! I had a solace of a different kind, for both the late Sir Kingsley Wood and Mr. Churchill telephoned me at my country house the next day to express their regret and disappointment at my not having been given the post of Secretary of State for War, which was a very kind and friendly thing to do. Reliable information reached me later to the effect that, in the evening of November 21, Mr. Baldwin decided to offer me the War Office but altered his opinion in the course of the morning of the 22nd. He approached Mr. Duff Cooper instead. There must have been a leakage from official sources to the Press on the 21st, and this leakage, though I was entirely innocent of any responsibility for, or knowledge of, it, may have caused Mr. Baldwin to change his decision.

In the course of the year 1936, Mr. Lansbury, owing to disagreements with his party over the question of sanctions against Italy, resigned the leadership of the Labour Party and was succeeded by Mr. Attlee. When this unobtrusive little man was elected leader of the Labour Party, there were the same contemptuous criticisms of the inadequacy of his political stature as those which were directed against Mr. Baldwin when he became Prime

Minister and leader of the Conservatives in 1923. At least from an electoral point of view the critics were hopelessly wrong in both cases. The Conservative Party has long forgotten, and the Labour Party is, at the time I am writing these words, in process of forgetting, what it owes in electoral appeal to the two leaders in question. A study of the Conservative majority in the election of 1924 and that of 1935 and the Labour majority of 1945 would refresh their memories.

I suppose that, with the exception of Mr. Churchill, Lord Samuel and Lord Simon, I have had greater personal experience of elections in the last half-century than any man in either House of Parliament. I have fought thirteen contested elections and one uncontested election, and I have spoken at a very large number of by-elections since 1904. I have a theory, which cannot be easily proved or disproved, that the electors will vote in greater numbers for a party led by a man who appears to be of no more than average intelligence and who seems to resemble the "man in the street" than they will for some supreme genius of world renown. They will flock to the latter's meetings, cheer him to the echo, and treat him as a popular hero, but they are coy about voting for him. Critics of the British ascribe this coyness to the distrust of an unintellectual and slow-thinking people for Party leaders who possess great intellectual gifts, coupled with capacity for rapid decision and action. They prefer the plodders, it is argued. If my theory is correct, allowing for other factors which I have either described or shall describe later, the heavy defeat of the Conservative Party when led by Mr. Balfour in 1906, the equally heavy defeat when Mr. Churchill led it in 1945 and his inability to get a majority in 1950 or a sufficient one in 1951, and the sweeping aside of Mr. Lloyd George in 1922 with the subsequent elimination for the rest of his life of his influence, were all due to similar causes. Mr. Balfour, as I have stated earlier in this book, had probably the finest mind of his political contemporaries, while Mr. Lloyd George's and Mr. Churchill's surpassing gifts and services to their country in two periods of dire peril need no further emphasis, since this book, like every contemporary record, underlines them again and again.

Of course, Mr. Baldwin was, and Mr. Attlee is, not really the "average man" as popular opinion has painted them. There have not been two more astute political leaders in Britain within living memory. There is a faculty possessed by some politicians of giving physically and otherwise the appearance of being "just ordinary men" who, in a position of authority, prove to be far above the ordinary in maintaining their position and fighting their enemies within and without their party. Joined to a deservedly high reputation for disliking and opposing the hot-heads and extremists of their party, this quality is a very powerful magnet to attract votes. It could be termed "The Baldwin Touch" or "The Attlee Touch" or "The Truman Touch", for all three men, despite differences in circumstances, had, or have, it. It is a gift of the gods which enables its possessor, when victory is won, to sit in the White House or No. 10, Downing Street and laugh at or pity (according to his mood) the people who have called him a "poor, feeble fool" during the contest.

The Italo-Abyssinian war which broke out in 1935 was an event of profound importance. By many critics both then and later their failure to prevent the war has been cited as an instance of the weakness and futility of the British Government, and of the Foreign Secretary, Sir Samuel Hoare, in particular. It is treated as a precursor of "Munich" and as a step in the staircase of events which led inevitably to world war. Its real significance was quite the reverse. Taken in conjunction with the Sino-Japanese war of an earlier date, it demonstrated with finality the futility of reliance upon the League of Nations as an instrument to prevent war. Just as the name "United Nations" is a contradiction in terms because its member states are not united and are, indeed, arming against each other, so the term "League of Nations" was a misnomer. Leagues, such as the Hanseatic League, in the past were groups of nations or states united in the common purpose of protecting, in a military or economic sense, or both, their national existence; often the boundaries of their members were contiguous; always their interests were identical: but no such condition applied to the amorphous body known as the League of Nations. Whether Italy invaded Abyssinia or not, or whether, having invaded her, she succeeded or failed, did not affect in the slightest degree the present or future national interests of South American Republics. Even if any statesman in any of them had been bold enough to contend, that, unless the Italo-

Abyssinian war was stopped, a second world war was inevitable, he would have been met with the cynical reaction, especially in the richer ones: "so much the better; if we are neutrals in it, we shall make money out of it". The United States was not a member of the League, and even if she had been, her President and Government would have been unlikely to take extreme measures against Italy for fear of losing the Italian vote. The smaller countries of Europe, who were members of the League, were hostile to the idea of effective sanctions if they led to war. Germany was not a member of the League; Russia was unwilling to take any effective action, nor indeed was any other nation, as was shown by the fact that, after the invasion of Abyssinia by Italy, Britain alone took military precautions, with a view to possible armed action by the League, by alerting the British Fleet in the Mediterranean and sending reinforcements to Egypt, Malta and Aden.

In the circumstances, the efforts of Sir Samuel Hoare and M. Laval to induce Mussolini to refrain from attacking Abyssinia or to stop Italian aggression after the war had started were bound to fail. In October, M. Laval and Mr. Eden, in the absence through illness of Sir Samuel Hoare, did all that they could at the Council of the League to dissuade the Italian delegates from the contemplated invasion of Abyssinia. Shortly afterwards, Sir Samuel Hoare at Geneva appealed to all signatory member States of the League to treat the League as a reality, as we had always done, and prevent the threatened invasion by all means in their power. This speech, which was much praised at the time, evoked no effective response and, after the war began, only France and ourselves showed any signs of military activity in support of possible armed intervention by the League or willingness to apply sanctions. Since the League was powerless to prevent the war, and since Italy manifestly had the power to destroy Abyssinia, it is as hard to-day as it was at the time to justify the moral indignation directed against the Hoare-Laval proposals. It was, and is, based on what is held to be the cynical contradiction between Sir Samuel's Geneva speech and the proposals; but the Geneva speech had failed in its purpose; in the circumstances, Sir Samuel felt bound to try a fresh method to stop further fighting in Abyssinia. The Hoare-Laval proposals suggested to both combatants that the conflict might be ended by "international supervision of the area of conflict, by territorial exchanges and by opportunities for Italian economic expansion and settlement".

The suggestions were rejected, and they caused a Cabinet crisis in Britain, only averted by Sir Samuel's resignation. The following is an account of the sequence of events from my diary:

DECEMBER 10TH, 1935

Angry debate on the Hoare-Laval peace proposals which certainly give Italy a good deal but are only proposals to the two disputants and to the League to be accepted or rejected. Anthony Eden and the Prime Minister spoke well in difficult circumstances.

DECEMBER 16TH, 1935

The controversy over the Hoare-Laval peace terms still rages and there is a demand in some quarters for Sam's resignation.

Very wisely, despite the state of his health, he has come home to take part in the debate which is to take place on Thursday. Meanwhile there is rather tepid support for the plan which is to be put to the League of Nations on Wednesday. There are rumours of dissensions in the Cabinet.

DECEMBER 18TH, 1935

Heard from David Margesson[1] that he would put my name first to an amendment to be put to the Socialist resolution tomorrow approving the Government's attitude over the Hoare-Laval plan. Whilst I was at a public dinner at Midhurst I was rung up by the Chief Whip and heard the astounding news that Sam has resigned. As he assured me that there had been no change of policy I consented to propose the amendment which is in general, innocuous terms supporting the Government's policy.

The telephone conversation was slightly embarrassing to me for another reason, since it had to be carried on in the public bar which was the only place in the building where there was a telephone; however, I felt fairly confident that there were no Press reporters in the bar and that its occupants knew nothing of what I was talking about.

[1] Now Lord Margesson.

DECEMBER 19TH, 1935

There is clearly a first-class political sensation. The Beaverbrook and Rothermere Press furious, the *Morning Post* sad, the *Telegraph* and *The Times* remaining in a dignified calm. It appears that Walter Elliot, Billy Gore, Duff Cooper and some others give no support to the Hoare-Laval plan, despite the Cabinet's acceptance of it, and threaten to resign, so Sam, feeling his position impossible, went himself.

House crowded for the debate as it has not been for years. Sam made his personal explanation; it was the effort of his life and had an immense success. Briefly his point was that we are reaching the danger point (i.e. that further pressure on Italy might mean universal conflagration), and that in any event some compromise in Abyssinia was essential, that possibly in six months' time Abyssinia would get no better terms than she was offered now. He sat down almost in tears amid an ovation and afterwards slowly and totteringly left the House.

The Prime Minister spoke next—he was very bad. Began on his old too-often played note of sentimentality. Politics were a cursed trade; he had to part with his old friend. Said that he was out of touch with Sam on the Sunday. Only got his letter on Monday. Did not much like its terms. Must stand by an absent colleague. Put terms to reluctant Cabinet, who accepted them, then realised that public opinion against the terms, always bowed to it.

There was no explanation of the threatened Cabinet revolt and no explanation of his remark in the previous debate that if members knew what he knew no one would go into the Lobby against it; this was generally taken as meaning that war might easily follow from the enforcement of sanctions; however, he did not deny that we alone had taken military and naval action to support the League in the Mediterranean.

Attlee's subsequent allegation that S. B. ought also to resign did not lack point, but he went too far and said that the Prime Minister's personal honour was at stake. This gave Austen[1] the opportunity of opening by saying that the whole Conservative Party would take up the challenge.

Archie Sinclair[2] followed and made a long, melodramatic but dull attack on the Prime Minister and the Government. Then I moved my amendment which was not too well received, being much interrupted by the Socialists, but I think I gained a few votes for the Government and I received considerable private praise.

[1] Sir Austen Chamberlain.   [2] Now Lord Thurso.

Neville wound up unconvincingly. My amendment received a huge majority.

I had a casual conversation with two "diehards" and one left-winger after the debate, all of whom said Sam would be Prime Minister before the end of this Parliament.

In the course of my speech I challenged the Labour Party and the official Liberal Party to deny that they had never dared advocate the use of British Forces to go to war for the League of Nations at the recent General Election. I got most equivocal replies. Lord Simon, in a book[1] published in 1952, has effectively exposed by quotations from speeches and records of voting the humbug and hypocrisy of both Parties in attacking the Conservative and National Liberal Parties then, as they still do to-day, for their betrayal of League principles whilst at the same time using every endeavour, by vote and voice, in both Houses of Parliament and on platforms to prevent British rearmament, the most powerful of all factors in making such support effective; they wanted us to fight in a literal sense on the League's behalf, but they were too miserably timid to advocate the unpopular cause of providing us with weapons to do so. For this attitude, Mr. Attlee and Sir Archibald Sinclair, as leaders of their respective parties, have the prime responsibility. Their subsequent patriotic conduct and valuable services to the country in the Second World War should not obliterate memories of the mischief which they did before it. For such men and their followers to charge the Baldwin and Chamberlain Governments with lack of courage or prevision is like a criminal contending that he and the judge who is trying him should change places.

It might be supposed that, if Mr. Baldwin and the Government had effectively overcome the crisis caused by the Hoare-Laval agreement, he would have tackled the increasing seriousness of the international situation and the concomitant need for British rearmament with the same grip and intensity which enabled him to deal successfully with the internal differences and bitterness caused by the General Strike in 1926. Unfortunately, neither in public nor private did he give the impression that he was willing to do so. This unfortunate insensitiveness to

[1] *Retrospect.*

the danger of the external situation was exemplified by an instance which came to my notice at this time.

A friend of mine who was a French journalist of great repute in his own country and abroad, and a man of complete discretion who would never betray a confidence by publishing anything "off the record", sought an interview with him. It was made clear that my French friend wished to put certain points of view to Mr. Baldwin and would not, unless the latter authorised him to do so, publish the answers or the nature of the interview. I had a number of friends in French political and journalistic circles at the time and therefore knew, at first-hand, how distracted, disturbed and divided French public opinion was. No doubt for this reason the interview was arranged with the support of the British Foreign Office and the French Embassy in London. A personal and friendly exchange of views between Mr. Baldwin and the distinguished French journalist might reasonably have been expected to help in some degree Anglo-French relationship. My friend was duly invited to lunch at Chequers. After lunch, Mr. Baldwin asked him to come to his study, saying that he could give him twenty minutes. As soon as they had sat down, the Prime Minister plunged into an erudite eulogy of French art and literature with especial reference to the Châteaux on the Loire of which, according to my friend, he had a complete and surprising knowledge. At the end of fifteen minutes, the French journalist suggested that, as there were only five minutes left of the time allotted, they should leave the subject of French Renaissance architecture and allow him to put his points. Mr. Baldwin agreed and the points were propounded, though necessarily somewhat hurriedly. The Prime Minister made no comment on any of them, but punctually at the end of the twenty minutes rose, shook hands very warmly with my friend, and remarked that not for a long time had he enjoyed a talk as much as this one with so agreeable and distinguished a citizen of a great and friendly country. My French friend, who had a knowledge of English colloquialisms, told me afterwards that he considered our Prime Minister to be an admirable exponent of the national habit of "stone-walling".

Senior members of the Party, such as the late Colonel Spender-Clay, M.P., who, although not a frequent speaker in the House, exercised by his character widespread influence among the back-benchers, were very disturbed at what was obviously a decline in Mr. Baldwin's prestige so soon after he had won an election with a large majority. They felt, as I did, that it was partly Mr. Baldwin's own fault for the reasons which I have mentioned. Therefore, soon after the debate on Sir Samuel Hoare's resignation, we sought an interview with the Chief Whip, Captain (now Lord) Margesson, in order to put our point of view. Lord Margesson, as I have stated in an earlier portion of the book, was one of a succession of first-class Chief Whips of the Conservative Party. The Chief Whip who performs his task properly can persuade, advise and entreat his Leader to alter his attitude when it is obviously doing harm to the interests of the Party which he leads, but he cannot compel him to do so. It was not Lord Margesson's fault, but Mr. Baldwin's, that the latter's star continued to wane for the remaining eighteen months of his Premiership, though he momentarily recovered his full power and prestige by his handling of the Abdication crisis.

King George V died in January, 1936. The manifestations of most genuine and sincere national sorrow—which might be termed the cumulative effect of the sense of personal loss felt by millions of Britons at home and abroad—repeated and even exceeded those on the occasion of the deaths of his father and grandmother; they were, in turn, repeated when his son died in 1952. On all these occasions Parliament became for the moment a united body with a common grief and sympathy for the bereaved Royal Family. Even the Irish Nationalists, on the deaths of Queen Victoria and King Edward VII, did not dissent from this attitude. Foreign countries, remembering how Britain had treated some of its kings in the past, are greatly impressed by the modern affection and respect for the Monarchy, especially by the attitude of Parliament in this respect. Unquestionably, this relationship between the Head of the State and those over whom he or she reigns helps our prestige and strengthens our position greatly in the world. It has a direct bearing on the question of the Abdication, with which I deal later.

As a Privy Councillor I attended an Accession Council of the new King, little thinking that I should be attending another one within the year; I also was a member of a deputation to present

an Address from the House of Commons to Queen Mary—
the first of several deputations to different members of the
Royal Family in which I took part by virtue of my seniority in
the House.

On February 13, 1936, there was an important debate in the
Commons on a Bill introduced by Sir Murray Sueter, M.P.,
to constitute a Ministry of Defence. I described the debate as follows in my diary:

> Attlee made a brilliant speech in favour of the principle [i.e.
> co-ordination and a Minister to do it], but against the specific pro-
> posal. After one or two unimportant speeches Austen spoke well
> on the same lines as Attlee and then proceeded, amid cheers from
> Winston, to call attention, in so trenchant a manner as to savour
> (though I think it was not intended to be) of a personal attack, to
> S. B.'s two voices in debates—in November 1934 and May 1935
> respectively, as I had done in the latter debate. He also called atten-
> tion to the famous "If my lips were not sealed" phrase of the Prime
> Minister's in December last and the subsequent *volte-face*.

FEBRUARY 16TH, 1936

> There is great speculation on Austen's speech and its meaning.
> I think it meant no more than that he was seriously alarmed, like
> the rest of us, at the turn of events and at a certain (and characteris-
> tic) mental inertia on S. B.'s part.

Yielding to pressure from various quarters, Mr. Baldwin did
appoint a Minister for the Co-ordination of Defence in December;
his choice for the post being Sir Thomas Inskip.[1] I wrote at the
time in my diary:

DECEMBER 15TH, 1936

> Yesterday a calamitous appointment was made to the new
> Ministry for the Co-ordination of Defence in the shape of Tom
> Inskip, though it is true that various reasons (*The Times* spoke of
> "temperamental unsuitability", meaning Winston) made the
> appointment of Winston or Sam[2] (by far the most competent men
> for the job) impossible. To give Tom, a lawyer of sixty, who, though
> an able man, has had no administrative experience of any sort, the
> post is fantastic.

[1] The late Lord Caldecote.   [2] Sir Samuel Hoare, now Lord Templewood.

There was hardly a member of the Conservative Party, outside the ranks of the Government, who in private approved of this appointment. Sir Thomas, because of his inexperience in this particular sphere and consequent lack of authority, was not successful either in accelerating the pace of re-armament or in reassuring disturbed public opinion in Parliament or the country. The Opposition took advantage of his unfortunate position to deride and interrupt him whenever he answered questions or spoke in the House, a proceeding which he met with imperturbable courage.

CHAPTER XVI

URING the early months of 1936, a group—to which I
have already referred—of us who were interested in
pressing accelerated rearmament upon the Government
and studying the problems involved, met regularly under Mr.
Churchill's leadership. On May 22, some members of the group,
including the late Sir Austen and the late Lady Chamberlain,
Mr. and Mrs. Churchill, the late Sir Henry Page Croft (afterwards
Lord Croft) and Sir Edward and Lady Grigg (now Lord and
Lady Altrincham) came to stay at my home, Shillinglee Park,
for the week-end.

The party was a purely private one and, following my custom
in such matters, I sent no information about it to any press
agency or "social editor". To my astonishment, when we came
out of the dining-room on the Sunday to drink our coffee on
the front terrace, we found there a reporter of a London newspaper who wished to know what the purpose of the party was
and if it had any political significance. Mr. Churchill and I in
turn addressed some angry words of reprobation to him, a process which neither of us have ever found difficult, for an unwar-
rantable intrusion into a private gathering, and he hurriedly left
the premises with heightened colour.

Next day, the *Daily Express* and *Daily Herald* each "stunted"
the party, and the *News Chronicle* devoted three columns on its
front page to it; the general tenor of these sensational articles was
that we had constituted ourselves a "Shadow Cabinet" who had
met to plot the downfall of the Government. When the House
of Commons met on the Monday, there were several satirical
comments in supplementary questions upon the matter. Mr.
Maxton asked how long it would take the present Cabinet to
clear out for the "Week-end" Cabinet, and a Cabinet Minister
called out "Traitors" in reference to us; he was ready enough
to accept office from the principal "traitor", Mr. Churchill, a
few years later. Cartoons appeared in *Punch* and the *Daily Express*
about the episode as well as speculative references in weekly

papers. But the most absurd sequel to the matter came from Mr. Baldwin himself. Having, despite his well-known aversion to sensational journalism, swallowed whole all the completely unjustified allegations made by the Press about my party, he said in a speech, with obvious reference to it, that it was a "time of year when midges came out of dirty ditches", but he always ignored them. Mr. Baldwin, at his best, was a master of the English language; but it would be hard to imagine any opprobious description less applicable to Mr. Churchill than that of a midge. Those who want to insult him by comparing him to an insect could call him a hornet, a queen wasp or a scorpion, but not a midge!

I have devoted some space to this long-forgotten five days' political sensation, because it was indicative of the uneasiness of Mr. Baldwin at the time about his own position—an uneasiness shared by his Cabinet colleagues. Every student of British parliamentary government knows that there are two sure signs that things are not going well with a Prime Minister and the Government which he leads. One is when mysterious references are made by him or in the Party press to "stabs in the back". The other is when, following a meeting with him at the request of his parliamentary followers in order to state this disquiet, a communiqué is issued from No. 10, Downing Street or the party headquarters to the effect that there had been a "frank and full exchange of views" and that at the end, the M.P.s present had "unanimously expressed their confidence in the Prime Minister". Whatever Government is in power, the formula seldom varies. It is completely meaningless, since it embraces two very different types of meeting. One type will have resulted in those present leaving the meeting as angry and confused as when they entered, after paying at the end a purely formal tribute to their leader through the mouth of the chairman; at the other type of meeting the dissidents will be effectively "squashed" by the majority, and the Prime Minister's position will be at least temporarily strengthened. Outside of both, the "news hawks", in the shape of the lobby correspondents, will be assembled, eager, as is their business, to acquire information about the proceedings, but seldom able to do so; moreover, they are a very honourable and discreet body of men who accept at once a refusal to discuss what has happened at a private meeting.

The Conservative Party is, in general, more fortunate than the Labour Party in ensuring secrecy about the meetings of its committees, especially when the Leader has been present and has spoken. But, in the '30s there was a considerable leakage of information concerning the proceedings of its principal committee—then known as the 1922, now as the Conservative, Committee. Suspicion was directed against one or two well-known journalist M.P.s, but no evidence was forthcoming to support it.

There was a leakage of information concerning certain items in the Budget of 1936 before its introduction; and as a result of a judicial enquiry, this was traced to an indiscreet remark made by Mr. J. H. Thomas to a Conservative Member of Parliament. On the advice of the Law Officers no prosecution based on the finding followed. Mr. Thomas resigned his office of Secretary of State for the Colonies and his seat in Parliament. He made a proper and dignified statement in the House which earned the approval of political friends and foes alike; among the latter Sir Stafford Cripps was the only important member who pressed for prosecution. The M.P. was quite unrepentant, and considered that he had been badly treated by the enquiry. The House was unsympathetic to his plea. Mr. Thomas accepted his downfall with courage and equanimity; he told me once, without rancour, that for several weeks after it his Sundays and those of his family were made unpleasant by the arrival of specially organised coach-loads of trippers who went to his modest Sussex home in order to stand outside it and stare in the hope of getting a view of him. One of the many examples of how thin a crust divides the human race to-day from its more barbaric predecessors is the cruel and morbid curiosity of many people, even in this civilised country. They will flock to get a glimpse of any person about to be tried for his, or her, life on the way from gaol to court; if a tragedy has occurred in some humble home when two or three members of a family have been burnt to death, they will intrude on the grief of the survivors by standing outside it, even in pouring rain, in the hope of being able to stare at them with expressionless faces. Despite universal education and the improvement, in many respects, of conduct in this country in the last hundred years, I have no doubt that, if public hangings were reintroduced, huge crowds would go to see them, as they did of old.

Mr. Thomas occupied much the same position in public life in the '30s as Mr. Bevin did in the '40s. They were affectionately known to hundreds of thousands of people who had never spoken to them or seen them as "Jimmy Thomas" and "Ernie Bevin", respectively. Differing alike in temperament and character, they had many characteristics in common. Both were very shrewd men who mounted by a rough path from humble beginnings to high office in the State by their adroitness and courage in conducting trades union negotiations; sometimes theirs was the propulsion which caused a strike; sometimes they were the brake which stopped a strike; in office they had great successes and great failures. Neither could master the King's English; indeed, the speeches of both in the Commons were sometimes so ungrammatically fashioned and so badly expressed as to be incoherent; but each could, on occasion, show so much native wit and good sense with so high a purpose that the House was moved and thrilled. Many a member of the Labour Party, with no better education than theirs, is a master of impeccable English. One of these to-day, Mr. Bevan, is a first-class orator of the classic kind. But in their rough way these two men—the late Mr. Thomas and the late Mr. Bevin—had a hold over the House which was unique. Perhaps Mr. Thomas was sometimes playing a part in his speeches, by deliberately using Cockneyisms in order to live up to a reputation which he had acquired: Mr. Bevin had no such intention. He thought clearly enough, but clarity often left him when he tried to express his thoughts.

The career of Mr. Thomas and Mr. Bevin illustrates a fact which even opponents of political trades unionism, like myself, should admit. This country is fortunate to have in public life Trades Union leaders of the personal quality and integrity which they and many others in the past and present have shown—the late Mr. William Adamson and Mr. Stephen Walsh, for example, and Lord Hall, Lord Citrine and Mr. Isaacs to-day. Trades Union leaders who are not members of either House, such as Sir William Lawther and Mr. Deakin, also worthily uphold British standards at home and abroad. The pity is that, by an outmoded custom, they and their followers should consider it obligatory to support the Labour Party, especially as many of them are Socialists in nothing but name. Perhaps, however, by being so hopelessly illogical they are merely being typically English.

There was little of much interest in home legislation and administration on home affairs during the summer of 1936. There were stormy scenes, an all-night sitting, and several suspensions of Labour members during a debate on unemployment regulations. Abroad, the sky continued to darken; the Spanish Civil War broke out during 1936 with horrible cruelties on both sides. Its sequel and its effect on British politics is described in a later passage of this book. Immediately after its commencement, the *News Chronicle*, supported by the Liberal Party, demanded British intervention, if necessary by arms, on behalf of the Spanish Government. The same paper and the same party had condemned British rearmament, and the *News Chronicle* had invented the unpleasant title of "merchants of death" for the British armament industry. But, as I have stated earlier, to press the Government to bring British forces into action against various foreign Powers in turn, whilst at the same time opposing all the measures to make those forces adequate for the nation's needs, was the fixed policy of both the Liberal and Labour opposition in the '30s.

Some months prior to the outbreak of the Spanish Civil War, the Emperor of Abyssinia fled from his country, and the Italo-Abyssinian war was virtually ended; also Hitler broke the Locarno Treaty by sending tanks into the demilitarised zone of the Rhineland. There were the usual fulminations and protestations at the Geneva headquarters of the League of Nations and the usual abortive consultations between the British and French Governments, but nothing came of them. All these events strengthened Mr. Churchill's determination, and we, who were supporting him over rearmament, continued to put pressure upon the Government in order to obtain an acceleration of its pace. At the end of July, Mr. Churchill led an influential deputation of Privy Councillors, ex-Ministers and Service Chiefs of the 1914 war to see Mr. Baldwin. The names, which included mine, of the deputation and a general account of the proceedings are described in Volume One of Mr. Churchill's *The Second World War*.[1] Mr. Churchill truly observes: "This was a great occasion; I cannot recall anything

[1] P. 204 *et seq.*

like it in what I have seen of British public life. The group of eminent public men, with no thought of personal advantage, but whose lives had been centred upon public affairs, represented a weight of consultative opinion which could not be easily disregarded. If the leaders of the Labour and Liberal Oppositions had come with us there might have been a political situation so tense as to enforce remedial action; the proceedings occupied all of three to four hours on each of two successive days."

As Mr. Churchill states on the previous page of his book, he made a personal appeal to Mr. Attlee and Sir Archibald Sinclair[1] to come with the deputation or allow their parties to be represented. Their refusal to do so adds one more charge to the heavy indictment of their conduct in matters of national defence during the '30s of this century.

In this year Palestine made its contribution to the general world unrest. Disorder broke out between Jews and Arabs, and the position of the British as the mandatory Power became increasingly difficult; ten years later it became impossible. During the recess, Sir Herbert Samuel (now Lord Samuel), as a former High Commissioner for Palestine and one keenly interested in the fortunes of his race, of which he is so distinguished a member, asked me, who had taken part in the Arab Revolt and had other official contacts with the East, if I would arrange a meeting between him and General Nuri Pasha El Said, a prominent Iraqi statesman who is, at the time of writing, Prime Minister of Iraq, as he has been at intervals ever since his country obtained her independence. I served with General Nuri in the Arab War of Independence, and we are great friends. Sir Herbert believed that a talk between him and General Nuri might be beneficial and help towards a solution of the Palestine problem. We all three met in Paris and had a most interesting and friendly two days' discussion. But we failed to agree on any plan which would commend itself to Arabs as well as Jews. That is not surprising, for a whole platoon—one might say, a half-company—of British, Arab, Jewish, Egyptian and American statesmen have, during the last thirty years, tried and failed to find a solution of the Palestine problem. They include the late Lord Balfour, the late Mr. Ernest Bevin, and two former Colonial Secretaries—Mr. Churchill and Mr. Amery. Even the

[1] Now Lord Thurso.

Zionists themselves have not yet found the clue, for, at the time of writing these words, Palestine is in more dangerous and straitened economic and financial circumstances than any country in the Middle East except Persia. It is a tragic commentary on the human race that a land which is sacred to three great religions has had during the last 3,000 years a more evil record of bloodshed, treachery, cruelty and internecine struggle than any territory of comparable size in the world.

The new session opened on November 3, 1936. There were notable speeches by the mover of the Address, Miss Horsburgh, the first woman member to perform this task, and by Mr. Harold Nicolson, then a National Labour member, the seconder; Mr. Nicolson spoke without notes and with grace, ease and eloquence. But Mr. Nicolson's real throne, and one which he adorns, is literature; he only sat uneasily on the steps of the throne of politics. Publicity of a different kind at this period came to Mr. Day, a Labour M.P. interested in the theatrical world. Mr. Day endeavoured to break a parliamentary record by asking more questions than any member had done since the days of the Irish Nationalists. He had questions "on the Paper" every day, usually going to the limit allowed. He frequently showed, in his original and supplementary questions alike, some ignorance of the subject, which was not surprising, since the most erudite and painstaking member cannot possibly have a personal knowledge of the affairs of every Government department, and Mr. Day interrogated every Minister in turn. The process became a parliamentary joke. Members using a well-known House of Commons formula in connection with the deferment of Business called out "Another Day" when he rose; the Speaker, who clearly disapproved of this excessive use of the Question Paper by an individual, because it meant a curtailment of other M.P.s' opportunities, used to rebuke him sternly, amid loud approving cheers, when, as often happened, he asked a supplementary question which did not have the slightest relevance to the original one. *Punch* chaffed him constantly, political commentators in the Press attacked him; but Mr. Day, grim-visaged and determined, ignored all this ridicule and resentment and continued, without a smile, to ask his numerous questions until I, for one, began to admire his thick-skinned pertinacity.

During the debate on the Address there was an important discussion on defence of which a description appears in my diary:

DECEMBER 10TH, 1936

Kingsley Griffiths[1] opened—quite good. Then followed Tom Inskip[2]—long, tautological and unconvincing, who was followed in turn by Lees Smith for the Socialists, who was quite good. I got the coveted fourth place. Sam Hoare[3] wound up (only got notice of it the night before), did his best to retrieve a bad position.

DECEMBER 12TH, 1936

Winston made one of the best speeches of his life during the continuance of the defence debate, and attacked the Government for the inadequacy of their rearmament programme, or rather its slowness. S. B.[4] made no real attempt to reply, but instead made an amazing statement which he himself described as one of "appalling frankness". He said that he could not have rearmed two years ago as he had not a mandate to do so and if he had asked for one he would have been defeated. He added that democracies always lag two years behind dictatorships; this statement will do him grave harm.

The statement did very great mischief to Mr. Baldwin's reputation and is still quoted against his memory to-day; it is a sad thing that the beneficial results, both for the nation and for the Conservative Party, of the earlier years of Mr. Baldwin's leadership should have become dimmed and obscured by the grievous mistakes of the last two years of his Premiership.

In the month of December a very grave event, in the shape of the Abdication, occurred. In the debate in the House of Commons following the first announcement of the difference between the King and the Government, Mr. Churchill, against the advice of a number of his friends such as myself who had met him at dinner the night before, took a line at variance with the Government's view. He was received with one of the angriest manifestations I have ever heard directed against any man in the House of Commons, and he finally resumed his seat without having made any

[1] Mr. Kingsley Griffiths was a well-known member of the Liberal Party at the time.
[2] The late Lord Caldecote.
[3] Sir Samuel Hoare, now Lord Templewood.
[4] The Prime Minister, Mr. Baldwin.

impression at all upon the House; I have, however, no doubt whatsoever, from some inner knowledge of the circumstances, that he was actuated by no motive other than that of what he believed to be in the interests alike of King and country; it was a mistaken but most courageous action on his part to attempt to make the speech which he did.

Bitter controversy and recrimination about the Abdication still prevails in some quarters, though it is doubtful if the public of to-day is interested in the subject. The case can be considered and the issue disposed of far more simply than the protagonists admit. Let it be assumed that neither the Prime Minister nor the Archbishop had discussed the proposed marriage with the King, that the Bishop of Bradford had not preached his celebrated sermon, that there had been no reference to it in the Press and that the first public mention of the matter had been a statement by King Edward VIII that he was going to marry Mrs. Simpson. It is no reflection upon the Duke and Duchess of Windsor to say that the intention of a British Sovereign to marry a lady who had comparatively recently divorced her husband would have endangered the very existence of the Throne. Hundreds of thousands of the King's subjects would have been deeply pained, many would have been highly indignant; in both Houses of Parliament petitions to the King to desist from his intention would have been moved. Whether such protests would have been justifiable or not does not affect the point. They would have occurred. Similarly, whether a majority of the nation would or would not have supported the King is immaterial; the damage would have been caused by the split in the nation on an issue of the highest national and moral importance. A situation would have resulted as damaging to the prestige of the Crown as that caused by the trial of Queen Caroline. There would have been demonstrations and counter-demonstrations for and against the King's proposed marriage in the streets and in front of Buckingham Palace. The subterranean minority of republicans as well as the Communists would have seized such a golden opportunity to demand the abolition of the Monarchy. The splendid principle established by King George V, King Edward VII and Queen Victoria, in securing respect, personal loyalty and affection for the Sovereign, following a period when the Throne was merely tolerated as an institution whilst its occupants were disliked or despised, would have been jeopardised, not because the King was unpopular, but because a number of his subjects would have deeply disapproved of his marriage.

Had Mr. Baldwin not acted as he did, he would have deserved impeachment for having failed as the King's First Minister in his duty of protecting the Throne from an unwise act by the Sovereign. The unanimity of responsible opinion throughout the British Commonwealth and the action of its Parliaments astonished the world and secured its admiration for what can be truly termed democratic as well as constitutional monarchy, the principle of which has been further strengthened and stabilised by the reign of King George VI and that of Her present Majesty.

The parliamentary year of 1937 was not marked by any great projects or controversies in legislation or administration appertaining to home affairs, though there were some useful measures passed, such as the Civil Defence Bill. Both Houses concentrated attention largely on foreign affairs, with frequent debates on that subject. The Labour Party and the official Liberal Party alike continued to urge more forceful action against Italy, Germany and General Franco in Spain, whilst at the same time doing their best to prevent the British Government from developing the resources both for attack or defence which were necessary to protect Britain from defeat and obliteration if she were to go to war on behalf of League principles. They objected to the civil defence contribution in the Budget; the Labour Party opposed the modest provision proposed to protect us against air raids; and Sir Stafford Cripps made the monstrous suggestion that workers should refuse to make munitions. In a later passage I make my contribution of praise to Sir Stafford Cripps as a statesman and a man, but just as, in the trite phrase, "the evil that men do lives after them", so, in the interests of history and as an example of what to avoid, it should be remembered against them. No man in the '30s did more to foster the genuine belief of the Nazis that Britain was both degenerate and divided than the late Sir Stafford Cripps.

In the numerous debates on foreign affairs Mr. Anthony Eden replied with courtesy, clarity and vigour; whilst pleasing the House as a whole by his frankness, he avoided, with great skill and statesmanship, unnecessary offence to any country. I noted in my diary at the time that he "increased in stature with every speech". Other men and women in different parts of the House who, at the time, attracted its attention and that of the Press because of success in administration or debate included the late Dr. Burgin, Mr. Geoffrey Shakespeare, Mr. Scrymgeour-Wedderburn[1], Mr. Seymour Cocks, Mr. Bellenger, Mr. Bevan, the late Mr. Bernays, Sir Walter Womersley, the late Mr. Crossley, the late Captain Cazalet and his sister, now Mrs. Cazalet Keir, Captain McEwan, Sir Alan Herbert and Mr. "Shakespeare" Morrison. Mr. "Shakespeare" Morrison, like his friend and colleague and contemporary, Colonel Walter Elliot, has suffered from an alleged private remark of Mr. Baldwin's, made apparently about both of them, that they were future Prime Ministers. No greater harm can be done to any rising young man in the Commons than to say of him that he is a certain future occupant of No. 10, Downing Street. However, as Mr. Morrison is Speaker of the House of Commons and Mr. Walter Elliot a Companion of Honour to-day, they have little reason to repine even if, which is unlikely, as they are both modest men, they ever shared Mr. Baldwin's view of their future.

The House of Commons, as I have previously stated, is usually cold, possibly from jealousy, towards those who are highly successful with their pen; Mr. Churchill is an exception to this as he is to almost any other rule. Consequently, for all his wit and erudition, Sir Alan Herbert only partially captured the ear of the House during his time in it; for a similar reason the same might be said about Mr. Beverley Baxter and Mr. Michael Foot to-day. The "leftists" from Scotland in the shape of the late Mr. Maxton, Mr. (now Lord) Kirkwood, Mr. George Buchanan, Mr. McGovern, Mr. Gallacher and others were as vociferous as ever and, in some cases, notably Mr. Maxton's, reached a standard of mixed wit, eloquence and intransigence that was reminiscent of the Irish Nationalist Party. Indeed, some of his speeches produced in me a feeling of nostalgia, for the House of Commons has never been the same place since the Irish Nationalist Party ceased to exist.

To the grief of his friends and the sorrow of the whole House, Sir Austen Chamberlain died on March 16, 1937. As it happened, I was about to preside at a dinner in honour of a friend of mine—

[1] Now Lord Dudhope.

M. Paul Reynaud. We heard the sad news just before dinner was due to begin. M. Reynaud asked me to postpone it for ten minutes whilst he walked alone in meditation upon the terrace. In the course of his speech he made, without a note and in impeccable English, one of the most moving tributes by one statesman to another who has passed away that I have ever heard. Mr. Ramsay MacDonald also died in 1937—a man broken and worn out by the toils of State. The new King and Queen were crowned in the early summer amid great manifestations of delight, for they had already become the two most popular figures in the country.

Soon after the Coronation Mr. Baldwin resigned and became in due course a peer. Mr. Neville Chamberlain took his place. Sir John Simon went to the Exchequer, Sir Samuel Hoare to the Home Office, Mr. Duff Cooper (now Lord Norwich) to the Admiralty, Mr. Hore-Belisha taking his place at the War Office. The late Dr. Burgin became Minister of Transport and the late Sir Philip Sassoon became First Commissioner of Works, an office for which, by his administrative ability and artistic knowledge, he was admirably suited. The late Mr. (afterwards Lord) Runciman retired and the late Colonel Oliver Stanley took his place at the Board of Trade.

I was offered and accepted the Chancellorship of the Duchy of Lancaster. The only thorn in this Lancastrian rose for me was that having become a Minister, I had to resign the chairmanship of a Select Committee of the Commons on Financial Resolutions. To most people resignation of the chairmanship of a Select Committee, especially one dealing with so dull and abstruse a subject as Financial Resolutions of the House, would cause no pang. But to be chairman of a Committee of the House of Commons, whether an official or unofficial one, has always had a great fascination for me. Fortunately I was able to indulge very frequently in my strange taste during the many years I spent in the Commons.

I had two personal experiences in the summer of 1937 which are worth recounting because of their bearing, as it seems to me, on the question under review at the time of Munich a year later. I went to Paris with my wife to attend a fancy-dress ball and reception given at the Palais Royal by the French Government in honour of the Lord Mayor of London, who was paying an official visit to Paris. We had a number of French friends at the time, and we dined before the ball with one of them and his wife in their flat. He was a shrewd man and well known in Paris. During dinner he said that there was so much unrest and disquiet in France, so little sense of purpose or national unity and such hatred of the poor for the rich, that he doubted the wisdom of such a function. He thought that the Lord Mayor might be jeered at as well as the guests in general. To my astonishment, because I could not conceive of such a precaution being necessary in London, even after the General Strike, he said that he had told his chauffeur to keep the blinds of the car half-drawn and switch off the inside light. Outside the Palais Royal we found a big traffic block and a huge crowd of sightseers. They cheered us and the occupants of other cars impartially and called on us to pull up the blinds and turn on the light so that they might see the dresses, which we did. Having been a politician all my life, the temptation to address a crowd, especially one in a good mood, is irresistible. So, in my execrable French, I told the bystanders that I was an English Minister and also a "Milord Anglais" who had come to Paris with my wife to enjoy ourselves. The crowd were delighted and there were loud cries of "*Vive, M. le Ministre*" and "*Vivent les Anglais*". I could see from his face that my host thought my conduct both vulgar and unnecessary; but his previous words had filled me with apprehension, as had those of others on previous visits to France, because they exposed one of the cracks in the foundations of France's national structure; that is, for all her democratic institutions, the antagonism and mutual misunderstanding between rich and poor. No doubt my friend had reason for his apprehensions. In that summer our King and Queen visited Paris. The Government took such extreme precautions to protect them with police and troops from any danger or incident that the crowds in Paris, who were enthusiastic about them, could hardly get a glimpse of them. The excessive caution increased the anxieties felt in Britain about the state of French nerves and France's ability to face the possibility of a new world war.

The other incident, which also took place in the summer of 1937, was in Prague. At the request of Mr. Eden, the Foreign Secretary, I went to attend the funeral of the late President Masaryk, as the representative of the British Government. It was an impressive, if somewhat exhausting, occasion, as we walked in uniform nearly four miles on a hot day behind the gun-carriage bearing the President's body. The route was lined by enormous crowds, estimated at a million, showing the deepest manifestation of personal grief at the death of their national hero. I walked close to M. Blum, then Prime Minister of France, whom I met for the first and last time and under whose charm and agreeableness I immediately fell. On the previous day I went to pay homage to the dead President where he was lying in state and to place a wreath on his bier; I was informed that the Prime Minister, M. Benes, whose office was in the same building, would like to see me after I had performed this "duty". Both the British Minister, who was with me, and I made it clear to M. Benes that I was in Prague as a member—but not a Cabinet Minister—of the British Government to represent that Government as an act of courtesy and respect to the late President and to the Czechoslovak Government: I was not there as an envoy to discuss the relation-ship between the two Governments or international affairs in general. Quite undeterred by this statement, M. Benes plunged into a lengthy and vehement defence of his Government's attitude towards the Sudeten Germans. I knew little of the subject, though subsequently I learnt from official sources that M. Benes's asser-tions to me that the Sudeten Germans had no grievances were contrary to the facts. If M. Benes had not a weak case, I think he would not have spent nearly an hour in trying to "nobble" an unimportant member of the British Government who was visit-ing his country for a ceremonial purpose. I returned home unable to share the enthusiasm for this statesman which so many in England had at that time.

CHAPTER XVII

THE year 1938 opened with an appropriate prelude to the grave events which were to mark and, as some would urge, to defile it; this was the political and parliamentary sensation caused by the resignations of Mr. Eden and Lord Cranborne.[1] The cause of the resignations and the debate which followed are thus recorded in my diary:

FEBRUARY 20TH, 1938

Despite denials there have appeared to be some Cabinet difficulties or differences for some days past and there have been meetings of that body to-day and yesterday. At 4 p.m. news came through on the wireless that Anthony[2] and Bobbety Cranborne have resigned.

FEBRUARY 21ST, 1938

Immense excitement over Anthony's and Bobbety's resignations. . . . There was a personal explanation of the reasons for the resignation by both of them followed by an adjournment debate to-day. Great excitement in the House.

I was left to answer Indian questions in amity and comparative silence.[3] But John Simon was booed when he got up to answer Foreign Office questions. Both Anthony and Bobbety were restrained though Bobbety, being a Cecil, was more vehement than Anthony; in effect they objected to the conversations recently begun with Italy being made more formal until she had made amends or at least shown contrition for past faults. They suggested, which the Prime Minister subsequently denied, that Italy had adopted a "now or never" attitude amounting to threats or blackmail. The Prime Minister, who held the House, took the view, obviously supported by a majority of National Government supporters, that we must try at least to come to grips with the problem by finding out what Italy wants and will do.

FEBRUARY 22ND, 1938

The "Left" are in full cry and a great many other people are frankly aghast at Anthony's departure on the ground that he is the

---

[1] Now Lord Salisbury.   [2] Mr. Eden.
[3] At this time I was answering questions for the India Office.

one leading political figure of his generation. But the debate to-day, on a Vote of Censure, did a good deal to put things straight; Neville, though he had a rough House at the start, was listened to with obvious acquiescence even when he appealed almost in a Baldwinian strain for some further attempt to prevent what some seem to think (this is a paraphrase of his words) is the inevitability of war. Winston and L. G. made brilliant speeches, but each had little real effect on the House. Winston was the most effective as L. G. made a rude, unjustifiable and stupid attempt to accuse the Prime Minister of duplicity over a document; we had a successful division, despite about thirty abstentions. Vyvyan Adams was the only National Government supporter who voted against us.[1]

Mr. Eden and Lord Salisbury were an ideal combination at the Foreign Office, and it must have been as great a blow to them as it was to their friends and admirers to have to give up a task which was congenial to them and which they were performing so well. On the other hand, Mr. Chamberlain's reference to conciliation as a means of avoiding war should be noted; it was, I am sure, an indication of his intense feeling on this subject which in turn probably greatly influenced his views at the time of Munich. He hated the thought of the appalling suffering and cruelty which would result from another world war. He believed, further, that such a war would eventually ruin British economy, mean the end of our position as a Great Power and finish Western Civilisation as well. There is a lamentable accumulation of evidence, though it is happily not yet conclusive at the time of writing these words, that his triple prophecy was correct.

In the spring Hitler invaded Austria; there were protests from the Powers but no action followed.

In March, 1938, I was asked if I would accept a seat in the Cabinet in order to represent Lord Swinton, the Secretary of State for Air, in the Commons and act as Deputy Secretary of State. The offer from the Prime Minister, which I accepted, came as a complete surprise to me, as it did to the Conservative Party and the Press. The immediate and ostensible reason for my appointment was an unfavourable report by a Committee, known as the Cadman Committee after its chairman, on the Air Ministry's handling of Civil Aviation. It suggested the creation of a

[1] Mr. Vyvyan Adams, M.P., a man of independent mind and judgment.

new post of Parliamentary Under-Secretary for Civil Aviation. The Government accepted the recommendation of the Committee in principle, though not the appointment of a new Under-Secretary. It thought that "the object aimed at could be attained in another way". But I think Mr. Chamberlain, in asking me to join Lord Swinton at the Air Ministry, was also influenced by other considerations arising from a situation which I must briefly analyse in what follows. During his Secretaryship of State, Lord Londonderry ploughed the land for the new and renovated R.A.F.; Lord Swinton harrowed and seeded it. Without the work of these men there would have been no Hurricanes and Spitfires with incomparable pilots to fly them, and the Battle of Britain would have been lost; for, to continue the agricultural metaphor, that rich, magnificent property—Britain's R.A.F., which in 1918 was producing the finest crop of men and machines in the world—had in the '20s become choked with weeds owing to national apathy and parsimony towards defence. Not even Secretaries of State of the calibre of Mr. Churchill and Sir Samuel Hoare could persuade their colleague, the Chancellor of the Exchequer, to give them the money to remove those weeds. Now, Lord Swinton, in my opinion, should be bracketed with Mr. Churchill and the late Lord Haldane as one of the three outstandingly successful Service Ministers of our time in preparing the Forces for which they were ministerially responsible before a great war for the task which they had to perform. In earlier passages of this book I have already referred to Mr. Churchill's prescience, energy and tremendous drive in superintending and directing the instant readiness of the British Navy to meet the task confronting it on and after August 4, 1914; and the late Lord Haldane was, as I have already shown, the "father" of the magnificent British Expeditionary Force of 1914, though he had left the War Office a few years earlier. Under Lord Swinton as Secretary of State a magnificent body of public servants came together, whether as administrators at the Air Ministry, in command of formations, or in the capacity of scientists, designers and advisers, This body included Lord Newall, Air Chief Marshals Sir Frederick Bowhill and Sir Wilfred Freeman, Marshals of the Air Force Lord Portal, Sir John Slessor and Sir Arthur Harris, Air Chief Marshal Lord

Dowding, Lord Weir, Sir Henry Tizard, Sir Robert Watson-Watt, the late Mr. Mitchell, Mr. Cam and Mr. Chadwick. The combined efforts of these men and many others like them, coupled with the keenness, *esprit de corps*, and fine traditions of the R.A.F., produced a mass of magnificent achievements, to describe which in detail would require a whole book. Only a few can be mentioned here: namely, the fighter aircraft, Hurricanes and Spitfires, which won the Battle of Britain, the Blenheim and Wellington bombers, Radar—perhaps the most valuable of all the British peace-time inventions for defence in any war—the "shadow factories", and the installation of the power-operated turret in bombers and cannons for fighters.

However, notwithstanding these achievements, not only had Lord Swinton to contend, as had Mr. Churchill and Lord Haldane before 1914, with colleagues and a parliamentary majority who dreaded to face the possibility of a great war, but in the early months of 1938 his administration had got into particular difficulties *vis-à-vis* Parliament. Firstly, there was impatience at the inevitable delays in producing new types of aircraft off the drawing-board, and in having to build and equip new factories; some of this impatience, which was, as a whole, completely unjustified, came from dissatisfied manufacturers, whose tenders, for perfectly sound reasons, had been rejected by the Air Council, but who had succeeded in inducing gullible Members of Parliament to take up their grievances. Secondly, the great progress made in offensive and defensive methods and weapons for the R.A.F. could not be disclosed in detail to Parliament for security reasons; the invention of radar was a case in point. Had it been possible to disclose the extent of this progress, much criticism in both Houses could have been met. Thirdly, the Secretary of State and the Air Council had not a free hand to spend as much money as they would have wished in re-equipping, enlarging and modernising the R.A.F.; yet neither Lord Swinton nor his Under-Secretary nor I, during the short period when I represented him in the Commons, were at liberty to mention what the limitation was. Had I been free to tell the facts, I am certain that my task, in which I failed, of persuading the House that the Air Ministry should not be a target of abuse would have been easier. I should not have thought it proper to mention the matter at all but for the passages from two books which I quote without comment:

> Did we produce enough planes? It may be fair to state that we did not do enough soon enough; that the financial limits laid down were too rigid; that we should have insisted on some power in peace time to attract part of industry on to war production, a policy strenuously opposed by the Prime Minister and the Board of Trade. On these matters I shall not attempt to excuse myself; I accepted the decisions and I bear my share of the blame.
>
> *I Remember*, Viscount Swinton, P.C., G.B.E., C.H., M.C. (Pp. 117–18.)

> Dowding realised that in the early stages of any conflict with Germany the R.A.F. would be heavily outnumbered and would be forced on to the defensive. In 1937 and 1938, however, the star of offensive strategy was in the ascendant and the promised expansion of Fighter Command was delayed by the Treasury's reluctance to finance it. Simon, now Chancellor of the Exchequer, had evidently forgotten what he had learnt as Foreign Secretary from Hitler's own mouth.
>
> *The Struggle for Europe*, Chester Wilmot. (P.35.)

Lastly, there were difficulties of a more personal kind. Lord Swinton has never in his long public life in both Houses of Parliament sought or obtained popularity; he is a man of great ability, with a fearless persistence in what he considers the right course for the public weal, whether Parliament likes it or not. He has never been a giver of "sops to Cerberus". Moreover, at the time of which I am writing, he was no longer in the Commons but in the Lords. His Under-Secretary of State in the Commons, the late Colonel Muirhead, had ability and charm, was a good speaker and enjoyed the esteem of the Commons; but he was handicapped by his status as a Minister not in the Cabinet in fighting the critics of the Air Ministry in the Commons. These were among the reasons for my appointment.

I spent ten weeks in my new office; they were very happy though strenuous weeks, especially as I was made a member of the Committee of Imperial Defence and continued to take an active interest in the Duchy of Lancaster's numerous agricultural estates, which not all Chancellors before or since my time have

done. A new method of ordering aircraft was now devised. A
Committee of the Air Council, under my chairmanship, was set
up on which there was direct Treasury representation in the
person of Sir Edward Bridges, now Permanent Secretary to the
Treasury and therefore head of the Civil Service. This obviated
prolonged discussions with the Treasury on orders to manufacturers. My "junior partnership", for that is what in effect it
was, with Lord Swinton could not have been more agreeable to
me, for he was not only an old friend, but delightful to work
with. Unfortunately, in a debate in the Commons early in May of
this year 1938, I crashed, bringing down the administration of
Lord Swinton with me. Partly misled by the comparative ease
with which Colonel Muirhead and I had got the Air Estimates
through a little earlier, I underestimated the extent of the feeling
against the Ministry in the Commons. I thought I could easily
dispel the hostility which was obvious when I rose to speak.
But I was too "long-winded", too parenthetical, and too ready
to reply to interruptions by Mr. Duncan Sandys and others. He,
and Sir H. M. Seeley,[1] another critic, were wrong in their facts
and I right in mine, but my presentation of them had a very bad
reception in the House and the Press alike. Any Minister who has
thus failed in a big debate should resign and, accordingly, on the
Monday after the debate, which was on Thursday, May 12, I
asked to be relieved of my duties at the Air Ministry. Lord
Swinton had already resigned. Both he and the Prime Minister
had had in contemplation a change at the Air Ministry before
the debate, but waited to see how it went, though I did not know
this until later. When I learned of it, I was the more upset by the
knowledge that, had I done better, I could have preserved Lord
Swinton's Secretaryship of State for the country and the Air
Ministry. However, its greatest achievements, which I have
mentioned, had already been attained.

Two pleasant incidents do much to sweeten the sourness of
the memory of this unhappy failure of mine. On the Sunday
between the speech and my resignation, Lord Beaverbrook
'phoned me and begged me not to resign. He said that I had
been dead right in all that I had said and that the *Daily Express*
would support me and Lord Swinton with all its might. The other

incident is that Mr. Churchill, in his reference to the debate in *The Second World War* carefully refrains, with typical kindness and generosity on his part, from mentioning me by name; he merely refers to the Minister "who failed to convince the House". I retained my seat in the Cabinet and the Chancellorship of the Duchy, and soon after the crash went to the Home Office as the Under-Secretary of State to assist Sir Samuel Hoare, the Home Secretary, in his Ministerial duties. Mr. Geoffrey Lloyd, the Parliamentary Under-Secretary for Home Affairs, was deeply immersed in the organisation of air-raid precautions, and there was obviously work for a part-time Minister as well as the Home Secretary and Parliamentary Under-Secretary.

Soon after my connection with the Home Office began I went, in July, 1938, to represent the British Government at Evian at a Conference on Refugees called on the initiative of the United States Government.

Since the United States was not a member of the League of Nations, the Conference was not held under League auspices, though the late Mr. Winant attended as an observer. President Roosevelt's object was, in the main, to try to provide a place of refuge and safety for the 900,000 German citizens who were suffering from disabilities on account of their race or were under notice to leave Germany, the majority being Jews. Care, however was taken in the Conference to make it clear that the proposed creation of an organisation to deal with refugees was not exclusively concerned with the German problem, as indeed it was not, and derogatory references to Hitler's treatment of Jews and other minorities were avoided. This was wise and proper, for in the period between the creation of the organisation and the outbreak of the Second World War, the German Government did not in any way hamper the activities of the Inter-Governmental Committee in facilitating the movement and re-settlement of the persecuted persons in Germany. Indeed, of the calculated number of 900,000 persons at the time of the creation of the Inter-Governmental Committee at Evian as a result of the Conference who came within the category which the Committee was formed to succour, between 300,000 and 400,000 were found homes and settlement through various agencies in western democratic countries. This was due to the fine work of Mr. George Rublee, a distinguished United States lawyer, the first Director of the organisation, and Sir Herbert Emerson, an equally distinguished former Indian Civil Servant, his successor, and their very competent international staff.

Most of the Western democratic countries were represented by delegations at Evian. I had the great advantage of having as my official adviser Mr. (now Sir Roger) Makins,[1] of the Foreign Office, with the late Captain Cazalet, M.P., as my personal assistant. The United States was represented by the Hon. Myron Taylor, France by Senator Beranger. Since, though for different reasons, Britain, France and the United States were the countries most interested in and likely to be able to help the refugees,[2] it was necessary for Senator Beranger, Mr. Myron Taylor and me to work together in the closest confidence and amity, as we did. Indeed, as a result of the Conference, Mr. Myron Taylor and I became very great friends, and have remained so ever since.

The plan for the formation of the Inter-Governmental Committee, which was adopted at the Conference, was in fact created by us three. Mr. Myron Taylor was the first chairman of the Inter-Governmental Committee but, at his request and that of his Government, I was made chairman late in 1938 and remained so until 1945, when I resigned soon after the advent to power of the Labour Government. I felt that the work of the Committee would suffer and my position be embarrassing if I represented a British Government which I normally opposed from the Front Opposition Bench. Mr. Ernest Bevin was good enough to say, in his reply to my letter of resignation, that, whilst he appreciated and accepted my motives, he would have had complete confidence in my representation of the British Government and his Department had I wished to continue, since no Party issue was likely to arise therefrom. Mr. Hector McNeill, the Parliamentary Under-Secretary of State for Foreign Affairs, succeeded me in the chairmanship until the Committee and its organisation

---

[1] Now H.B.M.'s Ambassador to U.S.A.

[2] The term "refugee" was not a wholly happy one, for the people whom the Conference was formed to help were not refugees driven from their country, but persecuted persons about to be so driven. Had we used the term "persecuted persons", however, we should have so offended the Germans as to make any co-operation with them impossible.

were abolished and the work taken over by the International Refugee Organisation.

The Inter-Governmental Committee for Refugees did a great work for persecuted persons during its existence, and many Germans, both Jews and Gentiles, now happily settled in Britain, the United States and elsewhere, owe their lives to the Committee. Its work, and Great Britain's substantial contribution to it, which was proportionately greater than that of any other country, have received little public credit. This, I think, is due to two reasons. The succouring of those who were predominantly German or Austrian Jews made no great popular appeal; leaders of the Jewish Community themselves in Britain and the United States, though very helpful to our work behind the scenes, were not notably enthusiastic about it in public; some feared that, if they were, it would betoken a lukewarm attitude to the ideal of a Jewish homelan d in Palestine; indeed, some leading Zionists—though not Dr. Weizmann—in private were unfriendly to the Committee's functions. In their stubbornly unrealistic approach to the whole question of Jewish migration from persecution, they believed that all Jews who could escape from that persecution should go to Palestine. The folly of this policy is very visible to-day in Palestine. As I shall show later, when I come to the year 1939, the late President Roosevelt continued to take the keenest personal interest in the work of the Committee.

From the time I resigned office in January, 1939, until 1945, I was in the curious position of presiding over an Inter-Governmental Committee without being a member of any Government. Thus I found myself sitting in the Chair with Ambassadors or Ministers from other countries sitting under me. However, I got through somehow. Mr. Eden, the Foreign Secretary, and Mr. Morrison, the Home Secretary, the two British Ministers principally concerned in the matter in the 1940 Government, gave me every support, whilst the late Mr. Winant, the U.S. Ambassador, and I worked together most amicably. I had a great affection for him personally as well as real respect for his judgment. His one defect was such overwhelming shyness that he hated speaking at any committee, and, when he did, he spoke in such a low voice that neither his colleagues nor the stenographers could hear properly what he said.

Our Committee meetings were usually harmonious affairs, any little preliminary differences between the members having been "ironed out" in advance. The proceedings would open with Mr. Winant sitting on my right. A delegate would open the discussion, other delegates would continue the debate, and then there would be a pause whilst everyone looked expectantly at the United States Ambassador, who usually remained silent until I had to say *sotto voce*: "You promised me you'd say something on this matter, Gyl, they all want to hear you". He would then shake himself out of his brown-study and make some very shrewd and, at the same time, tactful and helpful remarks. Unhappily, they were generally, as I have said, inaudible and I had to restrain a tendency to giggle when I saw elderly Ambassadors leaning forward and "cupping their ears" in a vain effort to hear what their United States colleague was saying.

In September came the crisis over Hitler's threats to Czechoslovakia, the extreme international tension, the mobilisation of the British Navy and other action to meet the threat of war, Mr. Chamberlain's journey to Germany, and, finally, the Munich agreement. It would be repetitive to describe these events here, for tons of paper have been devoted to them ever since they occurred. It would be a breach alike of honour, the Privy Councillor's oath and the Official Secrets Act to give the slightest indication of the form or content of the prolonged discussions in a series of Cabinet meetings concerned with the crisis.

As he was entitled to do, by the permission granted in such cases, Mr. Duff Cooper (Lord Norwich as he now is) in his resignation speech threw some light on them. A reference to this speech and the debates which followed Munich are given in a later part of this chapter. In a lifetime of public affairs, including many crises, both domestic and international, and of exciting events in peace and war, I have never experienced a greater feeling of tension and strain than I did in those fateful days in September, 1938. It falsified a prophecy which T. E. Lawrence made to me exactly twenty years earlier when the Arab Forces made a junction with General Allenby's Army following a week of fighting and marching by day and night when we got little food and less sleep. This was to the effect that, whatever happened to me hereafter in the world of politics, I should never again be likely personally to participate in so thrilling a series of events, packed into a mere fortnight of time, which, by their drama and their impact on the future pattern of the Middle-Eastern world, would have such a high place in history.

Two Cabinet colleagues of mine at the time, Lord Maugham, in his book on Munich[1], and Lord Simon, in *Retrospect*, with the knowledge, authority and responsibility derived from their personal qualities and their former occupancy of the Woolsack, have given the reasons for the Munich settlement. Not a single reviewer of either book has accepted the views contained in them, but, what is more surprising, in none of the reviews which I have read has there been the slightest attempt to answer the massive arguments in favour of the Munich settlement of these two ex-Lord Chancellors. I state later what I believe is the reason for this nation-wide refusal to consider, even fourteen years after its occurrence, the Munich settlement on its merits. The reasons for the Munich settlement can be summarised as follows.

Czechoslovakia had a very weak moral and practical case in the matter of the Sudetenland. How weak it was anyone with a knowledge of men and politicians could have told both from the manner and the method of President Benes's lengthy personal exposition to me of his views on the subject when I went to Prague in 1937. Lord Simon[2] shows how the late Mr. Arthur Henderson, who was Foreign Secretary in the 1931 Labour Government, a very shrewd and fair-minded man, condemned that portion of the Peace Treaty which placed millions of Germans under Polish, Italian and Czech rule. He suggested by inference that it would sow the seeds of a second world war. Mr. Lloyd George and Mr. Churchill both expressed grave doubts on the wisdom of the Article in question. The Munich settlement secured the orderly cession of the Sudetenland under international supervision instead of its armed seizure by Germany. The fact that this settlement was subsequently destroyed by Hitler does not affect the point.

Mr. Churchill in *The Second World War*[3] gives reasons, writing with all his great authority, why in his opinion it would have been of advantage to us to fight in 1938 instead of in 1939. His con-

[1] *The Truth about the Munich Crisis.*   [2] *Retrospect*, p. 239.
[3] Volume One, p. 301 *et seq.*

tentions are based on military considerations, using the term in its narrower sense, of the proportionate size of the British, Czechoslovakian, French and German armies. He admits that the Hurricanes and Spitfires were not ready in 1938, but contends that the Battle of Britain in any case would not have taken place before 1940 because the "German armies were not capable of defeating the French in 1938 or 1939". I think that these contentions of Mr. Churchill's are very dubious. Victory in battle does not depend upon numbers and equipment alone; it rests upon the offensive spirit of the armed forces and of the nation to which they belong; and there is evidence that what can be termed the spiritual and mental preparedness of France for war was even lower in 1938 than in 1939. I do not believe that Czechoslovakia could have saved herself in 1938 or that France could have prevented her destruction.

No one who was in office at the time of Munich and had access to official papers can assert that there was any substantial ground for believing in 1938 that the U.S.S.R. would intervene to save Czechoslovakia and fight against Germany on our side. I got into trouble soon after Munich for a statement I made in a public speech expressing doubt about the U.S.S.R.'s willingness to go to war at the time of the September crisis. Mr. Churchill remonstrated with me in some private correspondence we had. Mr. Henderson, M.P., raised the matter on the adjournment in the Commons, when I was defended by the Prime Minister after I had expressed regret if my speech had caused misunderstanding. The U.S.S.R. was sacrosanct to the Labour Party until the German-Soviet pact in 1939, after which, until Russia entered the war, they did not know what to say about the Kremlin. A year or so earlier, when Mr. Alan Lennox-Boyd made a jocular reference to the Soviet Ambassador by expressing the hope "that he wouldn't be liquidated", the whole Labour Party in the House got into a passion; they yelled at Mr. Lennox-Boyd, raised points of Order and demanded that he should apologise.

Unquestionably, Britain and the whole Commonwealth entered the war in 1939 with far greater determination than they would have done in September, 1938, for they had seen Hitler's broken promises to us and his contemptuous attitude towards us. In the portion of Mr. Churchill's book to which I have referred,

there is an interesting and authoritative account of a military plot
against Hitler which, save for the Berchtesgaden talks, might
have succeeded. But would it? Military plots against Hitler before
and afterwards all failed. The year of respite from war which
Munich afforded was, perhaps, the most valuable in our history
for the defence of these islands. Without it, we should not have
had the Hurricanes and Spitfires to win the Battle of Britain. We
did not gain this respite by breaking any treaty obligations to
Czechoslovakia, as some fatuous critics suggest, when they talk
of "betrayal" of Czechoslovakia, because we had none.

The Munich settlement was regarded by the late Field-Marshal
Smuts, the late President Roosevelt and every Dominion Prime
Minister as the right and proper one. Parliament and the British
people alike were delirious with joy at what was believed to be
the avoidance of war. No Prime Minister in peace-time has ever
received in the House of Commons and the streets adjoining it
such a reception as Mr. Chamberlain did on his return from
meeting Hitler. He was never bamboozled by Hitler, as his critics
aver. He knew the risks, and he took them as a chance of avoiding
the immeasurable horror of a second world war. As it happened,
the Cabinet contained a greater proportion of men who had seen
front-line service in the 1914 war than any previous Cabinet. We
were not, as has been constantly charged against us, a body of
frightened cowards; all the parrots and copy-cats in Parliament
and the Press follow the example of some who should know
better in using the phrase "Munich made war inevitable", to
insult the memory of a dead statesman. What did make war
inevitable was not Munich but the Versailles Treaty and the subsequent failure either to implement its military sanctions, using
the term in its general sense, or withdraw its unworkable clauses,
with the result that Nazism and Hitler came into power. Once
the man and the system were backed by great military strength,
each alike, for their continued existence, had to get German territory back or perish. If there had been no Munich but a determination instead by France and Britain to resist Germany's entry into
the Sudetenland, war would have ensued then or next year; no
dictator could have stood such an affront to his position and
survived.

There is a resemblance between the late Mr. Chamberlain's

action at Munich and that of Mr. Churchill at Yalta. Both were presented with a terrible choice of evils; Mr. Churchill would have liked, as is clear from his speeches since, to resist the attitude of the United States and Russia; but he could not do so without smashing the Alliance. He, like Mr. Chamberlain at Munich, did what was best in the circumstances; Munich did not avert war and eventually, despite it, Czechoslovakia was destroyed. Yalta handed over, also eventually, millions of people to the foul and filthy tyranny of the Kremlin, with its torture alike of body and mind. Yet, it is easy to see why Munich and not Yalta is to-day treated as a classic example of a plan which failed. The numerous newspapers and the hundreds of present and past M.P.s and the millions of the public who applauded Mr. Chamberlain's policy before and at the time of Munich would like their action to be forgotten. So, in effect, they say: "Hitler deluded Chamberlain and he, in turn, deluded us; it is shameful. Let us attack both Chamberlain and Munich".

The Liberal and Labour Parties have a second and even more powerful reason for attacking Munich to-day. They hope that, as a subject of condemnation and censure, it will take the place of their own dreadful record of obstruction and opposition to rearmament in the 1930s, to which I have already referred. The Labour Party was, of course, far worse than the official Liberal Party. The L.C.C. Labour majority, under Mr. Herbert Morrison, was in such a frenzy of anti-patriotism that it prohibited alike Cadet Corps in its schools and the Territorials from training in Battersea Park. This action, like the Peace Ballot of the League of Nations Union, strongly supported the views of many Germans that Britain would not fight. If you have betrayed the interests of the land of your birth in this way, how nice to be able to have the memory of your shame obliterated by fixing attention on Mr. Chamberlain's policy and saying that it, and not you, bears the blame for the Second World War!

The debate that followed the Munich settlement is described as follows in my diary:

OCTOBER 3RD, 1938

A packed House. After questions, Duff made his resignation speech. Good, though rather egoistic at end; still, a fine effort.

Neville good and respectfully listened to. Anthony spoke later and was also good. He was, of course, opposed to the settlement, but voiced his opposition in friendly tones. Attlee fairly moderate as the Socialists do not want to force an election. Sidney Herbert made a very good speech against.

OCTOBER 4TH, 1938

The debate continued. Some powerful opposition from Dick Law. It is said that Sam H. was excellent yesterday evening, but I did not hear him.

OCTOBER 5TH, 1938

Some inspired talk about having an election; I suspect Kingsley[1] is the source. So many speeches have suggested (from our side) that it was wrong and unfair in the circumstances that I think it is receding as a possibility; Simon was one of prominent speakers for his party; Greenwood, who followed, was mild and rather good. Winston delivered a brilliant Philippic.

OCTOBER 6TH, 1938

Rather amusing series of sarcastic speeches by Harold Macmillan and others about a proposal to adjourn until November 1st. Harold said "no wonder we wanted a rest from the strain of resigning in the morning and withdrawing our resignation in the afternoon".

In the middle of October, Colonel Edward Stanley died, to the grief of his friends and the whole House of Commons. It is a tragic coincidence that he, his brother, Colonel Oliver Stanley, and his great friend and contemporary, the late Captain Wallace, died in the prime of life and in the plenitude of their powers; all three men had a fine record in the 1914 war and rose to office and positions of authority in the Commons through merit and not by reason of their birth or position; and no three men of their generation commanded greater respect and affection for their personal qualities among supporters and friends alike in public life.

DECEMBER 20TH, 1938

The popular Press has been full of statements to the effect that Rob Hudson,[2] on behalf of himself, Strathcona and Dufferin has been to see the Prime Minister to complain of Leslie Hore-Belisha's

---

[1] The late Sir Kingsley Wood.   [2] Now Lord Hudson.

administration of the War Office, as well as of Tom Inskip's[1] administration of his Department. It is added that he objected also to Walter Runciman's[2] and my presence in the Cabinet, presumably on the ground that he does not like us. Some excitement in political circles caused by all this.

Even at this distance of time I do not know if Lord Hudson (as he now is) did or did not go to the Prime Minister as the Press at the time suggested. His justification, as a junior Minister, in so doing would presumably be the precedent caused by the approach of the Conservative Under-Secretaries in the Coalition Government of 1918 to the late Sir Austen Chamberlain in 1922 to complain of certain aspects of Mr. Lloyd George's premiership. If I wanted the revenge which time so often brings, which I do not since Lord Hudson is an old friend of mine, it could be found in the fact that, when the 1951 Conservative Government was formed, Mr. Hudson, though he was a prominent member of the Opposition Front Bench from 1945 onwards and had attained merit and fame as war-time Minister of Agriculture, was not included in it. But perhaps he did not want to be.

In fact, there were changes in the Government in January which involved my ceasing to be Chancellor of the Duchy and having a seat in the Cabinet; I became Paymaster-General in order to continue the work I was doing as British Government Representative on the Inter-Governmental Committee for Refugees. Mr. Chamberlain generously offered to attach a salary to this post as has been sometimes done in the past when its occupant has had important work to perform.[3] But I did not feel justified in accepting this offer. I was sorry to give up the Chancellorship of the Duchy for two reasons. As I have previously stated, unlike some Chancellors, I took an active part in my role of the King's Chief Agent for his large and valuable properties belonging to the Duchy in various parts of the country. More than one farm tenant on the properties whom I visited said I was the first Chancellor they had ever seen. Equally agreeable to me was the

[1] Sir Thomas Inskip, the late Lord Caldecote.
[2] Lord Runciman.
[3] It is one of the many delightful anomalies of the British Constitution that the Paymaster has no duties to perform, save very minor ones such as being chairman of the Governors of Chelsea Hospital, and is unpaid.

fact that my work brought me into direct contact with King George VI, who took a real interest in the Duchy. I found, as did everyone else who worked directly under him, what a wise and delightful man he was and how strong was his sense of humour. All the shyness he sometimes showed in public disappeared when one had an interview with him. I went to one interview very angry with a certain statesman (not, I ought to say, Mr. Churchill) of whom I was fond as a friend but whom I found intolerable officially. Though it had nothing to do with the object of my visit, I unburdened myself to the King and said, "Really, Sir, . . . is the limit. I know that I talk too much, but he not only talks too much but when one does manage to get in a word by way of question or criticism he doesn't deign to reply, but continues his dreary monologue. It is a pity so good a chap and so able a man should make his job so difficult by this failing". The King laughed and said: "He is just the same when he comes to see me!!"

CHAPTER XVIII

THE melancholy events that affected the external situation from the beginning of 1939 until the outbreak of war on September 3—the virtual elimination of Czechoslovakia as an independent Power, Mr. Neville Chamberlain's and Lord Halifax's abortive visit to Rome, the Soviet-German Pact, and the rest—have been described by weightier pens than mine, including the weightiest of all, Mr. Churchill's; so they need not be repeated here.

Sir John Anderson,[1] the new Home Secretary and Minister of Home Security, got his Civil Defence Bill through the Commons; Mr. Hore-Belisha's Bill to impose a modified form of conscription was passed. I noted in my diary at the time as follows about this Bill:

APRIL 27th, 1939

Debate on conscription in the House of Commons—many futile arguments from the Socialists; the Liberal Party divided; L. G. *et famille* voted for the Government.

APRIL 28TH, 1939

Conscription well received on the whole, opposition by Socialists not likely to be very serious. The adoption of the principle has given immense satisfaction in France.

I remember recollecting during this debate how the Liberal Party, including Ministers, sneered and jeered at those of us who, before the 1914 war, had advocated conscription and the plan for it put forward by Lord Roberts, V.C., and the National Service League; yet, if it were needed before the 1939 war, it was equally needed before that of 1914.

Sir Samuel Hoare[2] produced his monumental Penal Reform Bill; though it met with little opposition, it was so lengthy and complicated that it did not pass the Commons before the outbreak of war, and was withdrawn. Most of its provisions were

---

[1] Now Lord Waverley. [2] Now Lord Templewood.

reproduced in Mr. Chuter Ede's Bill in the 1945 Parliament. As I had made a study of the penal system, by visits to a number of prisons, and in other ways, when I was working at the Home Office in the previous year, I was one of the Ministers appointed to the "Standing Committee" which considered the Bill. The new methods of approach to the treatment of crime now embodied in the Act of Parliament have not, as yet, been very productive: but the fact should not involve criticism of Lord Templewood, who originated it, nor of Mr. Chuter Ede, who implemented it. The real hindrances are to be found in the shortage of money and materials to build new, modern prisons, the inability of the prison service, like many other services, to attract sufficient entrants of the right type, and an increase of crime in general due to various reasons.

Though much was written at the time, and much has been written since, about the debate in the House of Commons at the outbreak of the Second World War, I give my immediate impressions from my diary, because they recall an incident of some interest which has been almost forgotten to-day.

SEPTEMBER 2ND, 1939

The House of Commons carried a number of emergency Bills of a most drastic character. It was thought that at any moment Neville[1] would come and say war was declared; but he did not. At 7.30, to everyone's surprise, the Prime Minister announced that though no answer had been received to our message, war had not yet been declared; there was much uneasiness in the House and, when Greenwood got up, there were shouts of "speak for England". He was restrained, but anxious. Matters were made worse by a pacifist speech from Maxton praising the delay and cheered by some of the "foolish virgins" on our side. Wardlaw-Milne,[2] chairman of the Conservative Committee and a man of influence in the House, then rose and, amid resounding cheers, gave voice to the anxiety of the whole House. Shared a taxi home with Ramsbottom.[3] Both of us agreed that the Government would fall if there was much further delay; it was subsequently shown that the whole position was due to the desire of the French for a longer mobilisation period.

[1] The Prime Minister.   [2] Sir John Wardlaw-Milne, M.P.
[3] Now Lord Soulbury.

SEPTEMBER 3RD, 1939

A lovely warm September day—this opening day of the Second World War with its terrific addition to the sum of human suffering and goodness knows what further burden upon a perplexed and impossible world, both from the point of view of economic and international relationship. The Prime Minister stated at eleven o'clock over the wireless that war had been declared; I did not hear it as I was sunning myself on the Terrace of the House of Commons and just afterwards an air-raid alarm was sounded and a number of us, including L. G., crowded into the passage outside my room; then the "all-clear" went and we proceeded upstairs. Neville and the other two leaders spoke well; Winston was magnificent and McGovern made a grave and sincere pacifist speech; the House was quiet, unemotional, determined and almost united, which was very different from the wild enthusiasm, emotion bordering on hysteria, and the self-righteous patriotism of August, 1914.

From that day onwards the House of Commons, in my opinion, played its important part in the sustenance of the war effort of the people whom it represented far better than did its predecessor, the Parliament of 1910, during the 1914 war.

Soon after the declaration of war, the new War Cabinet was created, which consisted of the three Defence Ministers (Mr Churchill having been made First Lord of the Admiralty in place of Lord Stanhope), Lord Chatfield as Minister for the Coordination of Defence, Lord Hankey as Minister without Portfolio, Lord Halifax, Sir Samuel Hoare[1] the Chancellor of the Exchequer, Sir John Simon,[2] and the Prime Minister.

A fresh Budget was brought in later in the month, and I see from my diary that I described it as "stunning, though I do not say that it is not right"; if I and others as well were stunned by the Budget in question, it was nothing to the terrific concussion which we received from some of its successors.

In a passage from my diary which I have already quoted, I made reference to certain "foolish virgins" in the Conservative Party in the House of Commons. There were a few Conservatives who, even at this time, were averse to the war with Germany, and there were a certain number of well-meaning people, some occupying important social positions, who came under great

[1] Now Lord Templewood.   [2] Now Lord Simon.

250 ORDERS OF THE DAY

suspicion and who were also Conservatives, because it was alleged that they sympathised with the German cause. When Stalin and Hitler issued a joint manifesto in October, after they had tortured and dismembered Poland, to the effect that the cause for which we and France began the war was lost and that we ought to make peace, Hitler being willing to consider terms, the elements to which I have referred again became active and they were joined by Mr. Lloyd George. The following is a description of the debate in the House of Commons on the subject:

OCTOBER 4TH, 1939

Almost a row in the House of Commons when L. G. said that Hitler's peace terms ought at least to be carefully considered and then harped upon his old theme that it was difficult to fight without Russia with us and that we had given pledges without really being able to implement them. He was strongly attacked by Duff Cooper[1] and others. There are, however, a few "weak sisters" in our Party —not many, but the movement might be dangerous.

In fact, it was not dangerous and no harm to the Party or to the National Government resulted from it.

In October, 1939, Sir Herbert Emerson and I went to the United States at the invitation of President Roosevelt to attend a meeting of delegates of some of the member States of the Inter-Governmental Committee on Refugees in order to consider the fresh aspects of the work of the Committee. On arrival at Washington we were entertained to lunch by Mr. Roosevelt, who had invited his Cabinet to meet us as fellow guests. Afterwards he had a twenty minutes' confidential talk with me in the course of which I gave him a private message from Mr. Chamberlain and in return he sent one by me to Mr. Chamberlain and another to his friend, the British "Naval Person". He then presided at the opening of the Conference in the White House and showed a clear and deep insight into the problems with which we were faced. He stated, to the obvious surprise of his State Department experts (one of them told me afterwards that he had never consulted the Department on the subject), that instead of the million refugees which when the Committee was formed at Evian we considered to be the number within our category,

[1] Now Lord Norwich.

we should have, before the war ended, to deal with anything from five to ten millions.

I was proud to have met this great man to whom the United States, Britain and the world owe so much. As I state in the preface to this book, I have been fortunate in meeting and working with many famous men. No one of them has impressed me more with his personality on a first meeting than Mr. Roosevelt. Here I found a man, with perhaps the greatest responsibility in the world on his shoulders, and suffering from a cruel disability, devoting a whole afternoon, with obvious sincerity and deep enthusiasm, to a great humanitarian cause and doing it without the slightest pomposity; he was ready, indeed—a rare quality in the great—to listen intently to views different to his own and not to resent their presentation. At the end of the two hours or so which I spent in his company on this occasion, I felt that I had known him for years. I realise that there was alleged to be a different side to all this. On my recounting what I have written to an American friend of mine, he remarked, "Yes, I know, it's the same story with everyone who meets him for the first time. He made you feel, didn't he, how important you were and how he had been longing to know you for years; that is his harlot's charm". He was a great and dear friend, so I controlled my anger. It is easy to be cynical about Presidents and Prime Ministers. As with the rest of us humbler politicians, their private interior often bears no resemblance to their public exterior. But I prefer not to be cynical about Franklin D. Roosevelt. I number him among the real immortals, as do millions of his fellow-countrymen.

Our conference achieved considerable success and facilitated the succour of refugees, which, in spite of difficulties, continued throughout the war. I was given every possible support and assistance by Lord Lothian, an old friend and my host in Washington; a more talented and charming man and a more successful Ambassador never occupied the British Embassy in Washington.

For the six grim years from 1939 to 1945 my narrative is concerned, not with the general course of the war, but with the effect of certain war events upon parties, policies and persons in Parliament. After the Second World War, as after the First, there was a big output of books describing the war as a whole as well as particular campaigns and personal experiences. But in neither case has there been a proportionate amount of writing devoted to supplying a consecutive and concerted account of the actions and reactions of Parliament in relation to the war. These cannot be dismissed as of no moment by the fatuous and dangerous belief of some people that in war time Parliament is of no value, except as a nuisance, and that there should be no attempt by either House to enquire into, comment on and criticise, if necessary, the conduct of the war. The cherishing of this belief by the Germans was one of the reasons that lost them both wars.

In the pages that follow I have tried to set down fairly and impartially an account of important occurrences which come within the ambit of parliamentary action and reaction. I am in a position to do so, for though, in addition to the chairmanship of the Inter-Governmental Committee, I was engaged in other war-work outside the House, I was a constant attendant at all important debates and many unimportant ones. Some of these occurrences need recital, because they have been already forgotten, although they have a bearing upon sociological and political problems to-day. The inner significance of some of the others was not realised at the time.

To begin with, however, I must speak of a sociological phenomenon that was not purely parliamentary but now emerged as one of national importance—I mean the contrast between the moral and social behaviour of the people of London and the other great towns in air-raids and, insofar as those who left were representative of those who remained, their behaviour as evacuees. The courage, cheerfulness and spirit of co-operation of the bombed population in Britain in the big cities merits the highest praise; there was no panic by the stricken people and very little looting; there were innumerable cases of great kindness and self-sacrifice. Yet the manners, standard of cleanliness and general attitude of hundreds of mothers and children evacuated from the great cities, by no means all from slum areas, astonished and disgusted country folk in England, Scotland and Wales. Making all allowance for the strain placed upon evacuees of having to share a house with strangers, there seemed to be an undue proportion of slatternly, irresponsible mothers who spent their time at the "local" or in less desirable ways, and of children who were verminous, filthy in their habits and with no sense of right or wrong.

The continued existence of numbers of these problem families
and individuals, despite the immense improvement in social
conditions of the last decades, is only too obvious to anyone who
reads the newspapers or studies the statistics of crime in general,
juvenile crime, and cruelty to children. Both Houses of Parliament have discussed the subject at intervals, and many articles and
more than one book[1] have been devoted to it. Accurate assessment on a statistical basis of the extent of this evil, in relation alike
to the past and to conditions in other countries, is difficult. Undoubtedly, evacuation illumined, as nothing else would have done,
the sharp contrast between the outlook and attitude of big towns
and those of country villages in all three parts of the United
Kingdom. I have in the last forty-eight years spoken at political
or other meetings at hundreds of villages south and north of the
Border and in the Principality. A big change has been effected in
that time. The old days have gone, when the Laird and the Minister in Scotland, and the Squire and the Parson in England ruled,
benevolently or otherwise, and patronised the village; so, very
largely, has class distinction. There was never much class feeling
in the true countryside, as opposed to the mining countryside;
and to-day it does not exist at all. Young and old of all classes
meet on a level in the village hall and Women's Institute, at
dances, socials and the like. There is a strong community spirit.
If a family is verminous, drunken and disreputable, they become
the subject of village talk and of united village condemnation,
which may or may not improve them; but in big towns, where
many people do not know who lives next door to them, such
conditions pass unnoticed by neighbours, though the social
worker and the police may intervene when things get too bad.
The trouble with our urban population, which, despite the defects
I have described, is in the main very stable and orderly with high
principles, is that it frequently lacks any local community feeling.
This, however, is less marked in the North than in the South.
The proportion of wage-earners to other sections of an urban
population is much higher now than it was even fifty years ago,
since, by reason of improved transport, so many business men and
traders live outside the towns in which they earn their living.
The resident wage-earners know little about, and are suspicious

[1] One being *Our Towns*, by E. E. Halton.

of, a different class to theirs. To them such people represent "capitalists" and the "bosses" whom fifty years of Socialist teachings have taught them to oppose. In these contrasts between town and country are to be found the reasons for some of the resentment between war-time evacuees and country folk, and for the failure of the Labour Party, which is essentially an urban party, to capture many country constituencies, and of the Conservatives to win many town seats.

Early in 1940 a political sensation was caused through Mr. Hore-Belisha's resignation of the Secretaryship of State for War. Considerable feeling was evoked by this occurrence. Some Commonwealth and foreign newspapers accused the Prime Minister, Mr. Neville Chamberlain, when he called upon Mr. Hore-Belisha to resign, of dispensing with his services because he was a Jew or because he was "not a gentleman". As noted in my diary at the time, "this fantastic theory is said to be supported by the fact that his successor, Colonel Stanley, is one of the old ruling families". In the debate which followed Mr. Hore-Belisha's resignation, Colonel Wedgwood took up this charge of anti-Semitism, but the House was not impressed by it. *Truth*, on the other hand, launched a furious attack on Mr. Hore-Belisha and published a number of articles about his business life before he took office. The man who seems to me to have come best out of the whole affair was Mr. Hore-Belisha himself, who made a dignified resignation speech in the Commons and, for reasons which do his sense of the public weal great credit, has never discussed either in public or in private to intimate friends such as myself, what the cause of the conflict was. There is some circumstantial evidence to show that it was due to his deep dissatisfaction with the state of the French army and his outspoken comments on the subject when he visited the French front.

The Chamberlain Government fell at the beginning of May after a debate which has been described so often that it needs no full description here. Mr. Leo Amery, in a speech in which he for once scaled the heights of oratory, contributed largely to the Government's poor majority which caused Mr. Chamberlain to resign. The Prime Minister himself, who was obviously very tired and strained and not at all convincing, did not help his own cause. About a month earlier, he had used an unfortunate phrase, when he said that Hitler "has missed the bus". In face of the disaster in Norway, which was the immediate cause of the debate that brought the Government down, this phrase was remembered against Mr. Chamberlain to his disadvantage. To make matters worse, he replied to an interruption by saying that he had friends in the House who would support him. As I have pointed out earlier in this book, the House of Commons is generally a very fair body, but sometimes when it has a "down" on a particular individual it is very unfair. Being in that state on this occasion, it placed a meaning upon Mr. Chamberlain's incautious reply that it was never intended to have; members seemed to think that he meant there were Conservatives who were so attached to him by personal friendship that they would vote for him whether he was right or wrong.

The Government formed by Mr. Churchill was a very strong one. The "new entrants" to statesmanship were, as I have already said, a better choice than those selected by Mr. Asquith and Mr. Lloyd George in the First World War. They included, at first or later, men such as Sir John Anderson (now Lord Waverley), Lord Woolton, Lord Leathers, Lord Cherwell, the late Mr. Ernest Bevin, the late Sir Andrew Duncan, Sir P. J. Grigg and Mr. Oliver Lyttelton. In time of war the nation needs in high political office men of high repute, who have risen to the top in their own sphere of work and are accustomed to making quick decisions involving immense responsibilities. It does not much matter if they are inexpert parliamentarians, as both Houses are lenient to such men in time of war. In peace time the situation is different. Then the man in high office, who has what may be termed an amateur status as a politician and has never been through the mill as a back-bencher in either House, is at a disadvantage. The representation of a great Department in Parliament is a difficult trade to learn in later life. Even in the Lords, where the standard of courtesy is so high, a question of devastating directness is sometimes put to a Minister who is addressing the House with the aid of a carefully prepared brief. The professionals, with years of practice behind them in addressing stormy public meetings, can find a ready answer, even if it is wholly evasive and is not referred to on the brief. The amateurs, equally accustomed by years of supremacy in their military or civilian jobs outside politics to give orders and make pronouncements but not to answer hostile or irrelevant questions, are often "flummoxed". They either make injudicious replies or none at all. In either case their reputation and that of the Government to which they belong suffers.

EXTRACT FROM MY DIARY, MAY 21ST, 1940

Very grave news. The Boches have now taken, or their advance units have entered, Amiens and Abbeville. Notwithstanding these events, the House of Commons at its very worst at question time—frivolity, foolish chaff and indulgence in ridiculous arguments as to who should sit on the Front Opposition Bench and who be Leader of the Opposition.[1]

Two completely different pictures of the British reaction to the grave events of May 1940 are shown in the following entries in my diary:

MAY 27TH, 1940

Went to a public meeting at Mannings Heath.[2] The old ladies present were all genuinely ready to "do or die" for the country; in Sussex the ominous thunder of the guns in France and on the Channel come nearer every day; but the nightingales continue to pour out their hearts in the Weald on the lovely still Spring evenings of May, 1940.

The old ladies in question, as well as the few men present, were magnificent—an epitome of the spirit of England; none were under fifty, many were over seventy, because the younger men and women of the village were on war service somewhere. I told them that, if the Germans invaded us, Sussex would obviously be very much in the front line; that we must, in that event, obey the military authorities implicitly and not worry about our lives and properties; it ought not, I added, to be difficult for our generation, as we had been through all this in an earlier war. We had heard the Flanders guns in the Weald before, and some of our best

---

[1] I have remarked before that the House of Commons sometimes shows its anxiety and nervousness on great and serious occasions during question time by behaviour reminiscent of an infants' school.

[2] Mannings Heath was in my former constituency.

friends' bones lay across the Channel. But England had survived then and would again. My speech was badly delivered and over-emotional owing to the tension we had all been going through, whilst Sussex audiences are not noticeable for their enthusiasm; but the fifty or sixty old people present cheered me to the echo, drowning the dull "thud-thudding" of the noise of the guns from across the Channel. This little incident and the ceremony of signifying the Royal Assent described below in my diary heartened me enormously in this period of grave anxiety.

JUNE 30TH, 1940

Went as a "front-bencher"[1] with others to hear the Royal Assent given to certain Acts; John Simon,[2] very handsome and dignified and with admirable enunciation, performed his duties as Lord Chancellor. Francis Lascelles[3] read the Commission as Clerk. Memories of Gallipoli came flooding back to me. The ceremony was as usual simple, dignified and impressive. The pageantry and custom of hundreds of years was completely unaffected by the frightful proximity of the war to London.

In July Sir John Anderson (now Lord Waverley) had a difficult debate in the House of Commons over a Bill designed to set up special courts, with certain characteristics which resembled courts-martial, in defence zones. In fact, Sir Ralph Glyn, the late Mr. Lees-Smith, who was then leading the Opposition, and I were almost its only supporters. I have no doubt that its opponents, who comprised members of all parties, were mainly influenced by legitimate regard for the liberties of the subject.

On July 30 there was a proposal in the Commons to hold another secret session on foreign affairs, and a number of us took exception to this course on the ground that there had already been five secret sessions since the war had begun less than a year previously, and that there were no more than seven in the whole of the last war. We also felt that Mr. Churchill had rather a *penchant* for secret sessions. He has, indeed, shown this taste in

[1] After the fall of the Chamberlain Government, I returned to the Opposition Front Bench.
[2] Lord Simon, the new Lord Chancellor.
[3] Mr. Lascelles, a Clerk of the Lords and a former brother officer of mine in Gallipoli.

recent years. For obvious reasons the Press was very much on our side, but Mr. Churchill, by a most adroit and amusing speech, in which his hold on the affections and respect of the House were plainly shown, easily won the contest, though he had such well-known parliamentarians as Sir Percy Harris and the late Lord Wedgwood against him. The opponents of the motion were greatly annoyed at the late Sir William Davison[1] moving "to espy Strangers" in the middle of the late Lord Wedgwood's speech, especially as the motion itself, moved by the Government, was a combined one of "espying Strangers" and going into secret session. The motion was worded in this way as a result of an amicable arrangement between Captain (now Lord) Margesson, the Government Chief Whip, and the opponents of the motion. We were very angry with Sir William who, throughout the war, was a most powerful supporter of Mr. Churchill and generally spoke in his support when there was criticism of him. On one of these occasions, when I was criticising the Government, I remarked of Sir William that so complete was his trust in the Prime Minister that, if it should unfortunately happen that the latter went mad whilst he was making a speech and proceeded to stand on his head on the floor of the House, Sir William would immediately follow his example by also standing on his head and justify his action by saying that, if it was right for the Prime Minister to stand on his head, it must be right for him to do so also; I added that such faithfulness deserved at some future date translation to a higher sphere. Sir William Davison did not appear to like this observation of mine, whilst Mr. Churchill was incensed by it; he shouted out "Shame" with a tone in his voice and a look on his face that he reserved in later days for Mr. Morrison or Mr. Shinwell. Perhaps the explanation was that I was being unduly accurate as a prophet.

Following the Battle of Britain and the destruction caused in London by bombing in the autumn of 1940, Mr. Churchill made, on October 8, a statement in the House of Commons that was notable for its eloquence; not even he has ever employed more clear, beautiful, simple and classical English in acquainting the House of Commons with the facts of a situation. He had little that was new to tell members, save on one or two points, such as the

[1] Afterwards Lord Broughshane.

bringing into operation of the War Damage Insurance Scheme, and he touched on one or two matters which he felt it his duty to mention, such as that we should not pass Germany in actual possession of aircraft for some time: but the main feature of his speech was the way in which it raised the spirits and morale of all of us who heard it. In this respect, though it has been far less written about, it was in some ways even more helpful than his earlier speeches containing his most historic phrases about "fighting on the beaches", "blood and sweat" and "the debt owed by the many to the few".

During 1940 there was some damage to the House of Commons by bombing, though the destruction of the Chamber did not occur until May 10, 1941. In consequence, the Commons sat in Church House, Westminster, which had been prepared at an earlier date for their reception in the event of the Palace of Westminster becoming uninhabitable. It was interesting to see how quickly members became accustomed to their new home in which the space was much smaller and the amenities less than in their usual one. The secret of the move was well kept and never mentioned in the Press.

Mr. Chamberlain died in December, and I repeat below what I wrote in my diary at the time, because I think it well describes his character.

DECEMBER 10TH, 1940

Neville Chamberlain died this morning. I experienced a real personal feeling of grief and sorrow. It is a tragic thing to die of cancer so soon after his crushing political fall, the effects of which the efflux of time and a more just balance of opinion, especially among those of "leftist" views, might have healed. Neville was a man of great strength of character, complete integrity and immense assiduity in the discharge of the high functions of administration with a quick brain (far quicker in the "uptake" than his predecessor) coupled to judgment which was on the whole very good. He was also a good speaker though lacking any real eloquence; but he made up for this by quality of expression, good command of language and excellent enunciation. His fault lay in a certain obstinacy and aloofness (here he resembled S. B.[1]) displayed towards any colleagues or others who did not share his views; his very strength of character

[1] Lord Baldwin.

and will were partly responsible for this obtuseness, for such it was; he hated war, though he was by no means a bad war Prime Minister,[1] despite the criticisms of him in that capacity, and he had little personal acquaintance with, or, indeed, liking for, the vast cess-pool of European continental politics. The world of Europe was a *terra ignota* to him; he had none of Winston's grand conceptions, which are sometimes a weakness to Winston, of the clash and blare of world events, Fundamentally, he was a sober, intelligent, very able business man turned administrator and Prime Minister in his later years. In private life he was a most affectionate and understanding friend.

In the winter of 1940 Mr. Shinwell and I had a talk, following one I had had with Mr. Hore-Belisha. All three of us thought that there was both justification and necessity for a joint presentation of views, after prior consultation, on certain aspects of defence, foreign policy and supply. There had been, in the 1914 war, a friendly Opposition—to use what appears to be a contradiction in terms—of both Liberals and Conservative ex-Ministers, sitting on the Front Opposition Bench. As I have previously stated, Parliament ought not to be considered a negligible factor in war time; no one, indeed, holds this view more strongly than Mr. Churchill, as is evidenced by the respect for, and regard to, the House of Commons that he showed in his war Premiership. There is clearly need for critical comment at times, alike upon the course of events and the Government's reaction to them. A Government as powerful as the National Government has particular need for such comments, and it is in the nation's interest that it should receive them. We did not seek to form a group in the ordinary parliamentary sense of the term. Indeed, we repelled the help of some whom we thought had ulterior motives—of a personal character—in seeking to work with us. We did not want to be the stepping-stones for anyone's ambitions to overthrow the Government in order to have a place in a new one. Our object was not to destroy or embarrass the Government; nor could Mr. Shinwell and I be accused of the motives colloquially known as "sour grapes", for he had been offered and refused office, for reasons I do not know and have never discussed with him, while I had been asked if I would allow my name to

[1] He was a very much better one than Lord Asquith.

be submitted to His Majesty for a high appointment overseas. I declined the offer for the simple reason that I wished to remain a Member of Parliament and be "Father of the House". Even had we formed ourselves into a large, influential, aggressive group, engaged to press certain important issues upon the attention of His Majesty's Government, Mr. Churchill could not, in logic, have objected; for he was the leader, as he has stated in *The Second World War,* and I have described in this book, of just such a group, in whose membership I was included, during Mr. Baldwin's Premiership. I think that he accepted our position and aims after some preliminary observations of acerbity to which we replied with equal acerbity. The relationship between Mr. Shinwell and myself was described by Mr. Kingsley Martin of the *New Statesman* as "Arsenic and Old Lace", the title of a celebrated play of the time. The name stuck. I found it easy to work with Mr. Shinwell, despite our differences on domestic policy; I liked his intelligence and integrity. His occasional bursts of unnecessary violence and invective did not repel me, as I share this tendency with him. In private we were each of us attacked by personal and political friends for our alliance, which was alleged to be sinister and unnatural. We were not, in the slightest degree, embarrassed or annoyed by these attacks. The House, as a whole, treated us well, and did not regard our efforts as ignoble or self-seeking.

The alliance virtually arose out of a debate at the end of November on man-power and production. The Government were not in a very happy position, as both Mr. Greenwood and the late Mr. Bevin failed to answer Mr. Shinwell's powerful plea for universal organisation and compulsion where it was necessary. Mr. Shinwell showed political courage in making such a speech at the time, though what he advocated was, in effect, afterwards adopted by the Government. He said that there had been failure to use the powers given in the Control of Persons and Property legislation, and he was powerfully supported by Mr. Clement Davies for the Liberals, and by Mr. Hore-Belisha. There was a good deal of criticism of Mr. Bevin in private following the debate. It was not until the next year that he established his position as a first-rate Minister of Labour in a war-time Government.

I took the same line as Mr. Shinwell when opening the debate on the Address at the beginning of the new session a few days later. I had the support of influential members of the House such as Mr. Seymour Cocks and Sir John Wardlaw-Milne; but the principal feature of the debate on the Address was not this discussion, but a pacifist amendment moved by Mr. McGovern, who was supported by Mr. Maxton. The former spoke well and Mr. Maxton was good in his usual form. In replying for the Government, Mr. Attlee made what I described in my diary at the time as the "speech of his life". He said that Mr. Maxton's "chief charm lay in his irresponsibility" which, I am afraid, is an only too true description. Mr. James Walker, the Labour leader, also made a fine speech, with the result that only some four or five members voted for the amendment and there were 440 against it. I have devoted some space to this part of the debate because it unquestionably had an excellent effect upon public opinion abroad. Here was the Parliament of a country which, it was argued, had just avoided complete destruction in the most dangerous war in its history and might yet be defeated and obliterated, yet was determined to fight to the last; foreign observers compared this vote to the much larger pacifist vote cast in the House during the First World War.

There was also an important debate in December, 1940, on a Report of the Committee of Privileges which had had to consider whether the internment of Captain Ramsay, M.P., was or was not a breach of privilege. Very wisely and properly, it found that to intern a Member of Parliament for reasons of national security did not constitute a breach of the privileges of the House of Commons. Some foolish criticisms by members in different parts of the House, and their unwarranted assumption that Members of Parliament should be free in war time to say and do things that would be punishable if said or done by any member of the public who was not a Member of Parliament, were spurned and rejected by the House, and the Committee's Report was carried without a division. I was a member of this Committee at the time and continued to be so until my retirement from Parliament in 1951. During that period we had more difficult and intricate cases with which to deal than the Committee had ever had in its long existence. Mr. Attlee was our chairman during

the war, and Mr. Morrison in the early days of the Labour
Government in 1945; both were first-class chairmen with all the
qualities required for chairmanship of a body with quasi-
judicial functions. In the debates that followed many of our
Reports, it was never suggested that, as a body or individually,
we allowed party motives to influence us in the slightest degree;
the only criticism of the composition of the Committee voiced
during the discussion on the Ramsay case was from a Conservative member who suggested that we were not the sort of people
in whom he had much confidence; but no one in the House
cared very much whether he had confidence in us or not. I think
it is true to say that the Committee of Privileges in recent years
has achieved a much higher status than it had in the nineteenth
century, when, on occasions, political bias seems to have affected
its decisions.

CHAPTER XIX

THERE were important changes in the Government in the winter of 1940. In November, Sir John Anderson became Lord President of the Council, Mr. Morrison Home Secretary, Sir Andrew Duncan Minister of Supply and Mr. Oliver Lyttelton President of the Board of Trade. There were also several other changes; Lord Reith became Minister of Works and Buildings, and Colonel Moore-Brabazon (now Lord Brabazon) Minister of Transport; at the same time Mr. Bevin became a member of the Cabinet. Lord Halifax ceased to be Foreign Secretary and was appointed British Ambassador to the United States; his Ambassadorship, after a difficult start, was as illustrious and notable as his Viceroyalty in India. I think that historians of the future will draw a parallel somewhat on the following lines between the two Foreign Secretaries who were respectively in office at the outbreak of each of the great wars. Sir Edward Grey and Lord Halifax possessed much in common beside their Christian names. They were men of the highest character; indeed, the much over-used adjective "saintly" could be applied to both. Both had culture, erudition and a wide range of interests; both belonged to families with a fine record of service to the State; both inherited the best traditions of English country gentlemen; both had troops of friends and admirers and a happy domestic background; each had discernment and judgment, and took decisions he believed to be right even when they were unpopular with the public and his Party. Both, however, failed in what must be the primary task of all British Foreign Ministers, to prevent a great war in which Britain had to fight for her life with inadequate preparation. Was theirs the major blame? Or did it rest upon the shoulders of the Prime Minister and their colleagues in the Cabinet in which they served? Or was the failure due to circumstances neither they nor their Cabinet colleagues could control or avoid? It is hard to answer the questions. But if the old proverb "Set a thief to catch a thief" applies in such a case, then these two high-principled men were ill-adapted to deal with the scoundrels who infested the Wilhelmstrasse in Berlin before both wars. Mr. Eden was made Secretary of State for Foreign Affairs. His tenure of this great office throughout the rest of the war merited, and received, praise from all parties in the House.

In the first few months of 1941 there was a number of debates in the Commons that have long been forgotten; 1941 is remembered for the tremendous war events which characterised it, and not for parliamentary discussions. Nevertheless, some of these discussions had an influence not only on public opinion at the time, but on the British Government's conduct of the war, and for that reason justify incorporation in this narrative.

On January 21, the late Mr. Ernest Bevin, Minister of Labour, in an adjournment debate, submitted to the House what, in his own words, were "the reasons for the changes that have been made with the object of co-ordinating and expediting our production efforts". He went on to say that his statement would deal with four points; these were the newly-established governmental machinery, the policy in regard to production, how the powers granted by Parliament had in fact been used, and the policy to be pursued in the further organisation and use of man-power. Though Mr. Bevin appeared to "knock" compulsion in the first part of his speech, in the second he spoke of much greater use of it; there was to be prevention of dismissal (save for misconduct), reorganisation in businesses and mills which were of national importance, and universal registration for male civilians, with a view to compulsory labour if necessary. I followed him and took the opportunity of saying that those of us who were working together were grateful to the Government for having allowed the debate to take place, and that we formed no organised group or movement. I added, "We represent rather a movement of public opinion which has been on a much more rapid scale than that of the Government during the last few weeks". I was opposed by Mr. Ellis Smith, the Labour member, and Miss Irene Ward of the Conservative Party; it implies no reflection on either of those two excellent Members of Parliament to say that their speeches have never carried very great weight with the House. Mr. Shinwell and Mr. Clement Davies supported me, as did Mr. Simmonds, a young man of enterprise and ability who himself was largely interested in a manufacturing industry. Mr. James Griffiths, the official Labour Party front Opposition bench speaker, was neutral. Mr. Jack Lawson,[1] another Labour member, made a good speech, though he appeared to be rather too fearful of compulsion. The end of the debate is described in my diary in compressed shape as follows:

> Winston summed up. Very brilliant speech. Points. Comments and criticism very life blood of democracy; strongly in favour of it. Thought I went too far, but felt no resentment. War-time munitions factories were many of them as to four-fifths or two-thirds finished. When they were completed all possible labour would be required. The fact that those factories are not completed reason why mobilisation of labour not yet carried out; he turned down a War Cabinet of Ministers without Portfolio as a result of his experience in the last war; in fact, all other Ministers concerned had to attend such a Cabinet in practice in order to hear the arguments; said in regard to one supreme Minister of Economic Effort to control the home front, "where could we find such a man? Would have really to be a deputy or even joint Prime Minister".

Those of us who organised and took part in this debate were gratified next day to find we had a good Press and a recognition of the fact that our efforts had done something to accelerate the nation's war effort and "ginger" the Government. This was, in fact, one of those occasions when critical and interrogative parliamentary debate was of assistance to the nation. Those of us who criticised and interrogated the Government were gratified by Mr. Churchill's reply and his obvious intention to consider the points which we had made while, at the same time, rebutting some of them.

To supply a contrast, where Mr. Churchill and a number of his followers came into angry conflict, I will quote from my diary of February 27, 1941:

> Winston in a curious and truculent mood at question time and throughout debate on Bill to alter the law relating to "offices of profit under the Crown" which is to be altered so as to allow Malcolm MacDonald to go as High Commissioner to Canada

[1] Now Lord Lawson.

without vacating his seat; the Attorney-General[1] and Winston, in an amusing and characteristically brilliant but irrelevant and rather irresponsible speech, suggested that it was necessary in war time to widen the area of the Prime Minister's choice for offices for M.P.s to positions outside the House; he even suggested that better service can thus be done than by attendance to parliamentary duties. All fudge! There is no necessity for the Bill; already we have a sort of "King's Party" adding to the swollen total of Ministers, Parliamentary Private Secretaries, M.P.s who are Regional Commissioners, etc. The real object of the Bill is to let Malcolm have a job as the other Socialists apparently object to this very competent man being in the Government. Winston also snapped at me at question time and suggested that Shinwell and I were trying to form an Opposition; he angrily announced that he regarded the Bill as a question of confidence; he made, in an aside, an unfair reference, though an oblique one, to the fact that I had been offered and refused a certain post; Pickthorn[2] made a good speech against the Bill, as did John Gretton, but there was no division.

Students of Mr. Churchill's unique career in Parliament will have noticed that there are occasions, fortunately comparatively rare, when he is, to use the phrase I used in my diary at the time, "in a curious and truculent mood". This has occurred again in recent years and, indeed, in recent months (at the time of my writing this book). It is a mark of the greatness of the man and of his generosity of character that he quickly forgives and forgets any counter-attack made upon him when he is in one of these moods; it is also a sign of the respect and affection the House of Commons has for him that it equally quickly forgives and forgets any irresponsible or foolish remark that he has made on such occasions.

In January, 1941, a Select Committee which had been appointed to enquire into certain charges brought against Mr. Boothby, then a junior member of the Government, found him guilty of conduct unworthy of a Member of Parliament. This Report was discussed by the House on January 27. Mr. Boothby, who resigned his office as a result of the Report, made a long and, in the circumstances, a good speech defending his conduct; he was followed by the Prime Minister who, I stated in my diary:

[1] Sir Donald (now Lord Justice) Somervell.
[2] Mr. Kenneth Pickthorn, M.P.

made a rather over-sentimental speech (I am unable to see in the fact that Bob has been proved to have behaved badly a great national tragedy), whilst Mander[1] and I complained, with the evident approbation of the House against Bob's suggestion, by inference, that other M.P.s were not above suspicion, after the Committee were agreed in thinking that he was guilty.

Soon after this occurrence, there was a debate on the suppression of the *Daily Worker*. The reference to it in my diary is as follows:

> Mr. Aneurin Bevan made the best speech against the Home Secretary's action, though Pritt[2] and Gallacher[3] were also good. But Morrison[4] had no sort of difficulty in answering them.

In February, 1941, I paid a visit, at his invitation, to Mr. Lloyd George at his house at Churt; he was by then beginning to show signs of age physically and did not often attend the House. Like most men over seventy, he liked to have a short nap after lunch; but he insisted on this occasion that I should remain with him for the greater part of the afternoon. I found in him all the old wit, charm and astonishing powers of expression as he expounded to me his views on the war situation. He was able to take a detached view, and it was quite obvious that he had ceased to have any political ambitions. He had refused office in Mr. Churchill's Government some time earlier, on the score of his age. My reason for mentioning this occasion is the fact that his main theme was that, whoever won the war, the end of it would see Western civilisation in ruins, with little chance of the re-emergence of Britain as a great Power within the lifetime of the youngest person alive. Though it was a dark and gloomy day, with deep snow on the ground, I left Mr. Lloyd George's house without any great feeling of depression about what he had said to me, because I thought it represented the views of an old and tired man who would be naturally inclined to look at matters in a pessimistic

[1] Sir Geoffrey Mander, a well-known Liberal M.P. of the time.
[2] Mr. Pritt, Q.C., a Labour M.P. who later did not accept the Whip of the Party.
[3] Mr. Willie Gallacher, a well-known Scottish Communist M.P.
[4] Mr. Herbert Morrison.

way; but I have often pondered on his words since then. It was not a fashionable view at the time, as everyone forced themselves to believe that when Nazism and Fascism were destroyed a great new era of hope would begin for the world, just as in the previous war it was thought that, when Germany had been defeated and the Kaiser deposed, there would be, in Mr. Lloyd George's own words, "A world fit for heroes to live in".

On May 10, 1941, the Chamber of the House of Commons was destroyed by enemy action. During most of the war I was a fire-watcher at the House of Commons on certain nights of the week. I rejoiced, by reason of my seniority and knowledge of the Palace of Westminster, in the imposing title of Assistant-Controller, which I shared with another senior member and one of the senior officials who were each on duty on certain nights of the week. Our designation was less impressive than it seemed, as the real work was done by the Controllers, who were all members of the custodians' service of the House. The custodians are uniformed officials who supplement the Metropolitan Police in looking after the comfort and security of both Houses of Parliament and members. They are mostly ex-Service men of high character and fine war records. In complete accord with democratic principles, I obeyed promptly and explicitly the orders of my chief—the custodian who was Controller on my night of duty—during the hours of "black-out" whilst he, during the day, when we met, saluted me, in accordance with custom, and called me "My Lord". The fire-watching organisation of the two Houses of Parliament included Peers, M.P.s and members of the staff of all grades of the Palace of Westminster. We were a happy, friendly body in which all social distinctions were ignored. We owed much to the tact, ability and good humour of Captain Victor Goodman, one of the Clerks of the Lords, who was Chief Air Raid Precaution and Security Officer of the Palace of Westminster. I still remember with pleasure an excellent Christmas dinner we had in our canteen on Christmas Day, 1941. The organisation was devised to meet every emergency; though, unhappily, the resident Superintendent of the House of Lords and two police constables lost their lives in earlier and minor raids and certain damage was done to the Palace before the Chamber was destroyed.

I was not on duty on the night when the Chamber was burnt

by a fire bomb, but I was there the following night. Next morning at "stand down", on a cold grey day, I went to have a look at where the place had been where I had spent so many years of my life; the fire had done its work in a most astonishingly clean fashion. The Chamber itself had completely disappeared, as had the voting lobbies, but the other lobbies and Ministers' rooms close behind the Chamber were untouched; the void gave the appearance of having been chiselled out with a knife. I wondered, rather morbidly, if there was anything symbolical in this clear, clean destruction of the home of the "Mother of Parliaments". I gave a broadcast on the subject in the B.B.C.'s war-time North American Service a few days afterwards, but I did not mention my morbid fears; in any case, I think it would have been disallowed by the censor.

The year 1941 and the greater part of the year 1942 constituted, as everyone knows, a period of serious set-backs for British arms which naturally provoked, in Parliament and outside, doubts and questions about the capability and organisation of the Government in dealing with the situation. In a later portion of this chapter I put forward the reasons why those of us, inside and outside Parliament, who had those doubts were fully justified in expressing them. The Government, and even Mr. Churchill himself, gave signs of being uncertain of the extent of the support they would receive in Parliament, despite the absence of any possible alternative Government, and the enormous majority they could normally command. No doubt, because of this feeling, the Government, early in May, demanded a vote of confidence. I described what occurred as follows in my diary:

MAY 6TH, 1941

The first day of the big debate on the Government's rather unnecessary vote of confidence; Anthony Eden opened and was neither very communicative nor inspiring; the new member for the Northern Ireland Universities, Savory,[1] made a good speech in which he detailed the political and strategical results of not stopping Germany in the Rhineland. Hore-Belisha and Shinwell spoke well; McGovern was very violent in his opposition to the war and Attlee ended in an unimpressive debating speech.

[1] Now Sir Douglas Savory.

MAY 7TH, 1941

The big day of the debate which was opened by L. G. He was critical of Anthony's speech and its lack of information. He condemned the failure to institute full agricultural production and the lack of a proper war Cabinet; Winston made a magnificent speech and got an ovation at the end of it; at the beginning he was very aggressive and unduly recriminatory about L. G.'s and Hore-Belisha's speeches; L. G. was an easy prey as he had unfortunately confused Irak with Iran. The Prime Minister accused Hore-Belisha of not having provided tanks and, though the latter gave a perfectly reasonable answer, it did not seem to satisfy the House or subsequently the Press. He praised Hore-Belisha's introducing compulsion and when I interpolated "which the Home Secretary[1] opposed", he made an oblique reference, as in a former debate, to my alleged failure at the Air Ministry.[2] The Government received an overwhelming majority.

There was a debate on the evacuation of Crete on June 10, from which the Government emerged with some loss of credit owing to criticisms not only in the House but outside, of the conduct of the war. In its "Impressions of Parliament", *Punch* mentioned that Mr. Churchill "looked worried and wary". There was a rather reluctant coolness in the cheer which greeted him; this was not surprising in view of the fact that a month earlier Mr. Churchill had declared that we should defend Crete to the death and with no thought of retreat. Mr. Leslie Hore-Belisha made a good speech in this debate, as did Mrs. Rathbone, whose husband[3] had been killed in the war, and Colonel Macnamara, a young man of great promise with a fine record in the war, who was, unfortunately, afterwards killed, also made a good speech. When I spoke, I said that it was increasingly difficult for

[1] Mr. Morrison.

[2] Though I was concerned in it, I must say that I think this was a perfect example of a good double parliamentary "tit for tat" of which the House as a whole is so fond; I was annoyed with Mr. Churchill for what appeared to be his unnecessary onslaught upon Mr. Hore-Belisha and therefore I made a reference, which I knew would be most embarrassing to him, to the fact that his own colleagues in the Government had done their best to make rearmament impossible before the war; he was equally entitled, as he did, to say in effect, "Well, you are the last person to talk about it in view of your own failure when you were at the Air Ministry".

[3] The late Flight-Lieutenant J. R. Rathbone, M.P.

the Prime Minister to blame his predecessors for the lack of arms to-day. I also pleaded for more Indian and African troops to be raised. I remarked in my diary:

> The Prime Minister was good in reply, though, as usual, he answered few of the real criticisms and, as usual, attacked Leslie Hore-Belisha for his alleged negligence as War Minister. He said "my Noble Friend has been urging us to look on the gloomy side of things—a kind of inverted Couéism. When you get up in the morning you say to yourself 'we can easily lose this war in the next four months' ". Maybe I do; but it happens to be true.

In the middle of June, by the courtesy of the House of Lords, the Commons occupied the Lords' Chamber. At first this vast, gloomy building had a discouraging effect on many members, to whom environment, when they are speaking, means everything; but, on the whole, the House adjusted itself very quickly to its new home as it had to its previous temporary home in Church House.

We had in July, like a gleam of light in the sombre sky of international events and the progress, or, as it seemed at the time so far as we were concerned, retrogression of the war, a debate on the question of greater food production in Britain. Mr. Hudson, who was by far the best of Ministers of Agriculture in either war, gave a very encouraging report of what had been done. He made it clear that, whilst he did not want to use unduly the very great powers conferred upon him by war-time legislation and Orders in Council, he was determined to see that farmers and landowners alike utilised every acre of soil to help keep the nation from starvation.

On July 29, there was a debate on war production. *Punch* wittily described the prelude to it as follows: "For this was the day of the great chastisement. The House was to be told just how wrong it had been two weeks ago to criticise the Government in general and the Prime Minister in particular".

Punch's commentator goes on to say that things did not turn out as was expected and "there was a dead silence when Head Master Churchill strode in. The assembled culprits looked at each other in surprise, for the Head seemed fully as apprehensive as they. He fidgeted on his seat. He looked over his notes and, with one mighty heave, tore a projecting key out of the Dispatch Box on the table before him. Then he sat silent, so did the boys". This witty description of the occasion was completely accurate. There is no doubt that Mr. Churchill intended, as he was, of course, fully entitled to do, to bring the House to heel, but, in fact, the debate failed of its purpose. A more satisfactory debate, from the Government's point of view, took place just before the adjournment for the summer recess on August 5. The Government owed this mainly to two of its members, Mr. Attlee and Mr. Anthony Eden. At the end of both speeches the House was in a considerably happier mood than it had been after Mr. Churchill's speech at the end of the production debate. A point of this kind should be made in a book such as I am writing, since an erroneous impression has grown up in recent years that, in addition to all his other great deeds, Mr. Churchill alone of all Ministers was able in the war to inform and inspire the House of Commons. Mr. Churchill is far too modest a man to make such a claim for himself and, if he did, it would be completely untrue. As a whole, his speeches in Parliament in the 1939 war excelled in vigour, eloquence, the use of memorable phrases, and general structure, even those made by the younger Pitt, or by Lloyd George, in former wars; but he also made some bad ones, and he owed much to the assistance of his colleagues: Mr. Attlee, in his quiet, unobtrusive way, and Mr. Greenwood (to mention only two examples among Labour members of the Government) helped very materially at intervals to reassure the House and give it the information to which it was entitled.

When the House resumed in September, Mr. Churchill, on the 30th of that month, gave a resumé of the progress of the war—a sort of war diary—during the recess; it was a very good speech and a most heartening one. By it Mr. Churchill recovered the slight amount of ground he had lost in the House in the last few weeks of the session before the recess. Before he made his speech, two Labour members of the Government made notable statements; Mr. A. V. (later Lord) Alexander, who was popular with all parties in the House as First Lord of the Admiralty, mainly because he was a good parliamentarian who always judged his audience well, gave most cheering news about the superiority of the British Fleet and its aeroplanes over the

Italians in the Mediterranean; while Mr. David Grenfell, that most popular member of the House, who is now its "Father", gave a most remarkable reply to a question that was greeted with shouts of laughter. Speaking in his capacity as Parliamentary Secretary for Mines, he said that "it is not my business to disagree with the policy of the Government". The House dispersed that day in a happy mood, having enjoyed a good joke at the expense of Mr. Grenfell and one or two other Ministers, and having had such reassuring news.

During the war an admirable official parliamentary body was created in the shape of the Select Committee on National Expenditure. Its chairman throughout the war years was Sir John Wardlaw-Milne, who did good work in many capacities in that Parliament. The Committee justified its creation in a number of ways; and still continues, as the Estimates Committee, to exist eight years after the war is over. In October there was a serious dispute between Sir John and some of the members of the Air Sub-Committee of the Committee, all of whom, in consequence, wished to resign: a long and rather acrimonious debate ensued. There is nothing the House likes so much as a really good, long and acrimonious debate on some domestic difference; such debates seldom interest the public and are usually granted very little space in the Press; but that never deters the House from embarking joyfully upon them. The debate in question was exactly of this description. I helped to bring it to an end by suggesting that the Sub-Committee should withdraw their resignations if the Government would promise to deal with their report, which had been submitted to the Prime Minister confidentially, at any rate to the extent of saying what action they would take upon it; the Government promised to consider this suggestion which was finally accepted by Mr. Harry Crookshank, the Financial Secretary to the Treasury, and the resignations were withdrawn.

The new session opened on November 12; very appropriately, the Address was moved by Captain Pilkington, who won his M.C. at Dunkirk, and Mr. Marshall, a Labour M.P. Mr. Churchill gave one of his usual resumés of events at home and abroad. I stated in my diary that it was not as good a speech as that which he had made at the Mansion House in the previous week, which was among the most brilliant he delivered inside or outside the House during the war. I went on to note that "he said little, was a trifle too full of 'wise-cracks' and of aggression towards actual or potential critics". I should perhaps have added, in justice to Mr. Churchill, that one of his "wise-cracks" was an extremely good one. He said that there would be an invasion of Britain when the weather permitted and that we should deal with it. He went on to say that there would be some criticism of the Government from time to time, as befitted an extremely active democracy, and that the Government would also deal with that. I have wondered since whether Mr. Churchill realised at the time that the danger of invasion was, in fact, remote, but felt that, nevertheless, it was a good thing, from the point of view of keeping the military and civilian defences at the highest point of efficiency, to suggest that it was a likely contingency. In the circumstances, it would obviously have been quite legitimate to make use of this ruse; on the other hand, he may have really thought that invasion was likely to take place, in which case the advice he had received from his military advisers cannot have been very good, for the result of the Battle of Britain was to remove all chance of such an invasion succeeding, and from Mr. Churchill's own book there is little evidence to show that Hitler contemplated the invasion of Britain in the spring or summer of 1942.

The House met at short notice on December 8 to learn from Mr. Churchill his account of the attack on Pearl Harbour and of the United States' entry into the war. Two days later he had the sad task of telling the House that the *Prince of Wales* and the *Repulse* had been sunk.

At the end of January, 1942, there was an important debate in the Commons, opened by Sir John Wardlaw-Milne in an able and critical speech. Mr. Henderson Stewart,[1] Sir Herbert Williams, Sir Henry Morris-Jones, Sir Archibald Southby and others also attacked the Government which was vigorously defended by the Prime Minister's son, Mr. Randolph Churchill, in an amusing speech. It was a good, provocative rejoinder to the critics, containing as it did some wounding references to many of us, including myself, but it did not capture the ear of

[1] Now Under-Secretary of State for Scotland.

the House. During his period in the House, Mr. Randolph Churchill made many brilliant speeches, but the House never treated him with the trust and affection it has shown to his father, at any rate in recent years. I think that the reason lies in this: if you are the brilliant son of a brilliant father, it is as well to dissemble your cleverness and not to display it too much. I made the final speech for the critics of the administration before Mr. Churchill concluded the debate, and was gratified by his friendly references to me and his acceptance of the legitimacy of the position, from a parliamentary point of view, which we occupied, however much he might deplore the particular line which we took.

At the beginning of February there was a "reshuffle" in the Government, and Lord Beaverbrook was made Minister of Production. This pleased those of us who had been criticising the Government, for it was exactly the point we had urged in debates in the previous year. Sir Andrew Duncan went back to the Ministry of Supply after having been President of the Board of Trade for a few months. Mr. (now Lord) Llewellin became Minister of Aircraft Production and Mr. Dalton President of the Board of Trade, whilst there were one or two changes in minor offices. This "reshuffle" was not very well received by the Press. There had been other previous Governmental changes in 1941. Captain Margesson[1] ceased to be Patronage Secretary to the Treasury, as the Chief Whip of a party in power is called, and was made Secretary of State for War. He was, however, superseded by Sir P. J. Grigg before the end of the war and made a Peer. Experience has shown that to give an important ministerial and executive post to a Chief Whip who has never been in any office but that of the Whips is seldom productive of good results. The qualities required to control a great department of State are quite different from those necessary to control a parliamentary Party in the Commons. In an earlier passage of this book I have praised the high quality of the Chief Whips the Conservative Party has had, from the time of Sir Leslie Wilson onwards. In merit there is nothing to choose between them. Of all of them the disgruntled in the Conservative Party have said to me "I don't like . . . and he doesn't like me; he sees to it that I am never "called" by the

---

[1] Now Lord Margesson.

Chair". That, of course, is nonsense. A Chief Whip, whether his Party is in or out of power, cannot prevent the Chair "calling" a member, however much he may dislike him. Then, too, I have heard the complaint so often made in private of all Chief Whips, "I don't like being ordered about and told what to do as if I was back in the army, and a private at that". I know that many readers of these words who are not in political life will violently dissent from my views on this subject, but, in fact, a Chief Whip must exercise a considerable measure of discipline over the members of his Party unless it is to disintegrate. Of all the boring and dangerous "bromides" of the opponents of the British parliamentary system, the phrase "voting at the crack of the Party Whip" is the worst. Those who use it should study some Continental legislatures where the doctrine they preach is practised. In these countries, with their absence of large organised political parties and the existence of a large number of small groups who form, dissolve and re-form, there is no "crack of the Party Whip". So members vote as they please, or as they think will please their constituents, whatever the interests of the country may be. This results in the average life of governments being a few weeks. "Old-fashioned Liberal", "Pro Bono Publico" and others who, in the correspondence columns of the Press, advocate either proportional representation or the destruction of the British Party System as it exists to-day, should be compelled to spend a year in France studying French electoral and political conditions. It would do them as much good as it would any British supporter of the Communist cause to spend a year in a Siberian labour camp. A complete reversal of view would be likely to result in each case.

I must, before leaving the subject of Chief Whips, mention two others; Mr. Whiteley, C.H., M.P., the present Labour Chief Whip, and his predecessor, Sir Charles Edwards, have justly earned the admiration of political friends and foes alike by their conduct of their office. There is not much wrong with British parliamentary life when a party of the "left", such as the Labour Party, has as its chief officers men of such integrity, wisdom, common sense, charm and courtesy as these two men.

In February, 1942, there was considerable excitement in the Press, and a lesser amount in Parliament, owing to a warning given to the *Daily Mirror* that it would be suppressed under

Regulation 2D if it persisted in certain aspects of its campaign against the capacity and conduct of officers in the Army. Some saw in this warning a threat to the Press as a whole, and considered that Mr. Herbert Morrison should have proceeded by Regulation 2C, which would have involved action by the Courts. Presumably, he did not do so because of the delay involved. I had plenty of opportunities of observing Mr. Herbert Morrison's conduct of his great office of Home Secretary, which is one of the most delicate and difficult for any man to fill in war time. I also had some small unofficial business with him in my capacity as chairman of the Inter-Governmental Committee for Refugees. I consider him to have been an extremely successful Home Secretary in time of war and a very fair one. He showed courage, discretion and statesmanship in his control of the intricate special powers conferred upon him. I think he was right to take action in the case of the *Daily Mirror*, though it was not wholly popular at the time, and I think he was equally right in releasing Sir Oswald Mosley, as he did later on personal grounds, from his internment under Regulation 18B—an action that was equally unpopular.

Another Minister who was much in the news in the early months of 1942 was the late Sir Stafford Cripps, who went on an abortive visit to India to try to find some compromise between the views of the Indian leaders and the National Government. He did not succeed. It was Sir Stafford's misfortune during the war to have consistently to try to reconcile the irreconcilable. He was, for example, sent as Ambassador to Russia in the belief, no doubt, that the presence as British representative in Russia of a man of great talent and high character who was very much one of the "left" in the Labour Party would make it easier to deal with Premier Stalin and generally oil the wheels of Anglo-Russian relationship: through no fault of Sir Stafford's, it had no such effect. Though he did not succeed in these tasks which he was given, he earned the praise and respect of the House of Commons during the war for his personal qualities; his outrageous speeches before the war, which I have no doubt proceeded from a genuine and sincere belief, but which, nevertheless, did the country considerable harm, were forgotten and forgiven; members of all parties admired his courage in stating blunt and unpleasant facts about the progress of the war, his self-sacrificing assiduity in the discharge of his ministerial functions, and the clarity and brilliance of his speeches.

A Conservative Minister also earned the praise alike of the House and the Press in February, 1942. Mr. Oliver Lyttelton opened an important production debate in that month in a speech of great clarity and incisiveness; he finally established himself as a parliamentarian, in addition to being a very able administrator.

During this period of the war London was full of members and Prime Ministers of Allied and Commonwealth Governments and statesmen on official visits. Senior members of the House, such as myself, had many opportunities of meeting such men as Dr. Wellington Koo, General de Gaulle, Mr. Van Zeeland, Mr. Harry Hopkins, and many others, either at meals arranged in their honour, at meetings which they addressed, or in private. From them it was possible to obtain not only most interesting information on the conduct of the war, but fascinating sidelights upon the British statesmen whom they liked and trusted as well as upon those whom they disliked and mistrusted. It was also interesting and fascinating to watch the effect of those men and others like them upon unofficial meetings held in one of the "Committee rooms upstairs" in the House of Commons; a number of such meetings, where the attendance was open to every member, were held during the war. Two of the best speeches I heard, in each case made to a packed meeting, were from the late Mr. Curtin, Prime Minister of Australia, and Mr. Harry Hopkins. Mr. Curtin told us frankly that he and Mr. Churchill did not always agree, a fact that was indeed obvious from other information we had; but he added that they had a mutual regard for each other and that in any encounter Mr. Churchill got from him (Mr. Curtin) "as good as he gave"; he thought that these encounters were probably good for both of them, a statement that was heartily cheered by those of Mr. Churchill's critics who were present. Mr. Harry Hopkins made the best speech I have ever heard made to a gathering of this kind by a man who had not himself been in the House of Commons. He seemed by instinct to understand exactly the method and manner M.P.s like of presenting a case, whether in a debate in the House or at a Committee.

Sir Kingsley Wood's Budget was produced in April and contained few surprises; the chief features of it were heavy additional taxation on entertainment, tobacco and drink, all of which were expected. Domestic trouble in the Conservative Party arose over the coal rationing scheme suggested by Sir William (now Lord) Beveridge in a report to the Government. The Conservative Party, through its powerful unofficial 1922 Committee and in other ways, opposed the scheme, and the Government had eventually to abandon it.

During the war, in common with other M.P.s of all parties, I spoke at a number of Ministry of Information meetings throughout the country. These gatherings were for the purpose of describing the war situation and proceedings in Parliament. There was an honourable understanding, to which there was strict adherence, that no statements of a party character should be made at them; as a rule, a local leader of the Labour or Liberal Party took the chair for a Conservative M.P. and vice versa. In the course of one of my tours in the early summer of 1942, I was in Worcestershire and went to call on Lord and Lady Baldwin at Astley Hall. There was a fascinating contrast between Mr. Lloyd George's attitude during my visit to him in the previous year, which I have already described, and that of Lord Baldwin. It reflected very clearly the differences in character and outlook of the two former Prime Ministers. Mr. Baldwin engaged in no dissertation on the war and what would happen after it. He hardly referred to it except to say, rather plaintively I thought, that he had little official information about it. I said a word subsequently in the proper quarters to have this remedied. He showed me his house and garden and the well-known landmarks in his beloved Worcestershire which could be seen from it. He was witty, urbane and charming, as he always was in private when you did not want to talk political business to him. It was only when you did that his oyster-like qualities were apparent. He appeared genuinely delighted to welcome an old friend to his house, even though that old friend had frequently attacked him in the Commons. Apart from a limp due to rheumatic trouble, he seemed well and cheerful. I left him feeling glad that a man for whom I had an affectionate regard was apparently happy in his retirement, and I hoped that he and Lady Baldwin would live for many years yet to enjoy the domestic felicity of their country home. But it was not to be; very soon afterwards, he was seriously crippled with rheumatism and arthritis and in December, 1947, he died, only surviving Lady Baldwin's death by a few years. The last few months of his life were clouded by poignant periods of self-accusation[1], during which he accepted all that his most malignant enemies said about his originating responsibility for the Second World War. This was a sad end to the life of a man whose great public career had earned infinitely more of merit than discredit.

[1] He told me when I saw him that he was often very introspective in these days when he was alone. I did not realise the significance of his remark at the time: but I did when I heard of these emotional stresses.

CHAPTER XX

THE closing months of 1942 and the first half of 1943 were a period of almost unrelieved gloom for Britain in the Second World War. Doubt and anxiety arose in men's and women's minds about the conduct of operations. Some believed that the failure of British arms, despite the heroism of the individual British soldier, sailor and airman, was due to mistakes by the Higher Commands; others, on the contrary, believed that those at the top in the three Services were not given a fair chance owing to bad direction and conflicting orders by their ministerial Chiefs and by Mr. Churchill in particular. All this anxiety was reflected in the Press and Parliament for very proper reasons with which I deal more fully later. In the late winter of 1942, at his invitation, there was a meeting at the house of a well-known newspaper proprietor at which were present several members of Parliament of all parties, including myself, and three editors of important newspapers representing in domestic politics divergent points of view; we had a long and interesting discussion. The consensus of opinion at the end of it was that it would be wrong and contrary to the interests of the country to attempt to "push the Government out", even if it were practicable to do so, which it was not, because there was no alternative Government that could command the confidence of the country. We preferred, in the words which I used in my diary at the time, to "push the Government on" in order to induce them to take the action which we believed to be necessary.

In the middle of May there was a two-day debate on the conduct of the war. It centred largely on the relationship of the Prime Minister to the Chiefs of Staff Committee and of that Committee to the Defence Committee of the War Cabinet. There was some criticism at the Prime Minister's non-appearance in the debate. Mr. Stokes, Sir John Wardlaw-Milne, Commander Bower, Mr. Shinwell, Sir Edward Grigg[1], Mr. Clement Davies, Colonel Oliver Stanley and Mr. Hore-Belisha all made critical speeches,

[1] Now Lord Altrincham.

but they were not in agreement with one another. Colonel Stanley, for example, was opposed to an independent chairman of the Chiefs of Staff Committee, though he hinted very broadly that the Prime Minister interfered too much with it and that the existence of the Defence Committee was an unnecessary interposition between the Chiefs of Staff Committee and the War Cabinet; at the same time, he made the point that our criticisms must not be based on public clamour. Mr. Hore-Belisha was more direct. Sir John Wardlaw-Milne made a strong attack on the Government for certain of its sins of omission and commission. The following is an extract from my diary a week after the debate:

Information has reached me from reliable sources that our demands, in last week's debate, to Winston to put a rein on his desire to be a "strategist-in-chief" has had some effect on him and will, I am sure, strengthen the hands of the powerful triumvirate in the War Cabinet—Anthony Eden, Stafford Cripps and Oliver Lyttelton—to exercise their influence.

On June 18, Mr. Shinwell and I raised at question time the matter of our shipping losses. They were known to be calamitous to us and to others, but were withheld at the time from the general public. I said that if this grievous but not irremediable position was withheld from the public there would be a great shock when eventually the losses became known; Sir Stafford Cripps, who was leading the House at the time, promised to convey our views to the Prime Minister. Next day our questions were supported by inference through leading articles in the *News Chronicle*, the *Daily Express* and *The Times*; it was pointed out that the figures of our losses had already been given in the United States.

All this apprehension and disquiet culminated in a motion placed upon the Order Paper of the House of Commons by Sir John Wardlaw-Milne which read as follows: "That this House, while paying tribute to the heroism and endurance of the armed forces of the Crown in circumstances of extreme difficulty, has no confidence in the central direction of the war". Very properly, the Government arranged for the debate to be brought on as soon as was possible and convenient, which was on July 1.

Mr. Churchill, in *The Second World War*,[1] describes Sir John's
speech as an able one, as indeed it was; but, unfortunately, Sir
John spoiled the effect of it, after his complaint of poor direction
of the war at the highest level, by suggesting that the Duke of
Gloucester should be appointed Commander-in-Chief of the
British Army which was, for a variety of reasons, an impracti-
cable proposal. From that moment he lost the ear of the House.
The motion was seconded by the late Sir Roger Keyes. Sir
Roger was a most gallant naval officer, but he suffered from three
disadvantages in the debate: he was never a good speaker in the
House, he had been removed from his position as Director of
Combined Operations and he had recently suffered a grievous
loss in the death in action of his son, Lieut.-Colonel Keyes, V.C.
It is hard, even for a man of great courage such as his, to be at his
best when he has suffered such a terrible calamity. Having failed,
as it appeared at the time, to discuss in advance with Sir John
the line he was going to take, he adopted an attitude the exact
opposite of that of the proposer of the motion, and said that the
Prime Minister did not interfere enough in the direction of the
war. After those two opening speeches, I was certain that the
motion would not commend itself to the House. Mr. Oliver
Lyttelton spoke for the Government after Sir Roger's speech
and had an easy task in demolishing it; but to some of us he
appeared to go rather too far in attacking a man who was in the
position I have described, and there was some resentment among
the supporters of the Government at his attitude, especially as
he read most of his speech from a brief. Mr. Aneurin Bevan
opened the debate on the second day with a well-delivered
attack on the Prime Minister and the Government; his speech
also contained a strong affirmation of faith in the vitality of the
British nation and our will to win. Mr. Hore-Belisha summed
up well in the closing speech for the Opposition before the Prime
Minister addressed the House. Mr. Churchill's reply was not, in
my opinion, one of his great speeches of the war. He complained
too much of the effect of the attack both by the Press and by
Parliament, whilst at the same time representing it as having
little or no backing. The House was not greatly impressed by this
line of argument, since it remembered that he himself had

<hr />

[1] Volume IV, p. 356.

constantly, with great courage and persistence, attacked previous Governments of which he was ordinarily a supporter, even when few were prepared to support his attack in the country. I spoke on the first day of the debate. Mr. Churchill devotes more than three-quarters of a page to a report of my speech[1]; since those remarks will have been read by the millions of readers of Mr. Churchill's book (unless they "skipped" the page in question, which I hope they did not) there is no need for me to quote from my speech in this book.

The gist of my remarks was that, if there were a series of disasters such as we had undergone, the Prime Minister must be held constitutionally responsible. If they continued, he should resign his post as Prime Minister, and take office, preferably as Foreign Secretary, under some other member of the Government. I am proud to think that Mr. Churchill should have quoted so fully from my speech. I do not wish to retract or recant a word of it. It emphasised an essential and fundamental principle of British democracy. No statesman who has taken so tremendous and momentous a part in the affairs of his country as Mr. Churchill has done for half a century can escape the aftermath of his previous mistakes or misfortunes. The fact that this participation has, in the main, been of unique and immeasurable benefit to the nation does not alter this fact. Mr. Churchill had a direct responsibility for the ill-fated Antwerp expedition in 1914; he had an equal responsibility for the Dardanelles campaign, though I, among many others who fought in it, believe that he was not to blame for its failure; and he had, at least, an indirect responsibility for the completely abortive efforts in 1919 to overthrow the Bolshevist régime in Russia by sending aid to the admirals and generals who fought against it. At the time of the debate we had suffered a number of defeats, beginning with Narvik, when he was First Lord of the Admiralty, and afterwards, under his Premiership, as grievous as any in our history. By every rule of our well-established though unwritten constitution he had to accept responsibility to the House of Commons for them.

In his reply, Mr. Churchill specifically referred to my views on the responsibility of a Prime Minister and accepted them as a principle. Nor was this all. A delicate question, affecting alike

[1] *The Second World War*, Vol. IV, p. 358.

Mr. Churchill's personality and the relationship of a Prime Minister in time of war to the armed forces of the Crown, was clearly involved and was discussed in the debate, as it had been in the previous one. Was his control of the fighting strategy too close, too personal and too military in a general sense? Could he or should he have interfered less in it? The question has never been satisfactorily answered because the experts, of which I am certainly not one, both military and constitutional, differ greatly, at least in private, about the answer. Some considerations can, however, be advanced. "Generals", we have often been told, "cannot be allowed to run a war". A more factual and less cynical way of putting the case is that the immense complexity of modern war and the inter-relationship of the three Services demands a far higher degree of ministerial direction than was needed in the past. Someone has got to quell the inter-Service disputes which inevitably arise; someone has got to correlate British fighting policy, as well as he can, with that of our allies. Only a minister has the authority to remove from the High Commands of all three Services those who have failed. Only the Prime Minister can be the impartial arbiter in such circumstances; for a Service Minister, in charge of a department, may be unduly influenced by his Service advisers for or against a particular man in High Command. Professional jealousy or favouritism is not unknown among them. By Common consent, Mr. Churchill performed this task admirably. He was far better equipped for it than was Mr. Lloyd George in the First World War. Mr. Churchill had not only been a soldier and a war correspondent, but he was a distinguished student of, and writer upon, the art of war. Mr.Lloyd George rendered great service to his country from 1916 to 1918 by dismissing incompetents in ministerial office, inspiring his colleagues and his fellow-countrymen and "bull-dozing" through appalling difficulties which would have stopped a lesser man. But he was no militarist and knew nothing of military history or affairs. There was, with some exceptions, mistrust between him and the highest-ranking officers of all three Services. He meant little to the fighting man in any of the Services. Mr. Churchill meant a great deal. Everyone from the top to the bottom in the Services was devoted to him. His frequent visits to the various fronts were of great value, but I think it would have been better, had it been possible, for him to have visited them in civilian clothes. Probably security reasons, because he would have been conspicuous, forbade this. Nevertheless, his appearance, on occasions, in uniform with ribbons, to both of which he was most honourably entitled, gave the impression that he was a Generalissimo and not a Prime Minister; further, it suggested that he was more directly responsible for strategy and tactics than either was the fact or ought to have been. This donning of uniform was not popular with the House of Commons when they heard of it. That body has a long memory and has neither forgiven nor forgotten Cromwell, or his threats to substitute military rule for its own.

In the circumstances of the time, those of us who voted for the motion of July 2, 1942, were fully justified in doing so. We were expressing not only our own doubts, as it was our public duty to do, about the situation and the Prime Minister's method of handling it, but also those of a large proportion of the Press and the public. The late Mr. Harry Hopkins,[1] in a cable to Mr. Churchill, described our action as follows: "Those who run for cover with every reverse, the timid and faint of heart, will have no part in winning the war". I think that "timid and faint of heart" is an inappropriate term to apply to the late Sir Roger Keyes and, I hope, to the rest of us. We were, in fact, saying what Mr. Hopkins's own fellow-countrymen have very properly, again and again in their history, said to their leaders: "You must be held responsible, under our constitution, for the nation's defeats in war; either you must do better or you must go". Little as his extreme admirers may like the fact recorded, Mr. Churchill was helped by having to answer a vote of censure on his Government in Parliament. The House in the debate in question gave him an overwhelming majority,[2] but showed plainly by the respect accorded to the speeches made by the critics that it reserved the right to overturn the most powerful administration if it failed to bring good results.

By a magnificent effort in the next three years, to which Mr. Churchill so notably contributed, those results were attained.

On the first day of the resumption after the adjournment for the summer recess Mr. Churchill made a statement on the war

[1] *The Second World War*, Vol. IV, p. 366.   [2] By 475 votes to 25.

situation. It was somewhat below his usual standard, and the House showed so little interest in it and in that of Mr. Greenwood, who followed him, speaking on behalf of the Labour Party, that a number of members walked out. Later in the day Sir Stafford Cripps made a reference to this which caused considerable offence, since the House does not like anyone adopting a professorial attitude towards it. His actual words were: "I think it is a most unfortunate thing that such disrespect should be paid to the Leader of the Opposition or that members should go out in the middle of the Prime Minister's speech, as a number of members did. I do not think that we can conduct our proceedings with the dignity and the weight with which we should conduct them unless members are prepared to pay greater attention to their duties in this House, which are just as great as those of men in the trenches at the front". From this time onwards, Sir Stafford Cripps, as the phrase is, "got across" the House in his capacity as Leader. It is odd that this should have been so, because in later years, when he held high office as Chancellor of the Exchequer, no one, however much they might disagree with his political views (as I did), could fail to admire his great ability as a parliamentarian and the tact with which he treated the House as a whole; perhaps, however, this was a result of a lesson he learned when he failed to satisfy the House as its Leader.

The new session opened on November 11. The late Mr. Walkden,[1] Labour member for Bristol South, moved the Address, and Major Thorneycroft seconded it; both made very good speeches. So did the Prime Minister, who followed; he entirely recovered the slight decline in his position and reputation that he had lost by his speech in September. Mr. Aneurin Bevan spoke brilliantly on the second day of the debate and, for him, in a restrained fashion; indeed, he paid a tribute to Mr. Churchill at the commencement of his speech. He made the point that several important contentions which the critics had put forward against the Government in the past had now been accepted by them; for example, that all armies should be subordinated to one commander. He also said of the critics: "We said that we lost the earlier battle of Egypt partly because we had the wrong weapons, and that is the first charge admitted by the Government;

[1] Created Baron Walkden in 1945.

the second charge was that our men had the wrong military leadership and that the military organisation in Egypt was bad. The Prime Minister said yesterday that we were right". The battle of El Alamein had been won before the debate took place, and the Government were naturally in a far stronger position than they were in the summer. Consequently, there was a disposition, both in the House and in the Press, for attacks to be made on those of us who had criticised the Government previously and to say that we were proved wrong; Mr. Bevan, in my opinion, made a good point in showing how in three important respects we were, on the contrary, proved to be right.

The post of chairman of the 1922 or, as it is now called, the Conservative Committee, is an onerous and responsible one which has been admirably filled in recent years by men of authority in the Party. Tact and good judgment are always required in this position, for the chairman, among other things, has to act, when disputes and differences arise within the parliamentary Party, as an intermediary between it and the Government; the position naturally becomes harder when there is a rift of opinion in the Party. At the time of which I am writing, the late Mr. Erskine Hill, M.P., was the chairman of the Committee. Though he was an ineffective speaker in the House, whose ear he never commanded, he was a man of great charm and ability, deeply respected by the Conservative Party. He did fine work in these years of stress and strain by his part in ensuring that differences of opinion among Conservatives in regard to the conduct of the war should not degenerate into personal feuds or cause bitterness. I have said before in the course of this book that a sad feature of parliamentary life (as, indeed, of most forms of activity) is the speed with which men and women who were once well-known members of the House of Commons become forgotten after they have died or retired. Probably a large proportion of the present membership of the House of Commons has never even heard of Mr. Erskine Hill; but those of us who were Conservative M.P.s at the time when he was in the House revere his memory, because we knew that we could always get wise and tolerant advice from him when we wanted it.

In January, 1943, I suffered a serious loss through the destruction by fire, while in military occupation, of my home, Shilling-

lee Park, a Georgian mansion of distinction. I should not mention
this incident, which has no connection with the purpose of this
book, were it not for the fact that Mr. Churchill, who was
abroad at the time, sent me a cable as soon as he heard of the news.
I was greatly touched when I received it. For a man, with his
immense responsibilities, to find time to send such a cable,
especially to one who, though an old friend in private life, had
criticised him strongly in recent months, showed in a marked
degree his affectionate nature and the generosity of his character.

Early in February the Prime Minister made a statement about
his recent meeting at Casablanca with President Roosevelt and
concerning his visit to Turkey. I noted at the time in my diary
that it was "one of the finest orations he has ever delivered, crystal
clear, not over-optimistic but not pessimistic either".

The Parliamentary year of 1943 was notable for the formation
and action of the Tory Reform Committee. This Committee,
like its predecessor, the Social Reform Committee of the Party in
the years before the First World War, had as its object the
advocacy of measures of social progress, and was composed
mainly, though not entirely, of young men. I was a member of
both Committees, so can assert with inner knowledge that neither
had any ulterior motives, such as hostility to the leadership, but
each was imbued with the spirit and tradition of Disraeli and
Lord Randolph Churchill. Both Committees were disliked by
some elements on the extreme right of the Conservative Party
and regarded as bodies of self-satisfied and over-ambitious young
men. Conservative M.P.s such as the late Sir Frederick (afterwards
Lord) Banbury regarded the Social Reform Committee with the
same abhorrence that Sir Waldron Smithers did the Tory Reform
Committee. They were entitled to their views, and so were we;
the Conservative Party, as a whole, fortunately for its continued
existence, favoured our views rather than theirs. The leading exponents of the viewpoint of the "Tory Reformers", as we were
called, were Lord Hinchingbrooke, Mr. Hugh Molson, Major
Peter Thorneycroft and Mr. Quintin Hogg.[1] Individually and
collectively, they made a great impression upon the House and
were listened to with respect. In the 1945 Parliament Major
Thorneycroft and Mr. Hogg, until he became Lord Hailsham and

---

[1] Now Lord Hailsham.

left the Commons, were two of the most formidable debaters on the Conservative side. Both had what might be termed an "F. E. Smith touch", because they infuriated many of the supporters of the Government by their irony and invective, whilst delighting the House as a whole and earning in private conversation praise from those whom they had attacked. When the famous report of the Committee presided over by Sir William (now Lord) Beveridge, M.P., on the future of the social services came under discussion, the Tory Reformers took a prominent part in it. It was held on February 16, 1943, and is described as follows in my diary:

FEBRUARY 16TH, 1943

First day of the debate on the Beveridge Report; Arthur Greenwood moved a colourless resolution of rather tepid support in the name of all parties; an amendment by the Liberals (which I supported) calling for immediate action upon the Report and another by Hinchingbrooke supported by forty Tory Reformers asking for the creation of a Ministry of Social Security was not called; John Anderson,[1] amid considerable interruption, made a speech for the Government which gave an unfortunate impression that the Cabinet "damned the Report with faint praise".

FEBRUARY 17TH, 1943

The debate went worse than ever for the Government; Kingsley[2] even vaguer and more inclined to administer a cold douche than John Anderson; the Socialists threatened to vote against the Government.

FEBRUARY 18TH, 1943

The Socialists moved, with his approval, an amendment to Greenwood's motion, thus creating, as 116 voted for it, a problem for Socialist Ministers in the Government. Several of us who were prepared to support the Hinchingbrooke and Liberal motions would have abstained but for a reassuring speech by Herbert Morrison who saved the situation for the Government. That body intends to do its best to bring about what is, as Barrington-Ward[3] of The Times says, "mainly an organisational scheme", into operation; it is the approach to it which has been so damping; there was

[1] Now Lord Waverley. [2] The late Sir Kingsley Wood.
[3] The late Mr. R. M'G. Barrington-Ward, then Editor of The Times.

O.D.—20

no appreciation shown in the debate of the fact that this plan, and especially the suggestion of the creation of a Ministry of Social Security, has, rightly or wrongly, caught the imagination of the public; the Government have now accepted the main principles of the Beveridge Plan, but they should have signified this acceptance by showing enthusiasm and not by over-caution and expatiations on the cost of it all.

There are several points of interest in this debate for students of parliamentary proceedings who are concerned with their real texture and not their outward appearance. There were obviously doubts in the Cabinet concerning both the advisability and the feasibility of a big advance towards the complete Welfare State when the nation was still far from final victory in the most expensive war in its history. Could we, it may be supposed the doubtful argued, spend on social reform at least within the next decade so huge a sum from the taxpayer without grievous harm to our economic position? That question, as I endeavour to show in a later chapter of this book, has not yet been decisively answered affirmatively or negatively. But, when the Government horse is in the ring and is expected to jump a number of difficult fences under the eyes of a critical public, it should, unless it has determined to refuse them, do so without appearing to require the application of whip and spur. The Ministerial spokesmen should have realised in advance, from the appearance of the Order Paper, that if they refused the fences there would be trouble; Conservative support from influential quarters for the Beveridge Plan ensured that the rank-and-file of the Labour Party could not afford to appear to lack fervour for it. Mr. Greenwood, speaking for the friendly official Labour Opposition, misjudged the temper of the House as badly as did the Government spokesmen at the outset. He finally had to submit to pressure from behind. I am aware that the argument which I have advanced lies open to the retort that successful parliamentary advocacy requires finesse and flattery rather than frankness and honesty. I would rather put it that a skilful parliamentarian, especially if he is a Minister, puts his case in a way which is palatable to the corporate sense of the House; provided the Minister is sincere in his presentation, there is nothing dishonest in such a method. But, even if he is obliged not to present a palatable case, but to ask the House to swallow a big nasty-tasting pill, there are ways and means of doing it which will please the patient.

Early in 1943, Mr. Churchill, to the dismay of the nation and the democratic world, had a serious illness. Suggestions were then plentifully made in private, with oblique and often favourable reference to them in the Press, that Sir John Anderson (now Lord Waverley) would, though he was an Independent, be the best successor of Mr. Churchill as Prime Minister. Of all the brilliant team of outside Ministers brought into Office during the last war, none exceeded Sir John Anderson in capacity and achievement. His record as a great Civil Servant, as an Indian Presidency Governor, and in high office during the war was magnificent. Joined to his qualities in public affairs, he has as a man charm, courtesy, humour and the greatest integrity. No man has a more balanced and wise opinion in council, as I know from having been his colleague for five years in Mr. Churchill's Shadow Cabinet in the 1945 Parliament. The House of Commons both liked and respected him; yet he and it never got on well together in the sense that he could easily sway or persuade it. The suggestion, which so far as I am aware, received no support from Sir John, was therefore quite impracticable.

Among war-time Ministers in the Lords, Lord Woolton was most at home with an all-party gathering of M.P.s, though, of course, he never addressed the House itself and might not have been so successful there. "Uncle Fred", as he was affectionately nicknamed, had a "way with him" which was irresistible. Urbane, humorous, calm and master of his subject, he could induce his audience to accept, without question or objection, the most unpleasant facts about the food situation and his measures to combat the dangers of starvation. He always pleaded rather than exhorted. No leader ever made a better appointment than did Mr. Churchill when he induced Lord Woolton after the war to be the Conservative Party organiser. His successor as Minister of Food, Colonel Llewellin, continued the Woolton tradition; there was little serious parliamentary trouble over food. It is right to add that Lord Woolton was greatly helped in his task by his Under-Secretary in the Commons, Mr. Mabane, who, until he lost his seat in the 1945 election, was a National Liberal member. Mr. Mabane was a popular and efficient Under-Secretary who never, despite the difficulties of his office, made a serious mistake in speeches or at question time.

In March, 1943, Mr. Speaker FitzRoy died; the House was deeply grieved at the loss of a great Speaker while still in his intellectual prime. An interesting situation arose over his successor; the Government made known, unofficially, that they favoured the appointment of Mr. Gwilym Lloyd George to the post. The Conservative Party strongly supported the claim of Colonel Clifton Brown for the Speakership. He had been a successful Deputy-Speaker. Eventually Colonel Clifton-Brown was appointed. Mr. Gwilym Lloyd George is a tall man with a fine presence. He has a pleasant, modulated voice with a good command of English and an hereditary aptitude for the appropriate phrase salted with humour to suit the occasion, though, unlike his father, he has never been provocative in debate: as a Minister he has always presented his case with tact and discretion and earned thereby the respect of the House. His friendly rival for the Speakership, Colonel Clifton-Brown (now Lord Ruffside) was also a popular member of the House. Lord Ruffside is a small man who lacks the commanding presence of Mr. Lloyd George. He had at the time of his appointment, and still has, a very youthful face. He usually has a smile on it, which gives the impression of a happy boy at school. These features of his outward appearance were a disadvantage to him when, in the Chair, he had to rebuke a member or the House as a whole for its conduct. On such occasions the Speaker should be grim and formidable. He must not give the impression, when he is bringing the weight of his authority to bear upon a culprit, that it is a small matter to be disposed of by a laugh. Equally, on other occasions when a soft answer may turn away the wrath which is accumulating in the House, he must be able on the spur of the moment to use an apposite phrase to that end. Lord Ruffside had not the command of the English language possessed by his immediate predecessor or successor. It was sometimes difficult to follow the meaning of his observations and rulings. As an individual he was a popular Speaker, and he is a very kind-hearted and fair-minded man; he bore no ill-will in public or private to those of us on both sides of the House, from Mr. Churchill downwards, who came into conflict with him over his rulings. The lesson to be learnt from his Speakership is that occupancy of the Lower Chair, despite tradition on the subject, should never be regarded as giving its holder any prescriptive right to the Speakership; the qualities required in the two offices are not entirely identical. A successful holder of the most onerous and responsible post of Speaker must not only know the rules of the House and how to guide and control it, but he must look the part and àct it.

Spasmodic bombing of London and other great towns continued in the early months of 1943, to be followed later by the far more formidable "buzz-bombs" or self-controlled planes. Parliament, like the public, became inured to these dangers and the House seldom adjourned because of an alert. In the spring of 1943 I was present at the fortnightly meeting of a dining club to which I belong. Its membership, which is a small one, includes, and has included in the past, Archbishops, Bishops, Prime Ministers, leading members of all political parties, Viceroys and ex-Viceroys, Royal Academicians, distinguished men of letters as well as lesser individuals like myself. After dinner, one of the *maîtres d'hôtel* of the hotel at which we were dining entered our private room and said impressively, like a toastmaster announcing a toast: "My Lords and gentlemen, an air-raid is in progress; a bomb has already fallen in the vicinity; the guests in the public restaurant have taken refuge in our shelter; there is a special shelter at your disposal below this room". All of us present were over sixty years old; there was an instinctive feeling, though no one gave voice to it, that we had accomplished our achievements in life, great or small, that not much time was left to us on earth, and that it would be difficult to find a better way of leaving it than to be killed by enemy action after an excellent dinner in the midst of pleasant conversation, amid cigars and old brandy. So none of us took any notice of the *maître d'hôtel's* well-intentioned efforts to preserve us, and we continued our conversation as if nothing had happened. The *maître d'hôtel*, who was a citizen of a friendly foreign nation, left the room with a look on his face plainly implying that the English were madder than even he thought them to be after twenty-five years among them.

CHAPTER XXI

In February, 1943, there was an important debate in the House on war pensions. Sir Ian Fraser, the blind M.P., who has done such splendid work on behalf of the British Legion and for ex-Servicemen in general in the Commons, made a brilliant speech which concentrated on two points: he said that the pension for the totally disabled was insufficient; and he asserted that there was need for a Select Committee to enquire into the Royal Warrant which lays down conditions for war pensions. There were a number of other criticisms of the Ministry; for example, it was stressed that hardship was caused by the official phrase "attributable to war service" and by the delay in setting up appeal tribunals. Lady Apsley,[1] whose husband had been killed in the war and who now sat for his constituency, made an excellent maiden speech. I noted in my diary at the time that Sir Walter Womersley, the Minister of Pensions, made an "insufficient and aggressive reply". Sir Walter Womersley was a very good administrator of his office; he was a man who had made his own way in the world, having risen from humble beginnings to a good position in his native town of Grimsby, and he was respected in and out of the House. The Ministry of Pensions has always been, for obvious reasons, a target of attack in the House of Commons. The late Major Tryon (afterwards Lord Tryon), who was Minister of Pensions for longer than any other man since the Department was created, was the most successful of his predecessors or successors in dealing with criticism; he adopted an emollient attitude towards the House. Sir Walter, on the contrary, was in favour of a more astringent approach. He always gave the impression that he thought—often with justice—that some members were concerned to make extravagant demands upon

[1] Lady Apsley, despite the fact that she was crippled by a hunting accident and had to be wheeled into the House of Commons in a chair, was a successful as well as popular member of the House during her short period of membership.

the Ministry because it was a very easy way of winning popularity with ex-Servicemen; but he did not ease the difficult position which a Minister of Pensions always has to fill in the House, and he had some difficulty in getting a new Pensions Bill through the Commons this year. It should, however, be added that Sir Walter was personally very popular in the House; and there should be more men in ministerial office and on the back benches of the Conservative Party whose earlier lives have been spent as his had been. In an era in which there are so many leading Labour Ministers "wearing the old school tie", the Conservative Party has a particularly favourable opportunity of showing that it appreciates the class which makes up the bulk of its supporters by giving office to men like Sir Walter. Led by Sir Ian, a number of us continued to press for the reforms which he had advocated in the debate in question; we did so at intervals all through the 1945 and 1950 Parliaments; it must be a source of satisfaction to Sir Ian, as it is to us who followed his lead, that to-day some of these claims have been met.

On March 23, 1943, there was a debate on a statement made by Mr. Randolph Churchill about the French in North Africa which was alleged to be incompatible with his position as an officer in the army. Mr. Churchill successfully defended his son from the attacks made upon him by Mr. Aneurin Bevan; and the late Miss Rathbone complained that Mr. Bevan showed feline animosity against Mr. Churchill. In fact, Mr. Bevan's action was in accord with the practice which has generally been followed by men who are increasing their reputation in the House by a series of brilliant and provocative speeches, namely, to make the Prime Minister the principal object of the attack. It was a method followed very forcibly by Mr. Churchill at the end of the 1900 Parliament. The late Miss Rathbone was a much-respected member of the House who had done admirable social service in many spheres. She was a woman of strong convictions who supported lost causes as well as those which succeeded. She and I came into occasional conflict at this period over the proceedings of the Inter-Governmental Committee for Refugees which she believed was not doing enough for refugees, especially Jewish ones. The House admired her pertinacity, but she was not a very effective speaker.

In June, 1943, the Speaker, Lady Megan Lloyd George, Mr. Lawson, the late Mr. Maxton and I took part in a transatlantic telephone talk (recorded and subsequently broadcast to the United States) with the Speaker of the House of Representatives, Mr. Raeburn, and two gentlemen representing the Democratic and Republican leaders in the House of Representatives. The question mistress on this side was Mrs. Vyvyan Adams and her opposite number in America Mr. Alistair Cooke; neither party knew in advance what the questions were going to be. I felt at the time how tremendously things had changed since I first entered the House of Commons in 1904. We were told afterwards that the broadcast was a success. It certainly stressed the closeness of the Anglo-American alliance at the time and the relationship between two great democratic Assemblies.

In July there was another statement by Mr. Churchill on the war situation in which he reported most satisfactory progress in Italy; and on July 27 a courageous speech, which attracted attention at the time, was made in the Commons by Mr. Shinwell on the subject of overseas trade, in which he appeared as a wholehearted advocate of Imperial economic unity and the treatment of the Empire as an entity. I felt that my old Chief, Mr. Joseph Chamberlain, would have been glad to return to the House for such an occasion, because here was striking support from unexpected quarters for the principles which he had always advocated.

On September 20, his many friends in all parts of the House were distressed to learn of the sudden death of Sir Kingsley Wood from a heart attack; he had been a highly successful war-time Chancellor of the Exchequer, as was his successor, Sir John Anderson.

On September 21, Mr. Churchill made another speech on the war situation which earned the commendation of the House; he defended our negotiations with the Italian authorities resulting from the successful invasion of that country, and our relationship with Soviet Russia. He warned the House that heavy and bloody fighting lay ahead of us, and he promised that there would be a Second Front in Western Europe "sooner or later". The Government at the time was having some difficulty in dealing with the demands in more than one quarter at home and abroad, arising partly from malice and partly from ignorance, for the opening of a Second Front.

The new session opened in November, and the Address in the Commons was moved by Commander Rupert Brabner, a young man who spent, unfortunately, only too short a time in the House (he was killed in an aircraft accident while flying on duty as Under-Secretary of State for Air) and had the distinction of winning both the D.S.O. and the D.S.C. in the Fleet Air Arm; it was seconded by a popular member of the House, Mr. George Griffiths, an ex-miner. Mr. Herbert Morrison, the Home Secretary, had during the recess very properly and fairly, on grounds of humanity, released Sir Oswald Mosley from internment owing to the serious state of his health. A number of Communists and others gathered outside the Palace of Westminster on the day of the opening of Parliament and endeavoured to cause a demonstration against this release; Mr. Morrison was also fiercely attacked in the House by some, at any rate, who ought to have known better. He defended the release vigorously and effectively. On December 14, Mr. Eden gave an interesting account of the recent Teheran conference, but it did not wholly satisfy the House. Mr. Aneurin Bevan and Mr. Hore-Belisha, with some prophetic insight, suggested that its ultimate result would not be as satisfactory as the Government claimed.

The House adjourned for the Christmas recess in a happier mood than it had been since the war started. Mr. Churchill's status and position in the eyes of members was completely restored, and there was also confidence in the other Service Ministers, Mr. A. V. Alexander (later Lord Alexander), the first Lord of the Admiralty, Sir James Grigg, Secretary of State for War, and Sir Archibald Sinclair (now Lord Thurso), Secretary of State for Air. All three men were very successful in safeguarding the interests of their great Departments in Parliament, though Sir James was at times unduly provocative and suffered fools more ungladly than any Minister I have ever seen on the Front Bench; however, as his great qualities, both of intellect and in administration, were well known, the House, though not his victims, forgave him.

Towards the end of 1943 Mr. Bevin met with some opposition when he announced that extensions of the age of the "call-up", especially for women, might be necessary; but he easily overcame it, for he was by then firmly planted on both feet in the Commons which had come to like him enormously. Mr. Gwilym Lloyd George had earlier suffered similar opposition to the rigidities of coal rationing, but overcame it. It is fair to say that good Ministerial direction and representation in both Houses during the war was a prime factor in persuading Parliament to accept the drastic treatment which all Departments had to apply to the nation. A foolish or unpopular Minister or his Under-Secretary could have so upset either House as to make it difficult to obtain parliamentary sanction for necessary severities at this time of peril. Very emphatically, too, the same considerations apply to Mr. Hudson's tenure of the Ministry of Agriculture.

Late in 1943 there was a debate in which Mr. Churchill, in a delightful speech full of Churchillian humour, induced the House without a division to agree to the appointment of a Select Committee to consider the rebuilding of the Chamber of the House of Commons on broadly the same lines as the one destroyed by enemy action.[1] To my intense pleasure, because of my deep interest in the matter, I was elected without dissent chairman of the Committee, though there were men on it such as Mr. Hore-Belisha, the late Sir Percy Harris, chairman of the Liberal Party, and Mr. (now Lord) Pethick-Lawrence, whose qualifications for chairmanship were equal to mine. We were a harmonious body who worked hard and swiftly, with the invaluable assistance of our Clerk, Mr. Strathearn Gordon, to produce a report[2] to which there was only one amendment on a matter of no great moment and this was rejected. In 1944 the House accepted our report without a division, and Sir Giles Scott, the distinguished architect, then carried out his momentous and historic task of rebuilding the Chamber, to the general satisfaction. The House and its Select Committee showed more wisdom, tolerance and sense of public duty than did its predecessors, the then House of Commons and the Committee appointed

[1] The actual terms of reference were: "to consider and report upon plans for the rebuilding of the House of Commons and upon such alterations as may be considered desirable while preserving all its essential features".
[2] There are no majority or minority Reports of a Select Committee as there are, in the case of dissent, of a Royal Commission.

after the fire of 1834 which destroyed the Chamber.[1] The new Chamber was opened with appropriate ceremonial, including the attendance of all the Speakers of Parliaments and Chairmen of Legislative Councils then in the Commonwealth.

The big measure of the 1944 session was Mr. Butler's Education Bill which extended and improved the educational opportunities open to all children irrespective of the class or financial position of the parents. In many respects it followed logically on an Education Act, also passed at the end of a war, and piloted through the Commons by the late Mr. H. A. L. Fisher. Some doubts, which have not yet been resolved by the Act in operation, were expressed by those of us in the House who were Governors of Grammar Schools. In general, the Bill was enthusiastically received; Mr. Butler and his Under-Secretary, Mr. Chuter Ede, conducted it through the House with great tact, skill and dexterity. Mr. Butler, by his handling of the measure, stepped into the front rank of successful Ministers; his political and parliamentary progress has been continuous ever since. Whether the Act will remove from future generations the appalling illiteracy and lack of intellectual interest which, according to the National Service statistics, characterise male adolescents to-day, remains to be seen. Its aim and object of making Britain the best-educated democracy in the world is a noble and necessary one. During the passage of the Bill the Government were defeated by an amendment moved by Mrs. Cazalet Keir for equal pay for men and women teachers. She had been one of the principal exponents of the "equal pay" principle for some time and, like the late Mrs. Tate, was one of the most energetic women members at the time. Mr. Churchill rightly treated the matter as one of confidence and

[1] As is well known, Barry's rebuilding of the Houses of Parliament was delayed by interminable wrangling and interference (see Maurice Hastings, *Parliament House* (1950), pp. 151–69). These arose largely from the failure to determine the original requirements; neither House was then adequately consulted, and no Select Committee was appointed at the outset to supervise detail. This initial mistake resulted, during the progress of the work, in a petition to the Commons from the architect's unsuccessful competitors, the subsequent establishment of a number of Select Committees in both Houses to settle *ad hoc* difficulties, and finally in a judicial arbitration and a Royal Commission. The building took over twenty years to reach anything approaching completion.

demanded a reversal of the vote, to which the House agreed on the report stage of the Bill.

The Government had also considerable trouble over the Town and Country Planning Bill which was another principal measure of the 1944 session. Indeed, but for the tact and wisdom of Mr. W. S. Morrison (the present Speaker), who was in charge of the Bill, and the Law Officers, it would not have got through at all. There was a serious difference of opinion among the supporters of the Government on the compensation to be paid to landowners under the Bill; this followed party lines almost completely. A number of Conservatives wanted a larger amount of compensation paid to landowners than the Bill allowed, and a number of Labour members wanted less to be given. Both sides were very stubborn, and the position became so threatening to the Government that Mr. Churchill intervened in a mild and mollifying speech to advocate the withdrawal of the clause which dealt with the matter so as to allow of discussion between the rival schools of opinion with a view to agreement on a fresh clause. This advice was accepted and a compromise reached.

The House was in a critical mood in 1944 in regard alike to Government measures and Ministers. The unbroken series of victories in the war might have been supposed to buttress the Government's position and make possible a continuance of it after the war had ended. It was known at the time that this was Mr. Churchill's wish, but there were no signs of any such desire in any Party; yet the Government was a good one hampered by less internal dissension than was Mr. Lloyd George's Coalition Government during the First World War. Mr. Shinwell, Mr. Hore-Belisha and I, who had taken part with other senior members in criticising the conduct of the war in the past, had no longer occasion to do so. In fact, in a debate on Empire economic unity and integration which we promoted we were praised by Mr. Churchill for our "most statesmanlike speeches"; in other debates, sometimes difficult ones for the Government, we supported them. Even Mr. Aneurin Bevan did so on occasion. Any opposition to the Government was spasmodic, and proceeded from rugged individualists, like Lady Astor, Mr. R. Stokes (who carried on at the time a one-man vendetta against Mr. Churchill), Mr. Austin Hopkinson and Sir Herbert Williams; but as they were not politically and, in some cases, personally, on speaking terms with one another, the damage they did was small. Many Ministers, too, increased the high status and authority in the House they already enjoyed. Mr. Eden was described, with justice, by Mr. George Buchanan, as the best Leader of the House for a generation. Mr. Hudson had the greatest triumph of his career in the Commons in January when, faced by a revolt alike of farmers and members for agricultural constituencies in favour of a further increase in farm prices, he persuaded the House, by a speech of sweet reasonableness, that the proposals advanced were untenable and unpatriotic in time of war. Mr. Ernest Bevin scored a similar triumph when he prevented a coal strike by drastic methods which commended themselves to the country, though not to Mr. Aneurin Bevan; Mr. Thomas Johnston was a most successful Secretary of State for Scotland; Mr. Brendan Bracken floored each of his parliamentary critics in turn with an uppercut, usually to the delight of the House, whenever the actions of the Ministry of Information were questioned. Many junior Ministers, such as Mr. Thomas at the Admiralty, were conspicuously successful.

Why, then, was there this general reluctance to continue the Coalition when the war was over, as everyone realised in 1944 it was likely soon to be? Mr. Churchill, in his speech on the Address at the opening of the new session at the end of November, stated that there was no agreement with the Liberals and Socialists to continue their association with the Conservatives at the election that would follow the war. The Conservative Party in the House showed by their demeanour that this announcement caused them satisfaction rather than dismay. The Liberal and Labour Parties cheered.

It is as difficult to read the inner thoughts of a corporate body as to read those of an individual. I am no thought-reader, but I think that the reasons for this feeling were many and various. The Labour and official Liberal Parties believed that they would "cash in" at a General Election on the unpopularity of the Conservative Party before the war. The Labour Party proved right in this regard; they were in fact on a bowler's wicket, for, as soon as the political truce was over, they could quote Mr. Churchill himself against the alleged incompetence of his predecessors and their responsibility for the war. The Liberals were proved inaccurate in their assumptions. Rightly or wrongly, nobody loves a Liberal in these days, and their leader himself lost what had always been regarded as a perfectly safe Liberal seat. Many keen Conservatives thought that certain causes in which they passionately believed would suffer if a Government containing many men of "leftist" views was in office after the war. This feeling partly centred round the question of Commonwealth relationship and development. They should have been reassured by Mr. Shinwell's motion on the subject to which I have referred earlier. The Government could have gone to the country after the war on the great conception of Imperial economic unity and on the Beveridge Plan in domestic affairs. Yet, even so, difficulties would have arisen. The belief that there is something inherently wrong in British control or direction of millions of people of other races and colours in different parts of the world was still alive in many Liberal and Labour minds in 1944 and is not dead to-day; but it is, I hope, dying slowly, because the Conservative Party have met them half-way by accepting self-government by gradual stages as a principle in all Colonies. Thus the Imperialists and anti-Imperialists do not openly attack each other in Parliament as they did in the 1900 Parliament. In domestic policy the difficulty of reconciling the views of the respective advocates of public and private enterprise sitting in the same Cabinet in peace time would have been enormous. A pre-view of how formidable those difficulties would have been was afforded by the inability of Mr. Willink, the Minister of Health, to satisfy the Commons over housing policy in 1944. Mr. Willink, though a new member of the House with no previous administrative experience, was a popular Minister of great ability. His proposals, which clearly suffered from a divergence of views in the Cabinet, were received with almost universal condemnation and derision.

But there were other and more intangible reasons why the continuance of the National Government after the war was unpopular despite the support which it received, in private council, from many of us. There was distrust of the immense power wielded by the Government; and suspicion was aroused by certain indications that, disregarding tradition, it was too fond of multiplying the "offices of profit under the Crown" which M.P.s could hold without vacating their seats and without being Min-

isters in the Government. A Bill to allow Sir Louis Spears, M.P.,
to be High Commissioner in the Middle East, Sir Samuel Hoare
to be Ambassador in Madrid, and Mr. MacDonald British High
Commissioner in Canada was angrily attacked. The old idea that
Mr. Churchill was anxious to start a "King's Party" was resusci-
tated. Sir Samuel Hoare was called "The Rt. Hon. member for
Madrid".

There was another source of opposition to the idea of the
continuance of the Government when hostilities ceased. 1944 was
the year of the V1s and V2s. There was evidence[1] to show that
Mr. Churchill had accepted advice at high level, given by a
civilian against that of Service Chiefs, that had delayed counter-
action to meet this form of warfare. The House was disturbed
over the matter, all the more so as Government spokesmen were
most uncommunicative on the subject and tried to burke discussion even when it was suggested it should take place in secret
session. People in private said, "We need a change of Government directly the war is over; the Old Man is tired, obstinate and
too fond of directing things himself". Considering his share in the
vast military successes of the war, this was a foolish and ungenerous view in 1944. But no Prime Minister in such power for so
long ever escapes this kind of attack.

Members of Parliament, like the rest of the population, were
suffering from a prolonged period of stress and strain which made
them irritable and unreasonable to the "Powers that be" despite
the near approach of victory. Happily, however, the House retained its rather schoolboyish sense of fun and could laugh as
heartily as ever at a piece of unconscious humour on the part of
one of its members, even when the doodle-bugs were falling
around the Palace of Westminster. One summer's day in 1944, a
well-known member for a Scottish constituency complained to
the Secretary of State for Scotland about the dirty state of Scottish fish markets and of one in particular. Every time he went
there, he said, there was a smell. This innocent and no doubt
factual statement was greeted with loud laughter. "There is, in

[1] It is only fair to state that Mr. Churchill in *The Second World War* denies
by inference that this is so, though he admits there was a difference of opinion
between Lord Cherwell and Mr. Morrison in regard to the precautions to be
taken.

fact", he said, looking round with bewilderment for the cause of the merriment, "an awful stench". Members laughed even more loudly and longer than they had on the first occasion. The spectators in the public gallery looked as surprised and disapproving as they always do when the House has a "fit of the giggles".

In the year 1944 I had a hard time presiding over two such important Committees as the Inter-Governmental Committee for Refugees and that for considering the rebuilding of the Chamber, since each involved much discussion with Ministers, official advisers and others outside of the actual meetings of the two Committees. Nor did that exhaust my parliamentary activities, for I found out late in the year, somewhat to my dismay, that my speeches in the House occupied more columns in Hansard than those of any member who was not a Minister. But in November, 1944, I was paid a great honour that amply compensated me for all the work I had done that year, when I was entertained to dinner by the Empire Economic Union to celebrate alike my forty years in the House and the fact that forty years previously I was the first M.P. elected to support the Imperial policy of Mr. Joseph Chamberlain. Mr. Leo Amery was in the chair; two ex-Dominion Prime Ministers—the late Viscount Bennett of Calgary and Lord Bruce of Melbourne—Lord Beaverbrook, Sir David Maxwell-Fyfe and a number of M.P.s were present, as well as Mr. Chamberlain's widow, Mrs. Carnegie, and my wife. I was given a very fine piece of silver as a memento of this occasion.

I was paid an even greater honour in 1951 after I retired and ceased to be Father of the House. I was given a dinner at the House by Ministers, ex-Ministers and others at which my health was proposed by Mr. Eden and speeches in support of the toast were made by Mr. Attlee and Mr. Clement Davies. No mention was made of the dinner in the Press at the time, and, except for this fact, modesty would prevent me from referring to the occasion of so high a tribute to myself. It exemplifies the great generosity, the absence of Party or personal rancour outside the Chamber, and the sense of comradeship among M.P.s. Though most of my hosts were personal friends, I had criticised and attacked almost every one of them in debate. Often there had been resentment alike by the House and by those upon whom I had made an onslaught. I had received some hard knocks in return. Yet here were my hosts, most of them far more eminent than myself, whom I had orally assaulted so often, entertaining me to dinner as a mark of esteem at the end of my time in the Commons! In few legislative assemblies and in few countries in the world could such a thing have happened.

CHAPTER XXII

O N January 1, 1945, I became Father of the House of Commons owing to the conferment of a Peerage on Mr. Lloyd George, who had occupied that position for some time.

There were two important debates on foreign affairs in the early months of 1945. On January 1, as a result of the critical attitude of a minority of the Labour Party in the House of Commons, including such well-known members as Mr. Seymour Cocks, Captain Dugdale, Mr. George Strauss and Mr. Aneurin Bevan, towards the Government's policy in Greece, the Government wisely decided to have a debate on the subject[1]. Mr. Churchill opened the debate, and in one of the best polemical speeches he delivered during the war, devastated the Opposition. Before the second day of the debate, the Whips privately suggested to me that I might care to open it by making an aggressive speech against the opponents of the Government, but I was unable to do so owing to an engagement elsewhere. However, there was no need for my help, as Mr. Eden in his winding-up speech was, very properly, more aggressive than he had ever been before in a foreign affairs debate, and challenged the opponents to divide, with the result that only seven could be found to enter the division lobby against the Government. In this debate, Mr. Eden exhibited one of his most valuable qualities; though normally a very calm and suave speaker, he can hit as hard as anyone when the circumstances justify it, as they did in this instance.

On February 28 there was a debate on the Yalta Conference. On this occasion an entirely different set of critics from among the

[1] At this period, and for a long time afterwards, a number of Labour members and some Liberals had a complete *idée fixe* on the subject of our policy in Greece; ignoring the fact that the Allies had to take certain action there in order to win the war, they accused them and the British Government in particular of supporting a reactionary régime.

back-bench supporters of the Government was involved; the principal of these were Mr. Maurice Petherick,[1] Commander Sir Archibald Southby and Mr. (now Sir) Victor Raikes, all of them being Conservatives. They made good speeches, though at the time I fundamentally disagreed with them. They were principally concerned with the effect on Poland's position after the war of the decisions reached at the Yalta Conference. Their fears proved to be only too well justified, but, had I known then what I know to-day, I should still have voted for the Government for the reason which I have previously given when referring to the Yalta Conference. Mr. Churchill made a very effective reply to the criticisms, and only the small number of seventeen voted against the Government; the minority included Conservatives, members of the Independent Labour Party and a few Independents. In the course of the debate Mr. Petherick had a good joke at my expense; at least it was considered a good joke by House of Commons' standards, though, as I have remarked before in the course of this book, what Members of Parliament think funny is not always so regarded by outside opinion. I made a friendly interruption in the course of Mr. Petherick's speech and he replied, "I thought I should have the Noble Lord's support, but all that I get is a backward eddy". This play on my Christian name produced shouts of laughter in the House.

On January 25 the House unanimously adopted the Report of the Select Committee on the Rebuilding of the House of Commons, which was very satisfactory to my colleagues and to me; but a less favourable event, so far as I was concerned, occurred during questions. For some time prior to this Mr. Austin Hopkinson, M.P., had made certain charges against the Secretary of

[1] Mr. Petherick, who possesses courage and intelligence, was always able to get the ear of the House, but was regrettably defeated at the General Election in June, 1945. Sir Archibald Southby, who was a popular and prominent M.P., unfortunately had to resign his seat from ill-health early in the 1945 Parliament. Sir Victor Raikes, M.P., still contributes worthily to debates. All three men are of a type which is valuable in any Party in the Commons. Normally loyal to their leader, they do not hesitate to incur unpopularity with him by criticism of their Party's attitude in public on big issues when they are in disagreement with it. They are very different to another type of member to be found in every party who grumbles and spreads disaffection against the leader and his policy in private, but are silent or acquiescent in debate.

State for Air, Sir Archibald Sinclair,[1] and the Air Ministry regarding the alleged illegal use of farm produce grown on land of which the Air Force was in occupation. He had also made certain charges against General Critchley and the B.O.A.C. Mr. Moelwyn Hughes, Q.C.[2] and I, in consequence, put a motion on the Paper asking for a Select Committee to enquire into the charges, not because we either agreed or disagreed with them, but because we thought that that was the proper and constitutional way of disposing of a serious matter. When the time for the motion was refused, I said that I wished to give notice that I would raise the matter upon the adjournment. Mr. Churchill was very angry at this announcement and, though told by the Speaker that it was against the rules of debate to talk on the matter now that notice had been given that it was to be raised on the adjournment, he protested against my action. I did my best to pacify him by explaining that it was not intended to be hostile to the Government but, amid uproar, he shouted out: "It is a cowardly thing to do. I have never known you to do anything like that before". This remark was reported in all the newspapers.

That night I met Mr. Churchill at a dinner at which a number of other Ministers were also present. At midnight we resumed the controversy that had agitated us both so much at question time, and we continued a furious argument until 1 a.m., when we parted the best of friends. I remarked afterwards to one of my fellow-diners, who was a most distinguished man, that I felt rather guilty at keeping the Prime Minister out of bed in altercation over a comparatively small matter; his reply was that for the Prime Minister to have a good "ding-dong" verbal fight with an old friend in the small hours of the morning was a form both of recreation and recuperation, and that therefore I need not blame myself!

Some weeks later, the question of whether or not a Select Committee should be appointed to enquire into the charges was again discussed in the House of Commons. On the whole, there was friendliness on both sides. Mr. Churchill refused to agree to the appointment of a Select Committee and, on reflection, I came to the conclusion that he had some grounds for doing so. After a half-flattering and half-satirical reference to my "Father-

---

[1] Now Lord Thurso.   [2] Then Labour M.P. for Carmarthen.

hood of the House" and my mistaken notions of procedure, he said, "Let my Noble Friend be careful he does not reach senility before he attains old age". This observation made everyone, including me, laugh, and the controversy was ended.

In March, 1945, I opened a debate in the Commons on the need of supplies of food and raw materials for the liberated countries in Europe; and, partly from the knowledge I had obtained as chairman of the Inter-Governmental Committee for Refugees, I expounded the terrible privations and sufferings of the countries concerned. Mr. Greenwood, speaking for Labour supporters of the Government, agreed with my views; Mr. Attlee, for the Government, after a friendly reference to the indebtedness of the House to me for raising the subject, gave a reassuring and helpful reply. I think this debate, with its unanimity of opinion, did something to stimulate interest in this poignant matter. The admirable organisation and effort of U.N.R.R.A., backed by the great generosity of the United States, was able in the next few years to alleviate much of the suffering of which we spoke in the debate. It so happened that Mr. Lloyd George had died in his sleep the previous night: I said, in the course of my reference to the nation's loss by his death, that he was there in spirit with us, for in no subject did he take more interest in his long career than "how to help those who were in dire need of help".

A month later another great statesman died in the person of President Roosevelt. The British people were as deeply distressed at this occurrence as were those of America. I stated in my diary at the time:

He was perhaps the most charming of all the many illustrious men whom I have known in a long public career.

In May came V.E. Day. After short speeches by the leaders, the House of Commons adjourned in order that members might attend a service of Thanksgiving at St. Margaret's, Westminster. Such thunderous cheers greeted Mr. Churchill in Parliament Square that one of the police horses, normally the most well trained of all animals, plunged straight at Mr. Morrison and me as we were were walking together just behind the Prime Minister in procession. With considerable agility, the Leader and the "Father" of the House jumped aside just in time to avoid injury. Even on V.E. Day it would have caused some interest if we had both been killed. I can imagine a "sob sister" in a popular newspaper remarking how strange was fate, how inscrutable the ways of Providence that, on this day of all days, there should be, lying side by side, beneath the shadow of the great building which they both so loved, the bodies of the London policeman's son who, by his own talents and enterprise, had become one of the best known of all the occupants of the great offices of State, and of the crusty old Tory Irish Peer M.P. who had been a familiar[1] figure at Westminster for more years than people could remember. In death at any rate—she might have ended—they were not divided.

There was, though nobody appreciated it at the time, a hideous irony, one of the greatest in all history, about V.E. and V.J. Day. Very rightly, the Allied peoples west of the Iron Curtain rejoiced at their deliverance. Those of us who took part in the First World War were deeply thankful, too, that casualties in the fighting Services were less in the Second World War, though civilian casualties were much higher. Mr. Winston Churchill, as his book *The Second World War* shows, strenuously and successfully devoted his energies to avoidance of the frightful holocaust among our ground forces incurred on the Western Front in 1914 to 1918. It was one of the greatest benefits he bestowed upon his fellow-countrymen in the last war. In the neutral countries of Western Europe also there was relief at the victory. But V.E. Day meant something quite different to the peoples east of the Iron Curtain. From that day onwards a chain was riveted upon the minds and thoughts of all of them which was more deadly, in the long run, than any of the cruelties Nazism imposed upon some of them. Two of the master-tyrants, Hitler and Mussolini, were dead; but a third, Stalin, who was far more dangerous because he was an infinitely more able man, was still very much alive and was able, under the treaties which the Western Powers had concluded with him, to treat those unhappy nations with ruthless barbarity far in excess of any practised by his predecessors, the Tsars. If anyone on that sunny day of May, 1945,

[1] I hope she would have added "and popular", but modesty prohibits me from suggesting it.

when victory in Europe was celebrated, had, at "Speakers' Corner" in Hyde Park, informed his audience that within less than a decade Britain and the United States would be re-arming not only themselves to the limit of their financial resources, but Italy and a large part of Germany as well, in order to fight a possible third world war against the U.S.S.R., he would have had to be rescued by the police. Probably, at the subsequent Court proceedings for "insulting behaviour", the Magistrate would have remanded him in order that medical advice on the state of his mind might be obtained.

The Labour and official Liberal members of the Government resigned just after V.E. Day, and Mr. Churchill's "Caretaker Government" was formed to hold office until after the General Election; no doubt, if the Conservatives had won the election, it would have continued much as it was in composition, since it was well chosen and gave full representation to the younger members of the Party, including the "Tory Reformers". The Labour Party in the Commons and the country was obviously pleased to be free to return to party polemics. I was writing at the time a weekly political column under my own name in a Sunday newspaper. I mentioned in it that on the day after the new Government was formed Mr. Ernest Bevin and Mr. Herbert Morrison took their places side by side upon the Front Opposition Bench with a happy and truculent look upon their faces. Many impartial observers at the time believed that this Labour confidence was misplaced. They thought that the electors, in an overwhelming majority, wished to retain Mr. Churchill in office and disliked a return to party politics. As before the 1906 and 1929 elections, few Conservative organisers foresaw or foretold in private how heavy our defeat would be. I met only two men of importance before the election who believed we should be defeated. One was Lord Templewood and the other the late Duke of Devonshire. The Duke, a shrewd man who had been both an M.P. and a Minister, astonished me by telling me just before the writs were out that he thought we should have a defeat comparable to that of 1906.[1]

[1] At the 1906 election the figures were Conservatives and Unionists returned 157; at the 1945 election the figures were: Conservatives 189, National Liberals 13, Nationals 2 and Ulster Unionists 9.

I think that it is difficult to ascribe any one cause for our defeat in 1945. The well-known *cliché*: "There is no gratitude in politics" was again shown to be true. The number of people who will vote for the leader of a Party or for an individual M.P. because he has done good work for the nation or the constituency, and is thereby deserving of gratitude, is always less than that which votes according to the prevalent national mood. Many of the hundreds of thousands of people who turned out to cheer Mr. Churchill in his election tour voted against his Party. Some in their ignorance believed that, even if they voted against the Conservatives, Mr. Churchill would still be Prime Minister. Others were influenced by motives to which I refer earlier in this book.[1] I consider that the allegation made at the time, that Mr. Churchill lost votes by his electoral methods, is untrue. His attack, for example, on the late Mr. Laski was fully justified. It is the paramount duty of any Conservative Leader to denounce views he considers subversive of the nation and constitution.

The electorate was adverse to the Conservative Party in 1945 for several reasons. A Party in power at the beginning of and during a war is usually defeated at the election after it. If Mr. Lloyd George had gone to the country in 1918 with the backing of the Liberal Party alone, he would most probably have suffered as heavy a defeat as Mr. Churchill did in 1945. The end of the National Government in the spring of 1945 released all the old pent-up feeling against the Conservative Party which the Labour and Liberal Parties had created before 1939 and which had been in cold storage since; it was responsible, so ran the tale, for unemployment between the wars; its support of Munich had "made war inevitable". Why, Mr. Churchill had said so himself. Yet he was now asking for votes to put that Party in power. Even he could not expect the nation to do this. Also, what is conveniently termed "Leftism" always flourishes after a war. When men and women have been for years under strict discipline, they have a natural inclination to vote against the Right which represents stability and the old order of things. They want change, reform, and a new set of supposed values. A large majority of Servicemen voted Labour in 1945 for these

[1] See Chapter XV, p. 207.

reasons, though few of them would probably have been able to explain what those reasons were.

On account of circumstances that are not necessarily derogatory to the Labour Party, since the prominent men in it are older on the average than those in the Conservative Party, more Conservative M.P.s and candidates were on active service in the war than their constituency opponents. This is reflected in the casualties in the war among Conservative M.P.s. Of twenty-two M.P.s killed, twenty-one were Conservatives. The constituency organisations suffered from the absence of so many of their active members on service; the Labour Party was more fortunate, for many of its most influential supporters were working at home. This was not due to any lack of patriotism on their part. Indeed, without the unstinted support of the Trades Union leaders and their followers, the war could not have been won. But Mr. A., the well-known local Labour leader, who worked at Mr. B.'s factory throughout the war and was personally acquainted with thousands of the electors, had a great advantage over young Mr. C. who only came home, after six years' absence at the front, to contest the constituency just before the election.

The Parliaments of 1945 and 1950 are too close to the present in time to make it desirable or necessary to give, as I have done in earlier chapters, a year by year record of the principal debates, speeches and legislation which occurred in them. Instead, I shall attempt, in the remaining pages of this book, the ambitious task of assessing and analysing the trends of opinion, both of the majority and the minority, and the policies that followed from them as well as their effect in the Commons. Such a survey necessarily entails some description of the contribution of individuals to these events, for without such a description it would be dull and meaningless.

But before entering upon my survey, it is necessary to write something about the general atmosphere of the Commons during the period and the relative merits of the Government and the Opposition in handling the situation which confronted both in the House.

The defeat of our Party, though heavy enough, was proportionately less severe in the 1945 than in the 1906 election[1]; we

[1] See footnote p. 313.

were united under a great leader; and we had two excellent Chief Whips in the persons first of Mr. James Stuart and afterwards of Mr. Patrick Buchan-Hepburn. They and their assistants were, in the main, a more efficient team than their Conservative predecessors when the Party was in opposition from 1906 to 1914. Moreover, in 1906 Mr. Balfour's leadership was disliked by many of his followers, and the Party was divided between tariff-reformers and free-traders. In the election of 1945 we had a better intake of new young members, men of brilliance and achievement in many fields, than we had in that of 1906. The Liberal Government in 1906 far outshone in ability the Labour administration which came into power in 1945, and made fewer grievous mistakes; yet, whereas we won many by-elections in the first two years of the 1906 Parliament, we won none in the whole of the 1945 Parliament, and, until the General Election of 1950, the transfer of votes was insignificant.

There was at the time, and has been since, little public discussion on the causes of our failure; my own view is that it was to some extent due to the failure of the Opposition to function properly on the floor of the House itself.

It is always difficult to analyse and then assess, during his lifetime, the nature of the contribution a statesman of great renown has made to the history of the world and to his own country and Party in a particular period of his career. You have to pick your way carefully through a morass of partiality and prejudice in the shape of contemporary speaking and writing. On the one hand, you have to reject the views of those who, from good motives or bad—Party and personal loyalty or sycophancy—will admit no flaw in their hero; on the other hand, you have to avoid the opinion of those whose hatred for the great man, whether personal or political, is so intense that facts are disregarded and malignancy substituted for them. From 1945 to 1951, Mr. Churchill carried out a task in international affairs, at home and abroad, which, alike in volume and importance, has never been equalled by any statesman out of office in any country at any time. Beginning with his speech at Fulton, he led British Commonwealth, Transatlantic and Western European majority opinion on to the road which it is now following; to him the co-operation and defence of Western Civilisation against Communist Imperialism, under the direction of the Kremlin, owes its original inspiration. The late Mr. Ernest Bevin followed, at first reluctantly, afterwards more enthusiastically, after Mr. Churchill had erected the signpost. If a third world war is avoided, Mr. Churchill will be entitled to more of the credit than any other statesman in the world. Also, on subjects other than international affairs he made a series of speeches, in and out of Parliament, which, for wit, pungency and brilliance of expression, have never been excelled, even by him. The quality of Mr. Churchill's speeches was of great benefit to the Conservatives in opposition, but the leader of a Party in opposition needs to have other qualities than that of the gift of oratory; he should learn to endure boredom without showing how hard the ordeal is, and he should watch and wait in the Chamber itself or be at hand in his room for instant recall by the Chief Whip during dull, ordinary debates. For no one can tell when a situation may arise which he alone, with his authority, can handle satisfactorily. A Minister, by an unguarded statement, may make a serious slip, to the embarrassment of his Party, or the ex-Minister in charge of the Opposition front bench may make a similar mistake. Excitement rises in the House, the Chamber begins to fill. Journalists flock into the Press Gallery, for this may be an incident which will mean headline news. If the Leader of the Opposition is not there, he cannot exploit the first of those situations nor mitigate the harm done to his Party's interests by the second. Moreover, his absence will be noticed by thousands of his supporters next day when the Press report appears. For reasons with which one can sympathise, Mr. Churchill, unlike most of his predecessors, was not a regular attendant at unimportant debates in the 1945 or 1950 Parliaments. There was an immense call for his services outside the House; he prepared his speeches most carefully after much meditation and reflection; he was writing a book; he was leading, as I have stated, world opinion on international relationship. Yet the fact remains that he was sometimes not in the House when his presence would have been invaluable.

There were other reasons for the failure of the Opposition to perform its functions. The younger members of the Conservative Party have, in recent years, become imbued with the belief that they can best serve the interests of the Party and advance the prospects of their own careers by becoming immersed in the affairs of the numerous committees and sub-committees of the Party which meet, during the sittings of the House, in a committee room. They are in the Chamber itself only when they want to speak or are interested in the particular subject.[1] So, all too often in the 1945 and 1950 Parliaments, the Opposition back benches were sparsely filled by a handful of M.P.s too engrossed in thinking out what they were going to say, if they were fortunate enough to be "called", to encourage by cheers those of their own side who were actually speaking. No impression of unity or enthusiasm was created. Old hands, like myself, could get over this tepidity by deliberately picking a quarrel with the Government spokesman which almost invariably produces cheers, counter-cheers, and an exhilarating excitement.

But the Party methods were hard on a young, capable, but nervous new member of it. He got too little encouragement. I have referred in earlier chapters of this book to the help which Mr. Balfour gave, in the 1906 Parliament, to those of us who were then young and told how he would come to our rescue when in difficulties and enthusiastically applaud our most jejune efforts by loud "hear, hears".[2] To some, the view I present may seem old-fashioned. They would argue that fantastically inadequate Press reports of its proceedings have reduced the value of constant attendance in, and attention to, the Chamber. They would contend that a good party speech over the wireless is worth in votes a dozen exploitations of a situation in the House by a keen Opposition in full attendance and out for blood. I hope and think they are wrong, for, if they are right, the certain decline of the House of Commons is inevitable. I am encouraged in the belief that I am right by the fact that, again and again, whilst writing this book, former colleagues of mine in the Commons have told me that the Labour Opposition since the 1951 election have been far more successful than we were when in a similar position.[3] Again and

---

[1] There were, of course, exceptions to this rule. Mr. Boyd-Carpenter, for example, was most assiduous in his attendance at debates which has helped him to become a most successful parliamentarian.

[2] See Chapter III, p. 21.

[3] These words were written in 1952; it is fair to add that the Opposition has shown itself less efficient in 1953.

again, the statement has been made to me: "You see, the Socialists are always there ready to seize on any situation to their advantage". My friends usually add that the Labour Party is very unscrupulous in opposition; this is a charge always brought by supporters of any Government against any Opposition which is effective. If my friends are right and if a Party, so split over "Bevanism" as the Labour Party are, is more effective than we were when we sat on the left of Mr. Speaker, this constitutes a reflection upon Conservative methods in the Commons between 1945 and 1951.

Mr. Eden had his difficulties, too. It is not easy to be second-in-command to a world-famous Commander-in-Chief. I do not suppose that those who performed that task for Alexander the Great, Cæsar or Napoleon were always happy. It is an occupational disease of genius to be occasionally petulant and unreasonable. Only the undistinguished sail the voyage of life on an even keel. Symptoms of this disease in a mild form occasionally afflict both Mr. Churchill and Mr. Eden. It is a tribute to the greatness of both men that their personal relationship, even when they have differed on matters of policy, has always been most happy.

The work of the Party in the constituencies during the years 1945 to 1951 was a striking contrast to that of the Party in Parliament. Lord Woolton began his task as Party chairman and chief organiser by collecting a brilliant band of young men and women with fine war records at the Central Conservative Office. Then he turned his attention to the constituency organisations. These are independent bodies in every sense of the term. They are suspicious of too much advice from headquarters; and in some constituencies their principal office-holders in the past have been old men and women devoid of political horse-sense. Lord Woolton, with a mixture of suavity and firmness, renovated the Conservative constituency organisations from top to bottom; he inspired enthusiasm for the cause in the most difficult seats; he raised a large sum of money to enable a poor man or woman to stand in any constituency without incurring any personal cost in the way of election expenses; and he induced by far the most able band of voluntary workers who have ever laboured for the Conservative Party to give their services everywhere. The old incompetents disappeared from their chairmanships and agencies; a new spirit imbued the "Young Conservatives". This superb organisation, which was thus created so largely by Lord Woolton, and the Party's policy as set forth in *The Right Road for Britain* were two of the factors which caused so large a turn-over of votes to the Conservatives at the 1950 election. One other factor, probably a stronger one, was disillusion with Socialism in general and with the Socialist Party in particular. In view of the disappointing results of previous by-elections, this turn-over of 1950 may seem strange; but it is explained by the fact that at by-elections the voters attach importance to the merits or demerits of the Opposition in Parliament, whereas at general elections this factor is generally ignored. Lord Woolton had an admirable coadjutor in Mr. R. A. Butler. He was responsible, in consultation with Mr. Churchill, for statements of policy and for a general supervision of relations with the Press and outside bodies. His brilliance and clarity of intellect, tact, firmness, urbanity, expository powers and shy sense of humour, were great assets to the Party. These qualities of his have subsequently been more prominently displayed in his Chancellorship of the Exchequer.

I have already referred[1] to the high quality of the new and young members in the Conservative Party in the Commons in the 1945 election. The same description applies to those who entered the House in the 1950 Parliament. One very satisfactory feature about these young men was that several of them came from humble homes, and had made their way upwards solely by character and brains. There is a wealth of support for the Conservative Party among wage-earners, small salary earners, and young men and women of outstanding intelligence with high academic qualifications obtained at the University *via* the elementary and secondary schools. None are more anxious than Mr. Churchill and the leaders of the Party in general to welcome such men and women to the Commons. Far too many constituency Conservative associations, who have absolute freedom of choice in such matters, have been inclined in the past to prefer candidates of a different class to represent them. Now that Conservative candidates are no longer either expected or allowed to pay the expenses of an election, there is good reason for hoping that this attitude will change. Certainly refreshing evidence of such a

---

[1] See p. 309 of this chapter.

change was afforded in 1945 and 1950 by the new crop of Conservative members. It would be an invidious task, and one beyond
my capacity, to give a complete list of all the young men of
promise on the Conservative side in either Parliament. They
include Mr. A. H. Head and Mr. A. R. W. Low, Mr. Anthony
Nutting, Mr. David Eccles,[1] Mr. W. S. Shepherd, Commander
Joynson-Hicks,[2] Colonel Hare, Mr. Walker-Smith, Mr. Maud-
ling, Mr. Angus Maude, Mr. Aubrey Jones, Mr. Julian Amery,
Sir Edward Boyle, Mr. Macleod, Mr. Hopkinson, Mr. Michael
Astor and Colonel Poole. Unfortunately, the two last named
resigned at the General Election of 1950. The Labour Party was
also fortunate in the quality of its new members, including as they
did Mr. Gaitskell, Sir Hartley Shawcross, Sir Frank Soskice, Mr.
Wilson, Mr. Crossman, Mr. De Freitas, Mr. Dugdale, Mr.
Maurice Webb, Mr. Younger, Mr. Michael Stewart, Mr. De-
largy, Mr. Bing, Mr. Wyatt, Mr. Gordon-Walker, Mr. George
Brown, Mr. James Callaghan and Mr. Paget. It would be inaccurate indeed to say there was much to choose between the
debating abilities of the young and new members on either side;
nor, indeed, contrary to the general opinion, was there more
unfairness in debate, more interruption of the minority by the
majority or more ill-feeling than in previous Parliaments. As I
stated earlier in this book, the 1906 and 1910 Parliaments had an
unhappy pre-eminence in this respect.

I was invited by Mr. Churchill, in August, 1945, to the Eve-of-
the-Session dinner which the Leader of the Opposition gives by
a long-standing custom. Save for one other member, I was the
only guest present who had not been in the National or Caretaker Government. I was in the same position in the Conservative
"Shadow Cabinet", which I joined at Mr. Churchill's invitation
in November of that year. These unimportant autobiographical
details would not be worth mentioning in this book if they did
not exemplify Mr. Churchill's quality of generous forgiveness.
I had criticised him freely in the Commons during the war, and
we had had more than one clash in the House; I had no sort of
prescriptive right, as had the other guests, to be invited to the
dinner, since, by custom, invitations for such functions are usually

[1] He entered Parliament in a by-election during the war.
[2] He also entered Parliament in a by-election during the war.

confined to Ministers in the last Government before the Party went into opposition. Mr. Churchill, unlike far too many people in high positions, is a most forgiving man. Another of Mr. Churchill's qualities was displayed at this dinner. He had just suffered one of the most grievous disappointments of his life in the heavy defeat his Government had sustained. After dinner we heard on the wireless the announcement of the Japanese surrender; in the minds of all of his guests was the thought, how sad it was that the man who had done so much to make this victory possible had just been rejected as their leader by his fellow-countrymen. Mr. Churchill could have been forgiven if he had been depressed and ill at ease on such an occasion. He was, on the contrary, in the best of spirits, looking extremely well and cherubic; he was a most charming and delightful host, and never once showed the slightest signs of resentment at his defeat or doubts about the future of the Conservative Party. At the end of dinner, in a few short and sensible remarks, he gave his views on the political present and future. My mind flew back to a similar display of courage after a grave defeat and of confidence in the future on the part of Mr. Chamberlain when I saw him for the first time after the 1906 election. I felt proud to have served under two men of such supreme attainments, who knew so well how to treat those "two imposters", as Kipling called them, "Triumph and Disaster".

CHAPTER XXIII

THERE was good debating talent on both the Front and Back Benches in the 1945 and 1950 Parliaments. On economic and financial subjects, for example, the speeches of the late Colonel Stanley, Mr. Harold Macmillan and Mr. Lyttelton for the Opposition Front Bench and those of the late Sir Stafford Cripps, Mr. Dalton and Mr. Gaitskell bear favourable comparison with those delivered on both sides in the famous "Lloyd George Budget" fight. In accord with tradition, there were also in these two Parliaments a handful of members who attracted notice by the singularity of their views or by the methods which they used to force them upon the attention of the House. Such men and women, even when, as is often the case, they are slightly eccentric in their outlook, are valuable to the House; some eccentricity, or at least deviation from the normal, is very necessary in the legislative assembly of a nation which is so regulated and controlled as is Britain. Sir Waldron Smithers sincerely believes that the world in general, and Britain in particular, is suffering a serious moral and material decline through Socialist doctrine. Many millions of people agree with Sir Waldron at least in part of his thesis. Though he never attained the record of "Another Day" Day,[1] he showed great persistence in pursuing this theme at question time. His questions, especially his supplementary questions, were often embarrassing to his fellow-Conservatives, who repudiated the extreme nature of his views at one of their Party conferences. There is always, however, a law of compensation in such matters. When the Labour Party pointed to Sir Waldron as a typical Tory who, unlike other Tories, dared to say what he thought, we could cite Mr. Emrys Hughes as a typical Socialist who was not afraid to voice the real views of the Socialists. Sir Waldron sometimes recalled Lord Salisbury, in his most unguarded moments, in the '80s; Mr. Hughes, with his hatred and denunciation of war and armaments and his belief in the universal brotherhood and goodwill of man on either side

[1] See Chapter XVI, p. 222.

of the Iron Curtain, reproduced exactly the views of his Party in the '20s. The House was delighted with the embarrassment which both these good and sincere men caused to their respective Parties.

Mr. De la Bere [1] was also a frequent questioner in the 1945 and 1950 Parliaments. He had strong views on the iniquity of the Labour Government, especially in respect of their treatment of agriculture and horticulture. He was never satisfied by the answers he received. At the end of the supplementary answer he would invariably shout, at the top of his voice, an epithet derogatory to the Government's policy. The House loved this weekly or fortnightly performance. As the time of Mr. De la Bere's questions drew near, members waited as expectantly for them as children wait at the Zoo to see the lions or the bears fed. They were never disappointed. With a roar, reminiscent, indeed, of a caged lion, Mr. De la Bere would shout "Scandalous", "Disgraceful", "When *will* this nonsense stop?" Thunderous cheers from all parts of the House invariably followed.

Mr. Evans, the Labour M.P. for Wednesbury, then Parliamentary Secretary to the Ministry of Food, had a different method for registering his disapproval of the agricultural policy of the Government, which he normally supported and from which he resigned because of his disapproval. He charged the Government with paying such high subsidies to farmers that the industry was encouraged to be, and was, inefficient. In his original speech on the subject he spoke of "feather-bedding" agriculture, and was henceforth known as "Feather-bed" Evans. He returned to his charge again and again in debate, and since he is an able and sincere man and a good speaker, he made it appear more substantial than it really was. One could not help admiring his pertinacity.

Mr. Sydney Silverman used yet another method for attracting attention. It consisted of rising frequently during any important speech by a member of the Opposition, especially when Mr. Churchill was speaking, in order to ask a question or put a point of order. He did not invent this method. It has been practised by many in the past, including the writer of this book. To achieve its object, which is the dual one of embarrassing the person in

[1] Now Sir Rupert, Lord Mayor of London, 1952-3.

possession of the House and acquiring some notice, favourable or unfavourable, in the process, it must be carried out with discretion. If the interruptions and points of order are too frequent and wholly impertinent, in both senses of the term, the House will show its resentment by shouting the interrupter down and eventually relegate him or her to the category of a bore or a mere nuisance. But if the questions are relevant and directed by a back-bencher of acumen and intelligence against some important figure on the front bench of the opposite side of the House, they are tolerated, provided that the interrupter himself can hold his own in debate against similar treatment. To the public it may seem wholly wrong that a great statesman when he makes a speech in the House of Commons should be subjected to any interruptions. "Why does not the Speaker", I have often been asked outside the House, "stop . . . interrupting . . . ? Surely a man of his position should not be subjected to cheap sneers on the part of someone of no importance?" But a great man outside the House is only *primus inter pares* within it. The Chair and members very properly recognise that, within limits, he may be questioned even when he is speaking in an important debate. If he knows his job, he will turn the tables on his questioner. The whole process embodies the spirit of a democratic assembly. It is fair to Mr. Silverman to say that he practised the art which I have described very successfully in the 1945 and 1950 Parliaments, and still does so.

He was less happy in his persistence in suggesting that breaches of privilege had been committed. In some quarters there was a tendency in the 1945 Parliament which, if it had not been checked by the good sense alike of the House and the Committee of Privileges, would have brought both ridicule and odium upon the Commons. This consisted in believing that the House should treat as a breach of privilege something which might be so interpreted by precedents established in the seventeenth or eighteenth century, but which is harmless, or necessary to-day. Very wisely, the Crown and the Courts of Law do not insist upon the observance of rights or legal processes which have fallen into desuetude. The House of Commons must do likewise.

In debates on foreign affairs, Mr. Churchill, Mr. Eden and Mr. Bevin held a predominant position in the 1945 Parliament. The

Prime Minister, for the Government, and Mr. Butler, from the Front Opposition Bench, together with other Ministers and ex-Ministers, made valuable contributions from time to time on this subject, and helped to maintain the non-party national front upon it; but they never possessed the authority of these three men. Mr. Churchill and Mr. Eden derived this authority from their high position in world politics which the loss of electoral support for their Party at home did not injure. The House as a whole recognised this fact. Mr. Bevin obtained his authority from his great position in the Labour movement and his personal qualities: his courage, integrity and belief in Britain, of which, in respect alike of his virtues and faults, he was so typical a representative, earned him deep affection and respect in the House and in his department. Without these three men, I do not think the maintenance of a non-party foreign policy would have been possible. Proof of this can be found in the calamitous, though happily short, period in 1951 when Mr. Herbert Morrison was Foreign Secretary. It is strange that a man of great ability, who had been a very successful Minister in a most difficult office during the war as well as, in the main, a fair and reasonable Leader of the House in the 1945 Parliament, should have failed so lamentably as Foreign Secretary. He never once made a speech worthy of his office or of the occasion, with the result that debates on foreign affairs degenerated, in an astonishing degree, from the standard attained in the time of his predecessor. This appreciably injured our national prestige abroad. Some brilliant speeches were made from the back benches of all parties in debates on foreign affairs, but none of them had the influence which similar speeches on the same subject had had in previous Parliaments. Throughout the 1945 Parliament, it was the front-bench speeches which counted on international policy. That is not surprising, for it was those speeches which emphasised the bi-partisan character of British foreign policy and, indeed, made that policy possible.

Insufficient emphasis has, in my judgment, been laid in contemporary writing upon the magnificent and dramatic achievement of the British, United States and Commonwealth Governments[1] and of their respective legislatures since Mr. Churchill's Fulton

[1] I refer only to Canada, Australia, New Zealand and South Africa, not to the other self-governing Commonwealth countries.

speech in the matter of foreign relationships; save for a small lunatic fringe, which is powerless to do much harm, they have reached a unanimity on this subject which transcends the fierce party differences on internal issues. These Governments and legislatures represent between 220 million and 230 million people of the Caucasian race endowed with great virility and enterprise and possessing immense manufacturing and raw material resources, both actual and potential; they occupy most of the strategic keypoints of the world. In addition, they have the co-operation of a number of the most civilised and renowned of European and Asiatic countries. This formidable alliance, for such it is, constitutes a balance of power to counteract the Communist bloc of countries with a view to their containment until such time as their leaders are willing to enter into genuine negotiations for the preservation of world peace. Whether that day will ever come or whether, on the contrary, a third world war will intervene no one can foretell with certainty. Nor is it possible to be sure whether the "cold war" will not, by its prolongation, so weaken the spirit and resources of the democratic Powers so as to enable Stalin's successors to attain his long-term object, which is the Communisation of the Western world, without war. Meanwhile, the alliance is the only effective system of collective security in existence. That of the United Nations exists only on paper and in the perorations of politicians. It is the United States and the Commonwealth countries who supply the vast bulk of the troops who are fighting Communist aggression in Korea; it is the French, the Dutch and ourselves who are fighting it elsewhere in the Far East. Only the alliance, working, of course, in harmony with like-minded Powers, can attain the noble objects which the United Nations Organisation was founded to support. The "United Europe" movement and the Council of Europe are a valuable, though indirect, aid to the alliance. That it should be necessary to start a fresh armaments race so soon after the Second World War to achieve this balance of power is not only a hideous irony, as I have stated earlier in this chapter, but has justified, at least in part, the forebodings of two former British Prime Ministers to which I have previously referred.[1]

[1] See Chapter XIX, pp. 268 and 281.

Mr. Attlee and the late Mr. Bevin should be praised for their action in inducing the Labour Party, during the 1945 Parliament, to follow the new path which President Truman and Mr. Churchill had taken. It represented a complete *volte-face* to the Party's attitude in the '20s and '30s alike on foreign affairs and armaments. Between the wars Soviet Russia was still a promised land to Socialists in Britain and elsewhere, despite rebuffs and disillusions. National armaments were anathema to some of their leaders and to nearly all the rank-and-file. The 1923 and 1929 Labour Governments were full of pacifists and conscientious objectors of the 1914 war. The Labour Government, in view of the pacifist views of the majority of its members, is to be commended for the passage of the two years' National Service Act; it has strikingly proved its worth and necessity in Korea and elsewhere; but the commendation thus earned by Mr. Shinwell, first as Secretary of State for War and then as Defence Minister, has been entirely nullified by his subsequent statement, whilst in opposition, that the period should be reduced. This, to use a hackneyed phrase, is "playing politics" with a vengeance. When the great change-over of opinion began in the 1945 Parliament, the Conservative Party and the Conservative Press were too polite to mention, except obliquely, what had happened in the past; but the Labour malcontents, Communists and fellow-travellers did so very often. The witty and irrepressible Mr. Emrys Hughes constantly quoted in debate the pro-Soviet and pacifist speeches of Ministers in the past. Mr. Gallacher, Mr. Pritt, Mr. Platts-Mills and Mr. Zilliacus, who were a formidable quartet if only because of their fluency in opposing the bi-partisan policy, made this one of the points in their speeches. Their disappearance through defeat by the electors or through expulsion from the Labour Party in the 1950 election gave a good impression abroad of Labour solidarity in favour of the new anti-Communist front and Anglo-American co-operation. It was particularly satisfactory that, in addition to Mr. Gallacher, Mr. Piratin, the only other Communist in the House, was defeated. It is true that since 1951 the mild anti-Americanism of the "Bevanites" and their objection to the scale of re-armament have affected that solidarity to some extent; yet it remains true that the House of Commons is freer from pro-Soviet Communism than any other first Chamber in Europe.

That is a great achievement. However, if, as I have contended, Mr. Attlee and the late Mr. Bevin can share with Mr. Churchill and Mr. Eden some of the credit for the bi-partisan front on foreign affairs, they must also share with the Conservative and Liberal Parties the discredit for the failure of British policy in the Middle East. They inherited a thirty-two-year record of confused British thinking over Palestine and the Arab countries, but they added their own muddled ideas to it, with the deplorable results of the murder of British civilians and soldiers in Palestine and our hurried and undignified exit from it. It is, however, to Mr. Bevin's credit that he frankly admitted one day in debate[1] what no other British Foreign Minister had admitted until then, namely, that we had given conflicting promises to Jews and Arabs during the 1914 war. I, alone among Conservatives, cheered this remark loudly, to the astonishment, at the time, of some of my colleagues. But I had reason to do so, for, ever since I returned from the Arab Revolt in 1918, I had vainly tried to impress this fact upon the "Powers that be". If those who were ministerially responsible for British Middle Eastern policy in the First World War had consulted the appropriate authorities, both military and civilian, in the territories affected before they gave the undertakings which they did, Britain would not have been accused ever since by Jews and Arabs alike of breaking her word to them.

The Labour Party's record in the matter of Commonwealth and Imperial relationship during the 1945 and 1950 Parliaments was, in the main, an unhappy one. It was obvious after the Second World War that full self-government would have to be conceded to India and Burma within a reasonable time. But Britain had an obligation to see that the transfer of powers did not take place in conditions which endangered the lives of hundreds of thousands of innocent people. Yet this is what happened in the Indian Peninsula, where horrible massacres on an enormous scale occurred, and in Burma, where murder, rapine and widespread anarchy ensued. The Labour Party in Parliament, on the front and back benches, adopted in the 1945 Parliament an unpleasant self-righteousness in respect of their Indian policy. They talked of it always in terms which gave the impression that they alone had sympathy with Indian aspirations for self-government,

[1] See also Chapter VIII, p. 100.

ignoring the fact that Mr. Baldwin and Sir Samuel Hoare had risked the disruption of the Conservative Party for the same object.[1] Whenever Mr. Churchill referred, in any of his speeches, as he often did, to the sinister side of the transfer with its huge massacres, he was greeted with howls of indignation. Moreover, one feature of the attitude of the Labour Party "back-benchers" towards the great Peninsula has done, and is doing, harm, especially as it is shared to some extent by their leaders. It is always India that they praise; it is Mr. Nehru who is their "blue-eyed boy"; Pakistan is ignored. This has caused concern and, indeed, indignation among leading Pakistanis. One of them once said to me: "It is the old, old story with you British. Always in order to show your fairness, you are kinder to your opponents than to your supporters. It is *le défaut de vos qualités*. We in Pakistan are nearer constitutionally and in other ways to you than India, so your Government and its Socialist supporters go out of their way to appear to like India rather than us".

The cession of powers by the British Government to Burma was completely unjustified. Burma was entitled to full self-government only after certain conditions had been fulfilled. We annexed Burma within living memory, because the frightful cruelty and incompetence of the Burmese King and his Government endangered our valuable and legitimate trade there and were a menace to the stability of the entire Far East. Peace and prosperity, such as they had never known before, ensued for the Burmese until the Second World War; when war broke out, we were assisting them to advance by stages to self-government. There was in Burma infinitely less personnel available to provide efficient legislators and administrators than in India, although Burmans of all races are charming and delightful people with a highly developed artistic perception and sense of humour. We had just lost thousands of British lives in freeing the country from the cruel and ruthless Japanese invaders. But the aftermath of the upheaval was still painfully apparent. Mr. Churchill and I, who were the spokesmen for the Opposition Front Bench in the debate on the Bill conferring self-government upon Burma, warned the House that its effect might well be civil war and anarchy with resultant grave injury to Burma's national life and to the large

[1] See Chapter XII, pp. 158-163.

British investments in the country, as well as much individual hardship and suffering. Our warnings were unheeded but proved, in the event, to be completely justified. Britain lowered her prestige and the belief in her will and purpose in the East by this hurried evacuation. It may have been necessary for military reasons, as our ground troops were then, and still are to-day, very thinly stretched to defend our own and allied interests in the Far East and to protect our interests elsewhere. But at best it was a most regrettable necessity and not, as the Labour Party claim, a great act of statesmanship.

Every Secretary of State for the Colonies finds, on taking office, a mass of problems to be considered. They are more varied, difficult and potentially dangerous than those confronting a Minister in the most difficult offices concerned with internal problems, such as that of Labour. Mr. Creech Jones was faced by two major problems in the 1945 Parliament. The first was that of Colonial development. The world desperately needed food and raw materials. We were impoverished by the war, but we had under our direct control, in the Colonies, large areas which could supply both, to our advantage and that of the whole world. The Colonial Development Fund, instituted by a Conservative Secretary of State in the past, clearly needed to be extended or supplemented by further efforts under another form of organisation. So the Government acted, but the only results were the dreadful failures of the ground-nuts scheme, the Gambia poultry scheme and others of the kind. The rashness and incompetence displayed by those responsible for their carrying out were monumental; and a very ugly feature of the whole matter was that completely inaccurate answers were given in Parliament about them until their final collapse. Indeed, the answers and speeches of Ministers about them were so ludicrously remote from the facts that it might be supposed there was deliberate prevarication, though it is more charitable to suppose that the misleading statements proceeded from ignorance and incompetence. Mr. Attlee's handling of the matter was astonishing. He retained Mr. Strachey, the Minister responsible for the schemes, in another office after he had displayed his unfitness for a Ministerial post alike in the Commons and in his department, yet he compulsorily retired first Mr. (now Lord) Lawson and afterwards Mr. Bellenger from the office of

Secretary of State for War; though the latter was a competent Minister, at any rate in the House.

The other primary problem confronting the incoming Secretary of State in 1945 was the future form of government in most of the African Colonies. In the West African Colonies, where there is no permanent European settlement, an advance in African self-government was necessary as a result of the war and for other reasons; but every maxim of statesmanship required that it should be made by gradual though progressive stages. Within the lifetime of some old people still alive, the hinterland of these territories had been under the sway of blood-thirsty savages. The British, in the course of the last seventy or eighty years, have not only rescued these lands from barbarism, but developed their resources in an astonishing fashion. That development has immensely enhanced the economic status of the inhabitants; and it has played a great part in sustaining British trade during a period when we have suffered grievous losses of investments elsewhere—for example, in China and the Argentine. Now, if there is a lesson to be learnt from world events of the last twenty-five years, it is that democratic government simply does not function in a country where there is an illiterate electorate which has no understanding of democracy and where power falls into the hands of a tiny class of semi-educated agitators. Invariably, too, in such conditions, the owners of legitimate foreign investment in railways, mines, factories and plantations are threatened, harassed, blackmailed and frequently have their possessions taken from them without compensation. Ignoring all these considerations and without any sufficiently preparatory steps, the Labour Government conferred self-government upon the Gold Coast; and thus alarmed European opinion throughout Africa.

One other major problem which confronted the two Secretaries of State for the Colonies, Mr. Creech Jones and afterwards Mr. Griffiths, in the Labour Government of 1945 to 1951 existed in Kenya, Northern Rhodesia and the other Colonial territories in East and Central Africa. These, especially Northern Rhodesia, contained a growing number of European inhabitants, mainly of British or South African Dutch descent. The term "settler" is normally used to describe these people, but it is really an inaccurate one, since some of them belong to the second or third generation born in the Colony in which they reside, and the vast majority intend to remain there for the rest of their lives. A large proportion of the South Africans in these territories, both British and Dutch, are descended from families who have lived in Africa for a century or more. Naturally, after the war, these people demanded, as they were entitled to do, more self-government. The British Government had to safeguard, so far as it could, the interests of native Africans and Indian residents in these lands. Though their private character is beyond reproach, no two men could have been more unsuited to deal with this delicate situation than Mr. Creech Jones and Mr. Griffiths. They had no previous knowledge of Africa or experience of high office; like the majority of the Labour Party, both had inherited an evil tradition from the Liberal Party, when it was in its prime. This was a belief that Britons overseas in countries where there is a native non-European population cannot be trusted to regard the welfare of that population, and that they are exploiters who will bully the natives whenever they can. Mr. Creech Jones, Mr. Griffiths and Captain Dugdale, the Parliamentary Under-Secretary, made little effort to conceal their views when they visited the territories in question. I have friends in those territories and business interests in one of them; I was dismayed by the stories which I heard of the incidents and misunderstandings, on both sides, which occurred during these tours. In their speeches and in those of other Labour members in the Commons stress was always put on the interests of the Africans; the claims of the Europeans were hardly mentioned. In particular, there was failure to present the following undoubted facts. The best European opinion in Central and East Africa, under enlightened leadership, recognises the urgent need for reconciling the conflicting aspirations of multi-racial communities. It realises that without such reconciliation chaos and anarchy will eventually ensue. These territories are as much the homeland of their European inhabitants as they are of the Africans and Indians. Since 1948[1] there have been oblique references in Ministerial speeches and direct ones in those of their back-bench supporters to "Malanism" and "Apartheid" in the Union as a reason for

[1] The year that Dr. Malan's Government was formed in the Union of South Africa.

retarding any advance in self-government for Europeans in East Africa. Nothing is more calculated to infuriate the Europeans of these territories than the suggestion, which is wholly false, that they favour Dr. Malan's policy; but, as I have said in speeches in both Houses of Parliament, if British Governments in the next decade ignore the just claims of these people, they will look to the Union for support and possibly insist at some period on federation with it. In one of my speeches in the Commons on the subject I asked Labour members if they would dare to suggest, in such circumstances, that the British Government should send troops to prevent this happening? How else could they prevent it if the thousands of Europeans concerned unanimously demanded it? I got no answer to my challenge. The late Colonel Oliver Stanley and Mr. Lennox-Boyd from the Front Opposition Bench, and men with great knowledge of conditions in the Colonies such as Sir Ian Fraser, Mr. Gammans, Mr. Walter Fletcher and others from the Conservative back benches, in both the 1945 and 1950 Parliaments, constantly warned the Labour majority of the danger of their attitude towards Europeans in Africa, Malaya and elsewhere. But it had no effect on them or on the official Liberal Party. They completely ignored the lessons of the American revolution. It is distressing that, in consequence, many people of European descent in the Crown Colonies are inclined to regard the British Parliament as inimical to their interests. It is also most unfortunate that the unsympathetic approach of the Labour and official Liberal Parties towards their problems have caused many Southern Rhodesians to doubt the wisdom of the scheme of federation for the two Rhodesias; at the time of writing it appears possible that Southern Rhodesia may reject it in the referendum which is to be held.

Again, the impression among African Europeans that Britain is much less concerned with their fears and aspirations than with those of the native African inhabitants was not removed by the intense indignation shown by Parliament and the Press over the Seretse Khama case. This case, though it was made unnecessarily complicated by the evasion and equivocation of the Government in presenting it, was simple enough. A majority of the Bamang-wato tribe objected to the marriage of their Chief to a white woman. Their views on the subject of mixed marriages are

shared by other African tribes and by the whole European
population of Africa; for they have seen the social and racial
difficulties and dangers which result from such marriages. Now,
at the time when the case occurred there was a cumulative mass
of suffering, horrible to contemplate, in the labour camps behind
the Iron Curtain. The House of Commons, it is true, could not
do anything about that. But there was also much privation and
sorrow among displaced persons in Europe and the Middle East.
They had suffered from far greater hardships and injustice than
Seretse Khama. The House of Commons had, at least indirectly,
some responsibility for these unhappy persons. Its indignation
over the moral wrong done to Seretse Khama seemed, therefore,
excessive to me; I felt during the debate that some of it might be
diverted, for example, to the plight of the Arab refugees in Trans-
jordan; but the House of Commons would lose much of its
charm and be wholly unrepresentative of the British people if
it was always logical.

CHAPTER XXIV

ECONOMIC, financial and social questions were predominant in the domestic legislation and administration of the 1945 and 1950 Parliaments. But all of them were affected by external events and foreign relationships. The Labour Party, in general, never recognised this fact, despite more than one financial crisis and warnings by the late Sir Stafford Cripps and Mr. Gaitskell about the inadequacy of our own financial resources unless supplemented by aid from the United States. Nor, in their speeches in the House or out of it, did they admit that high wages and full employment from 1945 onwards were, in the main, due to the world hunger for goods and the continuance of conscription, supplemented in recent years by rearmament. Whatever Government had come into power as the result of the 1945 election, a great advance in social legislation, leading at the least to the partial completion of the Welfare State, would have been necessary; electors would have demanded it.

With the exception of Mr. Churchill, Lord Simon, Lord Samuel and a very few others, I can claim a larger experience of addressing public meetings as a candidate or M.P. than anyone alive to-day. During my forty-seven years in the Commons I had a large constituency, which made it necessary for me to hold many public meetings at and between elections. During that long period I spoke at numerous meetings in every kind of constituency outside my own all over the United Kingdom. A stupendous and revolutionary change has taken place in the public's attitude, irrespective of Party affiliations, in the last half-century. It demands the equalisation of opportunity through education, the levelling by the bulldozer of taxation of the extremes of wealth and poverty and adequate provision against sickness, unemployment and the hardships of old age. A cynic might claim that this demand has been over-stimulated by Party politicians, competing against their rivals for votes by promising benefits out of public funds. He might, indeed, go further and assert that what has happened justifies the fears of the opponents of the Reform Act of 1832, namely, that if you give voting power to the ignorant, they will eventually destroy the country's economy by their insatiable desire for more and more public money for themselves. But I agree with Dr. C. F. Garbett's views in *The Age of Revolution*.[1] Whilst admitting that there are dangers involved in it, he states that "the Christian Church should welcome the Welfare State". In a striking passage, he shows how many evils of malnutrition, ill-health, poverty and unemployment have been removed or alleviated by it, and says truly that "the Welfare State has brought hope to millions". To this might be added the fact that its existence, together with the good relationship between employers and employed, has appreciably reduced the power of the Communist Party to achieve its evil objects in Britain. There is infinitely less ill feeling between those at the bottom of the social scale and those at the top than in France or Italy. Nor is there the same unhappy contrast between the rich and the poor. We have no *zone septique*[2] in Britain, though it is only fair to admit that most of the disreputable rich inhabiting the French zone are foreigners; the international type in question does not come to live here because it dislikes our laws, our climate and our cooking.

The reasonable approach to the social, economic and financial problems of the nation at the beginning of the 1945 Parliament could have been stated broadly as follows. This nation, of 50 million people crowded together and perched precariously on a small island, which in order to avoid starvation needs to import much of its food and raw material, has suffered grievous losses in the two greatest wars in history. Even before those wars it was not in a wholly satisfactory economic position: it had lost its Victorian predominance; other countries were passing it in productive power. To-day we are poor. The Government fully recognises that the masses of the people, after the sacrifices which they have undergone and the heroism which they have shown, have a right to demand that everything possible should be done to avoid the evils of unemployment and to extend the opportunities for advancement through education as well as the social

[1] Page 151 *et seq*.
[2] The description of the Riviera which some cynical Frenchmen apply to it.

services. But we have much material damage to repair. There is desperate need for houses, for example. We are dependent at the moment upon the financial aid of our allies, the Americans. Without it our economic system would crash. If we try to do too much too quickly, we shall fail. We must advance by stages. Moreover, whatever the State does for the nation, the millions of individuals who comprise the nation must be prepared to work harder than ever before, because we are poorer than before the war. We must never suffer from the delusion that the world owes us a living.

It would have been difficult for a Government of the Right to make such a statement of policy to the electorate at the 1945 election; it would have been harder still for the Labour Party to do so. Had the National Government continued in office and appealed to the country on these lines, it could, without doubt, have obtained a majority, which justifies Mr. Churchill's wisdom and statesmanship in seeking its continuance; even so, it would have been subject to the fissiparous tendencies to which I have already referred.[1]

The unhappy truth is that the two major Parties in Britain are deeply divided on economic issues. It is not, as the official Liberal Party pretends, that Conservative views are of the reactionary Right or that Labour Party ideas belong to the extremist Left. Both Parties are far more moderate than most of their counterparts in continental countries. Even if they were not, the official Liberal Party could not act as a counterbalance until it has a leader who can command a following in the country and a policy which the electors understand. Mr. Clement Davies is a man who enjoys the respect of the Commons, but his task is made impossible by the internecine quarrels and confusion of thought among his followers. The division between the Conservative and Labour Parties lies in the fact that the former do not believe that nationalisation and state control are desirable as aims in themselves, though they accept the fact that some such measures are necessary: the Labour Party pursues both as ultimate ideals and as the real cure for economic dangers and difficulties. This fundamental clash of principle darkens the industrial sky at the moment, since the Conservatives intend, if the 1951 Parliament

[1] See Chapter XXII, p. 313.

lasts long enough, to de-nationalise road transport and steel, and the Labour Party intends to re-nationalise them as soon as it obtains a majority. That way lies industrial chaos, though the blame rests with the Labour Party for their gratuitous obeisance to an impractical ideal in nationalising both these industries. Had they been content with instituting public ownership of mines and railways in the 1945 Parliament, this clash on fundamental principles, threatening the heart and pulse of British Industry, would not have occurred. Nevertheless, there are gleams of light on the horizon. The very gravity of the differences will impel both Parties at some point to try to find a compromise as regards Government control and ownership in respect of land-tenure and of industry in general. Nationalisation has not fulfilled the expectation of the wage-earners engaged in the nationalised industries; it has, indeed, raised neither their morale nor their output; nor has it proved, as some opponents believed that it would, impracticable, and led to serious deterioration in railways or mines. These facts make for future compromise.

It was obvious, from the circumstances, that the main new burden laid upon the taxpayer in the 1945 Parliament, so far as home affairs were concerned, would be due to the housing programme and the National Health Scheme. To carry these two important projects through the Commons and put them into operation without unnecessary friction obviously required ministerial talents of the highest order; to make a success of his task, the Minister required to have many qualities. He needed to be a good House of Commons man, able to make a brilliant and provocative speech when the occasion demanded it, but equally to be prepared and willing, on other occasions when no party controversy arose, to give a conciliatory and business-like reply to points raised in debate. Previous ministerial experience, in high office, would make his task infinitely easier. He needed also to have a clear, cool brain, with a complete command of his temper, so as to conduct negotiations with the many interests involved with the minimum of friction; for anyone who has been in ministerial office knows that deputations representing important interests require careful handling in Whitehall offices. They are "kittle cattle", and if the Minister who receives them exercises his talent for sarcasm or dialectical skill upon them, they usually leave in a huff and report to their organisation that the Minister is arrogant and impossible.

Mr. Bevan certainly possesses some of the qualities which I have enumerated. He is the finest debater on the Labour benches and, at his best, can tackle Mr. Churchill himself with success; but he is sadly deficient in others. He has a most explosive temper, and often shows it in the House and in negotiations outside of it. He is frequently provocative when there is not the slightest need. Mr. Lloyd George, when fighting for his Budget, used two completely different techniques inside and outside the House of Commons,[1] respectively. He was very offensive to his opponents on a platform, but in the main mild and tactful in debate. If, as some allege, Mr. Bevan wishes to take Mr. Lloyd George's career as a model for his own, he has not studied it very closely. By his methods and temperament, Mr. Bevan created unnecessary difficulties for his department, for his legislative and administrative actions and for himself. He quarrelled gratuitously with many sections of opinion on other than political grounds, and he showed political bias against both the voluntary hospitals and private enterprise in house-building.

Mr. A. V. (now Lord) Alexander or Mr. Chuter Ede, with their long and successful ministerial experience, were more fitted for the key post of Minister of Health in 1945 than Mr. Bevan. Unlike Mr. Bevan, they had not, during the war years, attacked other Labour leaders in public with bitter reproaches and fierce denunciations. Why then was Mr. Bevan appointed? The answer probably is that Mr. Attlee thought that Mr. Bevan would be less dangerous to the Party in high office, where there was full scope for his many brilliant gifts, than he would have been in a comparatively minor one; for in such a position he would have ceaselessly manœuvred to secure promotion. This provokes the observation that some day a most interesting book is likely to be written, from inside knowledge, which will disclose the extent to which Mr. Attlee's influence and personality controlled the Labour Government of 1945. In the House he gave the same impression of unruffled tranquillity and equanimity as did Mr. Baldwin when he was Prime Minister. Neither man evinced, by the expression on his face, either interest or resentment when

_____
[1] Chapter IV, p. 31.

an attack was made upon the Government he led. Unlike Mr. Baldwin, however, who on occasions reached the heights of oratory, Mr. Attlee often failed completely to make a noteworthy speech in a big debate. Nevertheless, the House as a whole respected and liked him; and those of us who enjoy his friendship in private life can fully understand the reason for this. To return, however, to Mr. Bevan—as Minister of Health he had the advantage of the assistance of one of the ablest Under-Secretaries in the Labour Government, Dr. Summerskill. Despite her unconcealed dislike for her Conservative opponents, she usually handled an acrimonious debate more tactfully than the Minister.

Besides the complicated and controversial measures on nationalisation and on housing and health services, the Labour Government's programme in 1945 included a Trades Disputes Bill, which was bound to cause opposition, and a number of other important Bills, mainly of non-controversial character, such as the Criminal Justice Bill,[1] which would require a more lengthy consideration than I can give it here. In addition, there were a number of smaller bills, such as those brought in by Mr. Williams, the Minister of Agriculture, whose administration of his office, like Mr. Ede's of the Home Office, raised few Party differences; yet, however uncontroversial, the Bills could not be passed without discussion. For the fulfilment of this tremendous five-year legislative project, the Government obviously needed money and time on a bigger scale than is normal. They obtained the former by the most complete and ruthless taxation ever imposed in time of peace. However, some of the wiser members of the Labour Party are at last beginning to realise that there are no more financial hen-roosts full of fat chickens left to be robbed. Hereditary wealth is being rapidly eliminated; and so huge a proportion of the money earned by every person in the country is being taken in taxes of every kind that the incentive to earn is being seriously enfeebled. No one envies the task of the Chancellor of the Exchequer in the next Labour Government, if ever there be one, which is by no means certain, with the Labour Party so torn by internal quarrels as it is at present.

The Government stated at the beginning of the 1945 Parliament

[1] It was, in effect, the same Bill as that to which reference is made in Chapter XVIII, p. 247.

that they could not restore "Private members' time",[1] which was taken away at the beginning of the war, except gradually. Mr. Morrison, somewhat grandiloquently, also announced, soon after the new Parliament met, the Government's intention to "speed-up" the procedure of the House in order to make it more suitable for the times. To achieve this aim a Select Committee on Procedure was set up to report to the House what changes were possible and desirable. Captain Crookshank and I represented the Opposition Front Bench upon it. Though changes recommended by the Committee and enacted by the House were not very drastic, their effect was further to curtail the powers of the House over legislation and further to increase those of the Government. This process has been continuous ever since the '80s of the last century. The original reason for the closure and other alterations in the Standing Orders was the perfectly proper one of preventing obstruction by the Irish Nationalist Party which was endangering the whole machinery of Parliament. No such reason exists to-day. Indeed, Governments in recent times have made no concealment of the fact that they demand enhanced authority at the expense of the legislature to which they are responsible simply for their own convenience. In a country which has no written constitution and a Second Chamber with no effective power, this constitutes a most dangerous state of affairs. With an extremist Government in office commanding a big majority, it might conceivably lead to something closely akin to revolution.

To make matters worse, by the Parliament Act of 1949 the Labour Government further reduced to one year the period for which the Lords could delay legislation[2] initiated in the Commons. There were confidential discussions between the different Parties, prior to the passage of the Bill, to try to reach a compromise agreement on the functions and powers of the House of Lords. Had agreement been reached, which unhappily it was not, there might have been willingness on the part of all the Parties to try to produce a scheme for reforming the House of Lords, as regards both composition and powers. It is deplorable that, more than forty years after the passage of the Parliament Bill and Mr.

---

[1] This phrase comprises the time allotted under the Rules of the House for the introduction and discussion alike of "Private members'" Bills and Motions.

[2] Laid down originally in the Parliament Act of 1911.

Asquith's dictum that reform of the Lords "brooked no delay", Britain alone of the great powers outside the Iron Curtain still has no effective Second Chamber of a modern kind. Many Governments since 1911 have made vague and tentative promises to tackle this stubborn issue, but they have never been fulfilled.

As soon as the intransigence of the Kremlin became plain, a great deal of time in the Commons during the 1945 Parliament was taken up in discussing rearmament. The Korean war of the United Nations naturally increased the interest of all Parties in this vital problem. That war raised issues of great military and social importance which have been insufficiently discussed. When operations commenced, there was a great deal both of self-righteousness and over-confidence in some political quarters. The old familiar cockshies of the weak and wicked Baldwin and Chamberlain Governments were once again brought out to be thrown at. If only the action taken by U.N.O. had been taken when Italy attacked Abyssinia, or over the Spanish Civil War, or at the time of Munich, there would have been no Second World War—so ran the argument. We are going to show in no uncertain fashion, the argument continued, that aggression does not pay, as we ought to have done in the '30s before the Second World War. Unfortunately, it has not been possible so far to show, beyond peradventure, that aggression on the part of North Korea and Soviet Russia and Communist China who support her, has not paid. The maxim: "The United Nations must resist aggression wherever it occurs" should surely be qualified by the two following provisos: (1) that it is possible to resist effectively by military action without unduly weakening the capacity of the nations supplying the ships, planes, armies and man-power to defend their own vital interests elsewhere, and (2) that the victims of the aggression can be properly protected. Only a military expert can say if the first of these provisos has been fulfilled in the Korean war; but it is, unfortunately, completely clear that it has been impossible to fulfil the second. South Korea has been devastated and her inhabitants subjected to frightful losses and hardships: they could hardly have been worse off under a Communist dictatorship.

The Labour Government were fortunate to have an official Opposition that supported rearmament so firmly. Had a Conservative Government been in office, it is certain that, whatever Mr. Attlee's personal inclinations might have been, the bulk of the Labour Party would not have supported rearmament. As in foreign affairs so in defence questions, Mr. Churchill's great knowledge and authority were prominently displayed in debate. Also, there were a great wealth and variety of experience in both wars among his followers on the back benches. In the 1950 Parliament they included two V.C.s and a number of other members upon whom D.S.O.s, M.C.s, D.F.C.s or D.S.C.s has been bestowed. I doubt if any body of similar numbers outside the House had so high a number of decorations. Among the Conservatives were two known as "the two Brigadiers". These were Brigadiers Head and Low. Both were young men; one of them, at the time of his appointment, was the youngest of his rank in the Army. They contributed notably to Army debates. Very properly, Mr. Head was given the Secretaryship of War in the 1951 Government.

Towards the end of the 1945 Parliament, conversations took place, as the official announcement stated, between Mr. Churchill and some of his Front Bench colleagues and the Prime Minister and Service Ministers, on defence matters. I was one of the four members who represented the Opposition. It would, of course, be a serious breach of the Official Secrets Act as well as of decorum to state what form these conversations took, but it is perfectly proper to state this fact. They illustrated the exceptional mutations of political life in the last fifty years. Some thirteen years earlier Mr. Churchill had conducted similar conversations with Mr. Baldwin[1] and his colleagues in an effort to prevent the Second World War or, alternatively, if prevention was impossible, to create adequate British forces to fight it. He attached so much importance to this matter that he devoted three pages of the first volume of *The Second World War*[2] to it. Of those who took part in the later discussions only Mr. Churchill and I had been members of the deputation to Mr. Baldwin. Mr. Attlee and his colleagues had refused to take part in these earlier discussions, yet they had been members of Mr. Churchill's Government during the Second World War: whilst Mr. Shinwell and I, who sat on the opposite side of the table in the Prime Minister's room in the

[1] See Chapter XVI, p. 220.   [2] P. 204 *et seq.*

Commons, in which the deputation to Mr. Baldwin had also been received, had been frequent critics of that Government's military policy and preparations. Clearly, the discussions, from the form of their announcement, were concerned with the means of preventing a third world war and, if it could not be prevented, of defending this country in it. More than thirty years earlier some of us, including Mr. Churchill and Mr. Attlee, now sitting round the same table, had taken part as combatants in the First World War. The Government of that day and the then leaders of opinion in general had assured us and the nation at large that it was "a war to end war".[1] At least one Minister present at the conversations had opposed that war on conscientious grounds, believing then that war was wrong in itself, settled nothing and was caused by militarism and competition in armaments: but here he was in an important ministerial office which would take a most important part in the defences of the country in the event of a third world war. I felt that, if two most distinguished former occupants of that historic room, Mr. Disraeli and Mr. Balfour, had returned to earth and to that room whilst the latest discussions were in progress, they would have some sardonic comments to make on the topsy-turveydom of modern domestic and international politics.

The 1945 and 1950 Parliaments indeed illustrated the fact that this is an epoch of unsolved problems and unanswered questions. Statesmen and economists grope in the dark to find the solutions and the answers. They believe they have discovered some of them, and assert these as a principle with the support of the majority of their fellow-countrymen, only to find a generation later that they are not solutions or answers at all, and that their nation and the rest of the world rejects them.

Lord Grey of Fallodon, who was Foreign Secretary in 1914, wrote a book[2] which was published in 1925 and which rightly had a good reception. On page 92 of Volume II he writes as follows:

The increase of armaments, that is intended in each nation to produce consciousness of strength, and a sense of security, does not

---

[1] In 1914 it was the most popular of all *clichés*, alike for the perorations of politicians and speakers on recruiting platforms.

[2] *Twenty-five Years.*

produce these effects. On the contrary, it produces a consciousness of the strength of other nations and a sense of fear. Fear begets suspicion and distrust and evil imaginings of all sorts, till each Government feels it would be criminal and a betrayal of its own country not to take every precaution, while every Government regards every precaution of every other Government as evidence of hostile intent. . . . I shall suggest and examine, later on, what more effort could have been made by us to avert war in 1914; I shall explain how it seemed at the time, and still seems true to me, that the military power in Germany chose the time and precipitated the war; and that, had there been a real will for peace in Germany, there would have been no great European War arising out of the Austro–Serbian dispute. But, though all this be true, it is not in my opinion the real and final account of the origin of the Great War. The enormous growth of armaments in Europe, the sense of insecurity and fear caused by them—it was these that made war inevitable. This, it seems to me, is the truest reading of history, and the lesson that the present should be learning from the past in the interest of future peace, the warning to be handed on to those who come after us.

This opinion proceeded from an honoured elder statesman of great knowledge and authority; it also represented the views of an overwhelming majority of Britons and Americans at the time. To-day, an equally overwhelming majority of the two nations believe that only when, by an intense effort on the part of their countries and others in N.A.T.O., equality of armed power with the Soviet Powers is reached will lasting peace be attained. It is clear that there is an almost complete antithesis between the two views. Historians would agree that the heresy of the past has become the doctrine of the present, and vice versa, throughout our national history; but the reversal is much quicker to-day, which fact increases the difficulties of every British Government answerable to a nation enjoying universal suffrage, especially since a large portion of the electorate is imperfectly fitted[1] to understand either the doctrine or the heresy of the moment.

Governments and members of Parliament alike are overburdened with work. They have all too little time to consider and

[1] I am thinking in particular of the formidable amount of illiteracy among adolescents which the National Service intake and other evidence has disclosed.

afterwards explain to the electorate the complexity of the issues I have mentioned in this chapter and which confronted the 1945 and 1950 Parliaments. How to preserve peace, how to rearm without ruining the country's economy, how to maintain the British standard of life and the Welfare State, with the huge taxation involved in it, and at the same time compete in the export markets of the world to an extent necessary to save us from bankruptcy and starvation, how to reconcile by guidance and advice such serious differences within the Commonwealth as those between India and South Africa, how to treat future governance in multi-racial colonies—these are only some of the gravest of the problems. No sensible and impartial person can claim, with conviction, that the right clue to them has been found in either legislative or administrative action since the last war.

Far transcending all these matters in importance is the question of the moral fibre and sense of purpose of the British; have they improved or deteriorated in the period covered by this book? Have the House of Commons and politicians in general contributed materially to their development, if they have developed, or to their decline, if they have declined? A full survey and analysis of the subject would require a volume in itself; one can only state a few general considerations. A member of the Church of England, as I am, or, indeed, a member of any Church, must deplore the decline of attendance at public worship and in membership of the Churches during the last fifty years. This decline is mirrored in the greatly decreased influence of the Churches upon political parties; but that is not wholly a bad thing, since, when I first entered Parliament, it was neither edifying nor helpful to the cause of true Christianity to see Churchmen and Nonconformists squabbling angrily in the Commons over education, the licensing laws and other issues, and claiming in so doing to represent the views of their respective Churches. The decrease in Church support and membership does not necessarily, moreover, reflect less belief in Christ's teaching and in its practical application to the problems of this world than existed fifty years ago. Many would argue that the opposite is true; they would say that the Welfare State is itself an example of Christian principles in practice. The huge figure of those who listen to religious broadcasts is impressive. People do not listen on their wireless sets to something which does not interest them and in which they feel no concern.

Many people cite the serious increase in crimes of violence and indictable offences generally as evidence of a great deterioration in British moral standards. But it is difficult to be dogmatic when comparing the present with the past. The increase may be a temporary one due to the unsettling effect of two terrible wars and to the grave shortage of police[1]; there are, moreover, far more laws to break than there were in 1900. My colleagues of the Parliament of that year, in every part of the House, would have rejected with scorn and indignation proposals for many of the laws and regulations in force to-day. They would have argued that, not only were these enactments unnecessary and an insult to free Britons, but that enforcement of them would place such a burden upon the police that they would have no time left to deal with more dangerous law-breakers. Mischievous boys who broke windows, stole or damaged property in those days and who were caught often had summary justice administered to them on the spot in the shape of a sound beating, If they, through their parents, summoned for assault those who had taken the law in their own hands, the penalty imposed by magistrates' courts was usually only a nominal one. For the idea was then prevalent that a naughty boy needed to be hit and hurt.

A subject that has engaged the attention of both Houses of Parliament in recent years has been that of cruelty to children,[2] but the National Society for the Prevention of Cruelty to Children

[1] Neither the 1945 Labour Government nor the Parliament of that year can escape their respective share of the responsibility for the shortage of police. There were efforts by Mrs. Braddock and myself—acting together in a strange political alliance for this purpose only—with the support of one or two other members to get the Government and the House to realise the seriousness of the situation and to adopt remedial measures. We urged better pay and conditions for the Metropolitan and Provincial Forces and more housing provision for married members of it; slowly and with apparent reluctance, official steps were taken to this end, but recruiting is still bad. It is a serious thing that in London alone there is a shortage of nearly 4,000 police. The subject needs tackling at the highest level. It is difficult to believe that this gap could not be filled if a well-publicised recruiting campaign, with support from the most influential quarters, was inaugurated.

[2] I inaugurated a debate on the matter in the Commons and made my maiden speech upon it in the Lords.

are doubtful if there has been any real increase in the number of cases over the last half-century. Modern conditions, the Welfare State, and the system of control and inspection under it bring to full light and publicity some unpleasant things in the national life which were previously known only to a few who "worked in the slums", to use the cant phrase of the time. There is no doubt that, if there had been an evacuation of people from the towns to the countryside in 1900, country folk would have been even more surprised and disgusted than they were in 1939.[1] The population is physically far healthier and fitter than it was fifty years ago, and infinitely more sober. It is, in the main, better housed; despite the grave shortage of houses in many places, there is more room-space per person than there was twenty-five years ago.[2] For this improvement the House of Commons and all political parties in the last hundred years, but especially in the last fifty, can take a big share of the credit. Mr. Attlee's extraordinary suggestion in more than one of his speeches that social progress and betterment were practically unknown until the Labour Party came into power in 1945, and that the healthy babies of the last few years owe their long expectation of life to benevolent Socialism is fantastically untrue. This advance in physical well-being and the consequent rise in social standards are accompanied, as one would expect, by gentler manners and greater tolerance among the population in general. On the strength of a very extensive experience over nearly fifty years in addressing political meetings and coming into contact with people of all classes, I would support the assertion which I have just made against the most convinced *laudatores temporis acti* in the land. There are far fewer unruly mobs at public gatherings[3] of any kind; prostitutes and

[1] See Chapter XVIII, p. 252.

[2] In 1931 there was a ·9 of a person per room. To-day there is ·76 of a person per room.

[3] Up till forty years ago at village election meetings in country constituencies throughout the land where either the Liberal or Conservative Party had a big majority, the candidate of the minority party when he emerged into the dark after the meeting was frequently pelted with rotten eggs, and sometimes with sticks and stones. The village constable, if he were present, seldom took any action beyond advising the unfortunate candidate to get away as quickly as he could. Such conduct, which no doubt was a legacy from the bad old days of the hustings and was regarded as a legitimate "rag", would not be tolerated

drunken people do not annoy and jostle respectable members of the public coming out of a theatre at night, as they did within my recollection; and persons of unusual or deformed appearance are not stared at or followed by a crowd of jeering children in the streets as they once were.

All this does not mean that there is the slightest room for complacency or for any slackening in the attention which present and future Parliaments should give to social and industrial problems.

But have we, as a nation, lost one great quality which sustained us in the past, that of belief in our destiny and of our power to influence world events? Some of our best friends in the United States believe that we have, so that we admit our decreasing position abroad and are reconciled to taking a seat, if not in the back, at least in the middle row, and to vacating our former position in the very front. I think that this idea arises from a confusion of thought instigated largely by the British love of self-criticism. The United States is indisputably to-day the greatest world Power; and it is a splendid thing that, if we had to yield our place, it should be to her to whom we are tied so strongly by sentiment and a wealth of ideas and ideals in common. We have undoubtedly abandoned the old type of "colonialism", which was nowhere more strongly condemned than in the United States. But the British Commonwealth, despite the many changes in recent years in its internal relationships, with their inevitable stress and strain, is economically and in defence far stronger and more united than fifty years ago. It believes in its own future and in its immense potential developments. Great Britain, the parent country, shares in that belief, but admittedly with more reserve than most of the Dominions. This is the inevitable penalty of age. It is impossible to be dogmatic on such an issue, since nations, like individuals—so history teaches us—

to-day. A 'phone message to constabulary headquarters would soon bring a car-load of police on the scene, and those guilty would be arrested or subsequently charged.

At a meeting in my support at the 1906 election, a police-constable who tried to restore order was run out of the room by a gang of roughs; his helmet was removed and used as a football. Though he knew whom his assailants were, the County Police Authority took no Court action against them.

sometimes decay physically and morally with terrible rapidity. But it is difficult to believe that a country, composed of millions of individuals who showed such outstanding courage, composure, unselfishness, sense of public duty and will to win in the two most terrible wars in history, is decadent or on the road to decadence. It is more reasonable to think that Britain is tired and strained as she is certainly poor as a result of her exertions which led to such striking victories. It would be surprising if she were not. But there is much evidence to show that the young people of all classes do not feel that sense of strain and fatigue, and do not miss what they never experienced. For them, the egalitarian State, with its advantages and disadvantages, represents the normal. For them, too, the threat of the "hot", and the actuality of the "cold", war do not seem so terrible as they seem to their elders. They are inured to danger. The uncertain generation, which did not know what to make of the world, was that which grew up between the wars, though it acquitted itself magnificently when the crash came.

Finally, as I have endeavoured to show in various passages of this book, there is, in my judgment, no deterioration over the last fifty years in the quality of the House of Commons. Universal suffrage, payment of members and the consequent election of hundreds of men and women of humble origin have not affected its real character. It contains, as it has always done, persons of the highest character and attainments and others who belong to a different and lower category. Great orators as well as good and bad speakers are included in its membership in roughly the same proportion as they were fifty years ago; the admission of women to membership has not altered the proportion. It can claim, as can local authorities in general throughout the land, a freedom from personal corruption which is as great as that of any legislative or municipal body in any country in the world; indeed, the standard of public life in Britain is infinitely higher than in most countries.

The threat to Parliament and local authorities, as well as to the constituents whom they represent, lies to-day in another direction. The restrictive effect upon the freedom and initiative of the individual caused by the modern Welfare State, with its highly organised system of control, is recognised by every impartial person; unfortunately, its critics have as yet found no effective way of reducing the control whilst still maintaining the beneficial aspects of the structure. As long as the Parties are so closely balanced electorally, it is unlikely that they will do so: for the opponents of any remedy are on a bowler's wicket. What is less widely known is the great and hidden power which the system places in the hands of the higher permanent officials of the Civil Service and of Local Authorities. They alone possess the expert knowledge necessary to interpret and carry out the vast mass of legislative enactments and administrative powers which are nominally vested in Ministers, Parliament and Local Authorities. The fact that they are men of the highest character and attainments does not make the position less dangerous. They have, in many instances, far better and quicker brains than the Minister or the Mayor or the Chairman of whom they are the official advisers. Thus is bureaucracy enthroned. Young men and women seeking election to Parliament with the intention of spending, as I have done, a lifetime in it, could do no better service than devising how to reconcile the requirements of the organised State with individual freedom and true democratic institutions; for the issue which is involved therein vitally affects the position of Britain and her Parliament in the present and future; nor will it be settled easily or quickly.

INDEX

INDEX